3 6480 000075368

Labor's Story in the United States

In the series

LABOR IN CRISIS

edited by Stanley Aronowitz

Philip Yale Nicholson is Professor of History at Nassau
Community College and Adjunct Professor at the Cornell
University School of Industrial and Labor Relations, Long
Island Extension. He is the author of *Who Do We Think We
Are? Race and Nation in the Modern World*.

Labor's Story in the United States

Philip Yale Nicholson

TEMPLE UNIVERSITY PRESS

PHILADELPHIA

Temple University Press, Philadelphia 19122
Copyright © 2004 by Temple University
All rights reserved
Published 2004
Printed in the United States of America

⊗ The paper used in this publication meets the requirements of the American National Standard for Information Sciences—Permanence of Paper for Printed Library Materials, ANSI z39.48–1984.

Library of Congress Cataloging-in-Publication Data

Nicholson, Philip Yale, 1940–
    Labor's story in the United States / Philip Yale Nicholson.
      p.   cm. — (Labor in crisis)
    Includes bibliographical references and index.
    ISBN 1-59213-020-8 (cloth : alk. paper) — ISBN 1-59213-239-1 (pbk. : alk. paper)
    1. Labor—United States—History.   2. Labor movement—United States—History.   3. Labor unions—United States—History.   4. Working class—United States—History.   I. Title.   II. Series.
    HD8066.N53   2004
    331'.0973'0904—dc22   2003066317

2 4 6 8 9 7 5 3 1

To my parents,

Samuel and Gertrude Nicholson

Contents

Preface

Readers deserve an explanation at the outset of a new labor history book. How is it different from what has already been written about its subject? Certainly there are plenty of generalized books, along with hundreds of highly specialized works, about American labor since its conscientious study began early in the twentieth century.

When serious attention first turned to the subject of labor, its focus was on institutions, great conflicts, organizations, and leaders. For the next seventy-five years historians described the rising and falling fortunes of labor organizations and the people who made them. Unions were regarded as the logical or inevitable outcome of the unequal struggle between labor and capital for control of the wealth that labor created. Capital had organized into corporations, trusts, monopolies, cartels, pools, holding companies, and the like, and it was regarded as natural for labor to seek to build its own organizations. Indeed, it is worth noting that unions really came into existence as legal entities during the same period, around 1830 to 1850, that states passed general incorporation laws for business. Before that time unions were considered by courts to be illegal conspiracies; unchartered corporations were called conspiracies of capital.

Labor history as the history of labor organizations continues as many writers and labor leaders still seek answers to these questions: Why did some unions succeed and others fail? Which leaders made the biggest differences for their organizations and members, or, conversely, which betrayals did the most damage (e.g., Buhle, 1999)? What has been the place of ideology in the history of American labor unions? What lessons must today's unions learn if they are to play any part in the future (e.g., Aronowitz, 1998)? These questions remain an important part of labor history. Betrayal and failure are not casual observations, and success in organizing the workforce has eluded unions in the United States more than their counterparts in other industrialized nations. Why have American unions receded or been driven to the political sidelines as representatives of fewer than 10 percent of the private-sector workforce after two generations of prominence and power? Traditional texts did not anticipate labor's slow decline.

The sharp increases in the disparity of wealth in the last quarter of the twenti-eth century reversed nearly 200 years of democratic tradition and progress. After a century and a half of struggle to reduce the length of the workday and workweek, that trend has also been reversed for American labor. More workers are paid and re-garded as temporary or part-time than ever before. How have these dramatic setbacks come about? What, if anything, do they mean for the future of labor organizations, for democracy itself? Most of these questions still lack definitive answers. New ap-proaches to them may lead to a better understanding of current dilemmas.

Recent events add another dimension to labor history. The fortunes of labor during the nineteenth and early twentieth centuries appeared to rise during periods of eco-nomic prosperity and fall in times of economic decline. Since the Great Depression this pattern ceased to apply. Unions did well during those hard times and the good times of the postwar and cold war era. Their influence declined in the tougher eco-nomic times of the post–Vietnam War period and has continued to fall, nonetheless, in the unbalanced prosperity of more recent years. Nothing nowadays seems to help unions much.

The industrial age (1830–1973) was conflict-filled, stormy with strikes, rife with ide-ological challenge. Embattled unions, rising and falling, were a prominent part of the social landscape. The years since then stand in marked contrast to all of the previ-ous historic trends. Some critics have even suggested that the history of organized labor, as we once knew it, is over. Have labor organizations been made redundant by government agencies, personal or class-action lawsuits, and the end of an industrial economy?

Recent scholarship in the field of cultural studies has demonstrated the power of collective sentiments and perceptions in the shaping of group and individual actions and behaviors. The study of gender and race in the past thirty years has also expanded the boundaries of social history, including labor history. What American workers did or failed to do to build labor organizations now seems to have derived from what they believed was possible and what their dominant cultural forces enabled them to envision, rather than the corruptibility or brilliance of leaders, ideological shortsight-edness, or the economic circumstances that were present. The cultural foundations of labor action as found in ethnic traditions, the influence of celebrity and pop culture, and in all of their traditional social relations will have to be reconsidered.

Labor history has sometimes been portrayed as a subdivision of American history. There are even those who call worker organizations "special interest groups." What those who did the work thought of themselves, how they organized or why they failed to organize, and where they placed their hopes and loyalties is central to the history of the nation itself, as most Americans in history were either servants, slaves, or employees.

Even in an age of widely held shares of corporate stocks and mutual fund re-tirement systems, the vast majority of the American people must rely on the ex-change of their labor power to sustain their material well-being. More than 80 per-cent of the American people depend on wages, salaries, and tips, not capital gains, dividends, corporate profits, or earnings from self-employment to support themselves. That their labor sustains the entire edifice may be mysterious to many of them. It is not so obscure to those who depend on that labor for their wealth and power. As John C. Calhoun—like him or not—one of the most brilliant members of the U.S. Senate observed in defense of plantation slavery:

> It would be well for those interested to reflect whether there now exists, or ever has existed, a wealthy and civilized community in which one portion did not live on the labor of another; and whether the form in which slavery exists in the South is not but one modification of this universal condition. . . . Let those who are interested remember that labor is the *only* source of wealth, and how small a portion of it in all old and civilized countries, even the best governed, is left to those whose labor wealth is created. (Quoted in Hofstadter, 1960, p. 68, emphasis added)

The story of American labor is the story of the development of national social values, the cultural and political sentiments that most people shared. The energy and genius of laboring people in the United States and elsewhere has always been the great creator of new wealth, new goods, and now services for use and for an ever expanding marketplace. Yet, almost all of those whose intellectual and physical energies designed and built the transportation systems, transformed nature's bounties into products, made and still make the wealth of the nation, have never realized, by any objective standard, a fair share of it; nor did most of them really believe they should. While workers have placed enormous value on the goods and services that their labor has produced, they have been unable to challenge successfully the power of owners and managers who set the values for those products and the prices paid for the labor needed to make them. The successful organizations of labor, even when they were strong, usually asked for very little. The unions and political movements that presented a grander vision for labor or put forth an alternative social system were either defeated by their enemies or undermined by the loss of faith and affection of their adherents. In the pitched battles between labor and capital, the owners were eventually able to coerce or cajole most of the workers into abandoning any social values that contradicted the dominant national culture that preserved the supremacy of property rights.

It was the great and sometimes dazzling success of the owners and managers of wealth that has held the workforce in its political thrall throughout. Part of the history of the United States is the story of economic growth and geographic expansion as it became the single most powerful nation in the world. That success allowed, and continues to allow, resources to be available for the creation of new opportunities for strengthening the social hegemony of the owners of wealth. Selective material and social advantages have always been provided to workers. Elaborate hierarchies of privilege and reward have been maintained with the deliberate object of securing the loyalties of workers. The control of wealth also gave its owners the institutional power to maintain racial, ethnic, regional, national, and gender divisions among the laboring population, along with the ability to direct new technologies to their advantage. The only time when there were some significant exceptions was the period that followed the Civil War and concluded with the outbreak of World War I. Those are labor's heroic and socialist eras, which reached a pinnacle in challenging the hegemony of capital around 1912.

Throughout American history only those labor organizations most confirmed in their loyalty to the prevailing paternalistic social values of race, nation, and empire gained institutional succor in times of crisis or need. Even the Congress of Industrial Organizations (CIO) and the Communist Party, USA professed loyalty to the foreign policy aims of the United States during the Great Depression and World War II, though both dissented from the traditional racism of the past. During the war they were joined, at least in part, by the federal government's first challenge to Jim Crow restrictions in wartime industrial employment.

Patriotic labor organizations doubled their membership during the Civil War, World War I, and World War II, and maintained their wartime gains during the cold war. When such crises passed, so did their organizational gains. The American Federation of Labor (AFL) grew in prominence, if not always in numbers, from 1886, while labor organizations that contradicted prevailing national sentiments were attacked, destroyed, or displaced, with the assistance of the AFL. The social value of labor was always subsumed under the paternal authority of business, race, nation, and empire. All religious institutions confirmed that outlook. Any challenges to those values by either the gentle Knights of Labor, or the stridently militant Industrial Workers of the World, or the humane and democratic Socialists of the era of Eugene Debs, Upton Sinclair, or Norman Thomas, or the Communists of the pre-Stalinist, Stalinist, or post-Stalinist eras were incapable of reaching the American workforce with any kind of transformative cultural message for long.

By the year 2000 the fastest-growing segment of the American population classified as living beneath the nation's own meanly constructed poverty line were people and families who were fully employed. They were called "the working poor." Both the working and the "idle" rich were, at the same time, enjoying the most extreme statistical increase in their wealth in the nation's history. The gap between those who created the nation's wealth and those who owned or controlled it was never greater (with the possible exception of the era of plantation slavery), nor was there any other large industrial nation on earth where that social gap was expanding in any comparable way. No boiling point of explosive discontent was reached after nearly thirty years of radical redistribution of wealth away from its producers. Only the tepid plea, "America needs a raise," came forth in 1996 from a newly rejuvenated AFL-CIO leadership, one whose president was almost unknown in the working households of the nation.

This book seeks a better understanding of the origins and sources of the mythologies and cultural forces that have overwhelmed servants and slaves, builders of machinery, railroads, skyscrapers, and all of the miraculous technologies and goods of the past several centuries. Though the genie of contemporary abundance has been released, that abundance has not gone to those who created it. No new wealth of any social value has come into the world without the force and creativity of labor. Wealth, or capital alone, cannot increase itself. This simple observation remains, nonetheless, a dark secret or mystery, not to the owners and managers of wealth who have always understood it, but to those whose labor increases wealth. That inequitable blindness is not new. Its historical evolution is a continuing part of the history of labor in the United States.

This book rejects the claim that unions today would be stronger if some particular events in its history had been different. Unions would not be stronger today had John L. Lewis stayed loyal to the Democratic Party in 1940, or Trotskyists had somehow held onto the Teamsters Union instead of giving way to the mob guys, or Walter Reuther had not died in a plane crash in May 1970. Instead, I argue that, aside from some important and notable exceptions, labor has been able to organize when it has been in the interest of capital for it to do so. The owners have, for the most part, been able to call the shots.

The role of the state in shaping the destiny of labor has been crucial. Government is more important than voluntarist notions of American history usually allow. It has never been a neutral or passive influence in the history of the nation, certainly not in matters pertaining to labor and wealth. The promise of democracy has fueled every struggle by labor for social and economic justice. The limits of that democracy frustrated or reversed every one of those struggles.

Throughout the nation's past, the story of labor is a complex drama of resistance and struggle, of cultural integration and accommodation, of great victories and stunning defeats.

Acknowledgments

Before she retired from teaching and her duties on our union Executive Committee, Dorothy M. Cooke asked me to recommend a good up-to-date survey of the history of labor. She had become a laborite from experience, now she wanted to know the full story. This book was prompted by my inability to provide her with what she wanted. I regret that her untimely death prevents her from seeing what she helped to inspire.

When I asked the labor historian Irwin Yellowitz why there was no recent survey, he connected that void to the dismal state of contemporary labor, and encouraged me to undertake a new study. The sociologist and labor activist Stanley Aronowitz was also very enthusiastic about this project when I first told him about it. His support helped to sustain my efforts throughout.

Several critical readers have offered important suggestions. My sister, the distinguished feminist and philosopher Linda J. Nicholson, of Washington University, offered extensive comments, corrections, and recommendations on the entire manuscript. My academic friends Michael Ferlise, Richard Panken, Ed Boyden, Gene Glickman, Joe Harris, and Faren Siminoff read some or all of the chapters. Carol Farber's careful reading corrected many grammatical and stylistic glitches. As I did not always follow their advice, none of these readers is responsible for any mistakes that remain.

My students in American labor history in the Verizon Next Step Program and at the Cornell University labor studies program on Long Island were my most engaging critics. Along with their full-time (plus overtime) work schedules, these students read, discussed, and helped to improve this work while it was underway.

The vast literature on labor made me especially dependent on the inter-library loan services of the Nassau Community College Library. Alicia Sanchez helped me to locate hundreds of books and articles, and she promptly notified me when every one of them arrived. Her friendly assistance and interest in the project went well beyond her busy work responsibilities. The reference librarians, Charles Owusu and Marilyn Rosenthal, gave me time-saving suggestions and friendly encouragement throughout the project.

A sabbatical leave from teaching responsibilities, made possible through our collective bargaining agreement at Nassau Community College, enabled me to complete the book.

My wife, Linda, is a psychotherapist who helps people to increase their personal capacities. After forty years of marriage this book is as much a tribute to her patient endeavors as it is to mine.

Labor's Story in the United States

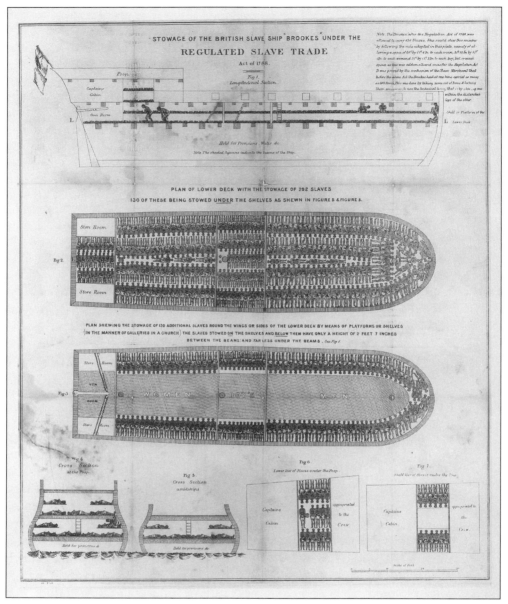

The slaveship *Brooke*. Skilled and unskilled labor built and manned the ships that carried slave labor to colonial America. The profit from all of that labor went to bankers, merchants, and planters. Abolitionists reproduced copies of this famous illustration to condemn the atrocious inhumanity of the slave trade, not the economic inequities that prompted its terrible efficiency. (Library of Congress, Prints and Photographs Division, Reproduction No. LC-USZ62-44000)

CHAPTER 1

European and Colonial Foundations to 1760

The poverty of the country is such that all the power and sway is got into the hands of the rich, who by extortious advantages, having the common people in their debt, have always curbed and oppressed them in all manner of ways.

———Nathaniel Bacon (quoted in Wertenbaker, 1958, v. 3, p. 135)

European Heritage

The Europeans who explored, conquered, and made settlements in the land mass of North America brought with them well-established practices of authority, particularly when it came to any form of productive labor or work. Agricultural wealth in Europe went to those who controlled the land. Control of property granted those who held authority over it power over those who worked it. Feudalism was the paternalistic institutional system that, with the laws of the Church, set the day-to-day pattern of life and supervised all social relations. The working population of peasants and artisans in most of Europe gave their emotional loyalty to the authority of the Church and the lord of the manor. People placed their faith and confidence in those whose power seemed to protect them from danger or offered some hope for the future.

Until about 1500 there were no nations or races as we know them, no national banks, passports, citizens, stock exchanges, or even Protestants. More than 95 percent of the people were "subjects" who lived under the power and authority of "masters" whose inherited social rank gave them their status. These subjects were called serfs. They had no access to courts, no voice or vote in any public matter, no right to make a contract or any legal claim whatsoever, and no right to testify in court or to claim legal ownership of any productive land or enterprise. There were no organizations or associations formed by them or for the purpose of acting exclusively on their behalf. They all worked, but had control only over their own gardens, personal livestock and possessions, and whatever they could steal. Religion influenced work habits, set frequent holy days, festivals, and celebrations, and mitigated punishments.

"City air is free air" was a well-known Central European comment about the absence of feudal bonds constraining craftspeople and merchants in the expanding towns and cities. Serfs were legally bound to baronial masters with a status similar to that of children. They could enter into no legal agreements, own no real property, or move about freely. In town the medieval guilds, also known as trade corporations, and guild masters were more autonomous. Guilds were intent on preventing competition among producers. They set firm rules and limits on everything from prices to the pace of work, and supervised the lives of apprentices and journeymen workers. Control of the secrets and the skills of the crafts that were passed on through the apprenticeship system gave added social power and importance to the masters, many of whom came to manage large workshops and build great fortunes. Emulating the landed gentry, they found ways to pass on their wealth to the next generation. The famous seventeenth-century painting by Rembrandt, *The Syndics of the Clothmaker's Guild (Staalmeesters)*, better known as *The Dutch Masters*, dramatically captures the importance and social presence of its subject.

Every craft had its guild and usually a guildhall. Weaving, building, stonecutting, furniture making, jewelry making, shipbuilding, armor and weapons making, and food processing or victualling were among the many crafts that formed guilds. These organizations set quality standards, established prices, trained apprentices, and provided security for their members. Guilds were often involved in political struggles to hold onto monopolistic privileges or fix prices for what they produced. Work stoppages were not uncommon as a tactic to achieve their goals. In most of the prosperous cities of Europe, however, the masters were on comfortable terms with the most elite merchants, bankers, and professionals with whom they worked closely. The masters were never significant critics of the society in which they enjoyed such status. They passed many of those same conservative sentiments and practices on to the skilled trade unions and the leaders that gradually replaced them as feudalism waned and capitalism gradually emerged. That relationship has been maintained consistently through the modern period. Other workers, the semiskilled and unskilled, and their organizations did not share the elitist identification of their skilled counterparts. Their loyalty and their identity with the dominant culture would more often be drawn toward the nation-state when it and their importance as part of the labor force emerged.

European guilds had their counterparts in medieval trade associations or monopolies such as the Hanseatic League of northwestern Europe. These trading guilds put profits into the hands of merchants and other middlemen such as bankers, insurers, brokers, and shippers and took them away from producers. Norwegian fishermen and Scottish and Irish sheepherders eked out a marginal existence while the codfish and woolens they produced brought fortunes to those who marketed them. As national governments gradually formed, they assumed the practice of granting patents to merchants or monopolistic trading rights to them in exchange for a share in the profits or tax revenues.

Another area of employment that began to open up as an alternative to feudal agriculture was the armed services. Military or naval service at the end of the Middle Ages (ca. 1500) was long-term and sternly disciplined, and the ranks of officers were restricted to those of noble birth, the aristocracy. When the longbow and gunpowder—both contributing to the end of the Middle Ages—made the heavily armored aristocratic knight almost useless, the ranks of soldiers were soon filled by long-term commoners. Then, as now, it was an uncertain career. Officers were handsomely rewarded for military victories. For common soldiers basic necessities were provided and a secure existence was promised unless death or injury on the battlefield soured the deal.

Since social status, or what later would be called class, was hereditary, the women of the nobility had authority over their social inferiors, but no legal or institutional power. A tiny patriarchal elite was confirmed in its authority by religious orders and law. Unquestioning obedience to a master or higher authority provided security and the comfort of a predictable relationship, like that of a man and his dog, for workers, serfs, soldiers, and women alike. For the European peasantry this dependent legal status meant ruthless exploitation, brutality, rape, and complete disregard for their human rights. Their only recourses were the peasant rebellions, thievery, and cheating on work that were all punishable offenses, but commonplace actions. Other forms of passive resistance were in the folklore that cheered renegades like Robin Hood, or the swindling of masters, but all of these were also outside the bounds of respectability.

The Expansion of Trade

Aristocratic and clerical control was gradually undermined by the dramatic expansion of trade in the centuries that followed the Crusades (1200–1500). Commerce disrupted the feudal centrality of economic life by conferring more importance on a new group or class previously of little significance in the early Middle Ages, the merchant, or burger, or bourgeoisie. The feudal aristocracy was dependent on wealth from control of the land, and began to fall behind the bourgeoisie in wealth and political influence. This new urban class included in its membership cartographers, guild masters, shipwrights, and early bankers or moneylenders. Their energy and ambition combined with their economic needs led them to give support to national leaders over local feudal barons, even to absolute monarchs whose navies and lawmaking powers coincided with their interests. When Thomas Hobbes wrote his influential work, *Leviathan*, in 1651 about the harsh necessity of governmental power, even absolutist power, he was echoing the widespread sentiment of a new age that had emerged in modern contrast to the decentralized and stagnant feudal order.

The wealth of the new commercial class came neither from birthright titles, inherited land, nor clerical privileges, though many rich merchants and bankers would ultimately seek these for themselves and their heirs. Through intermarriage with the aristocracy, bribery, and service to royalty, the new business elite gained status and legal security for their enterprises. The military and naval services they needed to protect and expand their business ventures were paid for in the form of taxes to a new agency created to advance the common needs of all who benefited from the expansion of trade. This new agency was called the state. It alone could provide the commercial and non-feudal property right laws, expanded banking and financial services, military and naval forces, commercial treaties, and laws that could govern and control the new workforce that were all beyond the boundaries or capabilities of traditional feudal and clerical power. The state could coin money, grant patents, charter corporations, set up secular courts of law, and establish claims to conquered territory for economic purposes beyond the grasp or scope of feudalism's religious, agricultural, and local military authority.

In some places the state was created even before there was a fully formed or unified national culture, as in some wealthy Italian city-states like Venice, or in prosperous trading towns like Pisa, Amalfi, and Genoa of the Renaissance era, or in the Dutch Republic of the late sixteenth and early seventeenth centuries. In other places, like Portugal, Spain, England, and France, the institutions of the state gradually evolved along with the cultural nation. Banking and insurance practices became centralized, along with new laws and agreements about property rights, maximum wages, trading rights, and taxes. Feudal forces could not compete with the wealth and power of those who had control of the more centralized system. Germany, devastated by the Thirty Years' War (1618–48), remained divided into many feudal kingdoms and lagged behind for two centuries as a cultural entity without a state until the era of its unification. The making of the modern German nation-state is usually credited to its Iron Chancellor, Otto Von Bismarck, in the second half of the nineteenth century.

The new wealth from trade and overseas empires was something that completely eclipsed the capabilities of feudal barons. None of them could raise a high seas navy, or establish a national bank, tax, judicial, or monetary system. Merchants and monarchs alike shared an incentive to trade. Naval power meant world power financed by expanded trade and new tax revenues. New routes to old markets were sought by rival states to increase their economic independence from one another, and explorers were sent all over the world to find them, especially after the capture of Constantinople by the Ottoman Turkish Empire in 1453. As a result, Europeans lost easy access to Asian goods and had to find new routes to them on their own or pay extortionate prices. Shipyard work expanded dramatically, especially in Portugal and Spain. Christopher Columbus was but one of many dozens of global seekers of wealth sent out on behalf of these new nation-states in search of direct routes to the fabled goods of Asia.

Prosperity in an age of increased trade was no longer primarily based on the feudal standard of land tenure. Gold and silver bullion became the new basis for the measurement of wealth. Land itself would soon come to have a monetary value. Brutal conquests and ruthless mining ventures in the "New World" (to the Europeans) were a crude way of gaining that wealth without having to trade anything for it. Nonfeudal forms of forced labor were improvised or imported to exploit the mineral wealth of America once the genocidal destruction and simple robbery or seizures from Tainos, Aztecs, and Incas, among others, gave way to regular mining operations. These native people were the first American workers. It was their confiscated land and coerced semifeudal and slave labor that created the wealth that contributed to the power of the modern European-based nation-states.

Since almost all labor was carried out in bondage or dependency in the 1500s, it is not surprising to discover the use of crude forms of enslavement of the native population. The murderous exploitation in mining operations and vulnerability to European diseases of native Americans led to the death and destruction of tens of millions of people in Central and South America by Spanish conquistadores and the viceroys that followed to govern in their wake. Devastation and genocide was so complete that in many cases only accounts of eyewitnesses and archaeological ruins remain. The poignant protests of some clergy, especially Peter Martyr and Bartolome de las Casas, continue to remind us of the price paid for the expansion of European global power. The rapid growth of every nation that became a great world power was similarly paid for with the coerced labor and seizure of the economic resources of another people. Every great nation's history is one of military conquest, expropriation of land and labor, and the development of racism. There never was an expansive modern nation that was free of militarism, conquest, and racism. Christian doctrine played almost no role at all in mitigating the harsh prerogatives of the aggressive nation-state. Most often clerical powers cheered on the conquerors and found ways to justify the harshness. Native Americans were cruelly worked to death, displaced and brutalized without mercy throughout the hemisphere by every European national power they encountered.

By many historically accepted accounts the Aztec population was reduced from about twenty-five million to one million during the forty years (1520–60) that followed Spanish conquest under Hernán Cortés. A similar devastation was carried out against the Incas of Peru. The conquistadores became spectacularly rich. No one can say for certain how many tons of gold and silver bullion were taken from the Aztec and Inca people, but one notable scholar, Ferdinand Braudel, argued in his masterful two-volume work, *The Mediterranean and the Mediterranean World in the Age of Philip II*, that it was enough to dramatically change the entire history of Europe and the modern world.

English privateers who enjoyed the protection of Queen Elizabeth brought some of this wealth home as booty stolen from the Spanish. From the time of Columbus until the defeat of its great naval armada in 1588, Spain enjoyed nearly a century-long golden age of prosperity and power. Spanish wealth flowed through the hands of bankers and merchants in the Netherlands and England who served the empire with the goods and services Spain could not provide for itself. The unpaid labor and wealth of the Aztecs and Incas made Spain one of the first great modern nations and one of the first great global empires in history. At the same time Portuguese and Dutch merchants were finding new ways of turning nonfeudal enterprises and unpaid foreign labor into gold.

Early Colonial Practices and Institutions

Old World slavery, as known and practiced in the Mediterranean world, had already been adapted for the production of refined sugar from cane in some of the Portuguese colonies in Africa. It was no secret that gold could be made from sugar, by selling the refined crystal for a profit. Portuguese and Dutch merchants took the lead during the sixteenth century in importing African slaves to their West Indian and Brazilian plantations to plant and cut sugarcane. Merchants quickly discovered that they could add to their commercial profits by selling slaves in other American markets as well. Sugar production flourished in the Caribbean and Brazil and, with the innovative legal authority of the modern state, turned the ancient custom of bondage into a modern labor institution that lasted until the late nineteenth century in the Americas. In the United States racial slavery finally was abolished with the Civil War and the passage of the Thirteenth Amendment to the Constitution in 1865. In Brazil and Cuba it lasted until the 1880s. Its social and cultural legacy is with us still.

Another compact way to process molasses for shipping, instead of refining it into sugar, was to distill it into rum. Rum could be turned into gold by merchants and enterprising distillers by using the labor of some slaves and, mostly, their indentured servants in colonial New England. Spices came from Dutch imperial plantation labor in the Far East and were turned into gold as well. Tobacco made by slave labor and indentured servants in Virginia soon followed. The enormous wealth made from American sugar, rum, and tobacco was greater than all of Spain's bullion and by the 18th century made the trade in slave labor the most profitable enterprise of the era. Once the English entered it in earnest after 1714, the trade in slaves soon became twice as profitable as the sugar carried in the same space on the return trip. Profits became so great by 1750 that more than a hundred English ships were regularly engaged in it, and many of them were now designed specifically for it (Davis, 1962, pp. 275, 293–95). Bristol, Bath, and Liverpool were prosperous new English cities built on the wealth made from this trade. Several historians have postulated that the wealth produced by slavery and the slave trade provided the economic foundation for the industrial revolution, and that plantation slave labor was the precursor to the propertyless industrial working class, or proletariat.

None of these things, gold, rum, tobacco, or slavery, was part of the feudal landscape. Neither was the tea or opium that came from the booming English East India trade of the era that followed (1660–1750). A new social structure with new hierarchies of power, new concepts of ownership and control, and new codes and laws of behavior was developed and imposed around these new forms of national and private wealth. The Dutch were the first to develop a national bank, a source of investment capital subsidized by the state itself, and a stock exchange. The English invented the "Poor Laws" of the sixteenth century, and later copied some of the Dutch ideas about business. The new English legal codes were designed to control the masses of impoverished peasants displaced from feudal estates after the conversion of the land system from subsistence agriculture to the more profitable sheep raising and woolens industry. In Ireland it was said that "the sheep ate the people" during the 1600s. Good agricultural land in Ireland was turned over to grazing while the people starved, fled, or were driven from the country. Following their military conquests, the English established plantations in Ireland as nonfeudal, agricultural enterprise zones and drove the population to the near barren and rocky cliffs of the western part of the country. Native Americans would soon experience the same displacement from their lands.

Race and Servitude in Colonial America

Just as the new European nations formed legal boundaries that separated and defined themselves as nations distinct from one another, they also established laws and treaties that separated and defined their control over foreign populations that came under their power. As merchants, bankers, and their royal authorities coined and printed their own money, they similarly marked and defined their own populations and those they dominated abroad by boundaries and laws. The concept of race gave legal definition to people under the political authority of European masters even in their own lands, or as transported slave laborers to European colonies abroad. Racial laws defined and limited legal marriage, land ownership, the right to own weapons or travel, labor practices, place of residence, and standing before the law in all matters.

The Irish became a race in their own country. They became subject to laws formed under the authority of their English conquerors as did native Americans in Virginia, along with Africans transported to work on the colonial plantations. The Dutch, Portuguese, and Spanish were making the same kind of laws in their sixteenth-century colonial empires in Asia, Africa, and the Americas. The modern idea of race was made by European states in an era of national colonial conquest. Old-fashioned empires (e.g., Rome, Egypt, China, etc.) were multicultural mixtures of people of varied ethnicity, cultures, and religions under a hegemonic imperial ruler. The modern domination of subject populations by military and legal institutions created categories of people under national, not religious or imperial, laws. These national laws were the foundation of racism in the modern world.

Citizenship, or membership in the state, defined those who were included in and protected by the laws of the nation. Usually it was based on the ownership of taxable wealth or land. All others, including women and children, were subjected to the laws of the nation or to the authority of masters or institutions that derived their legitimacy from the nation, such as the Church. Millions of Africans, Asians, native Americans, and Irish people were racially defined by their European national conquerors in the sixteenth and seventeenth centuries. They shared a common political inferiority and common masters. Together and separately they gave up their land and labor to their conqueror and took on a new human definition imposed by force. Terms of vilification were nearly identical, in spite of vast cultural and historic differences. Masters everywhere sought to instill values of sobriety, honesty, industriousness, and obedience to authority among their laborer-subjects, wives, and children. The new Protestant work ethic was much more congenial to these values than the traditional Roman Catholicism of the old aristocracy, and it flourished in the English colonies in America. There were fewer days off for holy days, and the use of alcohol was frowned upon. Masters imposed this ethic on their subjects. The masters said they were going to civilize their subjects, though eventually as racial mythologies became institutionalized, the masters and nation-states put that noble ambition aside. Masters assumed that the inverse or opposite of their virtues were the inherent characteristics of those under their power. Those held under racial codes often assumed these derogatory characterizations as a form of passive resistance. Many slaves and servants resisted exploitation by acting the way their masters assumed they would. Others found covert ways to resist, flee, or disguise their true sentiments.

Instead of being tied to a feudal or imperial entity, slaves and native Americans were bound to the legal systems formulated by the economic imperatives of the nation-state. Hence, treaties with native Americans were usually discarded when they became inconvenient, just as religious authorities likewise found themselves helpless to intervene against the violence or displacement imposed by the state on native Americans. The Protestant minister, Roger Williams, was forced from colonial Massachusetts in 1640 in part because of his defense of the property rights of native Americans. Some human beings, African slaves, for example, would soon have the legal status of private property. Native Americans would have their legal and property rights completely stripped away.

The Early English Colonial Settlement in Virginia

In their first few years the English colonies of North America lost money. The Virginia Company, which at first (1607) did not permit any private ownership of land and was the sole employer, became nearly bankrupt and the colony was taken over by the government in 1621. No gold or silver was found. No easy river passages to new markets were discovered and no great strategic harbors were secured. For the first few years adventurers, religious extremists, and ambitious speculators were the only significant groups with any wealth to dare the dangerous crossing and unknown circumstances that might await them in America. Convicts and prostitutes were sent to Virginia as bonded servants. English "Poor Laws" and judicially set maximum wage codes did nothing to assist an increasingly impoverished peasantry. Faced with famine and dependency on charitable services many sought any available alternative. Workhouses and debtor prisons housed thousands of people displaced by the Enclosure Movement. English law favored profitable sheep raising and the elimination of common grazing lands. The colonies became a natural and widely recommended dumping ground for these dependent laborers. Contemporary "workfare" or prison labor schemes are hardly original inventions. Kidnappers, known as "spirits," roamed the streets and alleys of English port cities looking to lure with inducements or coercion the unwary or vulnerable poor into making the passage to America as servants.

The only commercially worthwhile product in early Virginia was tobacco, though serious doubts were raised about its obnoxious and dangerous qualities from the start. Nonetheless, its profitability and immense popularity in England during the 1620s guaranteed tobacco a long, commercially successful life, even if the same could not be said for those who produced it or made use of it. Virginians gradually adopted the land and labor system used in the sugar plantation colonies of the Caribbean for their tobacco farms. It soon became the standard throughout the Chesapeake Bay region.

Nonfeudal colonial land took the form adopted by the English after their conquest of most of Ireland. It was called the plantation. The Dutch used the same kind of plantation system in their spice-producing regions of Indonesia. This kind of land was a grant by the crown or company (which held a patent or legal authority to do this from the crown) for the purpose of developing a profitable enterprise through its use. Plantation owners soon developed controls over other businesses related to their sugar and tobacco trade. Planters and their descendants became the merchants, lawyers, land agents, and political leaders of their communities. They soon came to dominate the emerging society in the colonies.

Just as slavery became one response to the great need for labor in the English colonies, its opposite, freedom, was simultaneously developed for the same reason. To encourage settlement and more diverse economic expansion the Virginia Company began to offer land under the "headright system" to anyone who was under no bond or obligation. Fifty acres or more were promised to any freedman. If that freedman was married, he could claim an additional fifty acres, plus fifty more per child. Only a small quit-rent, or yearly fee, had to be paid to the Virginia Company, then later the Crown Colony, to maintain ownership. The incentive worked to attract twice as many laborers to Virginia in the six years that followed 1619 as had arrived in the previous twelve and the new system was quickly adopted with variations throughout the Chesapeake Bay area. The system eventually spread to the Carolinas and Georgia as well.

One explanation frequently given for the absence of class consciousness among European American workers in comparison to their European counterparts is the abundance of land and opportunity for upward social and economic mobility that was missing in the Old World. The new Americans always saw opportunities for property, and later business ownership or the professions, as available to them. This opportunity set them apart from the more rigidly fixed class order of the Europeans, or the legally set and exclusionary racial codes that were imposed on slaves and native Americans. As "whites" by law they could hope and plan for a future quite different from their past, one that was in sharp contrast to the harsh limits imposed on "blacks" and "red" native Americans. That they also adopted the cultural attitudes and mythologies that went along with their legal status seems a natural consequence of that circumstance. Thousands of dispossessed English peasants came to the colonies as indentured servants, debtors, convicts, and redemptioners. Those who survived the crossing and term of service were quickly in search of the independence and opportunity that land ownership offered.

The New England Colonies

The Plymouth Plantation and the Massachusetts Bay Colony were originally settled in the religiously rancorous 1620–40 period as theocratic sanctuaries. Calvinist ideas of secular purity were merged in New England with economic enterprise. After a period of careful planning, thousands came to the area with the hope of finding a religious haven for the practice of their dissenting views. Indentured servants, convicts, debtors, and slaves soon added to the population. In spite of religious motivations, these people treated native Americans and slaves in New England not very differently than their counterparts in Virginia. As Mark Twain later observed, the New Englanders "first fell on their knees, and then on the aborigines." Day-to-day economic realities, not religious pieties, made colonial social relationships. The initial civilizing mission soon gave way to harsh racist attitudes as land ownership and slavery placed native Americans and slaves in a legally inferior status.

Of course the advertising and inducements for all of this did not mention the enormous death rate suffered in the early decades of the colonies. Nor did the promoters point out that the land that would become theirs if they survived their term of servitude was on the dangerous frontier of the colony, in close proximity to those native Americans who had either been swindled or displaced by brutal force. An early form of American liberalism was present in the promise of greater political (or religious) liberty and economic opportunity through land ownership. In exchange for scantily compensated or uncompensated labor, servants and other bondsmen were given hope for a better future. Unfortunately for many of them, their dreams were offset by the harsh reality of continued social inferiority and economic and political dependency on established authority. This dependency on established political and economic elites was an early form of American conservatism that most immigrants were forced to endure.

Forms of Resistance

Native Americans, slaves, bondsmen of various types and description, and other workers that were subject to the will and abuse of conquerors and masters expressed their discontent in several ways both individually and collectively. Theft of property, flight into the wilderness or to other colonies, rebellions, slowdowns, strikes, mutinies, and suicide were overt manifestations of opposition to the physical abuse and unfair distribution of the wealth that most of these laborers endured. George Washington complained that for every bottle of good wine that he drank from his abundant cellar, his slaves stole five. Expressions of hostility toward socially imposed circumstances included depression, despair, violence, and self-loathing, all well known sentiments in any society of sharp inequities. More generalized cultural forms of resistance included music, humor, and a folklore of righteous confidence still identifiable among many groups of the working class. Many people adapted to their cultural circumstances by internalizing the codes and practices espoused by their masters, especially when there was any hope or opportunity to gain even a small benefit from doing so. Servants and workers sought to please employers and masters by emulating the values and practices they thought were desired. Often these were feigned, done with a wink and a nod. Religion and English codes and laws pertaining to servants offered some protection from abuses. Servants, for example, had access to the courts, but other formal institutions and organizations awaited later development as no political power was in the hands of the propertyless in the seventeenth century.

That their property or labor was the source of the great wealth of their masters was not always apparent to those who gave up the land and did the work. Mythologies of entitlement that were enforced by social power and political legitimation took the place of obvious material realities. A sense of irreparable loss or intolerable physical harm was what initially drove workers to resistance, flight whenever that option was possible, rebellion, or suicidal despair. On the island of Hispaniola, almost immediately after the voyages of Columbus, the first significant slave revolt took place in 1519. Imported African slaves banded together with native Americans. This rebellion lasted more than a decade until Spanish authorities finally reconquered the island in the 1530s (Sale, 1990, p. 156). Harsh Spanish repression was accompanied by laws and codes designed to segregate and divide the loyalties of these dangerous allies in the future. In early colonial Virginia, New England, and Dutch New Amsterdam rebellions of native Americans were met with similar repression and massacres.

The Use of Force

Almost all of the work that formed the new wealth for Europeans was imposed by force. No people freely gave up their land, their labor, their gold or silver, or anything they treasured. Columbus expected tribute in gold or the consequence was death. The Taino people of Hispaniola who were completely destroyed by Columbus and his successors may have been the first genocide in the modern age, the age of national conquest. The price of modernity was paid for in gold and death. Every colonial enterprise of the sixteenth and seventeenth centuries, the English in Ireland and North America, the Portuguese in Africa and India, the Spanish in Central and South America, the Dutch in Indonesia and Brazil, was carried out with military repression, terrifying brutality, and racial exploitation and slaughter.

Some cultural confusion led to bad trades and misunderstandings. The actual price paid by the agents of the Dutch West India Company for Manhattan Island may not have been $24.00, but it was certainly a swindle no matter what trinkets were exchanged for it. It was a swindle since the people who lived on it did not share the same concept of private property as those with whom they traded. Once native Americans began to realize what was lost forever, they began to resist and suffered punitive and near or actual genocidal consequences. They were called "Indian givers" because, lacking the European sense of private property in land, they continued to trespass on what the newcomers claimed and defended with deadly force as their own. Those who were not destroyed in this process either found a way to assimilate into the dominant culture, died of European diseases, or moved into the unconquered territories beyond the reach of the intruders.

Slavery had no racial justification or definition in the Virginia and Maryland colonies at first. Africans, native Americans, and English servants shared a common bondage in the early years. Old World slavery carried on, following two existing traditions. One was the system of coercive codes and practices of European servitude that included whipping, branding, and other severe forms of corporal punishment. Master and servant behaviors had typically included servility and arrogance, grace and vulgarity, each dependent on the other. The other tradition was the mixture of ancient Roman and African codes regarding the ownership and treatment of slaves. Near the end of the Roman Empire, the emperor, Justinian, established a legal code for slavery. The code's most notable and enduring feature was its conferring on masters the power of life and death over their slaves. Slaves were the chattel or private property of their masters. What is equally important about Roman law from a modern point of view was its complete indifference to ethnic or racial characteristics of slaves. These codes had been modified by the actual Portuguese, Spanish, and Dutch experiences in Africa, the Far East, and America. In the modern era racial slavery placed restrictions on just about every important aspect of life. Race and racial slavery was an innovation of the conquering nation-state. Once such a racial identification and division was made, as the English did first in Ireland, the Dutch in Indonesia, and the Portuguese in Africa, Asia, and Brazil, the treatment of servants and slaves was altered accordingly, with the worst punishments reserved for slaves, native Americans, Asians, the Irish, or Africans. Nonracially designated servants enjoyed specific legal rights denied to slaves. Torture and horrific punishments beyond the norm of accepted law have always been associated with race. A racially stratified culture of coercion, accommodation, and resistance formed patterns of relationships that shaped collective behaviors and the social psychology of all who were part of it.

Forming a New Culture

From the very beginning the colonial experience reshaped the cultural heritage of the newly arrived Europeans, their servants, and their slaves. Far removed from the feudal influences of Europe, the people who labored in the English colonies of North America were forced to adapt to their new habitat. In addition to what they brought along with them or learned from earlier colonial enterprises, the colonists also absorbed much from the people they destroyed and displaced. Native American agricultural practices were freely adopted, if their more casual work discipline was not. Crops were made of native corn, peas, squash, beans, pumpkins, and melons. New Englanders learned how to clear land, tap maple trees for syrup, fish, trap game, make bark-covered canoes, and use fish as fertilizer. Later, Americans successfully used the native American hit-and-run tactics of battle in their own war for independence against the English. On the frontiers where European newcomers shared an uneasy existence with native Americans, the working interaction between the two was even greater. Both wore the same kind of animal skins as clothing, the new settlers learned to track and trail game from their neighbors, and they may even have borrowed some of their decision-making habits and powwows as early representative and democratic ways of governing themselves.

The need to improvise and adapt to harsh and remote rural circumstances led to clever methods of home manufactures, as American workers did remarkable things with simple tools and materials. Frontier people also enjoyed the liberties that distance from established authorities provided. When they exceeded the brutality and confiscation practices of the elites against native Americans, they were simply pushing the limits of established practice. Taxes were easily evaded on the frontier, but coastal merchants and businessmen did the same thing when it came to royal authorities and costly mercantile regulations. While the racial/national codes, laws, and mythologies were making the institutional and legal identities of the settlers, their cultural reality was shaped by interaction with the people they disdained, emulated, and destroyed. Fishing, farming, and hunting practices of native Americans were copied and adapted to European practices by the colonists. So were customs of preparing food, making clothing, warfare, and some social practices. In spite of the cultural borrowing and close, even intimate contact between the two groups, the legal domination of one over the other set up the emotional relationship. Racial contempt became the colonial standard whenever native Americans were legally displaced from the land. In another time white American racists would dance to and enjoy the music, artistic, and athletic contributions of descendants of slaves their forebears once dominated.

The resources in front of the newcomers were vast. It is difficult to imagine the magnificence of the American landscape as it appeared to the European settlers. The forest itself must have seemed a gold mine. Wood was used in shipbuilding, construction, and as the principal source of fuel for heating and making iron, glass, and copper. Early Dutch ships were deliberately designed for hauling lumber back to the Netherlands from their Hudson Valley colony of New Amsterdam. Fish and game seemed endlessly plentiful. The Hudson, James, Potomac, Delaware, and Charles rivers were safe harbor estuaries for tired ships.

Back home in Europe every river or creek had been accounted for, every hill and valley was under aristocratic or royal authority. All wildlife was subject to royal or aristocratic controls in the forests of England. None of these restrictions or prohibitions were found on the frontiers of colonial North America, or easily enforced in the settlements. After the whale was declared a Royal Fish and subject to tax in 1696, Long Island fishermen reported no more catches of whales for the remainder of the colonial era. No feudal aristocracy compelled obedience to inherited privileges in most of the colonies. Very little authority was imposed on settlers in frontier areas just a few miles from coastal settlements. The American class system that emerged in the colonies contained no rigidly fixed hereditary aristocracy, no titled nobility. There were, however, clear and frequently hostile clashes between back country farmers, (debtors) and the elite coastal authorities (creditors). If American labor and union organizations, when they formed later, became less class-conscious than their European counterparts, another reason is the historical absence of inherited and permanent class status. For the conquerors and settlers the only missing part was an adequate stable labor force and a way of organizing it systematically to turn the region's raw potential into the kind of wealth that might bring them the power that would allow them to compete with their rivals. This vision of abundance and economic potential came to be shared by elites and commoners alike. The only people excluded from this vision of a land of opportunity were slaves and native Americans.

Trade and the Nation-State

Trade, the wealth made from obtaining goods in one place and carrying them some-place else to be sold for a profit, became the new way nations sought their fortunes by the middle of the seventeenth century. The greatest English monarch, Elizabeth I (r. 1558–1603), launched several trading ventures, including exploratory openings to Ivan the Terrible's Russia and to Thomas Moore's Utopia in North America. Her successors, James I (r. 1603–25) and Charles I (r. 1625–49), helped launch the Virginia and New England colonies, but the European Thirty Years' War, the civil war in England, and the brutal Cromwellian conquest of Ireland postponed the development of a real systematic program for the American colonial project until the reign of Charles II (r. 1660–85). That political and economic system we now call mercantilism was constructed in his reign. It was a century-long era that served as the great nursery for the development of capitalism and the free markets that would follow. Slavery and indentured or bound labor were the standard in this highly controlled system. The gradual decline of the indenture system and the emergence of free labor, along with both the expansion and decline of slavery, took place after a century of mercantile enterprise.

Maturing Colonies in an Age of Trade, 1660–1760

The settlement of the English colonies was from the first an economic enterprise, a national business venture. That important worldly objective is sometimes obscured by the varied motives of so many of those who made the daring journey. Many thousands fled religious persecutions in Europe. It was a time of religious conflict, war, and intolerance. The concept of religious freedom gradually developed as the result of economic necessity, the pressing need for labor, not from moral enlightenment. The Thirty Years' War in Europe (1618–48) and civil strife in England slowed down the Atlantic migration until about 1660 and the coronation of a new king, Charles II. Then the English colonial enterprise got underway energetically with plantation crops of tobacco and rum driving the rest of the colonial economy in North America for the next century. England enlarged its empire through the East India Company's conquest of India during the same period. Liberty and slavery, servitude and freedom, poverty and prosperity were characteristics of this dynamic age. It was a highly controlled economic greenhouse of commercial laws and regulations, enforcement practices, and national imperial policies aimed in the same direction: the increase in measurable national wealth in bullion made from profitable trade. It was the age that nurtured into existence the modern world system of industrial capitalism.

Racial Slavery Institutionalized

Almost all colonial labor in America came under one form of bondage or legal dependency, or started that way. Servants and slaves in the colonial world were the first propertyless nonfeudal working class. The great historian, Richard Hofstadter, estimated in his book, *America in 1750*, that half the population by that year had started out unfree. To the good fortune of many thousands who came later, the mortality rates had improved as better housing and more reliable food supplies allowed more indentured servants, convicts, and redemptioners the opportunity to survive their term of service, gain their independence, obtain some land, and enjoy the legal status of free persons who were entitled to the protection of the law. Slavery, on the other hand, according to Edmund S. Morgan's careful study, *American Slavery, American Freedom: The Ordeal of Colonial Virginia,* became a strictly racial institution by law during the 1660–1710 period. Now the labor force in North America became permanently divided by the authority of law, one sector—white, by law—the beneficiary of specific liberties and economic opportunities, the other—black and slave, by law—denied the same.

The laws that established slavery and freedom (really liberty, or rights under the law) in North America evolved side by side. Access to courts and the right to enter into legal agreements, including the right to transfer property, were among the emerging civil liberties granted to whites and not to black slaves. Native Americans became racially identified in the same way during this era as similar laws and hue differences were contrived to set them apart. Until the new racial laws were set up after 1660 native Americans were not thought of or described as "redmen." Their so-called redness was actually the result of their use of red dye to color their skin, more an arbitrary assigning of distinction than a fixed reality. Of course, few "blacks" were actually black, and no "whites" were really white. Early English and Dutch settlers originally wrote descriptions of native Americans as tawny, as though they were Europeans who had endured more exposure to the sun and elements. Once color became incorporated in the definition of slaves and masters, color was also used in the racination of native Americans. Now everybody had a color, white, black, or red, by law.

In contrast, but by the force of similar laws, the Irish were made a colorless race in their own country. The Penal Laws were put into effect in Ireland after the Protestant Ascendancy restored the English monarchy after the Glorious Revolution of 1690. These new laws stripped the Irish Catholic population of legal and political rights in Ireland. The same kind of racially hostile sentiments and vicious characterizations of these behaviors prompted the historian, James Muldoon, to write an essay entitled "The Indian as Irishman." The Irish only became "white" under the laws of the

United States when they became citizens after immigrating in large numbers during the nineteenth century.

As mortality rates in the English southern colonies in America fell, the impermanence of a labor force based on indentured servants and slaves gradually gave way to one dominated by slavery. Indentured servants became a greater expense and were a less reliable labor force than slaves in a plantation economy. Servants, in the closing period of their obligation, were never as productive as in the first phase of service, and they were not always easy to replace, train, or trust. In a strictly plantation environment, as in the European sugar- and rum-producing colonies in the Caribbean, slavery almost completely displaced other forms of labor. In spite of its obvious contradictory moral and religious aspects, slavery was reliable, stable, and profitable. It was in these Caribbean colonies that the racial legal codes, a legal division of labor among slaves and nonslaves was formed, then, gradually after 1660, transferred to the English continental colonies. These codes established the ownership of children born to slave women as the property of masters, regardless of the status of the father. Such codes reversed the traditional English right of paternity.

Mercantilism and Labor

It was during this same period (1660–90) that the laws and enforcement practices governing trade were also established that earned the era its name, mercantilism. Laws and restrictions were carried out by special vice-admiralty courts and customs officials. The laws sought to benefit English merchants by directing imports from rival national trading systems through English shippers, and to increase the trade in English manufactured goods in the colonies. Trading companies were granted monopolies, patents, and specified rights to markets under legal protection. Colonial raw materials were to travel first in English vessels, and goods intended for the colonies had to travel the same way, with legally specified exceptions or exemptions.

The trade in slaves was itself one of the most profitable enterprises of the British Empire, especially after 1714, when the Spanish were forced by treaty to turn over monopolistic control (the *Assiento*). Thomas Jefferson actually blamed the profitability of this trade for promoting the expansion of the deplorable institution of slavery in the American colonies in his initial draft of the Declaration of Independence. Only the political concern for winning the approval of southern planters and New England slave traders for the document convinced him to edit out the phrase that blamed the greed of the king for the slave trade:

> He [King George III] has waged cruel war against human nature itself, violating its most sacred rights of life and liberty in the persons of a distant people who never offended him, captivating and carrying them into slavery in another hemisphere, or to incur miserable death in their transportation thither. This warfare, the opprobrium in INFIDEL powers, is the warfare of the CHRISTIAN king of Great Britain. Determined to keep open a market

where MEN should be bought and sold, he has prostituted his negative for suppressing every legislative attempt to prohibit or to restrain this execrable commerce.

Each colony likewise established laws and brought forth court decisions governing internal practices. The colonies imitated English laws that set maximum wages for labor, set prices, and restricted competition to protect fledgling enterprises. But these laws were not always followed. The chronic labor shortage in the colonies contributed to much higher wages for workers in comparison to English or European rates. As early as 1636, one frustrated employer complained that continuing high wages would turn masters into servants and servants into masters. In 1666 a New Englander wrote that "Help is scarce and hard to get, difficult to please, uncertaine, etc." In Pennsylvania one observer noted that workers "can here get three times the wages for their Labour they can in England." A report in 1694 stated that "labour costs but one sixth of the price (in Sweden and Denmark) as it does in New England" (quoted in Morris, 1965, pp. 46–47). The need for skilled workmen in the colonies and local communities prompted many of them to offer incentives. Tax exemptions for a specified number of years, exemption from labor on roads and military training, special land grants and leases, and even subsidies and bounties were offered to attract artisans.

While slave labor is most commonly associated with plantation crops and agricultural labor, slaves were also employed along with indentured servants and free laborers in every craft and form of manufacturing of the colonial era as well. Enterprising landowners in all of the English colonies soon discovered the value gained from developing and diversifying the skills of all of their laborers. Labor was varied and diverse in every colony. So was the pattern of free, slave, and native American labor.

By 1708 the total population of colonial South Carolina, for example, was counted as 9,580, of whom about 1,400 were native American men, women, and children. Of the 4,080 nonslave white population, only about 120 were under indentures at the time. The remaining whites included 1,320 free men, 900 free women, and 1,740 children. Black slaves, most of whom were employed in agricultural pursuits, comprised a population of 4,100, of whom 1,800 were men, 1,100 women, and 1,200 children (W. B. Smith, 1961, p. 128). By the end of the colonial era, the files of the *South Carolina Gazette* tell us that slaves there were trained in and practicing at least twenty-eight different crafts. Of seven different kinds of slave woodworkers there were sawyers, squares (the paper doesn't tell us what these were), coopers, house carpenters or shipwrights, cabinet makers, and wheelwrights. Leatherworkers included tanners, curriers, and shoemakers. Similar specialization of slave labor was noted among cloth workers, in the building trades, and there was at least one slave silversmith. Slaves also worked as navigators, boatmen, and pilots. Many masters found it more profitable to hire out their skilled slaves than to employ them themselves. There seem to be few, if any occupations, from which the skills of slave laborers were completely excluded. Racism and slavery went together, but job discrimination was not yet part of the picture.

The Idea of Liberty

The ethnic, cultural, and religious distribution of the population also varied. Predominantly Protestant, though Maryland was founded as a religious sanctuary for Catholics, colonists were divided into a multiplicity of sectarian groups and ethnic or cultural factions. Several colonies were identified with specific religions, though only a few maintained a majority religion for very long. The Catholic influence remained strong in Maryland long after Catholics became a minority of the population, a development that took place in less than one generation after the founding of the colony. Ownership of land and control of economic resources led to political power and social prestige, not simple numbers. Consequently, though numerical minorities, Catholics dominated Maryland and Quakers dominated Pennsylvania.

The plurality of religious groups and the varied ethnicity of immigrants meant that no single faith or cultural heritage gained a majority in any of the colonies. The common fear of a religion established by a majority played more of a part in religious toleration than fondness for the more abstract concept of religious liberty and the separation of church and state. Pennsylvania was established as a proprietary colony after 1681 by William Penn, a member and proponent of the small, but the influential sectarian group, the Society of Friends (more commonly known as Quakers). Penn favored the idea of religious liberty and was rewarded for his progressive views with the economic growth of his colony in spite of his otherwise poor business skills. Immigrants flocked to his and other American colonies for both the religious liberty and economic opportunity that was unavailable in most of Europe. That dual promise continued to fuel the hopes of immigrants to the United States throughout its subsequent history, with religious rights enlarged to include their secular counterpart, political liberty. That uninterrupted and unrestricted flow of (white) newcomers, until the exclusion of Chinese in 1882 and controls and ethnic origins quotas imposed on immigrants after World War I, is often noted as another explanation for the absence of the same kind of class and political consciousness among American workers as found among their counterparts elsewhere.

Newcomers usually accepted the practices of the nation that welcomed them with less criticism than the one they had fled. They worked under laws that held them as temporarily inferior politically to established citizens in exchange for the promise of a better future. Grateful for their newfound economic opportunities and the promise of civil liberties, immigrants gave their loyalties to the governmental and social authorities which granted them, in marked contrast to the denial of the same in the places from which they came. As newcomers they had to adapt their own personal and cultural habits, languages, and customs to the new society. As long as immigrants were hopeful about their newly adopted future they accepted the loss of old ways and took on those of the already existing Americans. Recent arrivals were also more vulnerable than citizens and worked for less, and their plentiful availability served as a brake on the demands of established labor groups. More than in any nation, except perhaps Canada, the labor force of the United States has been shaped and changed by the regular flow of a diverse pattern of new immigrants from every corner of the world to its ranks.

Culture

In spite of the increasing secularism and practicality of everyday life, religion played a powerful part in shaping the cultural world and emotional responses of the people to the possibilities within it. Religion was a dynamic cultural glue that bound family, community, and society together. In the colonial era the direct power over everyday life and labor held by religious authorities, most notably in the New England colonies, gradually gave way to the legal power of the state and its civil authorities.

The fastest-growing profession in the colonies was the law. Practical skills, science, and invention were distinguishing features of the era, known philosophically as an age of reason (in contrast to faith), and scientifically as one of Enlightenment (in contrast to ignorance). Nonetheless, religious influences held the loyalties of most of the population and unfailingly sustained the prevailing property and power relationships. Insofar as religious institutional influences played an important part in shaping the limits of the public imagination and the popular consciousness of power relationships from the colonial period to the present, they have played a conservative role throughout in spite of the benevolent and often radical work of humanitarian individuals in matters of justice and compassion. Labor could not form itself as an independent social entity separated from the religious institutions of the colonial age.

Each class and population segment found a religious denomination with the emotional, intellectual, and inspirational features that best served its interests. Frontier and libertarian sentiments helped extend the Great Awakening, a populist and universalist religious revival of the 1730s–40s that challenged most traditional Protestant sectarian groups, and led to new splits and divisions among them. In spite of the multitude of sects and groupings found among this vast array of immigrant, frontier, and ethnically diverse people, the most dominant religious influences came from the owners of property and leaders of this undemocratic society. It was the religious beliefs of such leaders that shaped the prevailing attitudes on work, law and government, race and patriarchy. Servants, slaves, laborers, and women expected the reward for their obedient service to be found in the pleasure it brought to their masters and their god, or in their afterlife. Few received much in this one.

Labor and Society

In every colony domestic institutions, including colonial assemblies, courts, churches, schools, and militias, soon claimed the loyalties of most of the population. Craft associations were few. England eventually restricted the migration of skilled artisans, and the colonial manufacture of a variety of goods, including specified woolens (1699), hats (1732), and iron (1750). Men and women in farm families took responsibility for the various household crafts, including soap and candle making, weaving, and carpentry. Fishermen and farmers built their own homes, and fashioned many of their own tools and implements. Women made clothing, preserved and prepared food, nurtured and raised large families. The relative absence of established artisans outside of the large settlements made for a simpler, even crude level of household refinement long into the American national experience. Whiskey and beer drinking among Americans, for example, was more common than wine consumption until the last decades of the twentieth century. Available free or inexpensive land was another disincentive for the growth of a large or organized artisan population.

Most artisans worked alone, traveling from place to place in the early colonial years. Many had varied skills, and could repair or make many things. Little hard currency was found in frontier regions and barter was common. Fish, tobacco, and grain were among many items traded for other goods or services. As settlements grew, and craftsmen could sustain themselves in one place, artisans or mechanics opened workshops in the larger towns and cities, took in apprentices, offered their services, and sold their wares. Craft shops, mills, and foundries were mostly small until the end of the colonial period, with masters working alongside apprentices and a few journeymen employees. Masters expected large fees for taking in apprentices, who worked for their food and shelter from about age fourteen to twenty-one while they learned the "secrets" of the trade or craft.

The products of colonial craftsmen eventually came to meet the highest standards of their European counterparts, especially in metalworking, furniture building, printing, shipbuilding, and construction. Profits were good and wages high for these skilled craftsmen compared to the European standard of the time, and abundant land and game provided inexpensive and plentiful food supplies. Products like iron, made in colonial foundries, gained an advantage in competition with iron made in Europe because of the inexpensive fuel that was provided by the vast forests of America. Finally, in 1750, the British passed an Iron Act to protect their domestic makers from cheaper colonial imports.

There were no unions, though various clubs, societies, and fraternal orders sprang up in the more prosperous decades of the later 1700s. Most of these associations professed an interest in promoting benevolent activities or the advancement of knowledge in their pursuits. For the most part they were social organizations or "friendly societies," and met in the homes of their members or in local taverns. Strikes or turnouts were more like family disputes or arguments over specific issues. Sometimes they could be quite intense, even violent. But they were more likely to be treated as local personal quarrels without larger significance or connection to other disputes. Examples of work stoppages are found throughout the colonial period, beginning with a strike of Maine fishermen in 1636. An English court decision in 1731 held that strikers could be prosecuted for criminal conspiracy, though such cases were extremely rare in the American colonies. Labor conflict took on other forms as well as the strike.

Conflict: Servants, Slaves, and Native Americans

No land or labor in the English or other American colonies was easily taken. The use and threat of violent force was always present. Native Americans felt this from the first, and massacres and brutal repression took place in every colony. A category of local military men, or militia, emerged in the settlements and on the frontier to provide local defense against remaining native Americans. Each colony had its more regular military force as well. These were used to drive native Americans farther into the wilderness and maintain frontier defensive fortifications. They also served in war on behalf of the British. Lacking the fire power of guns unless they could trade pelts for them, without technology to produce steel, and a vulnerability to European diseases, local native populations were destroyed or swept from their land. The process continued unabated until the final confinement to reservations, income from some specific crafts, then gambling casinos, of the few survivors two or more centuries later.

As a more clearly delineated class order took shape in the colonies, protests, uprisings, and rebellions of servants and slaves likewise followed. Slaves had already found innumerable ways to protest and resist. Onboard ship in the horrifying confines of the "middle passage" transport to America, and packed without room to turn and hardly enough air to breathe, they resisted. Dr. Falconbridge, a surgeon aboard slave vessels, testified to Parliament in London that when he entered the slave deck he followed the custom of removing his shoes to "avoid crushing the slaves." When he exited he "had the marks on his feet where (the slaves) bit and pinched him" (Mannix and Cowley, 1971, 104–7). Slaves ran away, committed suicide, stole, and found innumerable ways to cheat their overseers and masters of time and labor. They paid dearly in whippings, chains, branding, and tortuous punishments intended to discourage similar behaviors among other slaves. Servants and debt-ridden farmers, along with runaway slaves, joined together in conflicts against masters or creditors in almost every colony. There were enough of these uprisings to alarm and persuade the propertied masters that something had to be done.

Resistance and Rebellion

Colonial newspapers, once they were widely established after about 1690, frequently reported on runaway slaves and servants. Rewards were offered, descriptions given. Runaway slaves almost always were said to show the marks of brutal whippings in scarred necks and backs. Newspapers and handbills also noted that slaves and servants often ran away together, or in groups. Work slowdowns, the deliberate breakage of tools, mistreatment of work animals, and feigned illness were also commonly complained about in the correspondence of irate masters. Various techniques to combat these expressions of resistance included rewards and privileges, along with punishments that ranged from mild reprimands and deprivations reserved mostly for servants, to severe whipping and horrifying tortures reserved mainly for slaves.

Rebellions and the uncovering of plots of slave and servant rebellions were also common throughout the colonial period. These frequently included servants and slaves acting together, as in the plot in Gloucester County, Virginia, in 1663. In the plantation areas after 1690 and the creation of distinct racial laws, such unity declined. Nonetheless, dozens of plots were reported. One, originating in St. John's Parish and aimed at instigating a general uprising against the planters in nearby Charleston, South Carolina, in 1730, was said to be of such magnitude that "had not an over-ruling Providence discovered their Intrigue, we had all been in blood." The plotters were killed by the militia, with just a few escaping that fate (P. Foner, 1947, 1:21; Grant, 1968, p. 37). A real uprising that took the lives of nine whites took place in New York City in 1712 when twenty-three slaves acted to avenge their harsh treatment. The revolt was finally put down by superior force and the rebels executed with particular brutality. One was broken to death on a wheel, the others either hanged or burned alive. Whites and blacks were implicated in a huge planned uprising in New York in 1741 that resulted in the hanging of eighteen slaves, the burning alive of thirteen more, and the hanging of a white Catholic priest who was their accomplice. A white man, accused of providing the weapons for the plot, and his entire family were also executed.

Class Conflict

English policy, law, and tradition in every colony concentrated political and economic power in the hands of the few. Royal authorities, proprietors, and trading companies were in charge. Next in line came the large landowners, merchants, bankers, and businessmen. The plantation system gave advantages to large landholders who could more easily withstand price fluctuations in tobacco and other commodities. Coastal elites extended credit to back country farmers and dominated colonial assemblies that set tax and currency rates. As soon as this social system was in place, by about 1660, revolts and rebellions of small farmers, sometimes joined by runaway slaves, broke out in almost every colony. One of the most dramatic of these took place in the Royal colony of Virginia in 1676.

Led by Nathaniel Bacon, who gave the rebellion its name, the westerners challenged the undemocratic and corrupt royal governor, Sir William Berkeley. The governor was reluctant to carry out aggressive military measures against frontier native Americans because of his fur trading policies. Bacon, though only a resident of the colony for two years, defied Berkeley, raised his own military force, led a series of frontier battles, and demanded new elections for the colonial assembly, the House of Burgesses. When elections were held, Bacon, though condemned for his illegal actions, was elected from his district, but rebuffed again by Berkeley when he sought a military commission. Bacon railed against the authorities in class-conscious terms: "The poverty of the country is such that all the power and sway is got into the hands of the rich, who by extortious advantages, having the common people in their debt, have always curbed and oppressed them in all manner of ways." Bacon led an insurrectionary force of farmers, runaway slaves, and servants that seized and burned the capital, Jamestown, and drove Berkeley to flee the colony. For a couple of months Bacon governed the colony, he said, as "general by the consent of the people" (quoted in Nettels, 1938, pp. 332–35). Bacon himself set fire to the Anglican church in Jamestown. However, he suddenly sickened and died shortly thereafter. His organization disintegrated and the revolt was brutally put down by Berkeley's military, soon joined by regular English forces sent to quell the rebellion. Laws that racially separated the rights of servants and slaves immediately followed the uprising. So did the dismissal of Berkeley, who died in England less than a year later. The frontiersmen also won a negotiated settlement with the native Americans that brought temporary peace to their region.

Five revolts took place in Maryland before the end of the century, and the Catholic proprietors, the Baltimore family, which remained the most prominent landlords, did not regain control until 1714, and then only after significant concessions were made to the rebels. Similar struggles took place in the Carolinas between the proprietors and settlers. They battled over quit-rent payments, control of the fur trade, and opposition to the aristocratic system of government, which was closed, hereditary, and arbitrary. The Fundamental Constitutions of Carolina, drafted in 1669 by the great political theorist, John Locke, placed control exclusively in the hands of the proprietors and the few largest landholders, called nobles or landgraves. Opposition to aristocratic absolutism and the appointment by the proprietors of a new governor rendered the Fundamental Constitutions essentially defunct by 1691.

A similar protracted struggle for greater political liberties and against proprietary privilege and monopoly took place in New York between 1664 and 1685, and culminated in the suppression of Jacob Leisler's Revolt and his execution for treason in 1691. The same kind of grievances of settlers against proprietors and their monopolistic trading practices, policies designed to enhance the wealth of powerful merchants, led to similar conflict in New Jersey. Acts of resistance took place in the colonies of New England as well. In Pennsylvania in 1763 frontier farmers who called themselves the "Paxton Boys" took up arms, attacked and killed some native Americans, then stormed into Philadelphia to demand relief from tax and other perceived injustices of the proprietary system and coastal elite. Benjamin Franklin was sent to England to seek assistance from royal authorities to take power away from the proprietors and impose the authority of the Crown to restore order. From 1761 to 1771 a frontier faction known as the Regulators defied coastal authorities in North Carolina, and even won electoral control of the colonial assembly in 1769 until the governor dissolved it. A small army was finally needed to crush them in 1771. Seven leaders were quickly executed. By 1776 proprietary governments themselves had been eliminated and replaced by royal authority in every colony. Opposition to government authority from then on was opposition to the Crown.

None of these conflicts was, in the modern sense of the term, a labor struggle. No demands were put forward for higher pay, shorter hours, or improved working conditions. No permanent organizations of workers were built and no elaboration of alternative ideologies was put forward. A self-conscious labor movement did not exist. American society was still largely agrarian. More than 90 percent of the people lived in small towns or rural areas. The chief products of colonial life were still made by farm and plantation hand labor. Nonetheless, a conscious sentiment about economic and political justice was evident among the people. Colonists made the connection between political liberty and the distribution of wealth. Economic wealth and political power went together. Real liberty was impossible if monopolistic economic controls, tax, and currency policy rested in the hands of the few. This observation was commonly made as well among those at the top of the colonial social pyramid when they expressed their discontent at colonial regulations that put them in debt to or under the control of British banks and trading companies.

Colonial elites could either fend off the angry claims made by their fellow countrymen against the privileged positions they occupied, or try to redirect that rage against a common foe, the British Empire, and its monarch, King George III. Wealthy planters and merchants would need the economic and political support of their countrymen to challenge the British monarchy and its imperial forces. Though no one knew it at the time, after a century of colonial preparation, the Americans were almost ready to dare such a challenge. American officers commanded troops and won distinction in the French and Indian War. The colonial population was over two and a half million. Even though most of the people made a living from agriculture, the American economy was growing quickly in every colony. The great English economist, Adam Smith, observed on the eve of the American Revolution: "There are no colonies of which the progress has been more rapid than that of the English in North America. Plenty of good land, and liberty to manage their own affairs their own way, seem to be the two great causes of the prosperity of all new colonies" (Smith, 1937, pp. vii, 538–51).

What They Made

Walk through any old American East Coast city. Cobbled and carefully laid out streets still testify to the wonderful skills of colonial brick layers, stone masons, and early city planners. Buildings with delicate steeples and symmetrical Georgian shapes (named for the Hanoverian kings George I, II, and III who reigned then) were constructed by a vast array of craftsmen, designers, and architects employed by men who made their fortunes from the labor of these artisans and that of shipwrights, clerks, servants, and slaves. By about 1750 that wealth and those cities were comparable to those of England, and the society was as literate and as interested in the most advanced ideas of science (which they called natural philosophy) and the arts as that of any place in Europe. Philadelphia became known as the "Athens of the New World." Every ship brought journals and books, scientific implements, gorgeous fabrics, and household luxuries to an eager audience of American scholars and consumers. If anything, the

Americans were more modern, less restrained by aristocratic and clerical traditions than their creditors and business counterparts in England.

The workforce had made this possible. No feudal obligations, tithes, or titles restrained or drained the wealth from this new society. The opportunities for economic independence offered by abundant land were joined with the political concept of civil liberty itself. Slave labor enriched several generations of planters who compared themselves to ancient Greek and Roman patricians. That their wealth and power came from slave labor made them sensitive to the delicacy of their own liberties when threatened by newly enforced tax, monopolistic, or other onerous mercantile policies. Slaveowners knew firsthand what the loss of liberty meant. That recognition placed slaveowners in the forefront of the struggle for national independence.

The American workforce was more literate, the universities as up-to-date as those of Europe, and the population more aware of the sources of social power than any other on earth. Indentured servitude was beginning to fall off as more immigrants arrived without obligations to repay, and the institution of slavery was starting to generate serious criticism from among slaveowners themselves. Slaves and freed slaves were beginning the agitation toward abolitionism that would touch every corner of the nation and reach a conclusion a century later in the Civil War. The battle for political independence that grew out of the colonial experience was both public and private, institutional and personal, economic and psychological. The rights of labor, the debate over the morality and political incongruity of slavery, and the early glimmerings of a sentiment favorable to the expansion of the rights of women gained momentum under the banner of liberty as the independent nation was formed.

Conclusion

Many historical streams converged to create the beginning of an independent American laboring population. European worker and peasant traditions of faith and craft were joined with new circumstances presented in a harsh land of opportunity for some and brutality and servitude for many. The imperial conquest of the lands of native Americans led many poor servants to accept the political leadership and protection of those who could bring land ownership their way. Frontier life for farmers mixed economic independence with political dependence and military necessity. Racial slavery made sharp social and political distinctions among workers, and psychological and cultural loyalties were tilted toward those who granted newfound liberties. In spite of the formidable power of trading companies, proprietors, and royal authorities, their more humble servants, slaves, farmers, and artisans all found ways to resist or rebel against what they perceived to be abuses or injustices. The results of these efforts were always mixed with small gains, legal adjustments, and harsh reprisals.

Every institution or legal structure in colonial America came under the authority of those who controlled the wealth that labor made, with some notable temporary exceptions, as in the case of Bacon's rebellion. Scarcity of labor in contrast to the abundance of land and resources influenced the lives and circumstances of the entire workforce. Bountiful goods and high wages, land and liberty were available for some whose labor helped to make the wealth of colonial America. Racial slavery, extraordinary brutality, and near genocide marked the destinies of others whose labor and land did the same. The tremendous variety and diversity of circumstances among the people who came or were brought to the colonies added to the creative energy and economic vitality of the culture. What united this mixture of people was the growing recognition that economic opportunity and personal independence were inseparable from political liberty.

THE TRIAL

OF THE

BOOT & SHOEMAKERS

OF PHILADELPHIA,

ON AN INDICTMENT

FOR A COMBINATION AND CONSPIRACY

TO RAISE THEIR WAGES.

TAKEN IN SHORT-HAND,
BY THOMAS LLOYD.

PHILADELPHIA:

PRINTED BY B. GRAVES, NO. 40, NORTH FOURTH-STREET,
FOR T. LLOYD, AND B. GRAVES.

1806.

The indictment of boot and shoemakers. This notice reflects the law that finds the audacity of workers who wish to combine to "raise their wages" an illegal offense. (M. B. Schnapper, *American Labor: A Pictorial Social History*, p. 25)

CHAPTER 2

Labor and Liberty in the Formation of the Nation, 1760–1830

In the very first session held under the republican government, the assembly (of Virginia) passed a law for the perpetual prohibition of the importation of slaves. This will in some measure stop the increase of this great political and moral evil, while the minds of our citizens may be ripening for a complete emancipation of human nature.
—Thomas Jefferson, *Notes on the State of Virginia*, p. 87

With Liberty for All

Liberty was in the air. For the last hundred years of the American colonial era the idea of liberty, of rights established in law, was the common political objective of those who sought to change their standing in the world. Popular protests, rebellions, and petitions put the concept of liberty at the forefront of every struggle. Charters of "Liberties and Privileges" were sought in several colonies, including New York. John Locke's famous essay, "Two Treatises on Civil Government," published in 1690, though written earlier, argued that the fundamental reason for government itself was the protection of "life, liberty, and property." Locke's ideas justified the overthrow of the monarchy. When governments failed to fulfill their very reason for being they had to be changed or even overthrown by the governed. Without political liberties, no other rights could be claimed.

Until fundamental political liberty was achieved by workers, no rights to the control of their own labor could be secure. Slavery, indentured servitude, and the illegality of concerted labor action were the commonplace standards for workers of the colonial and early national period. Once political liberty was realized by some workers, independent labor organizations and contracts became possible. A strike by labor to achieve a contract agreement with an owner or manager of property was legally possible only when the workers were free of legal restraints to combine and act together. The contract or agreement that resulted from their interaction established rights as well as responsibilities. It was a miniature version of John Locke's social contract between government and the governed. Without legal rights, or liberty, workers who combined to act were in a state of revolt or rebellion against the state itself. It was natural to find workers among the most ardent members and organizers of radical groups like the Sons of Liberty in the movement for American independence.

Merchants and planters dominated the colonial society in the mercantile age, a period devoted to the increase of national wealth through trade. The liberties enjoyed by property owners were clearly superior to those codes and practices that denied comparable liberties to slaves, servants, workers, and women. Merchants and planters were granted patents or given the right to set up social and political institutions of their own from the start of the colonial age. Some practices, like slavery, for example, developed gradually and became more formalized in colonial law and judicial decision making under the limited British enforcement policy known as Salutary Neglect. A colonial elite was one of the consequences of the economic success of the plantation and trading system that developed. George Washington was known as one of the most prominent planters and wealthiest men in the colonies. John Hancock of Boston was one of the most powerful and wealthy merchants. Less eminent figures along with lawyers, bankers, brokers, and a growing professional and scientific middle class (e.g., Ben Franklin) were drawn to the fashions, political outlook, and business practices set by those at the top of the economic ladder. Those with less status took on the social ideas, practices, and values of the leaders whose success they sought to emulate. But liberty was something that cut across economic lines.

British laws and policy were designed to enhance the wealth of their own mercantile trading companies and producers of goods, so American upper-class habits and ideology looked very much like the Whig less feudal, more business-oriented aristocracy of England. The political ambitions of English Whigs were to reduce the arbitrary rights and inherited privileges of the remaining feudal aristocracy and royalty. Whigs, too, fought battles for liberty.

American workers, slave or free, did not constitute themselves as a self-conscious group at the end of the colonial era. Nor did women, in spite of their common lack of political rights. No organizations beyond fraternal societies spoke on behalf of workers. The propertyless had no direct or active political representation in any colony. Workers struggled with the allure of the culture that employed and enfranchised them, while at the same time they were creating a culture of resistance and autonomy of their own. Only a few workers advanced broad ideas or a vision of a society that would enhance their own class. Most workers built their own goals within the prevailing national ideal of liberty. For important parts of American history most employees eagerly embraced the ideological presumptions or worldviews of their employers. When the leaders of the colonial society began to challenge British policy as an infringement on liberty, the same sentiment coursed through large segments of the culture. Wealthy merchants everywhere resented the unearned privileges of birth enjoyed by the aristocracy.

Courts served as an extension of both the executive and legislative branches of government. The decisions of judges shaped colonial labor and social policies. Courts sustained the mercantile objectives of enhancing profitable trade practices with regard to the setting of maximum wages and prices. Courts defined and interpreted the laws and codes of servitude and slavery in the interests of planters. Strikes were considered illegal conspiracies, and it was not unusual for the charge of contempt of court to be used to end a work stoppage.

Just as there was no fully formed working class, there was no class of businessmen completely independent of government in this highly controlled economic universe. Both an independent wage-earning working class and a colonial capitalist, or property-owning class were still just emerging within the protective and nurturing confines of royal and proprietary controls in England and its American colonies. In both places the restrictive hand of government was generating criticism and resistance from those who objected to its royal and aristocratic authority. Resistance boiled over into rebellion and revolution after the great success of the combined English and colonial forces against the French in the Seven Years' War (called the French and Indian War by the Americans), and the Treaty of Paris of 1763.

Criticism from American planters, large landowners, and shippers arose from longstanding mercantile practices that were aimed at enriching English merchants and enhancing royal revenues. Take tobacco, for example. About 20,000 pounds were shipped from Virginia to England in 1617. By 1628 the Americans sent 500,000 pounds. The total colonial (legal) export to England and Scotland in 1763 was 35 million pounds. Tobacco was an "enumerated" product, so Americans were required to sell their entire export crop to England, where it was processed and sold there or reexported and sold abroad. American colonists could not sell their crop freely in the world market. The import taxes, or duties, on tobacco kept the price artificially high and forced down the prices paid to planters who had to stay competitive with other producers. These planters lived on credit extended to them by their English brokers and bankers. From 1685 to 1703 the duty on tobacco was four to six times the price paid to American planters for it. By 1760 the ratio had grown to fifteen to one. For every penny the planter got, the imperial tax collector got fifteen. While some or, at times, all of this duty was remitted on export, the only beneficiaries from the refund were the English merchants and businessmen who handled the crop and sold it, not the planters (Hacker, 1940, pp. 126–27).

Similar tax and commodity control practices existed on every item or product of value in this trading system. Tea got the most attention when a shipment of it from the British East India Company was tossed into Boston Harbor in 1773 by disgruntled colonists disguised as native Americans. Colonists, including local workers and artisans who did not have the right to vote in their colonial assemblies, protested the government tax which had been imposed without their representation in Parliament, and the privileged East India Company monopoly on tea. Liberty for planters and merchants meant freedom to trade outside of a politically oppressive and economically disadvantageous relationship.

Criticism of the imperial system by American workers and self-sufficient farmers (those without a significant crop for export) came from their desire for greater access to cheap western land and for more political rights and liberties. Liberty to farmers, mechanics, and artisans meant expanded legal and property rights along with greater participation in government, which in turn were seen as steps toward greater economic opportunity. All these groups equated the idea of liberty with economic rights. They sought the removal of mercantile restrictions and impositions on their liberties. The Writs of Assistance (generalized search warrants of 1761), imperial tax policies like the Stamp Act (1764) and the Townshend Duties (1767), maximum wage laws, and price setting on manufactured goods stirred angry passions. A baker's strike, for example, in New York in 1741 was carried out by master bakers in the city opposed to the setting of prices by the colonial legislature that kept profits down. The strike was not a struggle by workers for a higher wage, but one of small businessmen for a more open market. Liberty to the bakers was both political and economic at the same time.

Frequent rebellions, as noted, struck at proprietary, royal, and corporate restrictions on liberties. By 1760 wage earners, a growing segment of the colonial population, began to take up the struggle for themselves and shared the general sentiment that placed liberty and economic opportunity together. Among artisans, the journeymen began to regard the masters as employers, not as fellow craftsmen. Workers in iron foundries and the large shipbuilding industry of the coastal cities of Boston, New York, and Philadelphia were becoming a permanent class or group of wage earners. Lacking any apparent political remedy to their condition, a work stoppage by free black chimney sweeps in Charleston, South Carolina, in 1763 over working conditions is sometimes noted as the first modern strike in American labor history. The action of the chimney sweeps was reported as "insolence" by the *Charleston South Carolina Gazette on* October 29. It is probably more accurate to call the action an uprising or rebellion, no matter how justified or successful, since the strikers had little legal standing or protection from their employers.

Though none could clearly foresee it then, the era from 1760 to about 1830 was one of transition. Economic and political life was shifting from the highly controlled, patent-issuing, monopoly-granting, craft-regulating, and indentured servitude based labor system of mercantilism to one of more independent capital and wage labor. Slavery survived the transition from mercantilism as a form of freed or liberated capital in the plantation states.

The great economist, Adam Smith, saw this new system coming in his monumental work, *An Inquiry into the Nature and Causes of The Wealth of Nations.* According to Smith, lifting the restrictive legal and monopolistic controls on wealth, and moving toward the making of laws that liberated or freed trading capital from government authority would advance the expansion of economic society. "Liberty and Property," a phrase used originally by John Locke in 1690 to describe one of the basic reasons for the need for government itself, was a slogan of the revolutionary movement for American independence. The same measures that would advance the expansion of wealth were perceived as advancing the liberties of the people. What was regarded as a leap ahead for the wealthy owners of colonial lands and businesses was presented as an improvement in the opportunities for all. While many workers, slaves, and women remained skeptical, the appeal of liberty mobilized many of them into action alongside the merchants and planters who led the struggle. When the battle for independence was won, new areas of conflict soon opened up.

The methods used to achieve the goals of liberty were also imitated or adopted from one group to another. One of those methods was to organize for action. Colonists were familiar with organizations of militia for mutual protection. Many had been involved in organized protests against colonial proprietors. Most colonial Americans were members of religious organizations, and were aware of the force of legal institutions such as colonial legislatures and courts, though there were no political parties and no popular participation in government. When a group organized for political action on its own behalf, James Madison called that a faction, almost all of which were formed, he claimed, because of "the various and uneven distribution of property" (*Federalist* no. 10). In the struggle for American independence both the method and the form for future political struggles were born. The liberation of the capitalist class was, it was argued at the time, the liberation of all. The rights of property and human rights were advanced as two halves of the same thing.

Organizing for Liberty

By 1770 just five colonial cities had populations of more than 8,000: Philadelphia, New York, Newport, Boston, and Charleston. According to the first census of 1790, more than 90 percent of all Americans still lived and worked on farms or plantations in rural areas, small towns, and villages. Slaves had increased to approximately 20 percent of the total colonial population in 1770, rising from about 10 percent in 1700. Manufacturing had been restricted and crimped in the American colonies by British mercantile policies. It was royal policy to reduce competition with English producers, so an industrial working class was nowhere to be found in the American colonies. Steam power was in use in English mills long before it was adopted by American manufacturers. American artisans, mechanics, mill workes, foundrymen, shipyard workers, and slaves all played important parts in the struggle for independence, but not in combination as workers acting as a class.

The struggle for liberty grew out of opposition to English mercantile policy and the desire for autonomy over land policy. It was not a battle for workers' rights. It was antiaristocratic, antioligarchic, and pregnant with democratic values that touched every segment of the colonial population. It is worth noting, however, that John Adams was probably close to the mark when he estimated that only about one-third of Americans actively supported a complete break with England. The division among those who favored, opposed, or were indifferent to independence does not show clear working-class preference.

Those workers who did join in the movement for independence formed local and national organizations. These organizations became precursors for unions, trade associations, and political groups that emerged during this period (1760–1830) and later. In Baltimore an association of merchants and mechanics (craftsmen) was organized in 1763 to oppose the conservative and royalist policies of the colonial assembly. A New York association of mariners, the Sons of Neptune, may have been the model on which the Sons of Liberty was based. Some of these groups, the Regulators, for example, had previously formed in opposition to colonial proprietors. In Pennsylvania an organization was formed called the Associators. In Connecticut they called themselves the United Company. Generally, these groups were called Sons of Liberty or Liberty Boys, and a women's' organization known as the Daughters of Liberty added an early feminist presence to the protests and boycotts against British goods, taxes, and restrictive practices. Mechanics and artisans in some cities organized their own independent groups, especially when there were political differences with merchant leaders. In New York, Charleston, Boston, and Philadelphia, mechanics and artisans formed such associations to add some of their own goals to the struggle against England. In every case the objectives of these groups were political, whether in opposition to British mercantile or colonial domestic policy. To advance their economic and labor specific goals during the period leading to the American Revolution, workers took other actions.

Several strikes are cited from this period as the first of their kind in American labor history. The Charleston chimney sweep action of 1763 has already been noted. "Bespoke work," that is, goods made to order for specific customers, was giving way to wholesale manufacture for sale by retailers. Journeymen were becoming the wage-earning employees of masters. A strike of New York journeymen tailors in 1768 in protest against a reduction in wages by master tailors led to their forming a collective tailor shop in competition with their employers. Carpenters at the Hibernia Iron Works in New Jersey struck their employer in 1774 because of a delay in the payment of promised wages. New York printers struck in 1778, as did members of a Charleston, South Carolina Marine Anti-Britannick Society. The latter were prosecuted for rioting in 1777 instead of the usual charge of conspiracy for striking.

So-called friendly societies or box clubs were the only continuing labor organizations formed prior to and during the War for Independence. Their chief activity was to provide benevolent aid, illness benefits, and funeral arrangements for recently arrived immigrants and workers. Labor combinations and actions were still illegal. Nonetheless, many of these organizations carried out practices that anticipated the activities of labor unions. One of these, The Friendly Society of Tradesmen House Carpenters, was organized in New York in 1767. Its membership, limited to carpenters, had to pay a small initiation fee, followed by regular monthly dues to provide benefits to members in need. If organizations or groups took actions beyond the philanthropic, they faced sharp legal reprisals. A Marine Society was broken up and its officials arrested by

Pennsylvania state authorities after a strike of 150 Philadelphia mariners took place in 1779.

Workers who engaged in organizational activities in their own interest prior to and during the American Revolution did so mainly in concert, in what would later be termed a "united front," with colonial authorities, or when they joined with other groups, as coalitions, in opposition to British mercantile policies. When they formed such groups and organizations, like the Sons of Liberty, they were racially exclusionary. Even the first formal organization to oppose slavery, later known as the Society for the Relief of Free Negroes Unlawfully Kept in Bondage, organized largely by members of the Society of Friends in Philadelphia in 1775, had no black members. Neither slaves nor freed slaves formed labor associations or organizations in their interests at the time. There were no fully independent labor organizations, no working-class associations, no unions capable of legal action in colonial America. There were thousands of skilled and unskilled workers, half a million slaves, and the beginning of industrial manufacturers. The War for Independence and the American Revolution advanced the common interest of all laboring groups in the expansion of liberty, but not all of them would enjoy the benefits of independence equally.

The Fight for Independence

Though workers and poor farmers have borne a disproportionate share of the casualties in the nation's wars, they have always been promised compensation for their efforts. The war will be worth the sacrifice. Combat is the ultimate form of labor. The soldier labors at death, his enemy's or his own. The work is to take the life of the opponent, to destroy the ability to resist. Goods and services of all kinds are more urgently needed in wartime, and all of these are made by labor. The outcome of a battle, or even of a war itself, may hinge on the availability of supplies. An important part of the reason for the ultimate surrender of General George Cornwalis to General George Washington at Yorktown, Virginia, in 1781 was the successful blocking of the arrival of English supplies and reinforcements by the French naval force under Admiral De Grasse.

Throughout American labor history wage rates and worker incomes always rose during war, though not always in step with inflation. Political rights were also enlarged, and organizational representation for workers expanded during national military crises. Employers and large-scale property owners made their greatest concessions to labor when they needed that labor most. At the conclusion of every great conflict, the material and legal gains were usually reversed or withdrawn.

National leaders needed the loyal and willing labor of their workforce in wartime, but could not command it the way feudal and aristocratic leaders commanded their forces. The Americans were merchants, planters, and businessmen, not princes, dukes, or lords. Until the War for American Independence most European wars had been fought for feudal or royal objectives, often with religious overtones. Armies had been relatively small, highly trained professionals in lifetime or long-term service. The colonial struggle against England sought to enlist the entire population. The idealized goal in this effort was freedom. Freedom usually means getting rid of a restraint or all restraints. It is not quite the same as liberty, the winning of legal inclusion and rights under the law. Freedom has an emotional appeal since it can be imagined as having no limit. Its appeal is universal as everyone welcomes the loosening of restraints and the gaining of greater personal autonomy. The war for American national independence raised the hopes and expectations of many for greater liberties as it sought to enlist their services.

Even before the fighting began, protests and actions against the most obvious restrictions on liberty within the colonies began to increase. In Rhode Island, for example, the colonial assembly sought to prohibit the importation of slaves by law in 1774. The preamble to that legislation combined the popular meaning of liberty and freedom when it stated: "Whereas the inhabitants of America are generally engaged in the preservation of their own rights and liberties, among which, that of personal freedom must be considered as the greatest; as those who are desirous of enjoying all the advantages of liberty themselves, should be willing to extend personal liberty to others" (quoted in Grant, 1968, 291).

Slave labor was the largest single segment of the colonial workforce. It was the mainstay of plantation agriculture and produced the principal export crop of the mercantile colonial economy, tobacco. Revolutionary and early national political leadership came largely from the plantation region. It is no exaggeration to point out that slave labor was responsible for building the foundation on which the rest of the successful colonial and early national economy was built.

Slaves and freed slaves were barred at first from American military service, though outstanding examples of heroic service by free blacks prior to the Declaration of Independence are well known. Crispus Attucks, a former slave, was among those killed in the Boston Massacre (1770), and freedmen fought bravely at Bunker and Breeds hills in defense of Boston Harbor in 1775.

Once the war was underway, the British, following Lord Dunmore's lead, offered freedom from slavery to those who would join their side. More than 65,000 slaves eventually gained their freedom, with 30,000 escaping to the British from Virginia in 1778. Few of the runaways were given weapons or combat duties. Most dug trenches, built fortifications, and performed other chores. Many, including some of George Washington's slaves, were returned to American masters at the conclusion of the war. So much for the good word of English officers and gentlemen. The war gave thousands more slaves the opportunity to simply run away. It is estimated that as many as 25 percent of all the slaves in South Carolina fled their masters for freedom behind British lines, mostly as families (Jones, 1998, p. 103). Finally, the Continental Army accepted the service of slaves and rewarded 5,800 of them with manumission when their service was completed. Free workers made similar gains.

The war just about put an end to indentured servitude for the duration. The practice did resume in the 1790s though new humane regulations crimped some of its harsh conditions. The flow of redemptioners, those paying for the cost of their passage with labor contracts, ceased entirely during the war. So did most immigration, which meant that existing labor had to both fight and produce. The unfree, slave, or bound part of the labor force in Pennsylvania dropped by more than 50 percent during the war years from 13 percent to 6.4 percent of the total. By 1800 it had fallen to just one percent. (Salinger, 1987, p. 180). New York, in the week that followed the adoption of the Declaration of Independence, put an end to imprisonment for debt. The struggle for American independence was good for both labor and manufacturing. Protests against trade and tax practices, nonimportation agreements, and boycotts against British manufactured goods before the war, and then the wartime needs for manufactured goods, stimulated colonial production and put a premium on every category of labor.

Wages of War

British forces in the colonies also had to rely on colonial workers, many of whom refused employment. General Thomas Gage was frustrated in seeking laborers to build fortifications for him in Boston in 1774. The impressment or coercion of labor was carried out by the British and the Continental Congress along with the states to supply some of their military needs.

Workers in revolutionary America continued to enjoy a much higher standard of living than their European counterparts during the war, and made further wage gains due to the wartime emergency, in spite of legal restrictions. Wage and price controls were imposed by the states and the Continental Congress during the war. Much contention and debate accompanied the application and enforcement of these controls, though American workers generally regarded these measures as protection, not restriction. In many areas the maximum rates turned into actual minimum wages as both prices and wages responded to tremendous market pressures. Protests and demonstrations broke out among workers when inflationary pressure lifted prices while wages were fixed. Workers were accustomed to payment based either on time or piecework, and both provided employers with methods to circumvent the controls. Other incentives, like overtime work or bonuses for extra work, also allowed workers and employers the means to get around the legal controls. Actual wages and prices both tended to rise during the war, though wages were not always able to keep pace against a depreciating currency.

The seizure of Loyalist land during the war provided some free white American workers with opportunities to gain property under tenant preemption rights. Thousands more gained land when the war came to an end and the entire Ohio Valley became available for settlement. Before the end of the fighting, land opportunities and liberties were advanced by the revolutionary forces that had been uncorked by the struggle. This was both a war for independence and a revolution, with most of the dramatic changes taking place in the states.

Labor and the Revolution

The colonies were only loosely united. What had brought them together was a common desire to win greater liberties, then independence from the British Empire. The Continental Congress that directed the war effort served as a governing body until compromises over conflicting western land claims allowed the adoption of the Articles of Confederation in 1781. The former colonies, now states, retained their sovereignty over almost all matters throughout the war and until the adoption and ratification of the new federal Constitution in 1789. Once the war was underway the states had to create new governmental structures for themselves. States had to make new constitutions, establish judicial systems, and confront the legacy of British laws they had lived with for almost 150 years. It was in the making of constitutions for these states that the political and social revolution was made.

Thomas Jefferson was proud enough of one of his accomplishments as governor of Virginia to want it to be remembered as one of the three most important of his life. He led the state to adopt his draft of a resolution that ended the establishment of religion. Taxpayers would no longer pay for the maintenance of the Anglican Church, or any church or religious institution in Virginia. Jefferson achieved separation of church and state, freedom of religion, and a step in the direction of freedom of speech. (Jefferson thought his other two great accomplishments were his authorship of the Declaration of Independence and his role in the founding of the University of Virginia.) Largely as a consequence of Jefferson's urging, the Bill of Rights constituted the first ten amendments to the new Constitution a few years later. Virginia's concept of the separation of church and state was confirmed for the nation, along with other rights that were first adopted by states during the revolutionary era. The right to assemble, petition, and speak freely, to due process and counsel, and to hear from a press free from government censorship would be vital for democracy itself and for the building of labor organizations. These civil liberties were a revolutionary achievement. Every movement for human rights and the expansion of the democracy of the United States depended on those civil liberties. Royal and aristocratic power had always been the final word. Now government itself was held in check when it came to certain specific rights of citizens.

States outlawed primogeniture and entail, two vestiges of feudal restrictions on the division of land. Primogeniture required an estate to be passed intact to the eldest son or nearest living male heir, and entail prevented estates from being subdivided at all. Holding large parcels of land or estates together prevented workers or small business owners from acquiring capital of their own. States also barred the granting of titles of nobility to prevent a new aristocracy from being formed. Bills of attainder, which imposed punishments on family members of those convicted of crimes, were outlawed. The Pennsylvania constitution of 1776 granted suffrage to every free adult male citizen. While hardly representing universal suffrage, the absence of a property qualification to vote extended political rights to every (male and free) worker and farmer, and made a new segment of the people a political force in the affairs of the commonwealth (which they called their state). Other states expanded the suffrage by reducing property qualifications for voting during the war. New Jersey went so far as to briefly grant women the right to vote.

Vermont barred slavery, an institution of no significance there, in its new constitution of 1777. Pennsylvania was bolder when it passed its Emancipation Act of 1780, a law that brought slavery to an end within its borders. The moral and social contradiction of slavery was arousing criticism from a more enlightened and literate population. Quakers had been raising moral objections to slavery for years. In spite of the commonplace defense of slaveowners about their benevolence, few doubted the obvious reality that slavery rested ultimately on brutal coercion. Wherever slavery existed, manacles, chains, whips, and tools of torture were commonplace items. The questionable economic efficiency of slavery in nonplantation applications was also becoming a serious controversy. Antislavery societies were spreading, especially in the South. Many asked: why invest capital—wealth that is used to increase wealth— into labor when it might be better spent on land, tools, or other more productive forms of investment? Adam Smith, writing in 1776, after much careful evaluation expressed his opinion: "I believe that the work done by freemen comes cheaper in the end than that performed by slaves" (Smith, 1976, p. 99). Wage labor, especially that of women and children in manufacturing enterprises, was showing itself to be an inexpensive alternative to the maintenance costs of keeping slaves.

The ideals of the Declaration of Independence also generated a broad criticism of slavery. To a society nominally devoted to the concept of liberty, the institution of slavery was its most striking contradiction. Antislavery societies sprang up everywhere, including the plantation South, where they were most numerous, at least for those few years before the invention of the cotton gin and the use of steam in textile manufacturing made slavery really profitable again. Prominent intellectuals, including freed slaves or their descendants, like the Philadelphia scientist, Benjamin Banneker, began to bring their criticism of slavery and racism to public attention during the American Revolution. That racism and controversy about it, though legally and institutionally changed, is with us still.

Without a large professional standing army, the new nation had to rely on volunteers and conscripts from the states. Though a regular Continental Army was formed, it was more of a people's army of farmers and workers than a royal or professional national fighting force. Thomas Paine complained of the casual habits of irregular "summer soldiers and sunshine patriots" in his wartime *Crisis Papers*. Unconventional tactics were used by Washington and officers like Francis Marion (the "Swamp Fox") to harry and wear down the British. These tactics relied on smaller, more self-sufficient units than the conventional royal fighting forces. They were more democratic and received the assistance of the local population in ways that the British could never match. Noncombatants served Washington's forces as spies. Of course, some served the British as well. Farmers and workers disrupted and plundered British supplies, sometimes without proper regard for who kept the booty. Privateers and whaleboat owners did the same thing along the shoreline. Morale was not always high during this long war (1775–81) but the republican spirit swept through the patriot side throughout the struggle.

At home, on the farm, in the workshop or business, the wives, daughters, and sisters of soldiers took on added responsibilities. Women managed and worked on farms and plantations, ran businesses, and worked in shops, mills, and manufactures in the absence of men. They found employment in places they had never been before due to the extra needs for wartime labor.

The dearth of British textile imports prompted greater spinning, knitting, and clothing manufactured by women in workshops or at home. In Philadelphia, 4,000 women and children were employed as textile workers in the "putting out" system. Employers put out or placed materials in the hands of local shop owners or as homework to be finished and returned. The factory system would soon replace putting out as a large-scale system, but the practice would be maintained until our own times as sweatshop labor on the margins of the textile and some other industries.

Women became "republican mothers" responsible for passing on the new virtues of a modern civil society to their children (Jones, 1998, p. 157). Their correspondence and diaries reveal the reach of the war and revolution into every aspect of life, even personal and family relationships. The Continental Army included black women, mostly slaves, as cooks and nurses. Several white women went along with their husbands into the battlelines, at least three of whom saw action on the front lines. One of these, Margaret (Molly) Hayes, got the nickname "Molly Pitcher" for supplying parched soldiers with cool water from a nearby stream during the Battle of Monmouth, June 28, 1778. She worked an artillery piece as well during the battle and earned a warrant as a noncommissioned officer from General Washington (P. Foner, 1979–80, p. 16). The labor and sacrifice of free and nonfree men, women, and children helped bring success in the first of many modern struggles in what became an age of democratic revolutions. The problem for most revolutions, and this one was no exception, is what to do after victory comes.

Building a Nation

Many things helped win the War for Independence, not least of which were the popular energies and work of the people on behalf of liberty and new freedoms. Now bills had to be paid, a new noncolonial society made. The republican spirit inspired an active participatory movement throughout the American culture, most important, among farmers and workmen in towns and cities throughout the fledgling nation.

Philadelphia shoemakers and printers organized into unions and carried out strikes in 1785 and 1786, respectively. The twenty-six journeymen printers who struck their shop owners were protesting a cut in wages. They won their demand for a shop minimum of six dollars a week, and established a benefit fund to assist any other journeyman printer fired for refusing to work for less. These two strikes are sometimes called the first organized work stoppages in American history.

Baltimore artisans formed a Mechanical Society that gained a dominant voice and place in local politics. In spite of periods of reversals and electoral defeats, the candidates and officeholders endorsed by the Mechanical Society became the backbone for the struggle to expand democratic rights in Baltimore for more than the next generation. No actions were taken by states or combinations of states to invoke the conspiracy charge against worker organizations or their actions during the period of the Articles of Confederation. In England, during the same time and thereafter for several decades, such actions, or any action taken in combination to raise either wages or prices, were vigorously prosecuted as illegal conspiracies (Morris, 1965, pp. 138, 206).

Indebted farmers in western Massachusetts organized a rebellion led by Captain Daniel Shays against coastal creditors in 1786. This rebellion shook the political foundations of the state and raised alarms about the limits of state authority elsewhere. Continental currency issued during the war was rapidly becoming worthless. Protests were mounting over unfulfilled land grant promises. No revolutionary movement had appeared, however, calling for the abolition of private property or an end to a capitalist system. That economic structure had not yet fully emerged. There really wasn't a nation yet either, just a loose collection of independent states. The government, such as it was under the Articles of Confederation, had its hands full.

The long colonial legacy, along with a highly skeptical attitude about governmental power itself, led many leaders of the newly independent states to prefer keeping the noncentralized confederation they had. The libertarian sentiments that were hostile to strong central authority unleashed by the Revolution now stood in the way of those merchants and planters who wanted to build an effective national government. Disputes between states over land, trade, and borders, an inability to make foreign treaties, an absent judicial system, no financial system, and no real taxing authority were the increasingly obvious shortcomings of the government of the Articles of Confederation of 1781–89.

The one significant accomplishment for labor and democracy by this loose confederation was another achievement of Thomas Jefferson, the Land Ordinance of 1785 and the Northwest Ordinance of 1787. The latter was an expansion of provisions based on the original. These ordinances laid out the plan for the settlement of the land of the Ohio River Valley and the Great Lakes region south of Canada. Vast amounts of public land would be inexpensively made available to American citizens. Three features of these ordinances helped to form the American national future.

First, there was to be no slavery in future states formed in the region. The foundation for the controversy over slavery was set in motion here. Soon many states in the nonplantation regions likewise followed the lead of Pennsylvania and this ordinance and put an end to slavery. The free black population of the entire North amounted to only about a few hundred in 1770. By 1810 there were nearly 50,000 and their numbers were growing fast. Every northern state would soon be in the process of abolishing slavery by law. Former slaves helped to form and lead the abolitionist movement and Underground Railroad. Frederick Douglass ran from slavery to the free states as a teenager. He helped to lead the antislavery movement through to its conclusion in 1865, when the Thirteenth Amendment that abolished slavery was ratified.

Second, public education was to be a provision supported by land sale in the new territory. Neither democracy nor free and independent labor organizations can exist without universal education. Jefferson saw an "Empire for Liberty" in the geographic vastness of North America. His was an agrarian vision of independent, educated, self-sufficient, and self-governing farmers with little need of centralized government or big cities. He didn't see the industrial revolution coming, but did see that one of the roads to tyranny was an uninformed or misinformed public.

Third, the new territories, once populated enough by non-native Americans and organized under their own state constitutions, would be admitted to the Union on an equal basis with the established states. There would be no political inferiority for the new states, no colonial subservience as the nation grew, no population inferior to the authority of others based on geography. For its first hundred years the United States grew dramatically as a democratically inspired nation without colonies.

Of course, native Americans were uprooted, displaced, and destroyed in the process. Jefferson's vision excluded the well-being of native Americans and African Americans. They were consigned to the legal status of internal colonial subject populations with no real role in the determination of their destinies. Several states followed their termination of slavery with the disenfranchisement of freed black voters; New Jersey in 1807, Connecticut in 1818, New York in 1821, and Pennsylvania in 1837. Slaves and racially identified freed slaves remained, along with native Americans, as dependent, vulnerable segments of the population—the latter as racialized tenants with no legal rights to their land, the former as racialized workers and farmers with either no rights to their labor (slaves), or with legal infringements on their liberty (former slaves). That colonial and racist legacy continued to undermine the democracy and played a major part in restricting the success of labor organizations throughout the nation's history. Full citizenship meant an entitlement to political participation and economic opportunity that aligned vast numbers of American workers with the outlook of the state, which granted their liberties, and their employer, with whom they believed they shared a kinship and from whom they gained a preferential wage.

To be fair to Jefferson, it is worth pointing out that he was hardly alone in his thinking. His views, along with those of his most enlightened peers, were formed in a scientific age characterized by empiricism. Scientists and scholars studied just what they saw, and tried to understand what things in nature actually were. They had no clear time frame or sense of process for understanding either social or scientific changes. Darwinian concepts about the development or evolution of natural phenomena were still decades in the future. Jefferson did, however, recognize that things in both nature and society were subject to change, and frequently made comments about how "the earth belongs to the living generation, not the dead," and that, "all things are changeable except the inalienable rights of man." He imagined that each new generation might actually reconstitute itself based on its own reality, not be bound for centuries in the grasp of men even as well intended as he regarded himself.

Dynamic changes, however were taking place that would freeze some practices with institutional and social permanence and toss others onto the junk heap of history. One of those things to be tossed were the Articles of Confederation as a new federal Constitution, lasting until our own times, was created. The other newly emerging phenomenon was mass production of goods from a steam-driven factory system that would ultimately destroy slavery and replace the merchant with the manufacturer, the farmer with the worker.

Labor and the Federal Constitution

Workers enthusiastically joined the July 4, 1788 parades, known as the Federal Procession, that were a celebration of both independence and the new federal Constitution. In most cities, apprentices, journeymen, and masters marched or paraded their floats together in a spirit of unity with farmers and merchants. The new Constitution was linked with the patriotic sentiment of the day. Many of the problems of the old government, especially the obstacles to commerce among the states, had been discussed in the newspapers for months. Arguments in favor of ratification expressed in the essays by Alexander Hamilton, John Jay, and James Madison were also widely read at the time and are now considered among the classics of political theory. Those essays are known as *The Federalist Papers.* Anti-Federalist arguments won few adherents among workers in the commercially active large eastern cities. The Mechanical Society of Baltimore was one of the most outspoken advocates of ratification of the Constitution. Economic motives may have driven the founders, as later argued by Charles Beard in his *Economic Interpretation of the Constitution of the United States* (1913), but at the time the debate over ratification had more to do with the alleged libertarian benefits of a weaker central authority versus the dangers to liberties of a strong centralized one.

For labor the new Constitution was a mixed blessing. The Bill of Rights, adopted as the first ten amendments in 1791, and checks and balances of the federal system are well known achievements in the human endeavor to achieve responsive and nonarbitrary government power. The concept of civil liberties, universal specified rights protected by law, drawn from this era, may be one of this nation's gifts to civilization itself. Those of limited wealth are most vulnerable to abuses of power, and workers in the United States have enjoyed the protection from arbitrary infringements on their privacy, speech, press, and the like that were guaranteed by this kind of government, without always fully appreciating their good fortune.

The institution of slavery was given greater legal protection than it had been earlier. Now, as the result of various compromises, it was framed, not solely by state law, but by national law in three specific areas. (1) No action, the new Constitution stated, could be taken against the slave trade for twenty years following ratification. (2) The federal government was given the authority to pass laws to apprehend and return fugitive slaves. (3) Slaves were to be counted for the purpose of political representation as three-fifths of other people. So, while they enjoyed no rights whatsoever as citizens in their respective states, their masters gained congressional and electoral voting power from their ownership. For forty of the next forty-eight years, slaveowners occupied the office of the presidency and held commanding positions of leadership in every part of the national government. Slave labor, much of it highly skilled, leased or rented, under contracts with the owners, constructed the Capitol building and president's residence (later called the White House), along with many of the other buildings in the national city named for the first president. Slavery quite literally built the new government. When the political dominance of slaveowners was threatened by the increase in nonslave states, these slaveowners led a secession movement and fought a Civil War that sought to destroy the national Union itself.

Native Americans "not taxed" were given no representation whatsoever in the government that imposed its authority upon them. In 1790, in its first action that defined citizenship in contrast to those immigrants who would be permitted to enter the new nation, Congress limited naturalization to "free white persons." The door for newcomers was never fully open to "tired masses yearning to breathe free." From the birth of the nation, citizenship for immigrants was restricted to whites only until the revision of the law in 1952 (Lopez, 1996, p. 1).

Setting Direction

The new nation was still in transition from a dependent mercantile society to a fully independent manufacturing society in its own right when President George Washington took office in 1789. He put life into the Constitution by creating a cabinet, a body of executive branch leaders responsible to him but not mentioned in the original document. To maintain harmony among factions he appointed Thomas Jefferson his first secretary of state and Alexander Hamilton as secretary of the Treasury. Hamilton was charged with bringing forth a Report on Public Credit (issued January 1790) and a Report on Manufactures (issued December 1791). These reports urged that the power of the new government be placed on the side of an economic nationalism that ultimately reshaped the class and social structure of the nation.

Hamilton's work helped to establish the preeminence of an independent class or stratum of owners of capital, manufacturers with goals and political needs beyond the limits of traditional planters and merchants. A propertyless industrial working class also emerged, one that was far greater than Hamilton envisioned. Like Jefferson, Hamilton did not foresee the full impact of steam power and new technology. Hamilton favored public support for financial policies and tax measures that would strengthen domestic business interests, at the time still mainly mercantile. Among his recommendations were a publicly funded national bank, assumption of state debts, refunding the national debt, excise taxes on a variety of things (especially on tobacco, which he called "an absolute superfluity"), and protective tariffs on competitive imports (Morris, 1957, p. 258). These measures would be paid for by consumers, farmers, and workers in the higher prices, taxes, and interest payments that resulted from these policies. The general public was, through its sacrifices, expected to subsidize the accumulation of great private wealth for the few. This inequity was said to be for the good of the nation.

Hamilton and other Federalists, as those who favored his program were soon called, promoted a strict defense of the rights of private property and contracts. Though not as absolutely undemocratic as he is often portrayed, Hamilton regarded those with property as the only segment of the society trustworthy for service in government. Power among competitive nations, Hamilton understood, went to those of wealth. Government had an obligation to promote the expansion of wealth, not to manage its equitable social distribution.

The encouragement of manufacturing, Hamilton argued, should not divert workers from other economic pursuits. Women and children should be put to work in the new industries. Their labor would add to the household income and allow males to continue in their traditional labors. Coldly, he observed in his report: "women and children are rendered more useful, and the latter more early useful, by manufacturing establishments, than they would otherwise be." He noted with some envy that of those employed in England's cotton textile manufacturing, more than half were women and children, "of whom the greatest proportion are children, and many of them of a very tender age" (Morris, 1957, p. 279). Hamilton did not need to note the political inferiority of women and children. Their dependent status was confirmed by church and state. The cultural and legal division between men and women (and for more than the next century, children) workers has been a barrier to organizational and political unity among workers throughout the country's history. The political battle for equal legal rights for women began to gain strength in this era alongside the movement to abolish slavery.

The Treasury secretary also claimed in his report that immigration to the new nation should be encouraged to spur manufactures. Hamilton noted proudly that the United States offered the twin incentives of economic opportunity and personal independence, liberty and property. He observed that in the United States there was no mere religious toleration, but, "a perfect equality of religious privileges." Of course, he also pointed out that low taxes, plenty of cheap land, and abundant raw materials and water power were powerful incentives to immigration and to manufactures.

Hamilton and the Federalists argued that citizenship should be a reward after a probationary period of residency. Jeffersonian Republicans, who were enrolling more recent citizens as voters, argued for more liberal requirements. Immigrants faced a period of years during which they would not enjoy the full protection of the law, a form of national political indenture. This political and social division between new noncitizen workers and older citizen workers has been maintained throughout the nation's history. A five-year probationary period preceded naturalization for all immigrants with one notable exception. From 1798 to 1801 the Federalist Party won a temporary fourteen-year naturalization requirement to counter the advantage of the Jeffersonians for the votes of the new citizens. During the period of political inferiority the special cultural practices or religious differences of the immigrants would be exaggerated in importance in the public view, and contribute further to the insecurity and dependency of one group, and the conservative identification with the privileges of inclusion in the nation of the other. The deliberately constructed legal and social gap between citizen workers and non-naturalized immigrant workers has made it nearly impossible for them to attain organizational unity throughout the nation's history.

Hamilton anticipated Henry Clay's "American Plan" of the 1820s when he echoed Adam Smith in calling for the encouragement of the use of machinery. "It is an artificial force," Hamilton argued, "brought in aid of the natural force of man; and, to all the purposes of labor, is an increase of hands, an accession of strength, unencumbered too by the expense of maintaining the laborer" (Morris, 1957, p. 278). Workers have had to confront the utilitarian but destabilizing influence of technology ever since. The intellectual skills, imagination, and craft oriented capabilities of workers most often create the new technology. The innovative devices, from steam engines to computers, become property, a form of capital outside the control of labor, through either direct ownership or patent rights. Technology then is used to increase and augment the productivity of the worker without having to add anything extra or commensurate with what is added to the compensation of that worker. More product, same pay. The inventive mechanical worker or intellectual worker (scientist, inventor, or engineer) may enjoy a premium pay, may even share in the immense rewards of his creation as many did by becoming manufacturers themselves, but whatever the inventor is paid, it rarely equals the value made from it by the owner-employer. The government has historically protected patent rights, provided publicly subsidized research and development to owners of capital, and granted tax and depreciation allowances to promote technology. Capital could be said to be wealth created by labor, or found in nature as land or resources, which is converted to privately owned property by law. Law displaced American Indians and turned their property over to those with the weapons to defend that law. The new assertive government actions that grew from Hamilton's vision, aimed at the expansion of national capital, were not a vision that favored the equitable distribution of the wealth made by labor. To be fair to Hamilton (as we have tried to be to his counterpart, Jefferson), the young secretary of the Treasury did favor competitively high wages to attract skilled immigrant labor and to further the expansion of manufactures.

Control of new technologies by the owners of capital has caused worker discontent from the very first. Workers forced to adapt to machinery that dictated the speed and technique of labor resisted the innovations. Many workers took out their frustrations on the machinery itself. English workers, with no right to strike or organize in the early 1800s, smashed textile machinery to express their anger about low wages and long workdays. These workers were called Luddites after their alleged, perhaps mythical, leader, Ned Ludd, and their actions have regularly been invoked as examples of simplistic and foolish inhibitors of progress. The use of the death penalty for those apprehended and the widespread introduction of opium to company stores as a popular sedative diminished the frequency of Luddite actions in England, but their name has become a standard accusation against workers who stand in the way of new technologies or processes.

Federalism and Strikes: The Cordwainer Conspiracy Cases

Journeymen societies were fast-growing organizations of skilled employees who sought to improve their bargaining position against masters. By the 1790s, journeymen furniture makers, hatters, shoemakers (cordwainers), carpenters, and printers were among those organized in real trade union associations in coastal cities like New York, Boston, Philadelphia, and Baltimore. Strikes, or "turn-outs" as they were called, were usually the result of disputes over the price paid for labor, or wages. The new state constitutions and the federal Constitution said nothing about trade unions or strikes. It remained for a local court, in this instance the mayor's court of Philadelphia in 1806, to decide if the English common law prohibition on combinations of workers applied in their city to a strike of the previous year. The case is known as *Commonwealth v. Pulius*. English common law was not assumed to be in force after independence. It took what one author has called "affirmative action" by the various states, one by one, in their courts to reestablish it (Engerman, 1999, p. 222). In Philadelphia the defense argued that there was nothing in the law that justified the indictments against the shoemakers, and that the "spirit of the revolution" and the rights of man favored the striking workers. The presiding judge in the case, Moses Levy, disagreed. He clearly led the jury to his side when he sternly reaffirmed the hold of common law, and echoed then Supreme Court Chief Justice John Marshall's firm Federalist defense of contracts.

For more than a century state courts would be the agency of government that dealt most directly with the legality of the actions of American workers. The police and national guard units dispatched to break strikes by mayors, governors, and sometimes presidents were acting on the authority given them by courts. Unlike England, or any of the major European countries, it would be judges in state courts, with but a few federal court interventions, who set the legal framework for workers in the United States. Judges were the least democratically assailable government figures. Whether appointed or elected, they were far removed from the political debates that brought voters to the polls. The decisions of judges against workers almost never became public matters of debate.

In the original cordwainers' case the judge went so far as to make criminal the very act of association itself. It was the formation of the union that was illegal, as well as the strike action. That position mellowed a bit in the next cordwainer conspiracy trial in New York three years later. Those striking shoemakers lost too, but the judge did not find the act of association itself illegal. The legal door was opened a crack for unions. It was their action, the New York judge found, that was illegal, "the means they used were of a nature too arbitrary and coercive" (Engerman, 1999, p. 223). For more than the next thirty years courts impaled effective union action on these two poles: either the organization was an illegal conspiracy, or the strike was an illegal collective infringement on the rights of the employer. By 1840 universal (white) manhood suffrage had been achieved, or nearly achieved, in every state. But it was not until 1842 in *Commonwealth v. Hunt* that a striking union won a definitive decision in its favor. From the time of the original cordwainer cases to their ultimate reversal, great changes in the American workplace were taking place. So, too, were the changes in the thinking of many workers.

Industrial Innovation: James Watt, Samuel Slater, Moses Brown, and Eli Whitney

Alexander Hamilton may have recognized the value of technology in manufacturing, but it was among workers themselves that the actual industrial age found most of its creators. Shop floor craftsmen always looked for ways to refine and improve the work they did. The intelligent work of skilled mechanics was responsible for just about every new invention or improved technical process of the industrial age. James Watt was an instrument maker working at the University of Glasgow in Scotland when his refinements and improvements brought about the development of the first useful steam engine in 1769. British mercantile law recognized the value of skilled workmen by prohibiting the emigration of certain categories of artisans.

Since textile workers were among those prohibited from emigration, twenty-one-year-old Samuel Slater had to disguise himself to make the crossing from England to the United States in 1789. He was an apprentice textile worker who rose to plant supervisor and knew everything about cotton textile machinery then in use in English mills. Until Slater, the English were able to restrict drawings, plans, or models of their machinery from foreign eyes or hands. They could not hold onto Slater's memory, however, and he was in search of the money offered as bounty by American textile manufacturers who wanted what he knew.

Young Slater met Moses Brown in Providence, Rhode Island, and they went into business together making and using the first machinery that sharply increased cotton textile manufacturing in the United States. Slater and his new partner built a second mill in Pawtuket that employed a labor force made up of seven boys and two girls, from seven to twelve years in age, the children of local farmers and artisans and pauper apprentices. Slater's machine, a copy of the English Awrkwright, dramatically improved the spinning of raw cotton into yarn. That's all it did. The yarn was then sent out to the mostly cottage industry of hand weavers and cloth makers that continued making textile products with traditional methods. An all-children labor force in Slater's mills soon gave way to the family system, with adult men used as carpenters, teamsters, and outside laborers, and women inside the mills as workers along with children. Slater was said to be strict, but benevolent—coincidentally the same description slaveowners preferred.

Textile machinery and the family system of employment quickly spread along the river valleys and streams of New England. Steam-powered mills didn't come into widespread use until more than a generation later. The workday was dawn to dusk in summer, to 8:00 P.M. in winter with candle or lamplight, and the profits were enormous. These working hours became the standard throughout the factory system as it gradually evolved. Slater became one of the great men of new wealth of his day. He amassed a great fortune over the next forty years estimated to exceed $700,000. His success stimulated many would-be inventors and innovators to seek to do the same thing.

The first few years in the life of the new republic were influenced by many new inventions and the application of science and technology to practical purposes. Eli Whitney's device for cleaning or brushing the hard seeds out of raw cotton within a drum, called a cotton gin, drastically cut the labor cost of bringing the raw material to English, French, and New England mills. His built his first cotton gin in 1793, a year after his graduation from Yale University. He invented the device while a tutor on a cotton plantation and soon the demand for cotton gins outstripped his and his new business partner's capability to produce them. The cotton gin never made Whitney rich like Slater. Too many variations were made to enable him to patent his invention successfully. Eventually, huge steam-driven gins were in use throughout the cotton-producing regions of the South. The institution of slavery, instead of fading with the inefficiencies and low profitability of tobacco and similar crops from the colonial era, was given a new lease on life by steam power and the gin.

The demand for cotton grew sharply. Its cultivation by slave labor in the rich soil of the South proved immensely profitable. Western lands became vital for the expansion of cotton production. New England slave traders experienced a boom in their business too. More than 20,000 slaves were brought into Georgia and South Carolina in 1803 alone. Slavery underwent a vigorous revival instead of coming to a gradual end, in spite of what slaveowning critics of the institution had contended just a few years earlier. The demand for slaves forced a sharp increase in the price when the supply was crimped after the ending of the legal slave trade in 1809. Cotton production, and all that went with it, from field hands and house servants to horse trainers and craftsmen, brought about a new plantation era. The enslaved population of the United States increased from fewer than 700,000 in 1790 to over two million by 1830. The slave population doubled to four million by 1860, exclusively in the South and Southwest, while abolition brought the institution to an end everywhere else.

Whitney's other great innovation, though not his invention as he claimed, was his application of the concept of using interchangeable parts in the manufacture of firearms. He put this into operation in 1798 in his factory in New Haven, Connecticut. The craft of gunmaking was immediately reduced to one of assembling parts, each made repeatedly by an employee more easily trained to do the more specific task. Productivity increased, while costs of production dropped sharply.

The Threat of War

Disruption in trade with England and France during the Napoleonic Wars (1799–1815) forced Americans toward industrialization as well. Ironically, Jefferson the agrarian idealist as president helped to stimulate industrialism by his foreign policy. He led the nation, with much dissent, to accept an embargo, followed by a Non-Intercourse Act, that barred importation of foreign goods made in nations that refused to honor the neutrality of the United States. England and France both were guilty of that, and manufactured goods from them dropped off with important economic and political consequences. Many Federalists opposed to these policies were elected to office in the next elections, though Jefferson's successor was another Virginia plantation owner and Jeffersonian, James Madison.

The new president was eventually unable to prevent the drift toward war. Domestic manufacturing grew to meet the demand for goods blocked by the embargo, and later, to meet the needs of the nation at war. Merchants in New England states with trading ties to England threatened secession. "Home manufactures are increasing to such a degree there (in New England)," wrote one astute observer in 1808, "that ere long, in numbers as well as opulence, that class of the community will be a full match for the seaport merchants" (quoted in Bowers, 1936, p. 470). In Pennsylvania the effect of the embargo and war was called "magical." In Philadelphia in the embargo year, 1808, the Philadelphia Manufacturing Society proudly announced the opening of new mills and new machinery to produce woolen and cotton cloth. The Premium Society of Pennsylvania Manufacturers offered prize money as incentives to producers of quality goods, and three new paper mills opened in one neighborhood. By 1810 the secretary of the Treasury, Albert Gallatin, reported that there were 500 men and 3,500 women and children employed in the eighty-seven American mills in, or about to begin, production of textiles.

One New England businessman, Francis C. Lowell, traveled to England in 1810 to study manufacturing and brought his knowledge home two years later. Lowell convinced a group of his peers, later known as the Boston Associates, to start a Boston Manufacturing Company. They built a cotton textile factory in nearby Waltham that put all of the processes for making cloth under one roof. Mass production was underway in the first "modern" factory in the United States in early 1816. The Patent Office in Washington was soon swamped. During the 1790–1810 period about eighty patents a year were issued; by 1830 the number had increased to over 500. Women and children served as the mainstay of the new labor force.

The War of 1812

Warfare tends to speed up and stimulate existing social and economic processes for both winners and losers. The origins of the War of 1812 lay in disputes over trading rights, American aggressive land ambitions in Canada, and British reluctance to withdraw from their Ohio River Valley positions. Another war with England was highly controversial. Its most forceful advocates, known as War Hawks, came mostly from the West and South. Eastern mercantile interests, now largely Federalist Party stalwarts, opposed the boycotts on trade that preceded it, and the war when it came. Most workers were on the margins of the debates on this war, with some notable exceptions. The Mechanical Society of Baltimore, now avid Jeffersonian Republicans, opposed everything the Federalists stood for, and Baltimore workers destroyed one of the Federalists' antiwar newspapers, the *Federal-Republican* on the night of June 22, 1812. Some Baltimore workers apparently believed that war with England was a patriotic project, one that would drive up wages and make new work available. The same patriotic sentiment was present in most towns and cities where workers, black and white, turned out in support of the war effort. In spite of the cost in lives lost and casualties endured, wars through most of the nation's history have stimulated patriotic emotions among workers. Wartime patriotism was strongest when popular political and economic ambitions were linked with the goals of the war.

During the War of 1812 (1812–15) blockages on foreign trade stimulated domestic manufacturing and encouraged capital investment in industries instead of trade. Shipbuilding and munitions led the way, but every kind of manufactured item gained importance from the time of the embargo through the end of the war. Iron production in the United States was only about 55,000 tons per year in 1810. By 1830 it reached 180,000 tons. Even Jefferson became convinced of the value to the nation of manufactures. "Experience has taught me," he wrote in 1816, "that manufactures are now as necessary to our independence as to our comfort" (quoted in Peterson, 1967, p. 160).

The war encouraged advocates of other large-scale public projects favorable to economic expansion. Canals and roads were regarded as the best transportation means of reaching the immense resources of America's hinterland, but constructing them was beyond the capabilities or interests of private investors. A federal highway was built that crossed through the Cumberland Gap of the Appalachian Mountains and reached Wheeling, Virginia, in 1817 at a cost of $7 million. Canal building soared throughout the Northeast and Middle West. New York began the construction of the Erie Canal in 1817. That canal opened for business in 1825. New York City was linked to the Great Lakes by a canal network, including locks that overcame a 573-foot difference in elevation, between Albany and Buffalo, a total distance of 363 miles by man-made waterway. Other canals were linked to this great system. The new network opened up two-way markets in vast territories previously of little value because of formidable transportation expenses. At the outset of the Erie Canal project New York State authorized convict labor for the task. Eventually, thousands of Irish immigrant workers joined recently freed slaves in the hard physical labor of these projects. Their meager pay, set and varied by the contractors who employed them, was usually augmented by a ration of whiskey, sometimes as much as a quart a day per man. In southern states, slave labor was responsible for almost all canal building and river and harbor improvement projects.

The wartime and postwar boom, however, was soon offset by the return of foreign competition for the market of manufactured goods. Hundreds of American mills were unable to match English quality or price competition and were forced to shut down. The country was driven into its first industrial depression in 1819. Shut-down mills and unemployed workers proliferated. Many thousands, who were able to, joined the trek westward in search of cheap land and a new start. Industrial recovery proceeded slowly through the 1820s. The high wages and high standard of living that had won comparative renown in Europe were coming to an end, at least for a while. Pennsylvania was known in the 1790–1820s period as "the best poor man's country in the world" (Lemon, 1972, p. xiii). Harder times put that slogan to rest.

The Industrial Evolution

The industrial age was on, though it proceeded more as an evolution in development than the revolution that it was commonly called. Water power drove mills efficiently for decades. Woolen manufacturers resisted the factory system until the Civil War era. Cheap western land was more attractive to poor farm families than factories, mines, or millwork, and many tens of thousands moved into the Ohio Valley over the next twenty years. The trans-Mississippi West continued its appeal until the end of the century. Steam power drove many more boats than mills, and American production of coal and iron was still an insignificant part of the domestic economy until the 1830s. Permanent workers (those dependent on the exchange of their labor for their well-being) were the skilled and unskilled slave labor force of the plantation South, the freed slaves, immigrants, artisans and mechanics, and women and children in the mills and workshops of towns and cities in the North and West. This enormous labor force, with either no rights at all, or no legal rights to act together, had to find other means to assert their own desires.

Worker Action and Organization

Everything that had to do with wealth in the United States was protected or defined by law or institutional authority. Paper money had value only because of government legitimacy. Land ownership, contracts, the granting of bank or corporate charters, patents and copyrights, the institution of slavery, the prohibitions on the rights of nonslave workers, the legal inferiority of women, children, and immigrants (for a defined period) were codified by either federal or state governments. It is no stretch of analysis to suggest that the state itself was an agency of capital, no friend at all to labor. In these circumstances it is truly remarkable to review the ways which labor found to advance its interests in every sector.

Slaves found overt and covert means to resist, rebel, and finally (for some) escape. Slave actions were both broadly cultural collective responses that affected the entire society which sought to control them and deeply personal and individual. Slaves were aware of other historic groups who had escaped bondage. The Christianity they were taught included the popular story of Moses leading the Israelites out of Egypt. Spiritual music and popular tunes featured lyrical depictions of escapes from the hard injustices around them. Filled with subtlety and hidden meaning, the music of slaves included coded messages and guidance for those planning to run away. "Follow the drinking gourd" is how one song alluded to the way that the north star could be found in the night sky by locating the Big Dipper, since "the old man is a'waitin' for to carry you to freedom, if you'll follow the drinking gourd." Most ethnomusicologists argue that all of the spirituals of the pre–Civil War era included an extra covert meaning in their lyrics to at least some listeners. Music took on added importance in a setting where people were barred from literacy (by law in most states) and any other form of collective communication. Work songs and chants set a deliberate and tolerable pace for labor to follow. Theft and cheating of owners and overseers, in spite of harsh reprisals, became admirable accomplishments among those whose total labor power was arguably being stolen. Tools were routinely broken and work animals frequently beaten to death to interrupt the hard pace of labor. Arson was not uncommon, and the use of poison against masters was widely suspected and feared. Sometimes despair led to suicide and infanticide. Humor, folktales, games, everyday deceits, and petty sabotage lightened the awful burden of slavery and influenced the entire way of life of the society. So did plots of rebellion and escape.

Long before the appearance of the highly organized Underground Railroad that assisted thousands of runaways, slaves slipped away from masters and fled to towns or regions where they might make a new start. Before there were free states to escape to, slaves, alone or in small bands, fled to frontier regions and merged with communities of native Americans, or to lands under French or Spanish control. Once the Ohio River became a border separating slave and free states, clandestine traffic increased there.

Rebellion, or plot of rebellion, was always in the air. Every slave state had the experience of prosecuting slave rebels found in plots or after active uprisings. One of the largest in scale and audacity was the Gabriel plot on the plantation of Thomas Prosser in Virginia in 1800. It involved some 1,100 slaves pledged to fight, but betrayed by an informer. Federal troops were called in to aid Governor James Monroe in seeking out the last remaining rebels implicated in the Gabriel uprising. An uprising by several hundred slaves in 1811 about 40 miles north of New Orleans led to harsh battles and brutal repression before it was put down.

The War of 1812 heightened fears of uprisings among planters, and increased patrols and surveillance were imposed throughout the slave states. In 1816 four separate plots were reported in North Carolina alone. In Camden, South Carolina, in 1816 six slaves were executed for plotting an uprising that called for the burning of the town and the massacre of its population. A similar alleged plan to set fire to Atlanta, Georgia, was uncovered in 1819. Denmark Vesey, a freedman in Charleston, was charged with planning the capture and destruction of his city in 1822. Vesey's betrayal led to the capture and execution of thirty-five plotters and the sale of thirty-seven others out of the state. A slave uprising was suppressed by the intervention of federal troops on Talbot Island in Florida in 1819. Anyone who imagines that slave labor was readily tolerated needs to look at the actions of defiance, and the culture of resistance and rebellion slavery engendered. Those observers will also discover a culture of racial illusions, arrogance, and brutality that was increasingly needed to maintain control over slaves, especially as the idea of ending slavery was advancing nearby.

For those free workers who, in a few states, had the won the right to vote, but not to strike, rebellion took other forms. Strikes, of course, continued, often in defiance of the contempt charges that came from court rulings. Successful turnouts for higher wages or shorter hours were reported with the return of prosperity throughout the 1820s. Carpenters, painters, tailors, stonecutters, and cabinet makers won wage and hour settlements in several cities in the 1820s.

Most workers, especially women, children, slaves, and recent immigrants, had no vote and lacked protection under the law from various forms of abuse and exploitation. In Samuel Slater's textile center of Pawtucket in 1824, the textile workers went on what has been called the first organized women's turnout. A year later the United Tailoresses of New York organized a trade union for its women workers. Unionization, or the formation of trade associations or craft and labor societies, continued to spread throughout the urbanizing and industrializing parts of the nation.

Workies

To some workers, even the idea of unionization or strike action seemed too limited, too narrow in scope or ambition. Karl Marx was only nine years old when a Mechanics Union of Trade Associations in Philadelphia, the first of what came later to be called a city central federation, put forward its class-conscious program in 1827. A new kind of society was emerging, the Mechanics Union observed in its newspaper, the *Mechanics' Free Press*, one that was built on the wealth that labor created, but one that did not fairly share the product of that labor. The new organization claimed that strikes to get a little more money or a more limited workday were understandable, but not enough. Labor had to address the imbalance that unfairly rewarded those who lived as parasites on the labor of others. Labor deserved recognition and proper reward for the part it played in making the wealth of the new age; it should be at the forefront of society, not restricted to its fringes. Suffrage in Pennsylvania gave every male citizen the right to vote. Political power, claimed the Mechanics Union of Trade Associations, not just picket lines, was the way forward for labor. Historians frequently have pointed to the year 1827 as the point at which a class-conscious American labor movement was born.

A year later The Workingmen's Party, the first of its kind, was formed in Philadelphia, and a year after that The Workingmen's Party of New York was organized. The new organizations were riding the popularity of Andrew Jackson's election to the presidency in 1828. He, and they, attacked unearned privileges, leftover mercantile restrictions, and monopolistic and elitist concentrations of power. The national political consensus formed in the "Era of Good Feelings" (1816–24) after the War of 1812 was falling apart. Jackson used democratic rhetoric to his advantage on the national level; worker organizations did the same thing in the cities and industrializing towns.

These new parties were also influenced by the ideas of writers and social critics on both sides of the Atlantic. Some were finding their own voices in the radicalism and anticlericalism of Thomas Paine. Social critics assailed the sharp inequalities in wealth so evident in the society formed by expanding mills and factories. Some Workies read the words of Langton Byllesby, the author of *Sources and Effects of Unequal Wealth* (1826). Byllesby was a New York proofreader at Harper Brothers who blamed the rich, not the poor, for the spreading crime and poverty of urban life. Thomas Skidmore, a Connecticut teacher, machinist, and inventor, went even further. He extended the arguments of Thomas Paine to include *The Rights of Man to Property!*, a tract intended to become a book, published in 1829 in New York. Skidmore, like most utopian and early social critics contended that the unequal distribution of property was the source of all social ills. The answer, Skidmore argued, was in the equitable redistribution of property, mainly land, through inheritance taxes. Banks and factories, Skidmore said, should become public properties, and private land ownership abolished. Skidmore became the leading voice in the formation of the New York Workingmen's Party. Robert Owen, a pioneering utopian socialist, and Frances Wright, a Scottish-born utopian, abolitionist, and early feminist, joined with Skidmore in New York. Owen and Wright were advocates of universal free public education. They argued in their newspaper, the *Free Inquirer,* that education was the means to offset the unearned privileges of wealth. The new social critics, though widely diverse in their views of many things, generally agreed that the winning of public office by social reformers would allow the implementation of these humane and democratic proposals.

The workingmen's parties took up many of the new ideas, and added a few of their own. Workies pressed the demand for free public education. They sought an end to imprisonment for debt, and wanted a mechanics lien law to prevent the common practice of using bankruptcy as a way of forfeiting on unpaid wages. They favored more equitable tax laws, and saw an opportunity to gain greater influence in local government through abolition of property qualifications for officeholding. One organization, the Association of the Working People of New Castle, Delaware, advocated voting rights for women in 1831. The way to get public attention and to win elections, workingmen's parties believed, was through the press.

The Philadelphia party took the lead with the newspaper formed in 1827 by William Heighton. The *Mechanics' Free Press* was the official organ of both the Mechanics' Union of Trade Associations and the Philadelphia Workingmen's Party. The New York Workingmen's Party followed the Philadelphia organization a year later when George Henry Evans, who bought out Wright and Owens' *Free Enquirer*, started the *Working Man's Advocate*. Evans' slogan was printed in the first copy, October 31, 1829: "All children are entitled to equal education," he wrote, "all adults to equal property; and all mankind to equal privileges" (quoted in Wallace and Burrows, 1999, p. 519). The idea of a political party with a newspaper voice caught on and soon spread to more than a dozen states. Though strictly local, these parties were the first significant third-party organizations in the United States. In 1829 the New York Workingmen's Party elected the president of the Carpenters' Union, Ebenezer Ford, to the city assembly. The goals and ideas of Workies spread quickly and helped to shape the politics of the next generation and beyond.

Conclusion

The founding of the United States of America took place in a tumultuous era, a time of rebellion and world war. The emerging nation went to war with England twice. The remnants of hereditary feudal and aristocratic authority were swept away in the United States by wealthy slaveowners, their merchant allies, and thousands of people who recognized that there was something in the idea of liberty for them too.

The genie of liberty, once released, would never be easy to contain for the benefit of one group or class. Everyone wanted their place at the table where birthright or religious autocracy no longer held authority. The struggle for equal rights for women was launched. Abolition of slavery was also taken up across class and racial lines. Slavery, not racism, came to an end in the North and Northwest where wage labor seemed to be more suited to the new mechanical and industrial modes of production. Finally, workers began to create their own communities and their own cultural identity. Many recently enfranchised white male workers came to regard themselves as a distinct political and social entity. Without legal rights to act collectively in the workplace, these workers mobilized as a political force intent on realizing the promises of liberty loudly being proclaimed in the rapidly growing nation.

$200 Reward.

RANAWAY from the subscriber, on the night of Thursday, the 30th of Sepember,

FIVE NEGRO SLAVES,

To-wit : one Negro man, his wife, and three children.

The man is a black negro, full height, very erect, his face a little thin. He is about forty years of age, and calls himself *Washington Reed*, and is known by the name of Washington. He is probably well dressed, possibly takes with him an ivory headed cane, and is of good address. Several of his teeth are gone.

Mary, his wife, is about thirty years of age, a bright mulatto woman, and quite stout and strong.

The oldest of the children is a boy, of the name of FIELDING, twelve years of age, a dark mulatto, with heavy eyelids. He probably wore a new cloth cap.

MATILDA, the second child, is a girl, six years of age, rather a dark mulatto, but a bright and smart looking child.

MALCOLM, the youngest, is a boy, four years old, a lighter mulatto than the last, and about equally as bright. He probably also wore a cloth cap. If examined, he will be found to have a swelling at the navel.

Washington and Mary have lived at or near St. Louis, with the subscriber, for about 15 years.

It is supposed that they are making their way to Chicago, and that a white man accompanies them, that they will travel chiefly at night, and most probably in a covered wagon.

A reward of $150 will be paid for their apprehension, so that I can get them, if taken within one hundred miles of St. Louis, and $200 if taken beyond that, and secured so that I can get them, and other reasonable additional charges, if delivered to the subscriber, or to THOMAS ALLEN, Esq., at St. Louis, Mo. The above negroes, for the last few years, have been in possession of Thomas Allen, Esq., of St. Louis.

WM. RUSSELL.

ST. LOUIS, Oct. 1, 1847.

Reward announcement. Without any legal rights, escape became the only way out of slavery for this man of "good address," his wife and "bright" children. Note the immediacy of this printed bulletin following the escape. (Library of Congress, Prints and Photographs Division, Reproduction No. LC-USZ62-62797)

CHAPTER 3

Great Contrasts: Factory and Field, Slavery and Democracy, Civil War, 1830–1865

We have erected these cities and villages which smile where lately was the Indian's wigwam, or the lair of the wild beast.

We have called into existence American manufactures, and been the instruments by which Commerce has amassed her treasures; our labor has digged the canals, and constructed the railways, which are intersecting the country in all directions, and opening its resources.

We have built and manned the ships which navigate every ocean, and furnished the houses of the rich with all their comforts and luxuries.

> —*Third Grand Rally of the Workingmen of Charleston, Massachusetts, Held October 23, 1840*

The Making of Haves and Have-Nots

It was in the sharp contrasts, the immense asymmetries of social and economic wealth and power, that a conscious new outlook was formed among workers in the first decades of the industrial age. Democracy became the popularly accepted term to describe the political ideals of the nation while slavery, the antithesis of democracy, grew in importance to become the single largest labor formation in the country. Slavery dominated the national public debate until secession and civil war concluded the argument. Slaves and abolitionists challenged the idea of labor as property in words and deeds. At the same time feminists began the long struggle for women's legal and economic equality with men on their own and from within the antislavery movement. Political liberty came easily to neither group.

As soon as the franchise was extended to them, white workers formed political parties, enlarged their trade union organizations, formed citywide federations of labor, and launched the first national association of craft unions. Their leaders attacked the sharp contrasts between the lives of workers and the lives of those who profited from the wealth that workers produced. The boom and bust economic cycle made its harsh presence felt. Economic swings became more dramatic in an industrializing age that provided no refuge for the urban poor and unemployed. By the 1830s there were tens of thousands of working people in mills and factories who had no farm families to fall back on. Urban life offered enticing amenities, but few cushions against adversity. Immigrants and citizens (some recently naturalized) clashed in bitter disputes and riots following the Panic of 1837 and the depression that followed it. Employers and political leaders exploited the fears and suspicions of one group against the other. Class, gender, immigration, and race divisions became intractable centers of social conflict in national life. Finally, a dramatic social contrast emerged between the rapidly urbanizing industrial centers of the nation and the rural and small town agricultural way of life.

American labor, black and white, male and female, immigrant and native-born, rural and urban, took up a broad social struggle to find its face (what should a worker's nation look like?), its voice (what should a worker's politics sound like?), and a vision for the future (what should a worker's goals look like?). It is hardly surprising that no singular or unified conclusion was reached in this pursuit. There were many voices, many faces, and many visions. Workers of all kinds were not alone in seeking to form a new outlook for the nation. Landowners, industrialists, bankers, and businessmen of varied pursuits found themselves in sharp conflict over their opposing visions about the nation's future. Those employers were, however, united in at least one common objective: they all sought control of the wealth that labor produced. There was little that was serenely bucolic or pastoral in this stormy period except the work of artists and poets who idealized the natural beauty of the young nation. The conflict unleashed in these years concluded with the bloodiest war in American history, a war to determine, once and for all, the nature of the labor force for the nation's future.

Rise and Decline of the Workingmen's Parties

The greatest strength of the Republican Political Association of the Working Men of the City of Philadelphia was in the elections of 1829. Twenty of their candidates of fifty-four for city offices, with cross-endorsements from the two dominant parties (Federalists and Democrats), won election. Their votes were great enough to control briefly a balance of power, with neither of the two dominant parties holding a majority. The New York Party also peaked in influence and cohesion in 1829 when it was formed around the popular defense of the ten-hour workday. In Albany, Troy, and Salina, New York workingmen's parties swept to victory in 1830. At least twenty newspapers, mostly in New England and the Middle Atlantic states, were advocates of labor issues and candidates by the summer of 1830, according to one of them, the *Delaware Free Press.*

Leaders with widespread appeal were emerging among workers. One of these was William Heighton, an English immigrant who became a Philadelphia cordwainer. Heighton helped to organize the citywide party in Philadelphia, and founded its newspaper, the *Mechanics' Free Press.* Some of his contemporaries credited the brilliant speeches of Heighton, especially his 1827 "Address to the Members of the Trade Societies and to the Working Classes Generally," with launching the labor movement itself. Heighton, like many English immigrant workers in the Philadelphia area, added a new dimension to labor radicalism: working-class consciousness. He was known as a Ricardian Socialist for his joining of some of the labor theories of the English economist, David Ricardo, with the contrary democratic radicalism of Thomas Paine. In his famous "Address" he urged, in language that has continued to provoke debate ever since, political action as the best course for workers: "All our legislators and rulers are nominated by the accumulating classes and controlled by their opinions— how then can we expect that laws will be framed which will favor our interest?" Heighton said workers should "resolve to never give our suffrages to any but members of the working class, or to such others as will publicly pledge themselves to support our interest in the legislative hall." By the early 1830s, after just a few years of prominent leadership, Heighton disappeared from Philadelphia and the labor scene.

Seth Luther, a Rhode Island carpenter, was another worker advocate whose *Address to the Working Men of New England* went through several printings and was widely read by workers everywhere throughout the decade. Luther, like Heighton, tied the cause of workers to the ideals of the Declaration of Independence. Their ideological outlook came to be called labor republicanism. Both men urged the representation of workers in government to win what unions alone could not, especially when strike action was illegal. Stephen Simpson, another Philadelphian, was a journalist who became a leading influence in the workingmen's movement. Simpson's influential tract, *The Workingmen's Manual: A New Theory of Political Economy, on the Principle of Production the Source of Wealth* (1831), called for a "general system of popular education." New York, as already noted, boasted several radical leaders, including Thomas Skidmore and George Henry Evans. But even in its best year, 1829, the New York organization was beginning to show the symptoms of disintegration that soon overtook the entire movement.

Intraparty intrigues plagued all of the parties. The New York Party was split into three factions almost immediately after their first electoral success. Divisions about cross-endorsement of major party candidates, ideology, and organizational structure coursed through the movement. There was never enough money. Those who had it, or could get it, soon steered the parties back toward established parties. By 1831 the Philadelphia organization was falling apart. Their early success led to a massive attack on them in the city newspapers in 1830.

"Workeyism" was smeared everywhere with charges of atheism, riot, and rebellion. Many literate artisan and mechanic leaders were not traditional churchgoers.

They were deists and universalists in the tradition of Jefferson. Thomas Paine, known for his radical anticlericalism, was one of the Workies' most prominent heroes. The unions were attacked for their "monopolistic" imposition of terms on employers, and interference with the right of individual contracts made by workers and their employers. Frances ("Fanny") Wright was portrayed as the high priestess of the Workies. She was attacked as a danger to society for her advocacy of women's rights, abolitionism, and separation of church and state. In an article in the *Free Enquirer* on November 27, 1830, Wright joined her socially radical views to what she called a "war of class." She cheered "the oppressed millions who are making common cause against oppression," of "labor rising up against idleness." Her prophetic linkage of feminism, abolitionism, anticlericalism, and working-class struggle should not pass unnoticed.

Employers threatened workers with dismissal for their political activism. President Andrew Jackson's attack on the elitism and monopolistic power of the Second Bank of the United States won over the vast majority of workers to the Democrats in his reelection campaign of 1832. By then both major parties included most of the workingmen's issues in state and local platforms as they sought to win labor votes. Universal elementary public education gained support in many quarters. Those business leaders who recognized the value-added aspect it provided to their labor force were among its strongest proponents. Horace Mann was beginning to develop his idea that universal public education could promote a higher level of civic responsibility and public morality. Debtor prisons were abolished before the decade was over. Lien laws were enacted that protected wage claims, though immigrants always were vulnerable to employers who forfeited on wages. Corporal punishment (except for women and children), the whipping post, and branding soon disappeared outside of the slave states. President Martin Van Buren, by an executive order, brought the ten-hour day to workers on federal projects in 1840. The relative prosperity and western land boom of the early 1830s weakened the workers' political movement and shifted worker interest to more strictly union causes or personal goals. Finally, the democratic appeal of the nation itself bound workers to the rhetoric of the leaders of the major parties. The Workies didn't have a big or comprehensive enough program to compete with their rivals. They rarely did thereafter.

Democracy in America

Alexis de Tocqueville, the astute French observer of American life in 1831, was impressed with the vitality and energy of the rapidly growing nation. He found three noteworthy and distinctive features of special importance to labor in the United States. The first had to do with the division, specialization, and stratification of labor in the emerging mass production industries. The young French nobleman argued in his book, *Democracy in America,* that democracy favored the increase in manufactures in the United States, but feared that "as the principle of the division of labor is more extensively applied, the workman becomes more weak, more narrow minded, and more dependent." The worker, he claimed, must become more expert at smaller and more specialized tasks, while "the master surveys an extensive whole, and the mind of the latter (master) is enlarged in proportion as that of the former (workman) is narrowed" (1956, p. 218). De Tocqueville believed that the result of the expansion of the science of manufactures would be the reduction in the class and status of the workman to that of "brute," "born to obey," and the elevation of the class and status of the master to a new kind of aristocracy of "command." Even though wages for some workers in a democracy tend to rise, he issued a warning: "Hence, it would appear, on searching to the bottom, that aristocracy should naturally spring out of the bosom of democracy" (p. 219). This would not be a benign new manufacturing aristocracy, the Frenchman contended, but "one of the harshest which ever existed in the world." And finally, he cautioned, "the friends of democracy should keep their eyes anxiously fixed in this direction; for if ever a permanent inequality of conditions and aristocracy again penetrate into the world, it may be predicted that this is the gate by which they will enter" (1956, p. 220).

The second area de Tocqueville believed would continue to have a bearing on labor and democracy in the United States was the matter of race. He was not the only traveler in the youthful nation to observe the more specific forms of racial discrimination and the greater force of racial emotions in the "free" northern states than were evident in the slave states. "Race prejudice," he wrote, "seems stronger in those states that have abolished slavery than in those states where it still exists, and nowhere is it more intolerant than in those states where slavery was never known" (1975, V.1, p. 343). It was in the workplaces of the North, the Frenchman observed, that racial division and white hostility toward free blacks were the most sharply expressed.

De Tocqueville's third area of prophetic insight into labor is his conclusion about the relative position of women in the United States. While he acknowledged the dependent status of most women, and their confinement to what he called "the narrow circle of domestic life," he concluded on a very enthusiastic note: "I have nowhere seen women occupying a loftier position; and if I were asked, now that I am drawing to the close of this work, in which I have spoken of so many important things done by the Americans, to what the singular prosperity and growing strength of that people ought mainly to be attributed, I should reply, To the superiority of their women" (1956, p. 247). By 1831 women were doing more in the United States than anywhere else. They worked in industry and agriculture and were active in business and commerce. Women were taking the lead in the debates and organizations that were going to split the nation over slavery, and from that platform launched the most powerful movement in the world to end legal and social inequality with men. Women, children, and slaves were also in the vanguard when it came to labor action.

Labor Action

Two lines of labor action characterize the history of American workers. The one that is most quickly recognized, and the one most often thought of as the principal vehicle of protest action, is the trade union strike. Mechanics and artisans began that tradition when they became employees and lost their status as fraternal colleagues of masters. Other workers adopted the strike action as well, but it remained the organized union workers' mainstay, legal or not, throughout American history. The vast majority and the most costly of trade union strikes were, and still are, protests to prevent losses or abuses, not actions taken for greater gains.

The early trade unions excluded women and skilled black slaves or freedmen in the decades prior to the Civil War. Several early unions, tailors and typographers among them, actually struck against master journeymen to prevent the hiring of women in their trades. Trade unions, north and south, struck to prevent the hiring of free black workers in their trades as well. Skilled workmen, artisans, and mechanics as they called themselves, possessed a privileged social and economic status over noncitizen immigrants, all women, slaves, and freed blacks that only increased as their political rights were enlarged. Their unions and their leaders were trade- or craft-centered and most of them expressed little or no criticism of the political foundations of the nation for whose leaders they now voted, and on whose juries they now served. Their most radical leaders expressed their views in themes derived from the ideas of Thomas Jefferson and Thomas Paine. They acted as much to preserve their privileges from erosion as they did to prevent wage or other material losses.

The second line of worker action was that taken by the unskilled (often most recent immigrants) women, children, and slaves. Workers in this group had severely limited legal rights and no representation in any forum. Neither their labor or their lives completely belonged to them. Nonetheless, they too continued to find ways of acting in defiance of masters, both individually and collectively, though everything they did was a dangerous act of disobedience or rebellion.

Without formal organizations, with no legal standing, and dependent on or vulnerable to external authority, women, slaves, and recent immigrants frequently led the way for their skilled white male counterparts to follow. Individual acts of disobedience or defiance of authority were commonplace among them. So were secretive acts like theft, petty vandalism, arson, and feigned illness. Work stoppages by women mill workers were called mutinies, and more than a dozen serious strikes took place in textile mills where women led the action between 1824 and 1837. Children, supported by their parents and local artisans, struck the mills of Paterson, New Jersey, in 1828 over a proposed change in the dinner hour. They won back the old eating time, but failed in their bid for a ten-hour day when the state militia broke the strike. The young strike leaders were all fired.

Slavery and Racism

Slaves carried out similar individual and group acts of resistance, though risked far harsher consequences than the others. A distinct hierarchy of punishments and reprisals for labor action came into existence in this era, which further contributed to the social stratification of labor. Skilled white males, usually native-born citizens, were at the top, and though striking was almost always found to be illegal by the courts, their unions and political associations were legitimate and carried weight, with some variations from state to state. Workers' newspapers were read by merchants, small businessmen, and farmers, with whom they often associated for political purposes. Immigrants, unskilled men, women, and children followed in status with no real political rights or institutional structures of their own. Reprisals and punishments were sternly administered by the authorities who controlled the labor of women and children, though religious custom, family relationships, and social opprobrium limited the harshness of actions against them. Corporal punishment, the whipping post, and branding by government agencies, for example, came to an end in these years for men, but continued to be both acceptable and legal for women, children, and slaves.

Freedmen in the North and West occupied the lowest social ranking in the nonslave states, as they were systematically excluded from the various trades and crafts they had formerly held as slaves. State laws denied freedmen the right to vote or participate in political life in most northern states after slavery was abolished. The deskilling of freed slaves after the Civil War began first in those northern states that ended slavery before the war. Pennsylvania, for example, a state for which good statistical evidence is available, carried out the systematic exclusion of freedmen from skilled occupations from the ending of slavery to the outbreak of the Civil War. Freedmen in other northern states were similarly forced from employment as longshoremen, hod-carriers, coachmen, waiters, stablemen, bootblacks, and barbers by the vast numbers of newly arriving European immigrants, especially those from Ireland fleeing famine conditions after 1846. Slaves, the largest single cohort of the prewar labor force, continued at the bottom of the social pyramid, though a plantation hierarchy of privileges separated house servants, skilled workers, drivers, and field hands.

Once slavery came to an end in the nonplantation states of the North and West in the early 1820s, escape became an increasingly attractive, though dangerous option. Freed slaves led in the formation of northern antislavery agitation and set up networks of aid and assistance with friendly whites. The first newspaper to seek a black audience in the United States, *Freedom's Journal,* appeared in New York in 1827. The weekly paper was abolitionist and antiracist, and called for the confiscation of all slaves as property. As the northern abolitionist movement increased, many antislavery advocates sought to do more than just speak out against slavery. Their protection, money, and participation evolved into an extensive "underground railroad" system to assist runaway slaves. While abolitionists were in agreement about the evil of slavery, many of their organizations accepted prevailing views on race. The Fall River (Massachusetts) Female Anti-Slavery Society included many leaders drawn from the mill-owning families of the rapidly growing industrial center, but excluded blacks from membership when it was organized in 1825 (Blewett, 2000, p. 54).

David Walker, a free black merchant of Boston and agent for the distribution of *Freedom's Journal*, was convinced that the slave labor system could not be brought to an end peacefully or piecemeal. His *Appeal to the Coloured Citizens of the World* appeared in 1829 and was widely distributed in the tradition of Thomas Paine's *Common Sense,* hand to hand. Walker anticipated the inevitability of a violent conflict and suffered for his prophecy. His murdered body was found in the doorway of his shop soon after the publication of the third edition of the *Appeal* in June 1830.

Another Bostonian, William Lloyd Garrison, took up the abolitionist cause with almost as much risk to himself when he began the publication of his newspaper, *The Liberator,* a year later. Garrison was attacked by a mob in 1835, his press and office destroyed, but he continued his antislavery crusade until the Civil War. Elijah Lovejoy, an antislavery clergyman and editor of the religious journal, *Observer,* in Alton, Illinois, met the same fate as Walker when he was shot and killed in 1837. Like Walker, Garrison, and Lovejoy, there were many others willing to put their lives on the line in the battle against slavery.

Nat Turner

The slave Nat Turner led a murderous uprising in Southampton County, Virginia, in August 1831 that confirmed the worst fears and gave credence to the worst nightmares of southern planters. In the space of just a few days about sixty whites were killed by Turner and his band of fellow slave rebels. The ultimate capture and execution of Turner and his companions did little to allay slaveowner suspicions that agitation and resentment were smoldering beneath the superficial appearances of slave labor obedience and docility. Teaching slaves to read was now forbidden by law in states where slavery remained legal. Formerly there had been less statutory oversight on masters.

Labor, Racism, and Abolition

Few northern or southern workers or their labor organizations expressed any solidarity or identification with abolitionists or slave rebels. That indifference, or hostility, to abolitionism is an important indicator of the power of the legal division between slave and free workers at the time.

Citizenship and law divided slave from nonslave. Race was always made by law and divided labor no less in the nonslave states of the North and West than in the South. Union leaders distrusted the evangelism of many abolitionists and barred freedmen from their crafts. Free blacks were kept from union membership as well. One authority on black labor states emphatically: "But from the time the first trade unions were formed by white workers in the 1790's to the Civil War—in which period the free black population grew from 59,000 to 488,000—no free Negro wage earner was a member" (P. Foner, 1974, p. 4). Unions also demanded racially segregated workplaces in northern states when slavery ended there. White workers accepted racially segregated churches, schools, public gardens, playgrounds for children, and transportation on stagecoaches, steamers, and ferries. Mills and factories throughout the industrializing parts of the North and East restricted employment to whites only. In New York City at the time of slavery's legal termination in 1827, rigid segregation patterns applied everywhere in public life. Even the almshouse was segregated (Wallace and Burrows, 1999, p. 558).

Prosperity for Some

A western land boom in the early 1830s was part of the general economic surge that further exaggerated the growing contrasts between rich and poor, slave and free, men and women, immigrant and native-born. The new textile factories, mills, mines, and foundries placed matrons, supervisors, and foremen in positions of authority to direct the labor of the workforce. Owners, customarily stern but paternalistic authorities, were no longer present in the place of work. Their offices might be nearby, or even in the same building, but they seldom had any contact with the actual workforce. Slaves on large plantations likewise had to respond to the directions of drivers who were slaves put in charge of work gangs, or white overseers who were employees of the owners. Big projects like canal and railroad building relied on labor contractors who employed recent immigrants on short-term work agreements. Owner-operated shops, factories, mills, and farms were driven to the economic sidelines. Economies of scale favored the efficiencies and resilience to market fluctuations of larger production units over smaller ones. So did the new technologies of steam power and mass production. Larger aggregates of wealth were necessary to participate in the expanding markets.

The world of the worker was taking the shape that de Tocqueville warned about. The benevolence of the familial and personal workplace was being replaced by impersonal work rules and regulations. The short-term employment by New England factory girls and children that was expected to end with marriage or adulthood farming or independent shopkeeping was turning into permanent work. Wages for work, which had usually been low, now tended to fall even further as competition among producers forced them to trim costs or fail altogether.

The new wealth of this dynamic capitalist age was reflected in the booming cities of the Northeast and West and the great houses of the plantation South. The grim lives of the producers of that wealth were seen in the company towns, urban slums, and contract labor barracks, among prison laborers, and in the slave quarters of the great plantations. For labor this transition meant the emergence of a fixed working class, slave and free, which had only its labor to exchange for sustenance.

Manayunk

As the great civilization of Egypt was said to be the gift of the Nile River, the village of Manayunk, just outside Philadelphia, was the gift of the falls of the Schuylkill River.

Just six miles from the harborfront city, Manayunk was located on fast moving water, making it an ideal location for the early spinning mills and glass making factories that were starting up after the English model adopted by Samuel Slater and others in New England. By the mid-1820s, a flourishing collection of textile mills and factories was located along a two-mile stretch of water known as the Flat Rock Canal, built by the Schuylkill Navigation Company through the village of Manayunk. By the end of the decade Manayunk was bigger than Pawtucket. One Fourth of July orator in 1828 called it "the Manchester of America" (quoted in Shelton, 1983, pp. 54–55). More mills were under construction, and by the early 1830s eight large cotton textile mills were crowded together in the small industrial center.

Inexpensive water power and new technology concentrated the industry in Manayunk. The similarly inexpensive labor of immigrant children, who typically began work at age nine, and women generated the profits that brought investors there. A Pennsylvania government investigation of 1837 found wages for children at between $.50 and $1.00 per week. Some of the youngest, according to the testimony of the Manayunk schoolmaster, earned no more than $.75 every two weeks. Adults earned more. Women were paid about $2.00 a week; men could earn from $6.00 to $7.50 a week as mule spinners (Shelton, 1983, p. 71). Rooming houses charged women about half their earnings without including meals or fuel. Sometimes workers were paid in a discounted script. Pay period intervals were every four weeks with wages of a few days to two weeks always held back.

Philadelphia, a major port city, was the entry depot for thousands of English and Irish immigrants a year. Many of these newcomers had worked in the textile-producing centers of England and were imbued with the anti-Ricardian labor radicalism spreading in the mills there. Skilled immigrant workers had played a major part in the formation of the original Philadelphia Workingmen's Party. Harsh working conditions and six thirteen-hour days a week in the mills brought protests from middle-class reformers as well as the Mechanic's Society of Philadelphia. The *Mechanic's Free Press* railed against "the oppressive and degrading effects of machinery on the productive classes." The paper cried, "Look at Manayunk, the heart sickens to behold the remorseless system of infant labor obtaining foothold upon our soil" (November 7, 1828). A Germantown businessman, Reuben Haines, scolded the Manayunk manufacturers. He pointed to the mills of Lowell with their well-kept boardinghouses and "very ladylike females" who worked where "there appear none of the evils" of Manayunk (quoted in Shelton, 1983, p. 67).

Almost immediately after the passage of the Factory Regulation Act set a maximum ten-hour day for English textile workers in 1833, the demand for the same spread to the mills of Manayunk. The mostly women workers in the mills of Joseph Ripka and J. J. Borie in Manayunk left their machines and walked out over a 20 percent wage reduction in August 1833. The women protested over "thirteen hours of hard labor, an unhealthy employment, where we never feel a refreshing breeze to cool us, overheated and suffocated as we are, and where we never behold the sun but through a window [locked or nailed shut to maintain high humidity levels good for production] and an atmosphere thick with the dust and small particles of cotton, which we are constantly inhaling to the destruction of our health, our appetite and strength" (quoted in Shelton, 1983, p. 68).

The August turn-out sparked a series of strikes in the area over the next nine months and brought dynamic new leaders and organizations to the foreground. The first was the immediate formation of the Working People of Manayunk. Its goal was to mobilize other workers against the wage cuts. Other factory turn-outs followed. In November a citywide federation of labor organizations was formed with the clumsy name, Trades Union of the City and County of Philadelphia (TUCCP). Each trade union was its own association; together they formed a trades union, or union of trades. By May 1834 most mill workers were back at their jobs with a 5 percent increase over their former wages.

John Ferral, an Irish immigrant and handloom weaver, helped to lead the striking Manayunk workers. He gained more prominence that summer as one of seven Philadelphia delegates to a meeting in New York that formed the National Trades Union, the first organization of its kind in the United States. Ferral had not worked in the mills, but was moved by the harshness of the new factory system, especially the long workday and the unhealthful conditions. At the convention in New York he spoke out on behalf of women and children in the mills of Manayunk and their courageous struggle. A year later, on the heels of another labor victory, he was unanimously elected president of the NTU. Ferral was at the forefront of the battle for the ten-hour day when that victory was won in Philadelphia in the first general strike of workers in the United States.

The Philadelphia General Strike of 1835

Credit (or blame) for the radical idea of the general strike is usually given to William Benbow, a follower of the English utopian Socialist, Robert Owen. Benbow called for common concerted job action across occupational lines, a strike of all workers in the same place for a common goal. His argument, originally put forward in 1831, was spread in pamphlet form and found a sympathetic audience amid militant Baltimore, Boston, and Philadelphia workers. A coalition of seventeen trades unions struck for the ten-hour day in Baltimore in 1833; another similar coalition failed in an effort to do the same in Boston soon thereafter. Word traveled from city to city, and a Boston "Circular," when it reached Philadelphia, helped to set off the most massive labor action to that time in the United States (Commons, 1958, 6:40). In June 1835, 20,000 Philadelphia workers walked off their jobs and idled the city in a general strike for the ten-hour day. John Ferral, one of the strike leaders, lashed out at mill owners, calling them a "blood sucking aristocracy." A local newspaper fretted that the brevity of only a sixty-hour week would be harmful to workers, that all the extra time would be "applied to useless and unworthy purposes" (*Germantown Telegraph*, June 24, 1835).

The one-week general strike ended in a grand victory for the workers and spurred a massive increase in the size and importance of the TUUCP. Ferral singled out with praise the militancy of the women and children workers of Manayunk, employed, he said in "brutalizing emporiums of human misery" (Commons, 1958, 6:43). Other trade union leaders were drawn to the struggle of women and children workers. The president of the TUUCP, William English, in his first address to the delegates not two weeks later in New York, on July 4, 1835, called the cotton mills of the United States, "modern hells," and urged the organization of a Female Trades Union (Shelton, 1983, p. 165). During the strike Thomas Brothers, an English immigrant, began the publication of *The Radical Reformer and Workingman's Advocate* to further advance the ideas of the Philadelphia workers' movement. The unions got a boost. The ten-hour day became a mobilizing issue in every industrial city, for men and women, skilled and unskilled workers, immigrants and native-born alike. Workers everywhere, even in carefully constructed company towns, were asserting their demands for a fairer share of what their labor produced and more time in which to live the lives their labor earned. Within a year the Pennsylvania legislature began an investigation into unwholesome working conditions in mills and factories.

Waltham and Lowell

The textile mill town of Lowell, Massachusetts, where the Concord and Merrimack rivers join, and where the latter falls thirty-two feet in less than a mile, is one of the best examples of the economic success of the new factory system and the social consequences of that success. In 1820 the village, still known as East Chelmsford, had a population of only about 200. Nine textile companies, seeking to take advantage of the fast moving water for power, opened mills there between 1822 and 1839, and the population grew to almost 20,000. By 1850 there were 33,000 people in Lowell, which had become the nation's leading textile producer and the second largest city in Massachusetts. Most of the mill owners were members of a group known as the Boston Associates. They invested in mills throughout New England. None lived in Lowell. The mills were run by managers, most of the work done by "factory girls," young women between the ages of fifteen and thirty, who were recruited from the farm families of the nearby countryside. Because of the unity of ownership, the various mills were organized according to fixed standards that included work duties, supervision, wages, and hours.

In the first years of the Lowell project young women came to the mills eagerly. Often they came in kinship groups with sisters or members of their extended families already employed in Lowell. Paternalistic management policies were advertised as protective, almost utopian in their promises of a workplace and living "Garden of Eden." The letters and diaries of early Lowell women indicate that they viewed their employment as a source of independence, liberty from the unending drudgery of farm life. Many of them had seen their mothers broken by the constant burdens of childbirth and all of the labor that put so many of them into early graves. These women brought confidence and hope of self-improvement to the new way of life, and did not regard themselves as the social inferiors of their employers. They lived in either company-run or private boardinghouses. Some chose to have a portion of their wages sent home to their families. In the earliest years women came and went from their homes to their Lowell jobs every few months. For some women the employment was regarded as temporary, a way of saving money and engaging in self-improvement until the time of marriage. Matrons and curfews in company housing protected the young women from the dangers of worldly evils. Reading rooms and church services were provided. Infractions of strict social and moral codes were dealt with sternly, usually with dismissal.

Unlike the earlier "familial system" of the Rhode Island mills, work in Lowell quickly took on a harsh regularity. Work was twelve or more hours a day, six days a week. Workers signed a contract to work for a year, and agreed to give two weeks' notice before leaving after that. Failure to comply meant no "honorable discharge" would be granted. Lowell mills established an early "blacklist" by agreeing among themselves not to hire anyone without good papers from a former employer. Men, about 15 percent of the workforce, held all supervisory jobs, and were employed as mechanics, repairmen, and watchmen, and in some specific production work. Men were paid by the day, between about $.85 and $2.00 in 1836. Women tended the machines and were paid various piecerates by output of the machines they tended, or between $.40 and $.80 per day. Room and board was deducted in company-operated residences, or similarly charged by private homeowners.

When the Lowell mills cut wages by 15 percent in February 1834, women began to meet inside and outside the mills to protest. One of the leaders of the agitation was fired and her co-workers stopped working and formed a procession in the streets of Lowell to rally other workers. The *Boston Evening Transcript* reported that 800 women walked off their jobs in protest. The paper noted the militancy of the women and the stridency of their remarks. One woman was described as making a "flaming Mary Woolstonecroft (sic) speech on the rights of women," and the crowd was said to be willing "to have their own way if they died for it" (February 14, 1834).

The price of raw cotton was rising and competition from English mills was driving down prices for finished goods. Maintaining profits meant wage cuts. A similar number of women struck the mills of the Cocheco Manufacturing Company in Dover, New Hampshire, the same month. Both strikes were concluded without success for the women workers, but, as in Manayunk, the militancy and republican radicalism of the women was clear: "The oppressing hand of avarice would enslave us," said a circular passed out among the millworkers of Lowell (quoted in Dublin, 1979, p. 93). European radical and socialist protest was mixing with the democratic idealism of Paine and Jefferson among the industrial and artisan workers of the United States.

Two years later a much larger strike action swept through Lowell when the price of room and board was raised, effectively reducing wages by 12½ percent. More than 1,500 Lowell operatives went out in 1836, and, before this strike was broken by evictions, they organized more than 2,500 women into the Factory Girls Association. Women in nearby Amesbury, Massachusetts, were inspired by their Lowell sisters. They organized a victorious strike in March 1836 against a planned stretch-out, the doubling of the number of looms each worker had to tend with no increase in pay.

Labor Power

A high-water mark in labor activism in the United States was reached during the mid-1830s. There were more organizations formed than ever before. Unions and workers generally had never achieved more political influence either in their own localities or in both major political parties. In 1834 workers in New York formed themselves as a progressive wing of the Democratic Party and helped tip a close election for mayor. Two years later the president of the National Trades Union, a New Yorker, Ely Moore, was elected to the House of Representatives, the first outspoken worker advocate in that body. His powerful speeches were published by the Philadelphia labor newspaper, the *National Laborer*, and widely distributed nationally. Ely defended the rights of workers to organize unions and, like so many other Jacksonian Democrats, attacked privilege, monopoly, and aristocracy.

There were approximately 300,000 unionists in 1836. As a percentage of nonfarm labor, workers were better organized in 1836 than they would be until the New Deal era a hundred years later. Their main focus of attention in the mid-1830s was on the legalization of labor union actions, an attack on the conspiracy doctrine, and winning the ten-hour day. Union or worker newspapers proliferated, along with newspapers that favored worker issues but were associated with one or the other major political parties. The *Brooklyn Eagle* began publication in 1841. It was a stalwart paper for the Democratic Party and appealed to working-class readers for more than a century. Similar newspapers appeared in almost every industrial or urban setting. The Democratic Party and these newspapers were a powerful influence in drawing and keeping worker sentiment and loyalties within the mainstream of national life.

The building of the nation's canal system, now mostly completed, or soon to be outrun by railroad competition, was not a unionized project. Nonetheless, canalers were at the center of hundreds of strikes, militant labor uprisings, riots, and acts of sabotage in northern, southern, and western states. Even though much work on canals and railroads in the South was done by slave labor leased to contractors by masters, strikes and labor rebellions took place there as well. The peak of labor activism among canalers was reached during the 1834–38 period, when approximately forty strikes or labor riots took place. Dozens of workers were killed, hundreds arrested (Way, 1993, pp. 204–7). State militias were regularly called out wherever canals were dug and did most of the killing. The first time federal troops were used to break a strike was against workers building the Chesapeake and Ohio Canal in Maryland in 1834. Early railroad construction work followed the labor pattern set in canal building.

Several citywide labor federations were formed by the mid-1830s, and the first National Trades Union held regular conventions for a few years. Trade union leaders were becoming widely known in every major city of the Northeast. The trades achieved a virtual "closed shop" that prevented masters from hiring nonunion workers in several cities. European and homegrown utopian and socialist criticism of capitalism's harsh inequities was blended with the democratic and radical republican ideals of the early national experience.

The abolitionist protest was also reaching new intensity in its efforts to end the practice of slave labor. Alongside and within the abolitionist movement, feminists began the long struggle for women's rights. Some abolitionists put their lives and liberties at risk to assist thousands of slaves escape their legal bondage. Besides those helped by abolitionists and heroic figures such as Harriet Tubman, who went into the South again and again to help slaves, many slaves ran away on their own and were either captured and returned to their owners or fled to the wilderness. Though it may be impossible to know the exact number of slaves who ran away (or took brief excursions), one conservative estimate puts the number at 50,000 per year by 1860 (Franklin and Schweninger, 1999, p. 282).

Panic and Depression, 1837–1842

From this unforeseen, and at the time unknown, pinnacle of strength and influence, almost everything that had been built by labor fell to an unimaginable depth within the span of just a few years. The pattern of rising and falling labor fortunes entered the first of its many historic cycles with the onset of the Panic of 1837 and the five-year depression that followed. Economic realities regularly included boom and bust cycles. Foreign competition, the expansion of production faster than market capabilities to absorb the goods, and speculation in land, businesses, or financial instruments established themselves as inherent parts of the national marketplace economy. Prior to this era, however, most industrial workers could fall back on agricultural pursuits during business downturns.

In addition, the paternalism of small family-run and owner-operated workshops, mills, and foundries also helped to carry employees during times of business contraction. The larger size and impersonal design of the new industries paid scant attention to the consequences of shutting down for workers. Unemployment insurance or benefits were unknown. Most often workers actually lost back pay when employers shut down. The growth of big city worker populations, most of which were newer immigrants from Ireland and Germany with no nearby farms or families, meant miserable impoverishment to hundreds of thousands of unemployed workers, union or not. The urban freed slave population of northern and western states was similarly vulnerable, though domestic service work offered some familial protection.

High death rates from cholera epidemics in crowded cities and on industrial worksites and canal building projects were another part of the vulnerability of the newly forming permanent working class in the new society. In 1837 unions began to call on the government to create public works projects to alleviate the distress of unemployment brought on by the economic downturn. Other reformers called for the expansion of public sewer and water departments and the creation of departments of sanitation.

When workers formed organizations to represent their interests to owners and managers, there were always factors beyond their control that dramatically affected what they could accomplish. The very existence of unions depended on forces such as the business cycle, technology, and historical developments such as war. Unions represented workers in the workplace at the present moment. It was nearly impossible to imagine that the work itself might be coming to an end, or undergoing drastic change. The union was typically forced to focus on the most immediate and present material issues, wages, and the conditions of work.

The first consequence of the Panic of 1837 was a sharp rise in the already high prices for basic foodstuffs. Mills and factories cut production or shut down altogether. One-third of the New York City workforce, or approximately 50,000 people, became unemployed. The same situation applied almost everywhere. In Manayunk, Pawtucket, and Lowell the mills closed, some for a few months, some for years. Railroad and canal projects were halted for lack of financing, and the workers dismissed. Trade unions disintegrated, their newspapers folded, the yearly meetings of the National Trades Union ended. Some stalwart local craft unions persisted but their influence waned. Strike activity fell off sharply for almost a decade.

Those employers still in business took advantage of the hard times to take back the gains workers had won in better times. Wages were slashed, union activists fired, and long workdays brought back. Employer organizations gained new energy. Associations of masters had informally cooperated for decades, often in secret. "Masters," wrote Adam Smith, "are always and everywhere in a sort of tacit, but constant combination" to prevent wages from rising above certain acceptable levels. Businessmen organize to drive wages down as well, Smith added, and when they do this it is "always conducted with the utmost silence and secrecy" (Smith, 1976, p. 84).

From the beginning of the century associations of employers joined in the prosecution of conspiracy cases, made agreements to set wages and prices, and, in the 1830s, vigorously fought the battle against the ten-hour day. Government itself, shorn of feudal and aristocratic obligations, was becoming an agency formed by the owners of wealth to secure and advance that wealth. Strikes, rebellions, and riots of workers were regularly broken by state court injunctions and the use of militia. Can anyone point to the use of militia against employers for violating the rights of workers in the history of the nation? While master carpenters, tailors, shoemakers, and the like had once met informally and secretly, the new business leaders began to form more open organizations and raise funds for common antilabor activities by the middle of the 1830s. In 1836, a bitter struggle carried on by the Master Carpenter's Association of Philadelphia for the right to hire nonunion workers (the open shop), led them to form a citywide Anti-Trades Union Association. A New York Manufacturers and Retailers

Association was formed in April 1836 to "resist union demands and union regulations" (Bonnet, 1956, pp. 53–54).

It has never been completely clear in labor history which was regarded as the worst infringement by unions against management: material demands like wages and hours, or the setting of conditions of work and defense of worker rights. These demands often went together, though there were frequent instances where wages and hours were conceded to gain or enhance control in the workplace. The aftermath of the Panic and depression of 1837 brought forth a new wave of conspiracy cases against workers by employer associations on both fronts.

Commonwealth v. Hunt

The bootmakers of Boston clashed with their masters when they tried to bring unionism to all the shoemaking shops in the city in 1839. Instead of the customary charge of conspiracy for strike actions, the employer sought to reaffirm the old English common law concept that the union itself was an illegal conspiracy. The case was part of a revived management offensive that sought to expand the illegality of both union organization and activity. It was not a complete victory for unions when Judge Lemuel Shaw of the Massachusetts Supreme Court reversed a lower court decision and threw out the conspiracy charge against seven union leaders. Because the case involved specific charges of wrongdoing, that is, belonging to an organization that had allegedly unlawful rules, one that engaged in a conspiracy against an employer who hired a nonunionist, and one that conspired to harm nonunionists who worked for such an employer, many students of labor have found *Commonwealth v. Hunt* to have been a step forward in the legitimation of unionism. This positive reaction was a reflection of the popular sentiment of the time which had experienced widespread use of the conspiracy doctrine against labor.

Many unionists in 1842 had been fighting the conspiracy doctrine for years and hailed the case as a decisive victory. It was hardly that. It was true that allegedly illegal behaviors were, in fact, held to be lawful, as was the organization itself. But the decision simply restated the widely accepted premise that unions per se were not illegal conspiracies. What unionists really won in the case was the patina of respectability. Their organizations were legitimate in the eye of the state. Many of their critics felt that unions were not compatible with national economic policy and were an alien influence. In New York City, Judge Edwards declared in his finding of conspiracy against tailors for forming a union in 1836: "They [unions] are of foreign origin" (quoted in Boyer, 1955, p. 16). Throughout their history worker organizations have had to confront the dilemma of battling the prerogatives of capital in an aggressively and avowedly capitalist society, while at the same time craving a legitimate and respected place in an allegedly democratic one.

For the next hundred years, in spite of Judge Shaw's favorable decision, union-led strikes would continue to be broken by court injunctions holding them to be illegal actions. No business organization, and no actions taken by combinations of business leaders, suffered the same legal intervention for antiunion actions. Business leaders were never jailed for provoking illegal confrontations, or for hiring goons to attack or even murder union organizers. Businessmen formed combinations that routinely crossed the legal line in efforts to thwart unionism. They did so without fear of prosecution. Law and the courts are the defenders of property and the owners of that property. Those rare times, wartime, for example, when labor organizations or actions were protected by law to the apparent disadvantage of capital stood out as exceptions that serve to prove the rule. They were episodes when the longer-term interests of capital were at stake and caused a temporary lapse in legal interventions against unions and their actions. It is also worth noting that both political parties of this period, Whig and Democrat, were courting the votes of white male workers. Universal white male suffrage was, or soon would be, achieved in every state. Justice Shaw could not have been completely indifferent to political considerations when he ruled for the legality of the Boston Journeymen Bootmakers Society in 1842.

Nativism, Racism, Sexism

Anti-Catholic, anti-Irish, anti-immigrant, and antiblack agitation were rife throughout the lean times that followed the Panic of 1837. Mob assaults, lynching, and the destruction of churches and religious properties were common occurrences in big eastern cities until the economic revival of the mid-1840s. The anger was not simply the expression of irrational prejudice. The consequences of unemployment were as dramatic as life and death. Holding a job could mean the difference between feeding a child or watching that child starve. Worker resentment toward the most recent immigrants did not require the deliberate intervention or manipulation of employers or government. It was built into the very nature of the developing nation.

Workers opposed unrestricted immigration for years. Seth Luther's famous *Address to the Workingmen of New England* (1832) included in the Appendix on its final page the demand that Congress set more restrictive limits on immigration and the importation of wool. Luther wanted the government to protect workers and farmers the way it helped manufacturers through tariff policy. Competition for scarce jobs pitted native-born white workers against foreign or black workers. Antiabolitionist rioters murdered Elijah Lovejoy in Alton, Illinois, in November 1837, in part because of the fear of job competition that was potentially represented by millions of newly freed slaves. Irish workers fought each other in gangs for jobs. Such anger was political cannon fodder.

In every city local political figures tried to use those resentments to win elections. Native American parties pledged to new restrictions on naturalization laws sprang to life in several cities in 1837, the first in Germantown, Pennsylvania, then in New York, and Washington, D.C. Generally, these parties were anti-Catholic, but expressed other forms of bigotry and racism as well. The residence requirement for naturalization of all foreign-born should be raised, they said, to twenty-one years.

"Playing the race card" and the exploitation of anti-immigrant sentiment in politics in the United States have their origins in the fierce competition for economic security faced by enfranchised workers in hard times. Once universal white male suffrage was achieved, the emotional bond of patriotism was enhanced. Labor leaders eagerly embraced the concept of political liberty embodied in the right to vote. Now they sought to use the vote to advance their own interests, not to expand the rights of those outside their ranks, or those without the franchise.

Seth Luther was the most prominent labor leader in the United States before the Civil War. His militant speeches and writings were circulated wherever unionists gathered, especially throughout New England. When the struggle to win universal male suffrage in Rhode Island took the form of a rebellion led by Thomas Dorr in 1842, Luther went right to the front of the struggle as the representative of the Providence branch of the New England Association of Farmers, Mechanics and Other Workmen. Dorr's Rebellion, the brief seizure of government by constitutional reformers, was finally put down by military force, though the Dorrite goal of an expanded suffrage was ultimately won. Dorr was eventually pardoned from a life sentence for his part in the episode. Luther brandished pistols and a sword on the side of Dorr, while he successfully helped to defend the exclusion of free blacks from the suffrage in the new constitution, against the arguments of Dorr. In the course of the rebellion free blacks in Rhode Island opposed the Dorrites and threw their support to the defenders of the old charter. When the traditionalists regained power, free blacks won the suffrage. Once the vote was won, black Rhode Islanders gave their allegiance to the Whig Party, which opposed the reform issues of labor, including the ten-hour day. Though free black men won and exercised the right to vote in Rhode Island, segregation prevailed in most public places in the state, including schools, for many years to come. Workers were becoming a new class but their public consciousness was limited to what was possible within their national, racial, and gender identity. Though there were a few exceptions, workers, as they expressed themselves through their organizations and newspapers, were not at the forefront of the two great social movements of the time, abolitionism and feminism.

Humanitarian efforts on behalf of free slaves came from social reformers, some abolitionists, and feminists, almost all of whom also took up the struggle to improve the lot of workers. In contrast, few union leaders regarded free black workers with any class solidarity before the Civil War. Even when they adopted utopian socialist ideas of the period, labor idealists excluded black workers from planned communities or cooperative associations. At the same time, while the federal government under President Jackson was driving American Indians from their land, there was no significant public or union opposition. To the contrary, most workers and their advocates favored the idea of preemption, the right to settle on confiscated public land, improve it, and then have the right to purchase it later at a minimal price. The right of preemption for white citizens was first established in general terms in 1841. Freed slaves were denied such access to land in the territories.

A few years later, in one of his famous debates with Stephen A. Douglas, Abraham Lincoln expressed the popular sentiment on land: "Now, irrespective of the moral aspect of this question as to whether there is a right or wrong in enslaving a negro, I am still in favor of our new territories being in such a condition that white men may find a home,—may find some spot where they can better their condition in life" (Angle, 1991, p. 390).

The states granted land to canal and railroad companies and white settlers in the Jacksonian era. When union leaders expressed criticism of state or federal land policy, they only criticized the huge grants to canal and railroad companies. They expressed no opposition to the racial exclusion of black workers. Horace Greeley's famous journalistic admonition of the 1840s, "Go west young man and seek your fortune," appealed to thousands of white workers distressed by economic hard times, but was not an option for black members of the same class.

Cultural Formations: The Limits of Desire

It is tempting when looking back at an earlier time to impose values that are formed by the consciousness of the present. We make judgments that confirm the superiority of our own views. The deficiencies of the past seem exquisitely clear with the hindsight that comes from knowing the virtues of alternatives. Responses to the harsh contrasts of wealth and poverty, slavery and freedom, and white male authority of this industrializing era could only come from the cultural setting that formed them. At the time the nation and the sentiment of nationalism were powerful inclusive emotions for most citizens. Legal participation in the nation increased significantly for most citizens in this Jacksonian period. Democratic inclusion was so alluring that slaves, freed slaves, and immigrants naturally wanted to share in it. So did women. Democracy was the pathway to social justice, and the means to reform the apparent inequities of wealth and power within the nation. Political identification with the nation brought forth other sentiments, however. Slavery was a legally sanctioned institution in a democratic nation. So was the political inferiority of women, and the legal inferiority of new immigrants. Confiscation of the property of the native residents of North America was rarely challenged. Indeed, it was usually cheered on for having the conveniently twin virtues of advancing "civilization" and making inexpensive land available to white settlers.

The nation-state is the public expression of the collective private will. That will is not formed democratically, however, since private power varies considerably based on the distribution and concentration of wealth. The greater the wealth, the greater the institutional influence of its possessors in matters of cultural policy making. Men of wealth sat on church boards, were university trustees, owned or influenced newspapers, and were the visible leaders in their communities everywhere but on the frontier.

Of course, culture is not simply made up and passed down the social pyramid; it is made up of all the social interactions of participants in small and large groups, and the interactions between those with power and those without. Slaves and their masters together made the cultural life of the antebellum South. Masters dominated, or sought to dominate, that part of the culture they could control. The new industrialists of the Northeast and Middle-Atlantic states sought to extend their cultural values, their presumed virtues and visions, to the rest of the communities they sought to lead. Their success can be measured by the loyalties they cultivated from among those they dominated. Great social and political effort went into the battle to counter the union militancy, strikes, slowdowns, mutinies, and rebellions of workers, not least of which was cultural, the winning of "hearts and minds." In the United States, a society that appeared, and really was, successful in achieving its ostensible goals, credibility accrued to those who led or dominated it. The cultural hegemony of business and government was only challenged with force when internal economic crisis or serious setbacks undermined their leadership.

The *Lowell Offering*

In Lowell, Massachusetts, the Boston Associates sought to create a perfectly harmonious society, one that would produce wealth without conflict or interruption, and one that would reflect the higher cultural values they hoped to promote among their employees. Mutual self-improvement reading and writing circles, and a magazine called the *Lowell Offering*, were just the things they needed. The first few issues of the *Offering* appeared irregularly in 1840 when a Universalist minister, Reverend Abel C. Thomas, began to publish some of the poems, stories, and essays of the women's literary groups. It soon caught on as a monthly magazine that described itself as "A Repository of Original Articles, Written Exclusively by Females Actively Employed in the Mills" (quoted in Eisler, 1977, p. 34). The magazine helped to publicize the idealized image of Lowell as an industrial utopia in a democratic nation. Copies found their way across the Atlantic. Praise came from political and literary figures everywhere.

While the *Offering* was never officially a house organ, it was indirectly subsidized and controlled by the Boston Associates. Its contents were to be morally and spiritually uplifting. Working conditions and factory issues were excluded by an editorial policy that said simply, "with wages, board etc. we have nothing to do" (quoted in Eisler, 1977, p. 36). Controversy was inevitable, as wages for piecework were cut, a stretch-out (women were expected to tend additional machines with no extra pay) introduced, and cost cutting in the boardinghouses led to overcrowding. One of its contributors became its sharpest critic, and would soon become a prominent leader of Lowell workers.

Sarah Bagley had been one of the magazine's most talented authors. An early contribution of hers was entitled, "The Pleasures of Factory Life." Her delights with the factory culture, however, soon began to vanish, and she became angry when two of her essays were rejected by the *Offering*. Bagley founded the Lowell Female Labor Reform Association and became its first president. The new organization published her two unsigned essays as part of a series called *Factory Tracts*. Anyone caught reading "radical" pamphlets or newspapers was immediately dismissed and blacklisted everywhere in New England. Bagley was selected as one of five vice presidents of the New England Workingmen's Association at their July 4 meeting in 1845 and, in a speech that day, condemned the *Offering*. She attacked it as "controlled by the manufacturing interest to give a gloss to their inhumanity" (quoted in Selden, 1983, p. 157).

The ten-hour-day movement was generating renewed protest. The Lowell workweek was seventy-five hours over six days in 1845. In Pennsylvania, New Hampshire, and Massachusetts similar hours prompted humanitarian reformers to press legislators for laws to limit the workday, as English law had done. Petitions were submitted with thousands of signatures. In Lowell the petition was a scroll 130 feet long with 4,500 signatures. Sarah Bagley was among those who gave eloquent and moving testimony about the ill health and hardships that long workdays imposed on millworking women. The Massachusetts legislature could not act to regulate hours of work, several legislators claimed, because such legislation would "deprive the citizen of his freedom of contract," and would also be harmful to business. In 1847 New Hampshire took action to limit the workday when it passed a ten-hour law "in absence of a contract." Mill workers there were promptly fired and rehired only if they accepted a contract with the former longer hours. A year later the same thing happened in Pennsylvania. The loophole of a contract provision in Pennsylvania was eliminated for textiles, paper, and bagging mills in 1849 after a militant struggle, including a strike of Pittsburgh workers.

Employers were quickly turning to immigrant labor to replace the original local workers. The *Offering*, after losing both contributors and a large part of its original audience, ceased publication in 1845. The boardinghouse concept for employees was gradually terminated as employers recognized its dangerous contribution to collective culture and worker solidarity. No new boardinghouses were built after the mid-1840s. The planned paternalistic industrial utopia was finished. From less than 4 percent foreign-born women employees in 1836, Lowell mills employed over 60 percent foreign-born in 1860, about half of whom were Irish.

The benevolent paternalism of Lowell was permanently replaced by the harsh relationships found in the new industrial workplace. Bagley, until she found employment as the first female telegraph operator in the nation, briefly served as a founder and vice president of the Lowell Union of Associationists, a group that sought to establish the concept of communal living. Other worker activists turned as well—at least for the next few years—to larger visions, utopian schemes, and cooperative concepts made for the mutual benefit of all participants. They hailed cooperative associations and planned communities as an alternative to the oppressive economic and social reality of industrialism. Neither the paternalism of Lowell nor the bleak wage labor structures emerging in the nearby manufacturing cities of Lynn and Fall River, Massachusetts, offered any kind of desirable future vision for most workers. Many labor leaders and social reformers were frustrated as well by the limited possibilities for reform presented by the Democratic Party.

Utopian Reformers and The Cooperative Movement

For a few years during the economic recovery of the 1840s and early 1850s the concept of a planned or architecturally constructed society aroused excitement among critics of the sharp contrasts between wealth and poverty that were emerging. Enlightened thinkers wanted to carry the revolutionary political ideas of the founding fathers and democratic leaders of the American and French Revolutions a step further to include the economic and social universe. Few workers and almost no unionists were attracted to these plans at first. They were developed almost exclusively by idealists, social reformers, and intellectuals. Robert Owen was an English mill owner who won renown for his various humanitarian experiments in collective community ownership of productive enterprises. Nineteen Owenite communities were launched in the United States between 1825 and 1827 and failed for various reasons, but usually due to poor organization and leadership. They attracted little enthusiasm from workers.

Frances Wright made an attempt at planning a model community for freed slaves in 1825. She wanted to demonstrate a way to end slavery gradually by compensating masters with the product of communal labor. Her experiment in Tennessee went badly too. The plantation she and her supporters purchased, Nashoba, could not be made self-sustaining. Wright turned to abolitionism, feminism, and worker rights. But the idea of a better world through intelligent and humanitarian planning was not finished. Others were busy refining the project and a revival of utopian ideas accompanied the upturn of the economy in the mid-1840s.

The French utopian socialist, Charles Fourier, had the most influence in the United States after 1837, the year of his death. The natural virtues of humans were distorted by capitalist relations, he had argued, so existing institutions should be replaced by carefully planned agricultural and manufacturing communities. He was sure that without the competitive savagery and debasement of one class by another that were associated with capitalism, and with proper planning and organization, expanded social relationships could be made to flourish. These collective associations of producers could distribute the commonly made wealth in an equitable fashion so all would benefit from the enterprise and labor of all. Fourier's plans were very specific about the details of the living and dining arrangements, numbers of people, and responsibilities in what were called the phalanxes. It looked great on paper, especially to those frustrated and angry about the squalid lives of workers in contrast to the luxurious world of their employers.

Albert Brisbane, a wealthy landowner's son, brought Fourier's ideas to the United States when he published *Social Destiny of Man, or Association and Reorganization of Industry* in 1840. The liberal journalist and publisher of the *New York Tribune*, Horace

Greeley, promoted Brisbane's and Fourier's views to a vast new audience that included many workers of varied skills and crafts. These workers were looking for an alternative to the constant strife, poverty, and insecurity that seemed to be part of the industrial world. The concept caught on and for about ten years, from 1843 to 1853, almost fifty of these communities were launched by a variety of workers, farmers, and idealists throughout the Northeast and Midwest. The intellectually rich collective community of Brook Farm near Boston included some of the most prominent writers of the period. But the talents of men and women of the stature of Ralph Waldo Emerson, Nathaniel Hawthorne, Margaret Fuller, and many others like them could not offset the common problems all of these experimental socialist communities faced: chronic shortages of resources, internal divisions over important policy-making decisions, and the corrupting interactions between these communities and the larger society of which they were still a part. Friedrich Engels may not have gotten everything right in his collaborations with Karl Marx, but he did a masterful job in explaining the inevitable failure of these utopian socialist experiments in an essay, "Socialism; Utopian and Scientific." Similar problems afflicted the more modestly scaled producer and consumer cooperatives during the same era and thereafter. The larger society outside these projects was just too dynamic, too appealing, and too competitive. The utopians and associationists did contribute to raising awareness about the abuses and injustices of the rapidly emerging capitalist social order. They also raised the prospect of an alternative social vision for workers that might be attainable by democratic or voluntaristic means. They brought socialism to the table.

Immigration

Ireland lost about one-third its population between 1845 and 1855. More than a million starved to death due to a combination of potato blight and English land and relief policy. Almost two million people left Ireland for the United States or Canada. They were joined in migration to the United States by millions of Germans, English, Scots, Norwegians, and Swedes. Political liberty and economic opportunity, as Alexander Hamilton had foreseen, continued to be the main motivating factor for the newcomers. They brought a diverse mixture of energies, skills, and political ideas from homelands disrupted by economic crisis and political turmoil. After the revolutionary upheavals that swept Europe in 1848, immigrants included more political refugees and industrial workers who added their socialist and revolutionary experiences to the ferment in the United States. In just a single decade, 1845–55, more than three million immigrants, more people than the total number of Americans counted in the first census of 1790, entered the United States.

Employers eagerly put the newcomers to work on projects large and small. The immigrants continued to be more economically and politically vulnerable than native-born workers. A mining and railroad building boom was underway by 1845 that rapidly opened up the interior of the country to farmers, businessmen, and industrialists. New agricultural and industrial machinery was being utilized, helping in the expansion of the national economy. The rapid growth of cities and industrial centers was transforming the society. Most of the labor in the new industries was foreign-born, and, along with new technology and steam power, served to generally depress wages throughout the decade. Newspaper editorials cheered the immigrants. The *Chicago Daily Tribune* hailed the Germans as "fitted to do the cheap and ingenious work of the country." Edward Everett, later to be the featured speaker after Lincoln's brief address at Gettysburg, welcomed the Irish since "their inferiority as a race compels them to go to the bottom" of the job ladder, "and the consequence is that we are all, all of us, the higher lifted because they are here" (Levine et al., 1989, pp. 263–65).

Western Expansion and War with Mexico

The general economic recovery and rapid geographic expansion of the nation from 1844 to 1860 quieted some of the working-class opposition to the low-wage competition of immigrants. The isolation in specific wards or neighborhoods of big cities and on specific job sites also kept native-born and immigrant workers apart. Texas, the recently established Lone Star State, was annexed in 1845 and the war with Mexico that began a year later further diverted worker attention from immigration issues. Wars or other foreign policy actions, with the exception of immigration policy, were never initiated by workers or their organizations. The decisions to make war against England in 1812 and Mexico in 1846, the orders that set up the military seizure of Florida from Spain in 1819, the periodic wars against American Indians, or the final plans to fight to preserve or divide the Union in 1861 came from other debates and other class sources. The state moved to advance the interests of capital formation, not in the interest of labor. From time to time the two interests intersected or seemed to coincide.

The expansion of the nation added promised economic and social opportunities for workers. Union leaders favored western expansion and a cheap land policy to draw off immigrant and low-wage labor competition. Business leaders, North and South, favored growth into new territory for plantations and businesses. Democratic presidential candidate James K. Polk read the temperament of the nation accurately in 1844 when he favored an aggressive expansionist policy over the more tepid platform of his Whig rival, Henry Clay. Annexation of Texas quickly led President Polk to ask Congress for a declaration of war with Mexico. Artisans and trade unionists mostly responded patriotically during wartime crises, but often their newspapers and leaders added their own specific goals for war. Access to inexpensive land for white workers was one of these goals.

To the low-wage problems wrought by technology and immigration, labor advocates called for a generous public land policy. The land in a republic belonged to the common people, not the aristocracy, claimed the *Workingman's Advocate*. When the Free Soil platform that opposed slavery in the territories taken from Mexico was adopted by the fledgling Republican Party in 1854, workers and their unions were enthusiastic. They shared the desire to keep the western territories free of slavery in their own self-interest, not because they were sympathetic to the arguments of abolitionists. Tens of thousands every year, ultimately millions, of new immigrants joined the native-born in the trek westward to farm or seek their fortunes whenever new territories were added. Negotiations with England led to the peaceful acquisition of the Oregon Territory in 1846, an expanse of 286,541 square miles of new land. The Treaty of Guadaloupe-Hidalago ended the Mexican War in 1848 and granted the United States an additional 529,189 square miles of land.

The gold rush of 1849 drew thousands of newcomers a month and sped up the admission of the former Mexican territory of California to the United States in 1850. With California part of the nation, the argument to use public land to subsidize the construction of a new transcontinental railroad gained added momentum. The rush to California prompted the successful completion of the first railroad that linked the Atlantic and Pacific across the narrow isthmus of Panama in 1849. Now there were calls for another railroad line to connect the eastern and midwestern states to the West Coast. Technological improvements in steel production by the mid-1840s enabled railroad construction to enter a boom that lasted almost thirty years.

Coal, Iron, Steam

North America was rich in resources, but they were not always easy to get to or bring to markets. Agricultural products had no competitive market value without low-cost transportation. Public subsidy of road building, canal construction, railroad projects, river passage, and harbor improvements aided business interests in their efforts to profit from these resources and the products of agricultural labor. Farmers, laborers, and shopkeepers benefited as well from transportation improvements, along with land speculators, bankers, lawyers, professional gamblers, and prostitutes. The railroad age lasted about a century as the chief means of internal transportation for the nation. It was built on iron and steel.

The chief ingredient in the manufacture of iron and steel is fire—great, intense fire. Abundant timber for fuel made Pennsylvania and New Jersey iron profitably competitive in Europe before the American Revolution. Now coal, the highly concentrated organic material from an earlier age in the earth's history, became the energy source of choice. Hard coal (anthracite) and coke (distilled soft bituminous coal) became the chief fuel for open hearth iron and steel making before the Civil War. Coal remained the principal source of fuel for ships, homes, factories, and offices for many decades thereafter. Getting the coal out of the ground and to the mills became the hard and dangerous occupation of more than five generations and millions of miners and railroad workers. Turning the ore and coal into iron and steel was the comparably demanding job of skilled ironworkers who, working as great chefs above the molten iron, aptly named their early union for the ancient god of the hearth. These puddlers called themselves the Sons of Vulcan.

Coal mining, railroading, and iron and steel making, though relatively new as mass production industries, had more in common with some of the older crafts than they did with other industrial work. It was exclusively men's work. Workers were often completely autonomous on the job. They looked after each other and depended on each other. Some jobs among iron workers, coal miners, and railroad men required highly specialized skills. Various secondary crafts emerged as well. Leaders, and an on-the-job hierarchy, soon appeared among the workers. Their interdependence created a rough workplace democracy as well. Supervisors or foremen had little influence except in matters of discipline, quotas, and pay. Owners and stockholders were never in sight. In common with other industrial workers, these workers lived together in company towns or in private housing clustered near the worksite. They formed a culture from their day-to-day relationships, communities, and churches, all of which were often removed spatially from the rest of society. When they acted together in strikes, walkouts, or protests, their actions had a political quality since the entire community was involved, one way or another. Within a generation of organization, their unions and labor struggles shook the rafters of the industrial order. Their work and its product ultimately knit the disparate state and regional economies together into a truly national one.

In the southern states coal, iron, and railroads were used mainly to enhance the profitability of the plantation crops. Trunk lines from the interior to the coastal markets were built to bring cotton to port cities. In Virginia and Alabama, iron and steel making developed for a more limited southern industrial economy than it did for its increasingly diverse northern neighbor. Slave labor, along with free black craft and industrial labor, was used in industry and in the crafts in southern states to depress wages and frustrate or disable unionization among white workers, and, for the most part, it worked. After a major strike in 1847, the Tredegar Iron Works of Richmond, Virginia, the largest mill in the South, shifted from free to slave labor.

Union Revival, Worker Activism, 1850–1861

Rapid geographic and economic expansion stirred a revival of unionization during two periods in the years that followed the Mexican War, 1850–51 and 1853–54. In every city old labor associations were reorganized and new ones started up. City centrals were rebuilt as unions pressed the traditional goal of wage increases, and renewed their demands for the ten-hour day. During this decade the goal of the eight-hour day in a six-day week gradually became the new sought after standard. Elegant arguments rich in philosophical meaning about the object of life entered the debate about hours of work. With new machinery and steam power helping to increase dramatically the productivity of workers, it was argued that workers should have more time to enjoy the fruits of their labor. Prices, however, were going up every year, due in part to the introduction of huge quantities of California gold into the national economy. In one year alone more than $50 million in specie was added to the money supply. Wages were so low in contrast to prices that living conditions for hundreds of thousands of workers, including those in skilled crafts, were deplorable in every city. Many lived in unsanitary hovels. Immigrants crowded into urban slums in every port. It was a close argument, one that was frequently made in this era, as to which group of workers lived under worse material conditions, plantation slaves or urban and industrial workers. The big difference of course was in political liberty, not in material comfort.

New protests and activism became almost inevitable. Workers continued the tradition of setting practical and immediate goals mixed with a radical criticism of the economic inequities of capitalist relationships. Strikes were commonplace, north and south, east and west. Both native-born and immigrant leaders continued to project socialist visions of one kind or another for the nation's future. Most of the utopian projects were coming to an end and left only producer and consumer cooperatives in their wake. After the collapse of the revolutionary movements that swept Europe in 1848 a new wave of socialist immigrants, especially those from Germany, added the ideas of Karl Marx and Friedrich Engels to the ideological ferment that stirred workers in almost every city.

English and Welsh immigrants also brought experience in organizing coal miners. One of them, John Bates, an Englishman, organized the first miners' union in the United States in the Pennsylvania coal fields of Schuylkill County, just a few miles up river from Manayunk. Bates combined English and American practicality and individualism in his venture. After leading a successful strike in 1849, he named his union for himself, the Bates Union, paid himself a salary more than twice what a miner earned, and apparently sold out to the employer within a year. The union was gone by 1850. Union history is filled with leaders like Bates who used their positions for their own personal benefit. The entrepreneurial spirit and the greater emphasis on individualism in the United States, in contrast to European and other cultures, made every union leader vulnerable to personal ambition. Control of large dues treasuries and very little auditing of expenses encouraged union leaders to operate their organizations as businesses, with themselves as owner-managers. Their contact with employers also gave union leaders tempting opportunities to compromise their members' interests for their own. A new more longlasting miners' union, the American Miners Association, was organized by another English immigrant, Daniel Weaver, in 1861.

Several other characteristics of this period of renewal of unionization had lasting consequences. First, the organizational foundations were built for permanent national unions. In 1850 the National Typographers Union was established, and while printers had briefly organized in 1836, that original structure lasted only two years. The new one is still around more than 150 years later, though technology has changed the work and the membership. A larger dues base among the membership contributed to stability. National wage goals, work standards, and apprenticeship rules and restrictions were sought through bargaining with employers. The national organization kept locals informed of new developments, set targets for bargaining, and helped build organizational power through internal union structures. After 1850, telegraphic communication, usually along railroad lines, connected most cities. A national organization could keep in touch with its affiliates as never before.

The largest business organizations also became national, or expanded their regional structures. The idea of the corporation, of many shareholders participating in the ownership of an enterprise, was almost two centuries old. It had been a highly restricted practice under mercantile regulations. The number of corporations now experienced a sharp expansion. The technology and the scale of the new industries required huge amounts of capital, usually amounts that went beyond the capabilities of individuals or even large partnership groups to raise. Some of these industries, especially railroads, employed thousands of workers scattered in many worksites. The states that had not already done so passed general incorporation laws that freed capital to combine and act with limited liability to investors. Prior to such laws corporations were considered potentially dangerous "conspiracies of capital" that had to be carefully monitored and whose state charters had to be approved on a case-by-case basis. Industries that were national in scale suggested the need for the formation of comparable labor organizations.

Locomotive engineers organized a national union in 1854 which they called a National Protective Association. Hat finishers, plumbers, and a National Union of Building Trades formed national unions in 1854. Upholsterers, stonecutters, cigar makers, silver platers, lithographers, cordwainers, and an association of cotton mule spinners also formed national organizations in the 1850s. The Machinists and Blacksmiths National Union and the National Iron Moulders' Union were formed in 1859. The recording secretary of the Pennsylvania molders' union, William H. Sylvis, urged the creation of a national union to counter the advantages to employers brought about by the enormous changes in technology and organization sweeping his industry. He became the leading force behind the founding of the National Labor Union, an assemblage of national trade unions, after the Civil War in 1869. The words and sentiment of Sylvis, expressed in the preamble to the molders' constitution in 1859 have been widely copied by unions ever since: "In union there is strength and in the formation of a national organization . . . lies our only hope. Single-handed we can accomplish nothing, but united there is no power of wrong that we cannot openly defy" (quoted in Hoagland, 1913, p. 305).

For the most part, and with the exception of the printers, molders, and machinists, these craft organizations did little more than hold yearly meetings at which they passed various resolutions, made stirring speeches, and shared front-line "war stories" of their great triumphs on behalf of their members. One of these accomplishments was another milestone of the decade, the expansion of the concept of collective bargaining to establish more uniform wage scales.

None of the national unions were utopian or explicitly socialist in outlook, though their leaders were quite aware of these influences and not unsympathetic to them. Their newspapers and pamphlets show a great deal of political worldliness and sophistication. But these were practical men who sought to gain social and economic justice within the institutions that granted them their political liberties. They expressed little or no concern for the rights of immigrants, women, or slaves. For the most part they accepted their status as white craftsmen and skilled workers in a democratic republic. Economic slowdown in 1854 and the Panic of 1857 wiped out most of their fledgling national organizations, except for the molders, stonecutters, and printers. Employers reneged on agreements, fired unionists, cut wages, or simply shut down. Fragmentary organizational survivals among the others were on a state or local level. Conditions for nonunionized industrial workers were no better.

Lynn, Massachusetts

Steam power and the sewing machine drastically changed shoe manufacturing and propelled more dramatic social and economic contrasts. While production was increasing sharply, wages and working conditions among New England men and women shoe workers were deteriorating. Health officials in 1850 found that the average life expectancy of residents of Lynn, the center of the shoe industry, was forty-three years. In contrast, Massachusetts farmers posted an average life expectancy of sixty-five. By 1860 Lynn, Massachusetts shoe factories were producing 4.5 million pairs of women's and children's shoes annually, but wage cuts had reduced the earnings of men to about $3.00 and women to as little as $1.00 a week. Sixteen hours was the workday for many Lynn workers. Women workers were using machines introduced in 1852 to sew the tops of boots and shoes together. The factories employed women for other tasks as well. Men attached tops to bottoms and continued in various skilled and semiskilled tasks.

News of the collapse and fire in the poorly constructed Pemberton Mill in early January 1860, and the resulting death of 500 men and women workers sent a shock wave through the industry. Meetings were held in Lynn and a wage demand was presented to the manufacturers. When the employers refused to meet with the workers' committee or make any changes in the wages, a strike began on the agreed-upon date, Washington's Birthday, 1860. Within a few weeks the strike spread throughout the region and became the largest and longest sustained strike in the nation's history before the Civil War. More than 20,000 men and women struck for almost three months. Reporters from New York and other cities covered the massive strike. Marches, processions, and rallies in support of the Lynn workers were held. Local clergy and shopkeepers supported the strikers. By early April some wage concessions were won and the strike gradually ended with one group of workers after another returning to work. Little union strength was gained in spite of public sympathy for the workers.

The Civil War

In spite of his political astuteness, most voters rejected Lincoln as a presidential candidate in 1860. Almost 60 percent voted for a candidate (there were three others, including the Democrat, Douglas) who either favored the southern labor system, or were pledged to seek an acceptable compromise with its continued expansion. Only the Republicans, led by Lincoln, were unequivocally opposed to the further spread of slavery in the territories. Nonetheless, the electoral college majority that he won gave Lincoln the presidency and provoked the secession of ten southern states and the creation of the Confederate States of America. Rallies, parades, protests, and petitions came forth from workers' groups and unions in the North to urge a compromise to save the Union in the months that followed the election but preceded the inauguration. None came. Instead there was war.

The authority and appeal of political leaders, blue and gray, was strongest at the beginning of the conflict. Workers and farmers filled the ranks of the opposing armies alongside small businessmen, clerks, and schoolteachers, though on both sides it was legally permissible for the wealthy to avoid conscription for military service through the purchase of substitutes. The poor had fewer options. One southern shoemaker commented on his army's victory in battle in 1862: "What is gained anyway? It is a rich man's war and a poor man's fight, at best" (quoted in D. Williams, 1998, p. 195).

The Union was able to call on one group of workers for military service that the Confederacy could not. Only desperation in the face of immanent defeat led to a scheme to enlist black slaves as troops one month before Lee's surrender. Over 186,000 black men served in Union forces, of whom more than half were escaped slaves. So many thousands of slaves ran away to sanctuary behind the lines of Union armies in the South that emancipation may be said to have been forced on Lincoln by the end of 1862. What were his generals to do, enslave the runaways? The wealth lost to the Confederacy in labor power due to wartime runaways is difficult to calculate exactly, but it was considerable. Most of that labor went to the Union side in civil or military use. Discrimination in pay favored white workers in almost every area, public or private. A protracted battle for equal pay with white troops was finally won by two black Massachusetts regiments, the 54th and 55th, though a distinction was made that gave retroactive equal back pay to the time of enlistment only to freedmen. Slaves who enlisted were entitled to back pay equality only to January 1, 1864 (Grant, 1968, p. 104). In the course of the war black troops won great praise from their commanding officers, and suffered an estimated 35 percent higher casualty rate than their white counterparts. Admirals and generals like to take credit for it, but the Civil War was ultimately won by northern workers and runaway slaves, on and off the battlefield.

Once again the need for soldiers and workers proved advantageous for labor, especially in the more industrialized North. After the initial economic shock and brief depression caused by secession, the productive energy of industrial technology in the north began to bloom. Wages and prices increased sharply and immigration dropped off similarly. Inflation and war profiteering, workers noted, were responsible for most of the wartime strikes for higher wages. Unionization expanded as never before. By 1865 union membership was up 350 percent, rising to almost 300,000. Just about every northern and western city had a trade union council or citywide organization, usually called trades' assemblies or city centrals. New labor newspapers came to life and old ones revived. Women workers were organized into protective and relief associations, and some women were organized into several actual trade unions, among them cigar makers, sewing machine operators, and umbrella makers. The trend toward national organizations of trade unions accelerated. By the end of the war all of the original national unions of the 1850s were revived along with several new ones. Some, like the Moulders, took the name "International" because they included Canadian locals in their membership.

When capital needed labor for its own preservation, labor did well. Iron and steel were needed to win the war. In one year, 1863, in the midst of the war, William H. Sylvis, the president of the rejuvenated National Moulders' Union, happily reported that in his travels for the union he had organized nineteen new locals, rebuilt sixteen that had been defunct, and strengthened twelve others. His membership increased from 2,000 to 6,000 in two years, union income went from $1,600 to $25,000 a year. By war's end he was on his way to winning the closed shop throughout the iron and steel industry. Sylvis was a progressive reformer as well a model for labor organizers to come. He sought to raise the social status of all workers, to end the use of convict labor, to increase the political power and independence of workers, and to win the eight-hour day.

During the war Sylvis and other labor leaders fought back attempts by employers' organizations to break unions. Employer groups made systematic use of blacklists, "yellow dog" contracts also known as "iron clad oaths" (worker pledges of nonunion affiliation as a condition of employment), and brought in state and federal troops to break labor strikes or boycotts. Employers won legislation in several states to permit the employment of private police by railroad companies, a practice that was later used by the iron and coal industries. Unionists in many cities countered successfully with the use of boycotts against local companies that engaged in repugnant practices, and called on locally elected political representatives to intervene against employer-sponsored antistrike legislation. Their gains and setbacks led many labor leaders to begin to talk of a national organization, and the eight-hour day was put forward as a national labor goal. By the end of the war eight-hour leagues were formed, or soon would be formed, in every northern and western city. Free workers expanded their vision of the possible during the war against slave labor.

The war that began because of a refusal to allow the expansion of slave labor turned into one that would terminate the institution altogether. By their own actions slaves who ran away and joined the battle against the Confederacy forced the nation in the direction of its own noblest ideals, the political concepts expressed by Jefferson in the Declaration of Independence. President Lincoln captured that sentiment in various speeches, most poetically in his Gettysburg Address. In spite of much controversy about the war, the end of institutionalized slave labor was a monumental advance for all of labor, at least until a replacement structure of state and local legal racial segregation was put in place after 1877.

President Lincoln celebrated the importance of free labor in a famous observation that every labor advocate regards as a truism. He reminded a delegation from the Republican Workingmen's Association of New York of his profound recognition of the primary place of labor in a government of the people. The delegation had come to Washington to confer honorary membership on the president on March 21, 1864. Lincoln accepted the honorary membership and said, "the existing rebellion [which was what he always called the war] means more than the perpetuation of African slavery—that it is, in fact, a war upon the rights of all working people." He then read to the committee a lengthy selection from his December 1861 address to Congress that included this passage: "Labor is prior to, and independent of, capital. Capital is only the fruit of labor and could never have existed if labor had not first existed. Labor is the superior of capital, and deserves much the higher consideration" (quoted in Schluter, 1965, pp. 175–77). Not even Karl Marx, a journalistic advocate of the Union cause against the Confederacy who was living in England at the time, could have pleased the workers' delegates more.

The war, however, was not fought exclusively to advance the rights of labor. It was a conflict about the future expansion of capital, a future that was impeded by the political power of slaveowners. Free labor enjoyed a temporary coincidence of interest in joining in the battle against slave labor, a common ground that endured for a few years after the war. When labor was regarded as an obstacle to the expansion of capital, it too would experience the legal and, at times, even the military power of state and nation.

During the course of the Civil War, expansion across the Colorado plains was thought to be impeded by the presence of its residents, the native people who lived there. At Sand Creek, Colorado, more than 150 mostly women and children of the Cheyenne who were killed and mutilated there in 1864 suffered at the hands of the same unit of the Colorado militia that was used to crush Filipino resistance to the imperial conquest by the United States at the end of the century. That Colorado military unit, with another new generation of soldiers, found murderous employment again against the women and children of striking miners who were killed in their tents in Ludlow, Colorado, in 1913. Labor and capital made common cause most easily when they faced common enemies most fiercely.

Conclusion

The United States was still mainly an agricultural nation at the conclusion of the Civil War. More people worked the land, and more wealth was made from agricultural enterprise than anything else. But great changes were underway, and tremendous contradictory forces were in motion. In little more than the generation that preceded the war enormous technological changes in manufacturing unleashed productive processes that had profound consequences for every region in the nation and every segment of the population. The ultimate total destruction, or genocide, of American Indians as a viable part of the continent was undertaken in these years. A new class of mainly urban and industrial workers came into existence and was beginning to shape its own destiny, form its own visions of the future, and build its own institutions. There were now many women and some men who would no longer accept the political inferiority of women. The militancy and leadership of free and slave black workers, and women of the North and South, in labor struggles came from the growing contrast between what was possible with the acquisition of political liberty and what was impossible without it. Aligned with the invigorated union movement they sought immediate wage, workplace, and workday improvements as well as an alternative to the grim social costs of the new industrial order. Universal (white) manhood suffrage was won, the ten-hour day became the standard for federal contractors, slavery was abolished, and universal public education was introduced in most northern states. Immigrant and native-born workers disputed one another, sometimes fiercely, for the scarce opportunities that came with the economic instability neither controlled.

The two distinct and related forces that commanded the loyalties of most people were family and community. The safety and security of one depended on the other. Community was formed around work and living arrangements. Religion, regional and ethnic culture, work, and the legal construction of citizenship wove family and community together and helped to form and re-form both. State and national laws were the institutional glue that appeared to hold the social structure together, not identity with class, race, or gender. Family and community were part of this larger society and responded to its demands accordingly. Workers joined the ranks (for the most part) of contesting armies (sometimes with fear and uncertainty) in the same way that General Robert E. Lee rejected command of the Union Army and gave his loyalty to Virginia and the South. Common participation on the front lines of battle and industry brought about a temporary alliance between those whose labor created capital and those whose legal authority gave them control of it. Once the wartime emergency was over, and once the mutual interests of regional capitalists were reconciled, the clash of workers and owners resumed in earnest. When that conflict broke out again both sides were stronger and the conflict more severe than ever.

Mary Harris "Mother" Jones and Terrence V. Powderly were among those who nobly served labor in heroic struggles with no expectation of personal reward. (The American Catholic History Research Center and University Archives at The Catholic University of America)

CHAPTER 4

The Heroic Age of Labor, "The Days of the Martyrs and the Saints," 1865–1893

The working people of our nation, white and black, male and female, are now sinking to a condition of serfdom . . . The center of the slave-power no longer exists south of Mason and Dixon's line. It has been transferred to Wall Street.

—William Sylvis, president, the National Labor Union (Sylvis, 1968, p. 112

Two great mythologies sustain the story of the United States in the modern era. Both have been embraced by workers. The first is the creation myth of the founders, the celebration of the work of George Washington and Thomas Jefferson's generation to establish a new kind of nation, one that was, as Lincoln enshrined it at Gettysburgh, "of the people, by the people, and for the people." In that story, all individual citizens, like Lincoln himself, enjoyed liberties that could enable them to scale social and economic heights unthinkable in other societies. The Declaration of Independence, the Constitution and Bill of Rights, and the arguments found in *The Federalist Papers* express the basic logical and idealistic premises of the nation. They serve as moral political foundations as well.

The second myth is a romantic one, begun in the early national period and brought to a peak in the conquest of the far western frontier before 1890. It is the exciting story of how the taming of the wilderness forged the national character, contributed to democratic virtues, and provided economic opportunities for energetic individuals that were also unavailable elsewhere. Taken together the myths link political liberty and economic opportunity as foundations of the national structure.Like other myths, these were drawn from reality, and propagated because of the benefits they brought to their proponents. They are the simplified interpretations of otherwise dense realities. That story is certainly not one told or written by native Americans, or slaves and their lynch law and Jim Crow oppressed descendants, or most industrial workers whose interests during this heroic age were all obstacles to be overcome by those who wielded real power. None casually accepted the idealized story of the nation, all battled mightily for an alternative to that developing mythology

The period from the end of the Civil War to the closing of the frontier and the onset of the depression of the 1890s was a monumental age. The scale of the projects undertaken was enormous, the human conflicts of epic proportion. National folk heroes were made, and the nation became a great power in the world. Mythic figures were fixed here. Paul Bunyan, Pecos Bill, and John Henry became the legendary workers of the forest, frontier, and rail. Jesse James and Billy the Kid were among the heroic outlaws of the age. Wyatt Earp, the hero of the Gunfight at the OK Corral, and Wild Bill Hickock were among their legendary lawmen counterparts.

This was the age when tens of thousands of miles of new railroad lines were built to span the continent and knit the nation into one vast production and marketing unit. Astonishing bridges, like the one that joined Brooklyn to New York, were stretched across great rivers as never before. Settlements were made across vast expanses, and the United States left its debtor status behind and became a creditor among nations. The spectacular Rocky Mountains were explored, prospected, and mined for their mineral riches. Great cities grew rapidly from little villages. Almost like magic, electricity brought light, power, and the telephone into the everyday life of the urbanizing nation.

Every obstacle to the expansion of industrial capital seemed overwhelmed. When the frontier era was declared at an end by the Department of the Interior after the census of 1890, there were so few buffalo that the remaining handful would require the protection of zoos to maintain the species. After noble but futile resistance, the native American population was destroyed or placed on reservations; their great leaders, Sitting Bull, Crazy Horse, Chief Joseph, and the rebel, Geronimo, dead or defeated. The independent goals of labor were similarly attacked (sometimes by the same troops) when they were regarded as challenges or obstacles to the objectives of capital.

Sharecropping, convict labor, legal racial segregation, and lynch law replaced slavery throughout the nation. The Supreme Court, in a series of decisions culminating in the *Plessy v. Ferguson Case* in 1896, firmly upheld the legality of racial segregation laws, codes, and ordinances of state and local governments. The National Labor Union, the first great confederation of trade unions, and the Knights of Labor, the first all-inclusive industrial workers' organization, temporarily gained enormous power and influence but were gone or in ruins by 1893. At the close of this era, Booker T. Washington and Samuel Gompers were ready to seek a conciliatory relationship with the owners of capital after almost thirty years of the most heroic labor struggle in the nation's history. It was, as the great miner's advocate, union activist, and socialist critic, Mary Harris (Mother) Jones proclaimed, "the days of the martyrs and the saints."

Reconstruction and New Vistas for All of Labor

The Civil War put an end to slave labor in America, and raised the hopes and expectations of all workers for a better future. The Thirteenth Amendment (1865) abolished slavery, "except as a punishment for crime." The Fourteenth Amendment (1868) was intended to extend all of the rights of citizens to former slaves. The nation was on the fast track to industrial and civic unity at the same time as its future rivals established their programs of national unification: Bismarck's Germany (1870), Italy's *Rissorgiamento* (1870), and Japan's Meiji Restoration (1868). Radical Republican leaders quickly intervened in the South to prevent President Andrew Johnson from completely abandoning the freed slaves to the will of their former masters, still staunch Democrats. Civil rights laws were passed to protect the newly freed population from oppressive and discriminatory "Black Codes." Voting rights were (temporarily) guaranteed by passage of the Fifteenth Amendment (1870). Employment, education, and economic assistance were provided to former slaves through the Freedmen's Bureau. The civil rights, relief measures, and social services to the vulnerable population were under the protection of federal military occupation of the defeated states of the former Confederacy. It is no wonder that many white southerners still cherish the prerogatives of states' rights and resent any form of federal intervention. They maintain a cultural hostility toward the restraints imposed upon them by the federal government during Reconstruction. Despite their total abandonment by Republicans after the compromises made in the course of the election of 1876, most black workers stayed loyal to the party of Lincoln until the New Deal. That separated them politically from most white workers, who continued to give their votes to the party of Andrew Jackson. Those political allegiances confirmed the powerful public and social influences on workers that had little to do with their own class, union, or material considerations.

Protection of the rights of four million former slave laborers, while it lasted and as limited as it may have been, inspired confidence and raised expectations for other workers. In the South, public education actually reached more white children than black children as one result of Reconstruction. The division of some large plantations made actual landowners of tens of thousands of freed slaves and poor whites for the first time. A national labor movement and an expansion of labor and reform organizations accompanied the Reconstruction until its conclusion. The antislavery idealism that set out to enhance the rights of one large group of workers in the nation seemed to be good for all workers. Indeed, most of the Radical Republicans were staunch supporters of the rights of all workers, and included in their ranks the most outspoken advocates of women's' rights as well.

Eight-Hour Leagues

Almost every city had an Eight-Hour League by 1866. Statewide organizations were called Grand Eight-Hour Leagues. Ira Steward, a Boston machinist, was credited with having launched this national drive for a legal limit on the workday to eight hours. His union, the Machinists' and Blacksmiths', brought the issue to the Boston Trades Assembly in 1863 and they helped to make an otherwise sporadic and inconsistent idea a national issue for labor. Along with familiar arguments about equity and the opportunity to enjoy the fruits of one's labor, Steward linked the goal of a shorter workday to democracy itself. How, he argued, could workers really study and understand the institutions of their country if they spent nearly all of their waking hours at work? Without time to think, read, and reflect on their situation, workers would be vulnerable to the political influence of their employers. In a pamphlet published in 1865, Stewart argued: " . . . They (workers) will be found every election day, in company with master capitalists, voting down schemes for their own emancipation. Capital, with swift enterprise, can pay for heralding to the ears of ignorance favorite catch-words, while its control of the daily press and party machinery leaves the intelligent workingman, of slender means, in a mortifying minority" (Commons, 1958, 9:292). Steward's insight continues to shed light on the relative ease by which workers have been beguiled by the political and social visions of their employers.

The movement to seek legislation to limit the workday to eight hours without reducing wages spread rapidly and seemed to get results over the next three years. Unionists and nonunionists supported the idea. So did small business owners and even many farmers. Few politicians in working-class communities were staunch opponents. By 1867 four states and at least six cities had passed eight-hour laws for either women or government employees. Congress made the requirement a law for all government work in 1868, though all of these measures joined other Reconstruction-era protective legislation in their almost total lack of enforcement. Escape clauses, similar to those that accompanied earlier ten-hour laws, allowed individuals to make different contracts with employers, and drained meaning from the restriction. Managers simply made such contracts a condition of employment, and workers could do little but sign them. It is often overlooked by those who should know better that legislative victories are nearly worthless without effective executive enforcement, and that legal finesse can obscure or negate the full meaning of an apparent victory. But this was still an optimistic era, a period of social progress and union growth.

The National Labor Union (NLU) and the Colored National Labor Congress (CNLC)

The most important worker organization of the Reconstruction era was the National Labor Union (NLU), a confederation of national craft unions. The NLU was led by William H. Sylvis of the Iron Moulders' International Union from 1866 until his sudden illness and death at the age of forty-one in 1869. The NLU, which continued to hold annual meetings and lasted until 1875, was remarkable for several reasons. While it was comprised mainly of craft or trades unions, it allowed any group of at least seven workers to form a chapter and gain a charter so long as there was no alternative trade union in their area. The NLU took in secret labor and benevolent societies, mixed groups of millers and blacksmiths, and political reform groups of workers. Even some professionals, farmers, and politicians joined.

President Sylvis certainly deserves to be remembered as one of the "saints" for his unselfish devotion to the cause of workers and for his far-sighted recognition of the importance of gender and racial equality to the cause of labor. He warned the delegates at the 1867 convention that racial antagonism could "kill off the trades' unions unless the two [black and white workers] could be consolidated." The delegates tabled the inclusion measure as they had done the year before. A group of nine men, representing segregated black trade union locals in Maryland and Pennsylvania, responded to Sylvis's friendly invitation of December 1868, and was seated at the national convention in August 1869, a month after his death.

Racial and gender exclusion were probably desired by the majority of delegates to the NLU meetings. Their national organizations and locals were virtually all male and white and they shared the prevailing national legal and hierarchical sentiments about race and women. Sylvis himself expressed some of these racial feelings in his skepticism about some of the Radical Republican social measures in the South. In the absence of a labor party, which he hoped to see someday and was one of the expressed goals of the NLU, he usually supported Democrats for public office and condemned Republicans, to whom most former slaves were devoted, as the party of Wall Street.

Many of the black delegates seated at the NLU Congress went on to form a parallel organization in December 1869, the Colored National Labor Congress (CNLC). The CNLC was the first organization of its kind, and the first national labor organization to open its doors to all workers: men and women, skilled and unskilled, agricultural and mechanical, or industrial. The CNLC permitted white representatives from the NLU to participate in their meetings as their delegates had done, and were the first labor confederation to admit Chinese immigrant workers as well. The CNLC elected Isaac Myers, a delegate from the Colored Caukers' Trade Union Society of Baltimore, its first president, modeled its structure along the lines of the NLU, and held national meetings from 1869 until 1871.

The exclusion of freedmen from most of the white trade and craft unions kept their numbers nearly nil in those bodies and in those crafts in the North. The gradual termination of protection from white violence by the early 1870s made open labor organization impossible for the freedmen in the South. The primary emphasis on support for the Republican Party by most of the leaders of the CNLC took freedmen farther away from association with the mostly white and independent Labor Party or pro-Democrat NLU and soon weakened the CNLC. The CNLC ceased its national meetings, withdrew to a small office, and faded to insignificance. The great labor and class battles of the rest of the decade—and thereafter—were carried on with little racial unity or organizational solidarity, though many workers, North and South, expressed great personal and shop floor unity.

The overwhelmingly white NLU, a loose confederation to start with, permitted local organizations to make their own decisions on the matter of racial inclusion. The most elite and well paid craft and mechanical unions, such as the Sons of Vulcan, the Brotherhood of Locomotive Engineers, and the National Order of United American Mechanics (NOUAM), explicitly barred black workers from membership in their national constitutions. The last of these, the NOUAM, also forbade membership to foreign-born whites. Women, too, had no rights to membership in all but two of the participating member unions of the NLU. In spite of the limited numbers of union women, the NLU, with Sylvis prodding it before his death, linked women's rights with the rights of all workers.

From its founding in 1866, when it expressed support for "the daughters of toil in this land," to its convention two years later when it became the first labor organization of its kind in the world to pass a resolution calling for "equal wages for equal work," Sylvis's NLU recognized the stake that labor had in advancing the rights of women. In support of the right to vote, Sylvis successfully urged the seating of four women delegates at the 1868 convention, though one of them, Elizabeth Cady Stanton, as secretary of the Woman's Suffrage Association, was not a delegate from a labor organization. After the death of Sylvis a year later, Stanton was denied a seat on the grounds that her organization had endorsed scabbing practices against a printer's union strike in order to secure employment for women otherwise barred from that union and those jobs. Karl Marx, one of the recent (1864) founders of the International Workingmen's Association, was so impressed with the equal pay resolution and the treatment by the NLU in 1868 "of working women with complete equality," that he wrote to an American friend: "Anybody who knows anything of history knows that great social changes are impossible without the feminine ferment. Social progress can be measured exactly by the social position of the fair sex (the ugly ones included)" (Marx and Engels, 1942, p. 255). Would Marx have voted to seat Stanton a year later in spite of the scabbing charge? History is mute on this question, though evidence suggests that his labor sentiments might have overruled his feminism, unless an alternative compromise might have been struck. What is clear, however, is that the NLU, which encouraged consumer and producer cooperatives, was moving in the direction of some connection with Marx's organization and the creation of a labor party in the United States.

The End of the National Labor Union

The NLU was never really a union. It was a loose confederation of labor unions and reform-minded organizations. From its start, many of the trade union delegates objected to the introduction of what they regarded as irrelevant issues. They were unsympathetic to the revival of producer and consumer cooperatives, and unconvinced of the value of creating a national Department of Labor. Women's rights appeared to threaten the political advantages and domestic authority that many of the delegates enjoyed and defended. Socialism had a German accent for most of the nineteenth century because so many of its theoretical origins and organizational initiatives came from immigrants from there to the United States. Most daily newspapers reviled labor radicalism, even unions of any kind, and portrayed them as the result of foreign influences carried by immigrants. Leaders of comparatively comfortable craft unions favored what Sam Gompers later called "pure and simple" unionism, the specific improvement in the wages and working conditions of those they represented and from whom they collected dues, and upon whom they were beginning to impose more elaborate union rules and union discipline than ever before. By 1871 most of the delegates to the NLU convention were agrarian and social reformers. Only two of twenty-two delegates came from actual labor unions, though neither represented their unions at the convention. The NLU was almost finished.

The National Reform Party split the ranks of the remnants of the NLU when it was formed in 1872. The new party platform included a mix of labor (eight-hour day), currency (Greenback), public land policy (for homesteads, not as a gift to railroads), and contract coolie labor (end it) objectives among its various issues. A major obstacle in forming a labor party, or a coalition third party, was, and always has been, the federal political system itself.

Many unionists were ardent Republicans in states, cities, or localities where candidates to local or national office embraced their issues. Senator Benjamin Wade, a Radical Republican from Ohio, was as devoted to labor issues as he was to the rights of the newly freed slaves and women's suffrage. Others unionists and workers were Democrats for the same reasons and did not want to forsake leaders they had helped to elect. Big city political machines, their bosses and ward heelers alike, were becoming responsive to local union and working-class influences, and workers could not easily turn away from them for the vague promises and airy platforms of social reformers without any political base. When the NLU split into factions over the endorsement of a presidential candidate in the election of 1872, they were finished as a viable labor organization in spite of some meetings of a handful of stalwarts for a couple of years thereafter. Many of the strong craft union leaders who left the NLU were determined to learn from its mistakes and hoped to reorganize around what they called exclusively union and nonpolitical issues.

The Knights (and Daughters) of St. Crispins

The first large-scale union effort to organize on an industry-wide basis, and not strictly according to a specific craft or trade, was taken up by the Knights of St. Crispins. The Crispins (as they were commonly called) started in secret in 1867 in Milwaukee, Wisconsin. By 1870, with a membership estimated at 50,000 in over 300 lodges nationwide, they were the biggest single labor organization in the country. The shoemaking industry, largely concentrated in New England, was changing from a strictly craft and small shop dominated labor system of skilled handworkers, to one increasingly mechanized in larger and larger factories with labor processes broken into smaller and smaller semiskilled and unskilled tasks. The Crispins were primarily a defensive organization of existing shoeworkers who were organized to block the introduction of "green hands," the unskilled, from doing their work. Strike funds were used mainly to defend the organization, and to stem the reductions in wages that resulted from the introduction of green hands and new machinery. Their strike victories in several shoemaking centers (Lynn and Worcester, Massachussetts) and in Philadelphia and San Francisco in 1869 and 1870, quickly built their numbers. As the dues came in they expanded their activities, bought property, set up cooperatives, and took part in parades and public functions. But, in defending an obsolete method of making shoes, they were on the wrong side of history, and their defeat is illustrative of an ongoing dilemma faced by labor when the owners of capital control the new technologies and are willing to act in concert.

In 1872 a formal combination of boot and shoe manufacturers in Lynn, called "The Board of Trade," deliberately and with care set out to destroy the Order (as the Crispins were also known). The board raised money, recruited other manufacturers throughout the state, and vowed not to employ any union members. The manufacturers provoked a long and bitter strike by refusing to meet or discuss any matters with the union. The strike spread throughout the region and went on until the union was exhausted and individual workers crossed the picket lines and went back to work. Some of the struck manufacturers had made agreements in advance of the strike to send work out to other manufacturers, and, with the cooperation and assistance of state authorities, they also employed prison laborers. Imported Chinese workers were also brought in as strikebreakers and took over the machinery in many of the shops. Union funds were denied to strikers by former trustees of the union aided by the courts (through effective delay tactics) and manufacturers. The union was finally forced to submit to a complete surrender. The massive depression of 1873 devastated remaining lodges, though many of the Knights of St. Crispins became active members of the Knights of Labor during the period of its tremendous expansion a few years later. For now, the first great industrial union in the United States was busted, defunct.

An Unknown Workers' Pinnacle

The well-being of workers in the United States was never completely under their own control. Every group or segment of the workforce struggled to gain greater agency or self-determination measured against what seemed possible and in contrast to the political and social power enjoyed or exercised by employer groups. The era of the Civil War and Reconstruction was certainly a time of prosperity and expanded organizational strength for most workers, aside from the nearly one million who died in that war. The Radical Republicanism that helped the newly freed slaves extended rights and opportunities to all workers, whether they realized it or not. Freed slaves were protected in labor, education, landowning, and the exercise of their political rights by U.S. military forces that occupied large parts of the former Confederacy. Poor whites gained as much or more from that occupation than freedmen. The war and its after-math also opened the new occupations of teaching, government employment, and nursing to women. Women also had taken on the added responsibilities of farm and business management while men were gone. High farm prices, fueled by wartime needs and inflationary monetary policy, added wealth to farmers and agricultural workers.

At the height of the Reconstruction, in 1872, there were at least 300,000 workers rep-resented by labor unions, according to the Workingmen's Assembly leader in New York State, William J. Jessup. William Sylvis, more optimistically, estimated in 1868 that the number of unionists was twice that, or about 600,000, and growing. Coal miners rebuilt their small prewar organizations into a powerful Workingmen's Benev-olent Association of over 30,000 members by 1869. The skillful iron puddlers of the Sons of Vulcan reached a peak of influence in a successful contract in 1870 that in-cluded the setting of the pace and tempo of work. The Vulcans had not yet faced the full onslaught of the introduction of the Bessemer process for making steel, a technology that, in a decade, would transform their industry and render obsolete their well-compensated skills and authority. The distinguished labor historian, David Montgomery, estimated that "a larger proportion of the industrial labor force enrolled in trade unions during the years immediately preceding the depression of 1873 than in any other period of the nineteenth century" (Montgomery, 1967, p. 140).

For labor, the still uncontrollable forces of technology, national economy, and pol-itics all combined to reverse achievements made during the Civil War and Recon-struction. The continuing political, technological, and economic vulnerability of la-bor, combined with the pent-up ambitions of managers and employers to reverse the gains or concessions granted to workers during a period of economic expansion and military crisis, led to some of the most monumental labor struggles in all of labor history over the next twenty-five years.

The End of Reconstruction and the Deskilling of Black Labor

By 1872 the idealism and force of the Radical Republicans was fading fast. The Ku Klux Klan Act, passed in 1871 after congressional witnesses reported thousands of murderous attacks on recently freed slaves and their Republican allies in the South, gave the federal government the authority to protect the rights of citizens from south-ern violence. Enforcement, however, came to an end a year later as Radicals lost control of the Republican Party to Stalwarts and to a new group called Liberal Repub-licans, who were pledged to building a new South in economic and political cooper-ation with Southern Democrats. The original Republican Party, the party of Lincoln, was strictly a sectional political organization with no support or program in the South.

When the Civil War came to an end it was still under a sectional leadership intent on a punitive Reconstruction. The new Republican Party leaders saw no worthwhile gains in continuing a program on behalf of freed slaves. When they abandoned the defense of the political rights of freed slaves the Republican Party became a national party, not a sectional one. The gradual withdrawal of federal troops left the former slaves at the mercy of former masters and their Klansmen subordinates. Klan violence and vigilante lawlessness always enjoyed the subsidy and protection of elite groups, though from a respectable distance.

The fate of black labor in the South for almost a century was left to white landlords, white employers, and the racially exclusive Democratic Party. Sharecropping became a new form of landless peonage for most black farmers in the South. Few could escape near permanent indebtedness to landlords and merchants. Nonagricultural black workers were restricted almost exclusively to menial and service employment as they were barred from the skilled occupations and crafts that many thousands had practiced as slaves. In New Orleans, for example, where careful records of skilled craftsmen were kept, the number of black skilled craftsmen declined by over 90 percent from 1870 to 1900, or from over 3,000 to only about 300.

Convict labor was vastly expanded throughout the South, and was particularly brutal for black workers. Several states had no conventional prisons. They leased out all of their offenders. Whips, shackles, iron cages, and sweat boxes tortured workers throughout the South for over half a century with little outside protest or intervention. Convicts were leased out to contractors and were employed in mines, mills, quarries, railroad construction, and factories. They were leased out to work on sugar and cotton plantations, or worked in huge state-operated agricultural enterprises like the notorious Angola Prison Farm in Louisiana. It didn't take long before the loophole in the Thirteenth Amendment was found. Slavery, "except as a punishment for crime," was prohibited. Convict labor, then and now, was legal enslavement since existing labor standards, laws, or legal protection of citizens did not apply to convicts.

Disfranchisement and legally enforced racial segregation became the political and social standard for black workers in the South (and most in the North and West) within a generation of the formal termination of Reconstruction with the infamous Compromise of 1876. Disputed electoral votes in three southern states were all given to the Republican presidential candidate, Rutherford B. Hayes, in exchange for the promise to end whatever remained of the northern intervention in the southern states. The betrayal of the promise of freedom to former slaves was but the first step in the assault on the gains temporarily won by all of labor in the United States in the Civil War and Reconstruction.

Depression, 1873–1878

A general economic downturn, regardless of its origins, doesn't spread its misery democratically. Those in command of social and political power transfer as much of the costs of the slump as possible to those without it. This depression, touched off by the failure of the banking company of Jay Cooke and Company, was by every measure the worst and longest in duration in the nation's history up to that time. Banks and businesses failed, mines and mills closed, prices dropped, and farms fell into foreclosure by the tens of thousands. Businessmen opened an attack on the wages of labor to shore up falling profits in every industry that continued to function at all. On average, the wages of workers still employed were cut nearly in half. Following the lead of the Massachusetts boot and shoe manufacturers, unions were deliberately beaten down, many destroyed, and unionists blacklisted as never before. Unions were on the defensive everywhere. Strikes were bitter and usually lost. The thirty national unions in existence in 1873 were reduced to nine by 1877. Membership in unions dropped to less than 50,000 nationwide. Unemployment created desperation among hundreds of thousands of workers. Aside from private charities, most workers had almost nothing to fall back on when they lost their jobs. Faced with almost no viable alternatives, what could they possibly do?

Unemployment Demonstrations

The burden of temporary unemployment falling on the shoulders of workers is one of the great efficiencies of the age of private capital. It stands in stark contrast to the feudal or slave labor systems that preceded it. Feudal barons and slavemasters had the obligation of caring for those under their authority, the former as a feudal duty, the latter to protect their own investment. In contrast to serfs and slaves, free workers are also free to starve or perish for lack of adequate shelter or medical care. While no argument for a restoration of dependency, it is a tribute to the cultural hegemony achieved by their employers that so many workers accept their own misery as a normative condition, or, worse yet, assume responsibility for it. Not every worker, however, accepted personal responsibility for economic depression, and they sought government intervention to deal with the situation. One way to do this was to gather together in a collective effort to seek some form of relief.

Unemployment demonstrations took place in towns and cities across the nation. Labor unions were under siege, most were suffering defeats, and some of the worst living conditions fell on nonunionized women, children, and immigrant industrial workers. Consequently, unions were not at the forefront of the attempts to mobilize the unemployed. No dues could be collected from the jobless either. These demonstrations were often organized by social reformers and radical critics of what appeared to be a cruel and heartless economic and social order. Demonstrators wanted work provided by city authorities on public projects, rent relief legislation, or a public relief fund for the unemployed. In Chicago 20,000 people assembled for a march on city hall to demand that a fund of $700,000, the remains of a relief fund set aside for victims of the great fire of 1871, be used for victims of unemployment. Ultimately, almost 10,000 families received some assistance from that fund.

The most dramatic of the unemployment demonstrations took place in New York in Tompkins Square Park in January 1874. The surprising violence of New York mounted police clubbing their way through a peaceful crowd of about 7,000 in the ten-acre park is confirmed by accounts from both those who were its victims and those who witnessed it and reported it in the press. Despite the many eyewitnesses to the contrary, the crowd, not the police was blamed. Mayor William F. Havemeyer, the son of the sugar trust founder, and almost every voice of so-called respectable authority cheered the police attack on what they called a communist-inspired rabble, led by foreigners. Seventeen-year-old Samuel Gompers told about his own frightening experience in his autobiography almost fifty years later. He distinctly remembered cowering in a cellarway in the midst of the melee. He said he could never forget the relentless "orgy of brutality" he saw that day. He claimed the experience shaped his pragmatic and conservative methodology in building the American Federation of Labor several years later.

The men, women, and children in Tomkins Square Park and in surrounding streets were beaten and trampled for several hours for gathering without a proper permit. Most had not heard the news of the sudden revocation by the Police Board of the permit granted by the Parks Department the day before the gathering. Nor did they know that Mayor Havemeyer had rescinded his earlier sympathetic and positive response to speak before the assembled crowd. Because some in the crowd fought back, the event came to be known as the Tompkins Square Riot. In the aftermath of the event the city went further. It placed police spies in labor and socialist organizations, and brought pressure to bear on landlords to evict any labor organizations or radical groups from their properties. Labor organizations were quickly reduced to a tiny fraction of their size or influence in the city. While the depression was leading to consolidation among business organizations, workers and the groups they formed were under siege everywhere.

Crushing the Miners Union

Similar to the breaking of the Knights of St. Crispins, the assault on the Miners Benevolent Association was deliberate and calculated. The architect of the plan, Franklin B. Gowen, the president of both the Philadelphia and Reading Railroad and its subsidiary, the Philadelphia and Reading Coal Company, later boasted that he had spent more than $4 million to achieve his goal.

The MBA was formed in 1868 in the course of an unsuccessful strike by its mostly Irish members for the eight-hour day. About one-fourth of the miners were boys from ages seven to sixteen. During the presidency of John Siney the union soon represented nearly all the anthracite miners in the rich coal fields of southeastern Pennsylvania. The strength of the union increased after one of the great mining disasters in the nation's history, the Avondale fire, which took the lives of 110 miners on September 6, 1869. Miners knew that economizing on mining costs by not providing second exits could have disastrous consequences in the event of a fire or flood. With no way out, everyone in the Avondale mine perished in the fire. The health and safety of workers (and users of products) has always been a cost calculation for business and the result is an ugly history. Through most of these years it was not unusual for about 100 miners a year to die from injuries on the job among the approximately 22,000 who worked in the mines of Schuylkill County. Anger at their losses mobilized the miners and in 1870 the MBA, led by Siney, signed the first written contract between miners and coal operators in the history of the United States.

In 1873 Gowen set out to destroy the union by placing a hired private detective in its ranks. He consulted with Allan Pinkerton and, with a $100,000 retainer fee, helped advance what would become the most famous private industrial espionage and strikebreaking agency in the country. Gowen was sure that his Pinkerton spy would discover a band of Communists, agents of the Paris Commune, and members of the International Workingman's Association behind the union, and frequently made those claims publicly. He also claimed the unionists were terrorists, members of a secret organization called the Molly Maguires, a band named for an Irish woman allied with antilandlord uprisings in the old country. The mole, James McParlan, got no results after nearly two years, but continued to report his observations to his paymasters. Gowen raised the stakes of battle a little higher. The company announced a 20 percent pay cut in December 1874 and the union immediately responded with a strike called for January 1, 1875.

The Long Strike

In the course of this Long Strike several murderous attacks took place. Unionists were killed by gangs. Reprisals meant the killing went on. A mining company superintendent opened fire into a group of workers. Several were injured as they fled. Coal and Iron Police, a company force, were augmented by state militia to break picket lines. President Siney, in spite of his personal opposition to the strike, his field organizer, and twenty-five other union leaders were arrested, tried, and most were convicted of violating the existing Pennsylvania conspiracy laws. Siney was eventually exonerated and died in 1880 of the common ailment then called "miner's asthma," or "black lung disease." The convicted were sentenced to a year in prison. From every newspaper and pulpit the striking miners were attacked as lawless radicals. After six months of heroic suffering that included children grubbing for roots and edible herbs to stay alive, the strike was broken. So was the union. The miners accepted the pay cut and, enfeebled by hunger, went back to work. In the bitter aftermath of the strike and the destruction of the union, violence escalated.

Gowen wasn't finished either. Sometimes individual human agency plays an extraordinary part in the unfolding of events and people become more than marionettes to historical influences beyond themselves. Gowen certainly was a force. He convinced his agent, McParlan, to testify in separate trials against a group of men, mostly union leaders or activists, charged as murderers and members of the feared Molly Maguires. With incredible audacity, Gowen himself was named (or named himself) special prosecutor to try the cases. His evidence was almost entirely built on McParlan's testimony and that of several miners charged with or convicted of crimes, including murder. Roman Catholics were barred from the juries. One of the crimes had taken place fourteen years earlier. No independent evidence or testimony confirmed the men's guilt or even the existence of the Molly Maguires. Most of the accused miners were found guilty, and over the course of a year and a half twenty were executed by hanging. A group of four of these martyrs was put to death in January 1879 in spite of massive protests and appeals for clemency or pardon. A reprieve from the governor of Pennsylvania did finally arrive for two of the men, but it came too late to save them. Two final hangings were scheduled for October 9, 1879, and one was duly carried out. The last of the Mollys had his sentence commuted to life because of his being found to be "feeble minded."

The dead had their martyrdom officially certified a little more than a century later. The great-grandson of John Kehoe, one of the executed leaders of the MBA, succeeded in convincing Governor Milton Shapp of Pennsylvania of the injustice done to the men. Kehoe was officially pardoned by the governor, and on June 21, 1980, a plaque was formally dedicated at the Schuylkill County Prison in Pottsville to the memory of the rest, a group who were, the memorial proclaims, victims of "repression directed against the fledgling mineworkers' union of that historic period." Shapp said earlier in a letter that all Pennsylvanians "join with the members of the Pennsylvania Labor History Society in paying tribute to these martyred men of labor" (quoted in Kenny, 1998, p. 284).

In the same month as the first of the executions, June 1877, a series of wage cuts to railroad workers began on the Pennsylvania Railroad and was soon extended to other lines. A month later the greatest labor upheaval in the nation's history exploded.

The Insurrection of 1877

Unemployment, antilabor and antiunion repression, wage cuts, and the hanging of the Molly Maguires all played a part in the massive strike wave and labor uprising that began in July 1877 and spread quickly to major railroad and industrial centers around the country. No one planned it or could have anticipated it, though all of the conditions for an uprising were present. It had no real focus, though railroad workers ignited the spark and provided most of the leadership that emerged in the various cities involved. Hence, it is often known as a railroad strike, or series of railroad strikes. But it was much more than that. Several cities experienced nearly complete general strikes, total economic stoppage. There were few concerted demands or common actions from city to city, though entire regions of the country were suddenly brought to a near standstill by the strikes and the various attempts to put them down.

The conflict started in the little railroad town of Martinsburg, West Virginia, on July 16 (the first 10 of the alleged Molly Maguires were executed on June 21). Striking workers uncoupled locomotives and refused to allow any trains to operate unless a 10 percent pay cut was restored. Though never endorsed by the skilled Railroad Brotherhoods (Conductors, Firemen, and Engineers), before it was over, strikes of construction, maintenance, and other railroad workers quickly crippled railroad operations around the country. General strikes spread out from the railroad yards and brought economic activity to a halt for several days in Pittsburgh, Scranton, St. Louis, Chicago, Harrisburg, Baltimore, Louisville, and Buffalo. Strike activity on a lower level took place in dozens of other cities, large and small. In Galveston, Texas, and several towns in other parts of the South, black workers took the lead in railroad construction yards. They led or shared leadership in massive concerted actions that rallied all workers against pay cuts and for the setting of citywide pay standards for all workers. Racial solidarity was loudly proclaimed by a crowd of 10,000 mostly white workers on behalf of striking black workers on the levees of the Mississippi in St. Louis when they were asked for help by a black worker who addressed them. A parade of women in East St. Louis marched in support of the general strike, to which they added the demand for women's suffrage.

Local militia, police, national guard, and federal troops (hastily transferred from frontier battles with Indians) augmented local Law and Order Leagues, Civil War veterans, and company security forces to try to break the strikes and disperse the angry crowds. In several confrontations members of state militia units refused to report for duty, broke ranks and joined the protesting workers, or simply left the scene. After some members of the militia fired on crowds in Pittsburgh and killed twenty people, a massive outburst of popular rage overwhelmed the military unit, scattered them, and turned on the railroad yards. The crowds burned everything there. More than 2,000 railroad cars, and over 100 locomotives were destroyed. The outraged city was briefly in the hands of the strikers. Similar uprisings put temporary municipal control under strike leaders or, as in St. Louis, an "Executive Committee" of the Workingman's Party. No unified plan or cohesive program came forth from the workers, their unions, or political organizations. Nor did any singular leader articulate the common emotions that bound the workers together. A mixed expression of class and worker anger at wage cuts and general economic injustice was the common thread throughout the uprising.

Government and business leaders acted swiftly. They had no uncertainty about their objectives. Federal troops were quickly moved from city to city and joined with local authorities to end the strikes. More than a hundred people were killed in the suppression of what commanding General Winfield Scott Hancock called "this insurrection." Newspapers compared it to the Paris Commune. The *St. Louis Republican* called it a "labor revolution." For the most part striking workers gave up their struggle when faced with overpowering police or military presence. By the end of the month, or about two weeks after it began, the "Great Upheaval" came to an end. When it was over, President Hayes concluded simply: "The strikers have been put down by force" (quoted in Brecher, 1997, p. 21).

The Consequences

It is tempting to divide the nation's labor history into two parts, the period prior to the great uprising of labor in 1877, and the years that have followed. While that dichotomy may be overly simplistic, it may be a helpful way to understand some of the important changes and consequences that followed. After the uprising, great energy was expended by government, business, and labor to improve their position in future encounters.

Every industrial city and state undertook serious reorganization of its military and police. Most cities quickly began the construction or renovation of large armories or urban fortresses for maintaining national guard forces in the heart of industrial districts. Future clashes with workers were clearly anticipated. Military units were reorganized to assure their loyalty to established authorities. Now national guard units were structured to take into account ethnic, class, and religious considerations. States enacted more specific "malicious conspiracy" laws aimed at labor strikes to refine and update the old English Common Law standard. Employers made more aggressive use of these conspiracy laws, and by 1880, courts began to add the use of the injunction to break strikes. There were more conspiracy charges brought by courts against workers in the single decade of the 1880s than the total for the rest of the century (Commons, 1918, 2:504). Business also made more systematic use of blacklists and yellow dog contracts to combat union influences. Frank Gowen became a leading national proponent of the open shop, the right of an employer to hire nonunion workers in spite of the authority of a union in the place of employment. Gowen kept at it until scandal led to his fall from corporate grace; he committed suicide in 1889. Employer associations proliferated and expanded their antiunion cooperation. A cigar makers' strike, in New York, for example, brought together an association of thirty-two manufacturers when it started in September 1877. When the strike was over and lost, three and a half months later, the 7,000-member union had been reduced to 131 (Bonnet, 1956, p. 140).

Immigration was dramatically increased so that the nation changed its social composition over the next thirty-five years. Southern, central, and eastern Europeans accounted for most of the newcomers. In 1870 only about one-third of industrial workers were foreign-born and most of them came from northern and western Europe; by 1900 half were foreign-born and most of those came from south, central, and eastern Europe. Nearly all large-scale employers were native-born, and the vast plurality of them Protestant with northern European origins. In all of the nation's history prior to 1880, only 200,000 people had arrived from southern, central, and eastern Europe. In just the next thirty years, 8.4 million people arrived from that same region. Half the people in Chicago in 1890 were foreign-born, most from the new regions. Socially divided workers often took out their frustrations over scarce jobs, public services, and small markers of status on each other. The homicide rate in the United States tripled in the 1880s, and the prison population increased by 50 percent; both had a preponderant effect on the working class. The state was now the primary disciplinary agency for control of the labor force. Previously, masters of servants and slaveowners held sway.

The 1877 strikes prompted legislative hearings and the formation of state commissions to study and address labor issues. The idea of voluntary arbitration by publicly established labor boards to reduce conflicts was advanced, though not enacted. Stratification, or the division of labor through different pay and benefit structures, was increased. The elite railroad Brotherhood of Locomotive Engineers that had refused to strike, and maintained a no-strike pledge, made the first written contracts in the industry beginning in 1875. The BLE continued to gain high wage rates that specified additional pay for overtime; they won seniority provisions, established grievance and disciplinary procedures, and built a union-run benefit fund that set them apart as an oasis of labor tranquillity during the next, otherwise stormy, dozen years. Craft unions took notice and adopted similar negotiated settlements where they could. Several unions began to join business groups in lobbying Congress for higher protective tariffs on imported goods, to which they added their desire for curbs on imported contract labor, and immigration restrictions in general. The Chinese Exclusion Act was achieved in 1882 with bipartisan political support and the backing of business and labor organizations. Chinese immigration restriction was embraced by those business leaders who feared the competition of Chinese manufacturers who employed Chinese laborers, as much or more than it had been advocated by labor, though many of the employer associations formed to break unions opposed restrictions (Bonnett, 1956, p. 239).

In spite of the ultimate defeat of the labor uprising of 1877, thousands of industrial workers were invigorated by their temporary successes and made more aware of the need for organization. As the influence of the depression waned, industrial workers quickly began to fill the ranks of the Knights of Labor. The Knights were a formerly secretive labor organization begun by tailors in Philadelphia in 1869. It soon took the lead in many of the great labor battles of the rest of the century. Workers also enlarged their nonunion methods of building protective networks for themselves and their families in their urban and industrial communities

Company Towns and City Life: New Forms of Acculturation

Culture is the way people collectively explain and give meaning to everyday social life. It is made by influences that enter the community from the outside, from politics, newspapers, schools, and institutional leaders like clergymen and schoolteachers. These external and institutional influences then are mixed with the human needs and experiences of the people themselves. The new culture is also made inside the community as the external influences are melded and shaped by the immediate realities of the voices, sights, and smells of everyday life. A livable universe has to be made with the materials that are at hand. Slaves and their descendants made and remade family ties, took the religion that was given them, and made it serve with solace and songs of hope and escape. Humor and irony masked fearful risks; "roast pig," it was said, "is a wonderful delicacy, especially when stolen" (Genovese, 1976, p. 599). Miners, mill-workers, and factory operatives formed a functioning cultural universe in crowded company towns and the working-class neighborhoods of the rapidly growing cities. Workers mixed their traditions, folkways, foods, and beliefs with inputs from the bigger world of their city, state, and nation. Everything useful was kept, things that didn't serve faded. Unions, labor newspapers, songs, and politics grew out of the ferment of worker culture.

The dynamism and near constant growth of the country put small and large opportunities in front of workers all the time. City and country life was teeming with business enterprises, both legal and illegal, made from the circumstances and deficiencies of everyday life. Most farmers thought of themselves as small businessmen. With their urban retailers, farmers made illegal untaxed whiskey—moonshine—the largest cash crop in Kentucky by 1900. Business enterprises were everywhere workers lived. Workers, or members of their families, frequently opened and patronized simple shops, bars, and restaurants. If they knew anything about the building trades, many of them became contractors. Tailors became clothing manufacturers. Workers cared for each other's children, made or acquired things to sell, took in boarders, and provided subprofessional services. Workers formed business cooperatives to buy their necessities and sell their products. The working class imitated the speculative energy and excitement of capitalists as they produced their own loan sharks, gamblers, bookmakers, prostitutes, and politicians. There was always a business presence in working-class culture alongside the collective sentiments of ethnicity, religion, and union. Cities and large industrial enterprises brought new kinds of employment to workers in offices, as managers, clerks, and administrators. The application of electricity to everyday life created new skilled crafts and unions for hundreds of thousands of workers.

When workers went into politics, most imitated the property-owning classes and treated public offices as they did other forms of enterprise. For the services provided to their constituents they expected and received proper compensation. The same attitude often carried into union organization and leadership. Many trade union leaders accepted the political attitude of George Washington Plunkett of Tammany Hall, who said there was a world of difference between honest and dishonest graft, that he had simply "seen my opportunities and took them." The more that workers regarded themselves as upstanding citizens in the United States, the more they accepted the social codes of the nation, codes that included sharp racial and gender differentials. For immigrants, whiteness and social authority came with citizenship, a distinct advantage over their prior status, and the legal inferiority of former slaves and women.

Labor organizations that did not succumb completely to the values and civic codes of the dominant business culture were seen as renegades or radicals. These organizations expressed the frustrations of workers and put forward a vision of the future that condemned the permanent or inevitable subjection of what they called the "producing class" to the absolute power of the owners of wealth. While many Socialists and social reformers contributed ideas and energy to the ongoing discourses among workers about alternatives to the injustices they experienced, fewer workers in the United States were drawn to these theoretical alternatives than Europeans. The republic seemed to offer real opportunities to transform itself democratically.

On the other hand, workers in the United States acted more militantly when they confronted their employers than their European counterparts in this era. They appear to have wanted far less, but were willing to fight much harder for it. Strikes in the United States were more numerous, longer, and more often resulted in violent or legal clashes with police or military forces than the labor conflicts of their European and more outwardly socialist counterparts. When socialism and the reaction against it finally entered the picture in a forceful manner in the United States, it came on the heels of a great and heroic struggle by labor for a place at the table of the rich and growing nation. The first great all-inclusive industrial labor organization to challenge, without wishing to overturn, the prevailing business and capitalist order in the United States, The Noble and Holy Order of the Knights of Labor, began its meteoric rise a year after the great uprising of 1877.

The Noble and Holy Order of the Knights of Labor, 1869–1890

What happened to the Knights of Labor is both encouraging and discouraging to advocates of organized labor. From the economic and antiunion gloom of the depression of the 1870s the Knights rose to enormous national influence and power in less than a decade. Five years after that they were all but gone from the scene. In spite of the brevity of their prominence, they were by far the most important national labor organization in the United States in the nineteenth century. Their citywide assemblies, publications, and national organizational structure sought the inclusion of all workers: the skilled and unskilled, black and white, men and women, immigrant and native-born. Their idealism restricted membership a bit: "no person who either sells or makes his living by the sale of intoxicating drink can be admitted, and no lawyer, doctor or banker can be admitted" (Commons, 1918, 2:337–38). Gamblers and stockbrokers were also barred. The producer and consumer cooperatives of the Knights achieved such remarkable success at times that it required the concerted efforts of business groups to destroy them.

Expansion of the Knights became possible when secrecy was put aside after 1879 and locals were permitted to make their presence known in their districts. Leaders of the Knights of Labor sought to use reason and conciliation to settle disputes, not strikes or confrontational tactics. Though formally nonpartisan, at their peak in the mid-1880s, their endorsement secured the election of candidates for office in more than 200 towns and cities in thirty states. Third-party labor candidates were nearly elected mayors in New York and Chicago as a result of Knights of Labor support. Both major parties courted their votes. Nonetheless, and in spite of their gentle and humane approach to every form of conflict resolution, they were condemned by the popular press as responsible for the huge strike wave and the monumental labor conflicts that accompanied their period of greatest expansion. Their collapse was as stunning as their expansion.

Until the era of the New Deal, unions carried an illicit aura, since concerted action by them was usually found to be illegal, and there were no institutional sanctions or laws that protected them. Employers commonly placed labor spies or informers among workers to maintain tight control of the workplace. Uriah Stevens, one of the founders and the man behind most of the secret rituals of the Knights of Labor, had trained for the Baptist ministry before he turned to labor organizing. He never lost his missionary zeal; neither did the labor organization he helped to start. Terrence Powderly, who became the organization's first publicly known leader in 1879 with the title Grand Master Workman, carried on the salvationist message until he was forced out of the nearly defunct organization's leadership in 1893. Almost at the same time, in 1878, Powderly, with the Greenback-Labor Party endorsement, was elected mayor of Scranton, Pennsylvania. He defeated a fusion ticket of Republicans and Democrats who warned voters against communism and called his party a "Molly Maguire ticket." Powderly was reelected in 1882 and again in 1884. In office he favored temperance and sought a cooperative commonwealth that recognized and respected the legitimacy of both capital and labor. Neither Powderly nor Stevens could have predicted that the Knights would soon become a lightning rod for all of labor, and that its membership would grow from a few thousand members in and around Philadelphia to a national force of about 750,000 by 1886.

Pennsylvania miners, whose union was shattered in the Long Strike of 1875, became the first major group to align themselves with the Knights of Labor. In the aftermath of the uprising of 1877 thousands of industrial workers affiliated with the Order, as they were also known. Secrecy was appealing to those familiar with the railroad and mining companies. With the return of prosperity in 1878, and the dropping of the secrecy rule a year later, more workers formed local and district assemblies. Membership doubled from about 10,000 in 1878 to 20,000 in 1879. But the Knights were never a unified organization or a union that could act in concert on any matter. They were a democratic labor movement with a radical and republican orientation, not totally dissimilar to the Grange organized by farmers during the same period.

The American Federation of Labor

Skilled craft workers were divided about the Order. Some of them, led by cigar makers Adolph Strasser and Samuel Gompers, were scornful of associating with unskilled factory workers. They enjoyed the autonomy and better wages their crafts gave them in the workplace. Unlike factory operatives, their skills belonged to them, and they—

not the boss or manager—passed them on to new members. The two men preferred an exclusively trade union federation, and a much more pragmatic labor organization. In 1881 the two of them became associated with the Federation of Organized Trades and Labor Unions (FOOTALU). Though both men were educated as socialists in labor, they were convinced that the capitalist system that employed them and their countrymen was so powerful that the only practical course of action for labor was to make the best economic and political deals the strength of their unions allowed. For a number of years, they sought to avoid politics altogether. They favored the "voluntarism" of an open struggle between labor and management without any government intervention. They later modified this policy to accept most of the protective reforms of the Progressive era and the New Deal. Though they were openly critical of the social injustices they saw and experienced, they accepted the United States as it was, capitalist and racist. There was no great national war they couldn't support, though Gompers was an active participant in the Anti-Imperialist League that criticized the acquisition of the Philippine Islands and other territories in the aftermath of the Spanish-American War. Like the Knights, FOOTALU numbers also grew steadily, though never as spectacularly. In 1886 the name and the organizational structure were reconstituted into the American Federation of Labor (AFL). The AFL did not seek to organize labor unions or laborers outside of the trades, or skilled crafts. It would be a national assemblage of craft unions organized along the same lines as the federal and state governments. Autonomous local trade unions organized into state associations that affiliated with the national federation. The AFL was, itself, not a union, could not call or call off a strike, or mount a picket line. It was in business primarily to promote the expansion of craft unionism. The Knights are long gone, the AFL, a patriotic and practical organization of neither martyrs nor saints, is still ticking.

The Rise of the Knights of Labor

A series of successful strikes by Knights' locals, including several victorious actions in 1884 and 1885 against the notorious Jay Gould's Union Pacific, Wabash, and Missouri, Kansas, and Texas railroads, brought in new members by the tens, then hundreds of thousands. Gould was the infamous "robber baron" who casually boasted that he "could hire one half of the working class to kill the other half." A second strike against a Gould line resulted in the killing of seven workers by police in East St. Louis in April 1886. Enrollment in the Knights went up immediately afterward. A revived national struggle for the eight-hour day brought thousands more into the ranks. The essentially peaceful Order was the dominant labor organization in the country when the number of strikes, mass actions, protests, and demonstrations reached a level of intensity known as the Great Upheaval of 1886–87.

It wasn't the rituals, or a special knack for organizational structure, or charismatic leadership that made the Knights so prominent. Nor was it the mixed and sometimes contradictory viewpoints that were expressed in magazine articles and speeches by their leaders at their various assemblies. The Knights sought a radical transformation of the nation in the continuing idealistic tradition of Jefferson and Paine, through educational enlightenment and the mobilization of all producers. Women and black workers constituted approximately 20 percent of the membership of the Knights, or about 60,000 black workers and 50,000 women, at its peak. Neither group would be as strongly represented in a national labor organization until the formation of the Congress of Industrial Organizations (CIO) fifty years later. Workers rushed to affiliate because the Order was a popular and democratic expression of their own mixed sentiments, not because it was an effective union, though they all hoped it would be. With the return of prosperity in the early 1880s, the demand for the eight-hour day was on the mind of just about every worker.

By 1886, while the Knights and the AFL were contending for prominence and leadership of labor, millions of citizens of every description were challenging the imperatives of capital as never before. The farmers' alliances in the South (black and white together for now) and West were mobilizing millions of people angry at railroad rate discrimination and price gouging, bank foreclosures, and collapsing prices paid for their commodities. It was also the year in which the Apache leader, Geronimo, led the last significant native American uprising against the government of the United States. It seems that no one wanted to stay in the exploited and subordinated place assigned to them by their landlord, boss, government, gender, or race. Only the AFL, which knew its place, continued to make cautious headway. The rest, including most dramatically, Geronimo and the surviving native American people, black Americans, the Knights of Labor, and women, failed to achieve their objectives in the heroic battles that continued to the end of century.

The Haymarket Martyrs, 1886

Massive eight-hour-day demonstrations, with deadlines for implementation on May 1, were underway in dozens of cities in April. Strikes were hitting a crescendo of frequency never seen before. From 1881 to 1885 there were fewer than 500 strikes that involved an average of about 120,000 workers each year. Almost half of these strikes were not union-affiliated walkouts. In 1886 alone there were 1,432 strikes that mobilized over 400,000 workers, and the great plurality of them were union-sanctioned. Though down to under 1,000 in 1888, two-thirds of the strikes that year were union-sanctioned. The most dramatic and most publicized labor confrontation of all of these took place in Haymarket Square, Chicago. The decline of the Knights of Labor is often attributed to the Haymarket Square conflict and its outcome.

Eight-hour-day rallies had begun in earnest in Chicago with a march of 80,000 on Michigan Avenue on May 1. A day later two workers were killed by police in Haymarket Square. Workers gathered in the square on May 2 to rally for the eight-hour-day and to express support for striking shingle shavers in a shop near the McCormick Harvester Company. Labor radicals, including some anarchists whose literature extolled the virtues of dynamite, led the call for a rally in Haymarket Square on May 4 to protest the police killings. The rally was not heavily attended, though a large contingent of police was there. When a bomb was hurled by someone among the rapidly disbursing crowd of about 300, one policeman was killed immediately and seven others fatally injured. The bomb thrower has never been identified, but as the labor activist, Mary Harris (Mother) Jones said, "The city went insane." Sadly, she added, "the workers' cry for justice was drowned in the shriek for revenge" (quoted in Atkinson, 1978, p. 76). Samuel Gompers observed, "The effect of that bomb was that it not only killed the policemen, but it killed our eight-hour movement for that year and for a few years after, notwithstanding we had absolutely no connection with these people" (Commons, 1918, 2:386).

The national press and pulpit erupted with condemnation of all labor activism. Even the Knights shared in the blame despite Powderly's lack of interest in the eight-hour-day movement of that spring, and his consistent hostility to strikes or violence.

The Haymarket Riot, as it was called, resulted in the arrest and trial of those who were held to be responsible for the May 4 rally, not anyone ever identified as a bomb thrower. Eight men were charged and convicted, and seven of them sentenced to death in a trial that was quickly regarded by all of labor as baseless. Lucy Parsons, the wife of one of the well-known arrested anarchists, Albert Parsons, devoted herself to building a movement to save the men. For nearly a year she traveled the country, wrote letters, and spoke at meetings and rallies while the case was appealed first to the Illinois, then to the U.S. Supreme Court. Almost single-handedly she helped build a massive movement for clemency that included international protests. The appeals failed. Four of the convicted men, including Parsons, were executed for the crime. One other committed suicide or was killed in his cell. The other three condemned men were eventually pardoned by Illinois Governor John Peter Altgeld after his election and a careful review of the case seven years later. Altgeld found that "much of the evidence given in the trial was pure fabrication," and that the police had bribed and "terrorized ignorant men," or threatened witnesses "with torture if they refused to swear to anything desired" (Boyer, 1955, p. 98). Those who were executed are known as the "Haymarket Martyrs" and were commemorated thereafter at May 1 Labor Day parades and rallies around the world. Altgeld, shortly thereafter, took another brave step. He defended the American Railroad Union in the course of the Pullman Strike of 1894, and, though he was a popular Democrat, was excoriated by the business community and the press, lost the allegiance of his party, and was never elected to any office again. Altgeld's political martyrdom led his biographer, Harry Barnard, to refer to him as an "Eagle Forgotten."

The Collapse and Legacy of the Knights, 1886–1892

It wasn't the bomb hurled in Haymarket Square that destroyed the Knights, though the press of the day linked their labor advocacy with the event. The Knights adamantly repudiated violence and stayed as far away from the case as they could. Unlike Gompers, who persuaded the AFL Convention to pass a resolution urging mercy for the condemned, Powderly used his influence to defeat such a motion by his General Assembly. Leaders of the Knights decried the militant strike and union action that continued for the next several years. Concerted attacks on labor by employers and police raids were not the reason for the demise of the Knights either, though union busting by employers was intensified in the aftermath of Haymarket Square.

Many employers simply refused to negotiate with union employees unless they disaffiliated with the Knights. Many thousands of workers were forced to do that. Murderous attacks on racially mixed assemblages of workers in the South took the life of a white organizer for the Knights, H. F. Hoover, in May 1887. Thirty black sugarcane workers, who had been evicted from their homes, were killed when their shanty town was stormed by a vigilante mob in Thibodaux, Louisiana, in the fall of 1887. Labor activism always carried risks. Race consciousness always implied violence. The rapid collapse of the Knights of Labor was as much a consequence of internal labor conflicts as it was external public or business forces.

The Haymarket conflict brought to the surface disputes and fissures within the ranks of labor itself, and from among the Knights themselves. In the same months as the Haymarket crisis was making the news, the Knights went through a series of indecisive reversals on another strike of Gould's Southwest Lines. The organization lost thousands of members who, with justification, blamed Powderly and the Order for a complete capitulation to the railroad.

This Great Upheaval of the mid-1880s marked the time from which the battles within the ranks of organized labor matched those with capital. Like rival corporate entities of the time, labor unions began to compete with one another for the loyalties, political influence, and the dues of their constituents. The Protestant moral codes of the Knights may have helped inspire social idealism, but those codes also turned away many of the new immigrants who didn't share the same sentiments, especially with regards to temperance. The AFL drew off the craft unions anxious to disassociate from the unskilled. In their rivalry, Powderly became embittered at the AFL, lashed out at Gompers, and threw most of his energies into reform movements such as the Women's Christian Temperance Association and the farmers' alliances that formed the Populist Party in 1892. Socialists criticized Powderly as a naive middle-class reformer. In 1893 he was replaced as Grand Master Workman. Internal disputes about tactics split off other groups. Greenback-Labor candidates for public offices supported by the Order were losing out to major party coalitions. The Knights of Labor were quickly reduced to a few thousand loyalists scattered around the country. They were finished, but they left behind some worthy accomplishments.

Unionization of nonskilled and semiskilled workers achieved a permanence that it had never had before thanks to the work of the Order. Black workers, new immigrants, and women continued to seek recognition for collective representation and bargaining rights from employers. The Knights served as a school for labor organizing for those workers outside the traditional or newly emerging crafts and skilled trades. Industrial unionism quickly revived with the founding of the American Railway Union in 1893, and in the mines by the United Mineworkers Union and Western Federation of Miners, and in the needle trades, often by men and women who had formerly been members of the Knights of Labor. Eight-, nine-, and ten-hour-day agreements were accomplished for hundreds of thousands of workers during the mid-1880s where much longer workdays prevailed before. A federal Bureau of Labor, similar to those already in place in several states, was established in Washington, D.C., in 1884 as a fact-finding agency within the Bureau of the Interior. By the end of the decade women's' groups from the Order had built effective political lobbying forces that won factory inspection laws in several states, including Pennsylvania and Illinois.

Heroic Battles, Class Warfare: Burlington, Homestead, Coal Creek, Coeur d'Alene, New Orleans

Burlington

The strike by the Brotherhoods of Locomotive Engineers and Firemen on the Burlington Railroad in 1888 marked the end of tranquillity between elite engineers and a railroad company. Two years of frustrating negotiations had failed to produce any change in frozen wage rates. The strike also marked the first dramatic use of a federal injunction to break a strike since the passage of the Interstate Commerce Act a year before. The injunction, a court order to cease immediately an illegal action or risk the charge of contempt, was relatively new to labor struggles. The first such actions were taken by courts in the 1880s, but none had received the publicity that injunctive force attained in the Burlington strike. To a young railroad union activist named Eugene Victor Debs, the disastrous strike showed the hopelessness of separate craft defined locals in the railroad industry. At first switchmen, who were not on strike, crossed union picket lines, then Knights of Labor workers took on the jobs of striking firemen and engineers. Debs finally got the switchmen and Knights to support the strike, but the injunction frightened the engineers back to work. The firemen stayed out for a year until they were broken and blacklisted. The strike was the real launching pad for Debs, who became one of the most heroic figures in labor history. His first move, less than a year later, was to begin the organization of an all-inclusive industrial union for railroad workers, the American Railway Union. On the other side, the injunction was now a government and management staple for breaking strikes.

The national strike wave and labor militancy of the mid-1880s reached a new crescendo during the years 1889–93, before falling off in the deep depression of almost the rest of the decade. The number of strikes nearly matched or exceeded the former peak year of 1886 with 1,833 strikes in 1890 and 1,717 in 1891. In 1892 alone, the national guard was used twenty-three times to break strikes. Four strikes that year, of a total of 1,298, either gained extraordinary national attention or represented heroic milestones in labor history. They were strikes at Homestead Steel, a division of the Carnegie Steel Company, in Pennsylvania; a bitter strike of miners in Coeur d'Alene, Idaho; a militant strike against the use of convict labor in the mines of Briceville, in Anderson County, Tennessee (Coal Creek); and a biracial general strike in New Orleans. The first three strikes involved court actions, military intervention, and the armed resistance of striking workers. In New Orleans, racial solidarity led to the winning of a qualified victory.

Homestead

At Homestead, on July 6, two barges carrying 300 armed Pinkertons were confronted in a gun battle and captured by striking steelworkers. The workers, led by the skilled Amalgamated Association of Iron and Steel Workers, an AFL affiliate, mobilized the entire town of over 10,000 workers to protest the company's plan to end union recognition and cut wages 18 percent. The Pinkertons were forced to surrender after a ferocious exchange of fire that went on for several hours and left seven dead among them. Nine workers were killed, but their forces controlled the steelmaking plant and the town for several days, until the Pennsylvania militia arrived. Reporters swarmed into town and reported the events to an astonished nation. General George Snowden was shocked by the high level of organization and complete control of the mill and town achieved by the workers. Snowden had to order his troops to desist in fraternizing with the people. "Pennsylvanians can hardly appreciate the actual communism of these people," Snowden complained. "They believe the works are theirs quite as much as Carnegie's" (quoted in Wolff, 1965, p. 164). Actually, most of the leaders of the Homestead strike were quite conservative, patriotic, and overwhelmingly Republican Party stalwarts. In spite of criminal charges of murder and treason brought against union leaders, the strike held firm for four months. Workers everywhere identified and marched in "Homestead Day" celebrations to raise money for the striking steelworkers. None of the accused was ever convicted, but the time and money spent on bail and legal expenses exhausted the union in spite of the help they received. Technological advances in steelmaking enabled management to train strikebreakers more easily than ever, and, since none of the other large mills were out, production was shifted with little interruption to orders.

The union finally gave in and the strike was broken on November 20. Wages were cut 25 percent, and the workday was gradually extended from eight to twelve hours. Though defeated, class solidarity, rather than simply union consciousness, appeared to be on the rise. Labor leaders and their newspapers began a marked shift toward a socialist analysis and criticism of their circumstances in the wake of the harsh government and company repression endured at Homestead. A House of Representatives Committee, established to investigate the Homestead strike, reported: "Within the next decade we may reasonably expect a revolution" (quoted in Dubofsky, 1994, p. 28).

Coeur d'Alene

A similar armed confrontation and radical ideological shift was taking place between striking miners and armed detectives in the Coeur d'Alene region of northern Idaho. A strike in protest against falling wages was successful in preventing strikebreakers from entering the mines from January through May. In June, after an exchange of fire with guards, the seizure of several mines by armed unionists, and the taking of strikebreakers as prisoners, the governor declared martial law and sent in an unenthusiastic militia. When that failed to achieve the desired result the governor requested federal military intervention from President William Henry Harrison, who complied. The strike was broken by the combined military and the arrest of over 500 workers and many of their supporters. Those arrested were placed in stockade and barbed wire enclosures known as "bull pens." Nine men were eventually found guilty of contempt for defiance of a court-ordered injunction and sentenced to terms of six to nine months. Four others, who had been found guilty of conspiracy, had the charges thrown out on appeal to the Supreme Court. Indictments against almost 500 others were dropped. Once released, the men resumed the strike, and eventually achieved a victory with the discharge of all strikebreakers and the return to employment of all of the former workers. Those serving prison terms for contempt spent most of their time talking over their situation and came to the conclusion that a more unified organization of miners was necessary to match the power of the mine owners. As soon as they were released from prison they set to work organizing The Western Federation of Miners, a union described as "the most militant in the history of the United States" (Perlman and Taft, 1966, 4:172).

The same kind of strike, court-ordered injunction, military intervention, martial law, and massive arrests took place at Coeur d'Alene again seven years later. In both cases the U.S. Army helped the company take over its mines and run them with strikebreakers. The military was never used to protect workers from owners in the United States, no matter the outrages or illegalities carried out against them.

Coal Creek

Almost at the same time, a long-running struggle to stop the use of convict labor to break the coal miners' union came to a head in Tracy City and Bryceville, Tennessee, in an area known as Coal Creek. In July, regular miners were put on half-time while 360 convicts were brought in on lease full-time. After secretive meetings, miners organized into a military force. Inspired by what they had heard from Homestead, they stormed the convict barracks in three mining locations and sent the prisoners by train to either Nashville or Knoxville. Their siege of Fort Anderson was broken up by the arrival of militia, who quickly put down the uprising. Hundreds were arrested and locked up in temporary prisons in railroad cars, a schoolhouse, and a Methodist church. Local juries refused to convict any of the workers. The convict labor system soon came to an end in that region (Brecher, 1997, pp. 68–69).

New Orleans

Not all of the heroic battles of this dramatic year brought workers to violent confrontations with military authorities. For many years there was a racially aware labor structure in the busy harbor of New Orleans. The mix in the city of Spanish, French, native American, Northern European, and African people, both slave and free, was too complex for simplistic racial divisions, though consciousness of race was abundant. While the city was under military occupation for part of the Civil War, and for several years thereafter, freed slaves found employment in a wide range of jobs, skilled and unskilled. Though most of these jobs were racially segregated, labor unions representing different groups worked together through most of the 1880s in a Central Trades and Labor Assembly. This assembly, formed in 1881, was composed of about thirty unions. The Knights, never strong in New Orleans, had twelve assemblies, about half white and half black. Black and white dock workers struck together four times from 1865 to 1887, and set up a work-sharing system to divide work evenly. The first of these so-called half-and-half agreements was made by longshoremen in 1885, then extended a year later. Not everything was cordial in town. There were fights, even what were described as "race riots" and fierce competition for jobs during hard times.

Management on the docks didn't like the half-and-half rule, and objected when it was reaffirmed in March 1892. A strike of streetcar drivers in May included the demand for a closed shop. A newly formed Board of Labor Union Presidents replaced the former Labor Assembly and, with the support of the mayor, assisted the drivers in winning their strike. The new labor body changed its name again to the Workingmen's Amalgamated Council during the summer when it represented 30,000 workers in forty-nine unions.

When three unions in town, Scalemen, Packers, and Teamsters, formed their own Triple Alliance and struck in October, they drew harsh attacks from local newspapers and their employers because of their biracial composition. The Teamsters were a primarily black union. The new Amalgamated Council came to their aid, set up a Committee of Five, one of whom was a black longshoreman, and sought a negotiated settlement with the Board of Trade. The employers offered to negotiate with the white unions, but refused to deal with the biracial committee. The employers and the press waged a vicious and racist attack that sought to evoke the worst fears of "mobs of brutal Negro strikers." The committee decided to call a strike of every union member without a contract in the city. They set wage and hour demands for each, along with the closed shop, and led more than 25,000 workers on the most well-organized and unified general strike in the century. Workers acted more militantly than their leaders when thousands more violated their own contracts and joined the strike. By all accounts business in the city was completely shut down, all electricity and gas lines out.

The Board of Trade, an employers' association in the city, swung into action. They made plans to bring in thousands of strikebreakers from all over the region. They called on Governor Murphy Foster to send in the militia because the mayor was un-willing to use local police to break peaceful picket lines and protect strikebreakers. Foster threatened to put the city under martial law in spite of the absence of violence. A mediator was agreed on and an agreement that gave the Triple Alliance everything but the closed shop ended the strike after just three days. Samuel Gompers, still in his nonracist public posture, exulted in the unity of the workers. He called it "a ray of hope for the future of organized labor," that with "one fell swoop the economic barrier of color was broken down" (quoted in Rosenberg, 1988, p. 36).

Employers weren't satisfied. They wanted to break the unions. The Sherman Anti-Trust Act became law in 1890. It prohibited combinations that acted "in restraint of trade." Most people assumed that the law was designed to prevent the monopolis-tic power of business trusts from strangling markets. Just two days after the end of the general strike, the leaders of forty-four unions were charged under the new law with conspiracy "in restraint of trade," and an injunction was issued by the federal court against them should the action proceed. This was the first application of the new law against labor. After delays and appeals the case was eventually thrown out. An important precedent was set, however, and one of the most heroic victories in labor won.

Racism Federalized and Institutionalized

Along with its unions, New Orleans had an active civil rights movement in place in the early 1890s. Legally enforced racial segregation codes and ordinances were still in the process of being developed, especially in the South. Racism was entering its most rampant national and international stage. Lynching and political disenfranchisement accompanied the new Jim Crow laws across the South. Employers refined their ap-plication of racial and ethnic divisions of labor in mines, mills, factories, shops, and offices nationwide. Institutions like schools, churches, hospitals, theaters, and asy-lums throughout the country accepted the strictures and exclusions of race. In New Orleans a well-established middle class of people of mixed backgrounds known as Creoles, along with some local white and black leaders, opposed the new codes and ordinances that were imposing racial segregation practices. Their organization, a Cit-izens Committee, and a newspaper, the *Daily Crusader*, wanted to test the Separate Car Act of 1890 in court. A member of the committee, Homere Plessy, volunteered to challenge the law and sit in a "Whites-Only" part of a railway car in June 1892. His conviction for violating the law was finally upheld in 1896 by the U.S. Supreme Court in one of its most infamous decisions, *Plessy v. Ferguson*. Racial segregation now was sustained by the full authority of the federal government. It was the law of the land.

It is important to note that racial segregation, or racism generally, was not made by workers. Neither was capitalism or nationalism. All were structures of social organi-zation that were made to serve other interests. Workers only adapted to all of these as they became good citizens. Dissent from prevailing systems of thought and social practice meant alienation, or worse. The biracialism of workers in New Orleans held on heroically for more than twenty years, and withstood many challenges, including a major strike in 1907, but was finally broken after World War I. Other unions and their leaders fared less well on the matter of race.

In his early years of leadership of the AFL, Samuel Gompers was an outspoken critic of racially exclusionary practices, except for his consistent anti-Chinese position. By the time of the AFL convention of 1894 he capitulated to the prevailing racist sentiment of his organization and nation, and thereafter withdrew his advocacy of solidarity with black workers. Gompers even allowed himself the occasional derogatory racist remark. Black workers were not sought by AFL organizers. Those who applied for affiliation were placed in segregated locals. Since most of the crafts controlled apprentice admissions practices, black workers comprised no more than about 3 percent of the total AFL membership by the mid-1920s.

The Temptation of Politics, the Populists, and Labor, 1892

Unlike every other advanced industrial nation, the United States has never had a sustainable national labor party. Major parties were able to draw enough workers into their folds to prevent a serious challenge to their hegemony. Democratic Party leaders like Governor Altgeld and Governor Grover Cleveland of New York publicly sided with workers in various disputes and won their votes. Cleveland, though known as a conservative, or "Gold" Democrat, successfully drew off worker votes from the Populist Party in the election of 1892. He sided with the Homestead workers in their conflict with Carnegie Steel that year. Republicans consistently held vast pluralities among black voters until the New Deal won their allegiance in 1936. Immigrants had no vote until they were naturalized. By then they learned of the benefits that were available to them from big city political machines of both major parties in exchange for their votes. Ward heelers and district captains shared cultural roots with the newcomers. The political machines dispensed jobs and other forms of assistance in the neighborhoods in exchange for political loyalty on election day. Minor parties, no matter how appealing, had nothing tangible to offer practical men.

There were two serious national attempts at a labor party. One grew out of the Greenback-Labor coalition of the late 1870s. That political movement reached full bloom when Powderly, of the fading Knights of Labor, joined with farmers' alliance leaders in 1891 and formed the People's or Populist Party and nominated James B. Weaver for president in 1892. The other waited until Eugene Debs ran for the presidency in 1912.

The Populists' greatest strength came from the anger and desperation of millions of farmers and small business owners faced with discriminatory railroad rates, bank foreclosures, and high prices for manufactured goods brought on by business monopolies and rising protective tariff rates. The hostility to the giants in railroading, banking, and manufacturing temporarily united farmers, workers, reformers of various description, and small businessmen in a massive outpouring of popular dissent.

Most of the Populist platform expressed the mood of agrarian resentment, and held little appeal for workers. The goals of government ownership of railroad and telegraph lines, free coinage of silver to promote inflationary agricultural price increases, a graduated income tax system, direct election of U.S. senators, and a federal postal savings system stirred little emotion among workers. Populists expressed solidarity with the Homestead strikers, and all of their meetings and organizational efforts sought ties with labor, organized and unorganized. The Populist platform included labor demands for the eight-hour day, immigration restriction, a condemnation of the use of hired mercenary gunmen—Pinkertons—as strikebreakers, and a ban on the use of the convict leasing system. Both parties, Populist orators proclaimed, were in the hands of the giant trusts, and like the famous twins, Tweedledum and Tweedledee of *Alice and Wonderland,* candidates for high office couldn't really be told apart.

Gompers was hostile to the Populist Party. He thought of it as a movement of small business people with no real understanding of labor issues. The highly sectarian Socialist Labor Party leader, Daniel DeLeon, was even more critical. On the other hand, many socialists took part and claimed success through the party in advancing their views about greater economic democracy. Many AFL locals participated as well, and were heartened by the results. The railroad unionist, Debs, thought the Populist platform was too radical. He stayed loyal to the Democratic candidate, Cleveland, who won the election. Soon after taking office President Cleveland smashed the new American Railway Workers Union and jailed Debs for contempt as the federal government broke the great Pullman-inspired railroad strike of 1894. Debs subsequently changed his mind about politics.

The election results in 1892 were encouraging, some said heroic, for the new party. Populists elected ten representatives, five senators, and four governors in 1892, but carried no big cities. Populists did better in small towns and rural regions west of the Mississippi than in eastern urban and industrial centers. No third party had done better since before the Civil War. Skeptics remained skeptical, and the question of political party affiliation for most workers remained divided. The Populist Party was not a labor party, nor were Democrats or Republicans, though all claimed to favor the interests of workers. The battle for the endorsement of labor in 1892 showed the weakness of socialism and radicalism, and the strength of dominant political institutions in winning the votes, if not the hearts and minds, of most workers. Workers stood ready to do battle, to wage open combat if necessary, on behalf of immediate objectives, or to protect themselves from harm. Beyond that their vision was shaped more by the success of their nation and their perceived place in it than their hostility or alienation from it. The harsh nationwide depression that began with the bankruptcy of the Philadelphia and Reading Railroad soon after President Cleveland took office was soon to test that perception.

Conclusion

The end of the frontier and the onset of the depression of the 1890s marked the conclusion of the heroic age in national life. Industry placed the United States in the front rank among the wealthy nations of the world. Millions of people continued to seek refuge and opportunity within its borders. Its success was dazzling, awe inspiring. The human costs in thousands of lives lost in the building of railroads, extracting of minerals from the reluctant earth, and the destruction and displacement of the native American population were dimmed by the astounding achievements of the age. The repression and denial of full citizenship to the former slave population by the 1890s was accomplished with a lack of distress by the rest of the nation.

Science and ideology contributed self-serving justifications for these apparent deficiencies as inevitable, and natural. Some races (a relatively new concept) were more advanced than others, that was all there was to it, though there was no scientific agreement about what constituted a race. Similarly, Social Darwinism crudely endorsed the dominion of the industrial barons and all that they represented as a natural phenomenon. The political exclusion and social and economic inferiority of women were likewise endorsed and assumed by most people to have emanated from forces beyond mortal control. God and science were enlisted to defend the existing order. Few commentators reflected on the power of the courts and the use of the militia in a one-sided manner. If, as it has often been said a hundred years later, a strong judiciary was responsible for the creation of weak labor organizations in the United States, this was the era when that was done too.

To seek to alter the apparent realities of the age required olympian efforts and deserve to be regarded that way. New Orleans dockworkers joined Nez Perce Indians in successfully holding off the forces of capital for a time. Haymarket martyrs and Molly Maguires joined thousands of less well organized black workers hung at the ends of ropes for their real or imagined resistance to the social and political power of the dominating culture.

At the same time, the native people of the Great Plains and Northwest were either exterminated or driven from their homelands into confinement on reservations or into Canada. To convince the great chief, Sitting Bull, of the hopelessness of resistance, he was taken to see the booming cities of the East. It worked some of its overwhelming magic on him the same way it worked on most workers, native and foreign-born. Sitting Bull joined Buffalo Bill's Wild West Show for a short time thereafter, then made a few dollars before he went home and was killed by soldiers for allegedly resisting arrest in 1890. His heroic counterpart at Custer's Last Stand, Crazy Horse, was killed in custody in 1877 at the Red Cloud Agency and never had his consciousness raised by travel outside his own domain.

Were Sam Gompers and Booker T. Washington right? Was accommodation the only answer? Or, would it only work for either the privileged few or the millions who found their own ingenious ways of staving off despair and destruction?

Workers found hope and comfort in their communities. They shared scanty goods, and enjoyed the social pleasures of the games and music they made together. A protective subculture of slang, nicknames, and loyalties existed wherever workers lived. In a world where their labor power was stolen from them, many workers had little compunction about taking some things back from bosses. Petty and grand theft, techniques for slacking off at the job, gambling, bookmaking, and prostitution were all methods of indirectly confronting their circumstances and trying to gain some advantage. Beer halls and barrooms relieved workers of hard-earned money, and provided comradeship and escape from an oppressive reality.

Religious institutions and charities helped the same way that political machines did. They offered balm and comfort in exchange for loyalties to the society and world that contributed to the suffering that placed workers in need of such help. Professional sports and distracting forms of commercial (for profit) entertainment became established parts of urban life, and provided workers with heroes other than radicals, socialists, and union leaders. Many workers saw hope for themselves in the anticipated success of their children. There was ample evidence that opportunities for wealth and social advancement were really possible over time and generations.

At least one out of four manual workers gained a little status by becoming an independent farmer or by starting a small business in this period. One-third of Italian and Jewish immigrants moved from unskilled to skilled employment during the 1890s. The life of workers in the United States was as rich and dense with hope and possibility in this heroic age as it was often filled with contradiction, sacrifice, misery, and martyrdom.

Man in IWW hat card. This man's hat threatens a willingness to carry out extreme action for but a modest demand. (Library of Congress, Prints and Photographs Division, Reproduction No. LC-USZ62-22190)

CHAPTER 5

Challenges and Responses, 1893–1913

The golf links
Are so very near
The mills,
Where every day
The little children
Can look out and see
The men at play.
—Anonymous, ca. 1900

By the time of the closing of the Columbian Exposition and World's Fair in Chicago in 1893 the nation had made the transition from agricultural to industrial predominance. The heroic age was over. The great historian Frederick Jackson Turner proclaimed the end of the first age of the nation's history with the passing of the frontier when he addressed the recently organized American Historical Association that year. Turner said that abundant land and natural resources fueled a democratic individualism that made the country unique among nations.

Turner's thesis about the exceptional nature of the United States contained an argument that reemerged later to explain the relative lack of class consciousness and political independence of the nation's workers. According to Turner, the United States had no hereditary aristocracy that stifled or restricted class mobility. The frontier offered ordinary people the opportunity to own property, go into business, and enjoy class mobility the way no European or Asian counterpart could. It was a prosperous and growing nation formed of many ethnic and religious groups. Late-twentieth-century adherents to the Turner idea of American exceptionalism added the important history of slave labor and its racially segregated aftermath as additional elements in making the United States unique in comparison to other industrialized nations. Working-class unity or socialist politics, many have argued, could never be built on that kind of foundation.

Friedrich Engels, the well-known collaborator with Karl Marx on many socialist ideas and organizational activities, kept up an active correspondence with several friends on the class peculiarities of the United States. He frequently shared his views about the exceptional qualities of the United States with Friedrich A. Sorge, a German American who lived in Hoboken, New Jersey, where he earned a living as a music teacher, and was as an occasional writer for the German-language press. In one letter to Sorge, Engels noted: "the Americans are worlds behind (the Europeans) in all theoretical things, and while they did not bring over any medieval institutions from Europe they did bring over masses of medieval traditions, religion, English common (feudal) law, superstition, spiritualism, in short every kind of imbecility which was not directly harmful to business and which is now very serviceable for making the masses stupid" (November 29, 1886, Marx and Engels, 1942, p. 451).

Both Turner's concept of uniqueness and Engels's view of the workers of the United States as retarded in theory were in for a shock. Within just a few years of their comments, workers in the United States mounted the most dramatic class-conscious and socialist challenge to the political power of industrial capital in the history of the nation.

In less than a decade after its founding in 1901, the Socialist Party USA elected more than 1,200 of its candidates to various offices, including seventy-nine mayors in twenty-four states. By 1905 President Theodore Roosevelt believed socialism the most serious political threat faced by capital: "The growth of the Socialist Party in this country," he warned, "is far more ominous than any populist movement in times past" (quoted in Weinstein, 1968, p. 17). The revolutionary Industrial Workers of the World (IWW) led some of the most dramatic and successful strikes in the nation's history before World War I. By the end of this era women gained prominent and permanent leadership in labor organizations. New labor newspapers, unions, songs, and literature in dozens of languages proliferated as never before. Union membership more than quadrupled in the first decade of the new century. Radical and revolutionary leaders led historic strikes in mass production industries. Serious commentators called it the "era of the mass strike" and the "age of industrial violence." Turmoil touched every aspect of labor, government, and business relations. Even the more conservative Gompers was displaced for a year (1894) as president of the AFL by the more radical United Mineworkers of America (UMWA) leader, John McBride. Black and white workers won new battles together on the New Orleans and Philadelphia waterfronts, and in the mines of the East and South. The National Association for the Advancement of Colored People (NAACP) began its historic struggle for full civil rights after its founding by Socialists and Progressives in 1909. Liberal intellectuals and middle-class reformers pressed a broad agenda of progressive reforms that gave a large part of this era, the period between 1901 and 1916, its name.

Business and government responded mightily to the challenges. Seeking the appearance of neutrality, President Theodore Roosevelt, with the assistance of the great banker, J. P. Morgan, forced coal operators to negotiate with the miners' union to end a great strike in 1902. President Wilson went further than any of his predecessors in seeking the patriotic participation of labor in the Great War. New methods of settling labor disputes made their appearance alongside innovations in industrial efficiency. Old business methods of resistance and repression of labor were refined or expanded. New legal precedents were set by the Supreme Court that both protected and contained labor. As no other time before it or since, this was a time of challenge and response, and the first challenge for both labor and capital was the worst economic depression that either had ever seen.

Depression, 1893–1897

When almost every particular detail of economic activity in the nation can be shown to be the result of deliberate and conscious government or business action, it is astonishing that a catastrophic economic collapse is regarded as a natural phenomenon. Some business and government leaders defend economic slowdowns and large-scale bankruptcies as healthy weeding or pruning of overgrown industries. Of course, depressions are also wonderful opportunities for some businessmen to buy out the ruined remains of failed competitors at bargain basement prices. Labor costs fall, sometimes sharply, and the organizational strength of workers usually declines to the obvious advantage of employers. Generally speaking, though, nobody really favors a prolonged economic decline and the massive unemployment that accompanies it. Less new wealth can be created when labor is idle. The nation is at a competitive disadvantage with rivals who may not be struck by similarly hard times.

The panic and severe depression that began early in 1893 with the collapse of Frank Gowen's once prosperous Philadelphia and Reading Railroad was no act of God or nature, though many workers, small businessmen, and farmers blamed themselves for the loss of a job, business, or farm. Millions of others recoiled against the suffering they were forced to endure through no deliberate actions of their own.

Overexpansion in relation to income, built on excessive debt, is usually a recipe for disaster. Other businesses, in the same circumstances as the Philadelphia and Reading Railroad, quickly followed it downhill. The failure of the National Cordage Company in May provoked a general crash in the stock market. Within a few months thirty-two steel companies were among 16,000 businesses that filed for bankruptcy. Over 600 banks were insolvent. By the summer, massive unemployment led to breadlines in more than 100 cities. Immediate relief came mainly from private charities, religious institutions, and local governments. No state or federal aid was provided. Unemployment marches and demonstrations took place in dozens of cities. Municipalities provided temporary and short-term jobs on public works, parks, drainage projects, and streets for either subsistence wages or meal and lodging coupons.

Jacob Coxey led the nation's first march on Washington from his hometown in Ohio to the nation's capital. He was able to mobilize thousands of unemployed workers on behalf of federally funded public works and road building programs to create new jobs. He and his peaceful band, known as Coxey's Army, were clubbed by Washington police, scores were arrested, and the rest were dispersed. The federal government stayed consistent. It had nothing to offer labor.

For the next five years more than 20 percent of the labor force was unable to find any work. Short-term and temporary jobs were all that were available to hundreds of thousands of other workers. Railroads connected the industrial centers of the nation, and tens of thousands of workers in search of jobs rode the freight trains and habituated the "hobo jungles" that formed everywhere. Prices and wages fell sharply. A run on the country's gold reserves by investors forced the government of President Grover Cleveland to seek a bailout from private bankers in 1895, the first such rescue of government of its kind. Government returned the favor to business with a stepped up naval building program that, when completed, enabled the United States to make a successful war with Spain in 1898 and go beyond its continental limitations. Though relatively brief, the depression years witnessed several other dramatic changes in the state of labor and the direction of the nation.

Race, Gender, and the AFL

Racial segregation gained complete legal sanction at every level of government in the United States by 1896. Courts upheld state and local government segregation laws. Lynching, as noted earlier, went unpunished and became commonplace, with approximately a hundred people killed every year for the next three decades. Many lynchings were public spectacles attended by huge crowds. Fierce competition for jobs pitted white unionists against black workers to the benefit of employers in pursuit of lower wage rates. Under the leadership of Samuel Gompers, the AFL reversed its earlier approach to organizing black workers. At the beginning of 1893 the AFL and Gompers still urged the inclusion of black workers into usually segregated AFL labor unions, and refused to issue charters to unions that had racially discriminatory constitutions. All workers, they argued, should belong to unions. Most of the national craft unions objected; they wanted no black members. By 1894 the federation accepted a solution that allowed national unions to ban black workers from membership without officially doing so in their constitutions. AFL unions were permitted to allow racially restrictive initiation rituals for new members. Before the end of the decade even that charade was put aside. The color bar became part of the rituals or constitutions of all but a few of the affiliated AFL national unions for the next fifty years. When black workers sought a charter or were already organized into AFL segregated locals, they were routinely barred as delegates to central labor councils. Nor were they permitted to organize their own black councils without the consent of the established bodies. Booker T. Washington, the conservative and accommodating black educator, was not alone in condemning the AFL for its racism. Exclusion from the top trades and crafts meant that the only jobs available to black workers would be menial, unskilled, and low paid. Economic barriers would lead to the formation of a permanent racial caste system far into the future. Many black workers developed a long-lasting hostility to unions because of the AFL's racially discriminatory policies.

The railroad Brotherhoods also adopted a rigid color bar that drove thousands of black workers out of skilled work as engineers, firemen, switchmen, and brakemen, work they had been doing in the South for fifty years. Before the Civil War almost all railroad work, both construction and operation, had been done by slaves. The only jobs that slaves and freedmen had previously been barred from in the South were that of conductor and engineer. There were exceptions to even those restrictions

Women workers faced similar discrimination by the AFL, though a few women were given specific leadership positions by male officers. The emphasis in the AFL was on traditional craft unionism and, the union press and public statements frequently said, the ability of a man to properly support his household. At the very time when women were entering the wage labor force in retail sales, offices, service and educational jobs, and professions, the AFL newspaper, *The Federationist*, attacked the idea of hiring women in industry, and most AFL unions explicitly denied membership to women. The actual percentage of women as wage or salaried employees increased from 15 percent of the workforce in 1870 to 21 percent in 1910, but most women were channeled into gender-specific areas of employment under male authority, with little chance of representation by the AFL. Like black workers, when women did manage to form their own unions, they faced exclusion and discriminatory treatment inside their own organization if they joined the AFL. Women and black workers battled with the law for equal rights, their employers who exploited that inequality for profit, and the AFL, which defined its objectives for the exclusive benefit of skilled white male workers.

The AFL's vision was limited to the next pay envelope, dues deduction, and the provision of immediate services to its members, and only its members. Gompers proudly admitted as much in his often cited statement in reply to the question of what labor wanted: "More!" When he testified before a Senate committee looking at the relationship between capital and labor, Gompers said: "We have no ultimate ends. We are going from day to day. We are fighting for immediate objects" (quoted in Huberman, 1960, p. 231). Gompers and the AFL began their long history of discriminatory, antisocialist, and antifeminist politics in the depression years of the 1890s. Their anti-immigrant position went to their origins a decade earlier. Business leaders, religious traditionalists, and social conservatives could not have been happier with the racism and sexism of the AFL, though the former fought the labor organization for every dime. But the AFL was not unique in labor.

When Eugene Debs spoke later about the vote to ban black workers and women from the newly formed American Railway Union (ARU) in 1893, it was always with sincere regret. His experience in the great Burlington strike of 1888 convinced him that only industry-wide unionism could match the power of employers, that separate craft unions were too easily divided against one another to match the power of a major industrial entity. He and Gompers became arch rivals as national labor leaders for the rest of their lives. Debs left his successful activities with the old railroad Brotherhoods in 1892 to go to work building a union of all railroad workers, skilled and unskilled, men and women, black and white, immigrant and foreign-born. In this objective he was carrying on the ideals of the nearly defunct Knights of Labor. The vote to ban black workers and women from membership in the original constitution of the ARU was close, but Debs was on the losing side, 113–102. He later claimed that agents for the employers inside the newly forming organization had tilted the balance, and that had the vote gone the other way the outcome of the massive Pullman strike and boycott the following year would have been different (Ginger, 1949, p. 259). Even if Debs was mistaken, race and gender exclusion and discrimination certainly played an important part in shaping allegiances and blocking working-class unity for decades to come. Black workers and women workers became types cast in inferior roles by laws, customs, and institutional practices. It is hardly coincidental that the rising of one would coincide with and help to generate the rising of the other over the next century, just as runaway slaves and women built the abolitionist and early feminist movements together in the century past. Nor was it coincidental that the AFL (not the CIO) adamantly resisted both struggles until it was forced to relent by new laws half a century later.

The Pullman Strike and Boycott, 1894

Wage cuts during a depression were nothing new. What outraged the workers at the Pullman Palace Car Company in the model company town of Pullman, Illinois, was the maintenance of rent and company store prices at the same levels after wages were cut an average of 30 percent. George Pullman thought it was fair since rents in the nearby towns hadn't changed.

Pullman was a builder and a businessman. His success came from the manufacture of specialty cars for the nation's railroads, most famously the sleeping cars that bore his name. His peculiar form of paternalism toward labor was architectural and structural. He framed his vision of a perfect industrial community in a carefully planned company town built on a two-square-mile private tract of land on the southern outskirts of Chicago. His workers were not required to live in his community, but if they were ambitious and wished to rise in the company, they knew they had to live there. The lowest-paid entry-level workers lived in Pullman's rooming houses. Next up the ladder, workers found flats in tenement-style buildings. Senior workers and skilled craftsmen were able to rent small attached brick houses that had cellars, gas, and water, and got the most attention when visitors were given the grand tour. At the top, Pullman's executives and their families lived in individual houses with gardens. An arcade of shops, a church, and a hotel named for his daughter, Florence, were also rented to occupants by Pullman. (The town is a privately maintained, living museum today.) Pullman favored the hiring and advancement of what he and other employers called "Buckwheats," the white Protestant descendants of earlier generations of immigrants from northern and western Europe. He encouraged their residency in his community. Other workers chose to live in nearby towns where the rents were 20 percent less than the average $14.00 per month charged in Pullman. Nobody, wherever they lived, liked the pay cuts.

Most of Pullman's 4,000 workers had been organized into the new ARU by 1894. They joined what became one of the single largest worker organizations in the United States. After only one year's existence the ARU represented more than 150,000 railroad workers in 465 locals, and had scored one of the biggest labor victories in decades. With the support of surrounding communities of farmers and small business leaders, and the leadership of Debs, the ARU won an eighteen-day strike in April 1894 against wage cuts imposed on employees by James J. Hill's Great Northern Railroad. The new ARU took advantage of widespread public hostility toward the notoriously unfair rates and monopolistic practices of railroad corporations. Banks were also unpopular among debt-laden farmers and small business owners, especially during this time of falling farm prices and widespread foreclosures. Now, even some of the more elite Brotherhoods were signing up with the ARU.

When Pullman refused to make any concessions on the wage and rents issue to a committee of his workers, and after three of the committee members were fired a few days later, the union, with representatives from the ARU present, voted to strike in early May. Debs went to study the situation and decided the action of the workers was justified, that he was with them "heart and soul." He cautioned that "as a general thing I am against a strike, but when the only alternative to a strike is a sacrifice of rights, then I prefer to strike." He added, "I am against the paternalism of Pullman. He is everlastingly saying, 'What can we do for our poor workingmen.'" Debs stirred the audience by saying the real issue was, "What can we do for ourselves?" (quoted in Papke, 1999, p. 22).

What turned this strictly local strike of Pullman workers into a massive national conflict were the remarks of Pullman workers at the first national convention of the ARU in Chicago a month later, and the refusal of Pullman to accept arbitration as suggested by the ARU. Pullman's near feudal control over every aspect of life in his community enraged the delegates. One of the speakers at the convention was Jennie Curtis, a seamstress employed making carpets, drapes, linens, and seat coverings for Pullman coaches. She was president of the "Girls Union Local" and told the story of her father, who had worked for Pullman for thirteen years. On his death the company presented Curtis with a bill for his back rent of $60.00. Until the debt was paid her biweekly pay was reduced to about $9.50, out of which she had to pay $7.00 for room and board. She asked the convention "to come along with us because we are not just fighting for ourselves, but for decent conditions for workers everywhere" (quoted in Papke, 1999, p. 24). On June 22 the union voted to boycott, to refuse work on any trains carrying Pullman cars. Everyone in the union knew that this bold action held enormous potential for wreaking havoc on the nation's rail lines, but expected the railroad companies to compel Pullman to negotiate fairly or risk having his cars disconnected and put on the sidings. What they didn't know was how much anger and resentment workers throughout the country were about to unleash. The ARU also underestimated the determination of the railroad corporations in general, and Pullman in particular, to resist any negotiations. The union also failed to anticipate the crushing role the federal government was going to play.

The boycott went into effect June 27, a day after the deadline for a company response had quietly passed. The railroad companies challenged the union by keeping or adding unnecessary Pullman cars to freight trains, mail trains, and suburban carriers. Within three days almost all rail traffic west and south of Chicago was at a standstill, nearly 100,000 workers out. Soon, every part of the nation was affected, from coast to coast. The government and the railroads quickly swung into action.

Once the boycott began, Debs and the ARU were up against the combined power of the General Managers Association (GMA), an organization of twenty-four railroad companies with terminals in Chicago. The GMA was determined to break the boycott and the ARU, and brought in thousands of strikebreakers with the promise of permanent jobs, no matter the outcome. In the course of the struggle the ARU never had the full support of the elite Brotherhoods, many of whose members continued to work throughout the boycott. The union was also faced with an openly hostile attorney general, the prominent railroad lawyer, Richard Olney, who continued to receive his retainers from several railroad companies while in President Cleveland's cabinet. Olney's influence dominated the government's plan of action throughout the conflict. To protect mail service and counter what he said were conspiracies "against commerce between the States," President Cleveland willingly sent in the United States Army over the strong objections of Illinois Governor Altgeld. The troops were also expected to enforce the action of the federal courts, which finally broke the boycott and ended the strike by using injunctive power under the Sherman Anti-Trust Act. The boycott action was eventually found to be an illegal action in restraint of trade. Though probably not decisive in terms of the outcome, hundreds of black workers, excluded from the ranks of the ARU, joined the strikebreakers in taking the jobs of striking/boycotting workers.

At first Debs naively welcomed the presence of troops when they arrived in Pullman on July 4. Though no outbreaks of vandalism had occurred yet, Debs thought the troops would help to keep things calm, and prevent arson or acts of violence. He couldn't have been more wrong. Wherever troops were present furious responses to them erupted. The first railroad cars were set on fire a day after troops arrived in Chicago. Cavalry attacks and bayonet charges were the response. The rioting crowd grew to over 10,000. By July 6 more than 700 cars were destroyed in the Chicago area, more than a dozen people killed, and hundreds were wounded or injured. Chicago was gripped by a near total general strike. Throughout the West, Midwest, and Southwest trains were toppled, bridges blown up, and railroad yards seized by angry workers in defiance of Debs' constant telegrams pleading for calm. Debs, along with other ARU leaders, was in court almost immediately, and jailed for the first time July 23.

The case, finally decided at the Supreme Court in 1895, was complex and ARU staff lawyers were no match for the federal opposition. Clarence Darrow, then a young railroad lawyer, took the case for the ARU because of his belief in the rightness of the union cause. He was eventually joined by Lyman Trumball, one of the most distinguished legal minds in the country. Trumball, eighty years old, had served in the U.S. Senate, was a member of its judiciary committee when it drafted the Thirteenth Amendment abolishing slavery, and was the founder of the American Bar Association.

Attorney General Olney led the government side, which ultimately won a unanimous Supreme Court decision, presented May 27, 1895. The constitutional authority of the federal government to issue an injunction in the case was upheld. Debs's criminal conviction for contempt of the injunction was sustained, and he was sent to prison for the rest of the year. Newspapers reflected the enthusiastic approval of the business community, but Darrow fretted that the decision "left the law so biased that, in cases involving strikes, at least, a man could be sent to prison without trial by jury" (Papke, 1999, p. 79).

Darrow was right, and the business community was justified in its celebration. The injunction became the favored tool of business and government in breaking strikes until the 1930s. The use of injunctions against labor actions doubled in the decade that followed the Pullman case, and doubled again in the 1920s (Forbath, 1991, pp. 193–98). Though restricted by the Norris-LaGuardia Act of 1932, injunctions are still in use, primarily on the state and local levels, especially against public employee union actions.

The Pullman strike had other consequences. The strike/boycott was broken by the injunction and the first jailing of its leaders less than three weeks after it began. Pullman was back in business, though the image of his paternalistic model community suffered public scorn. The idea of the benevolent company town was never the same. All of the ARU leaders were blacklisted and the huge organization disbanded. The outcome of the strike convinced conservative AFL leaders of the rightness of their craft-focused accommodation with business, and the hopelessness of industry-wide confrontations by labor with capital.

On the other hand, Debs made good use of jail time. For years afterward, Debs enjoyed telling of his conversion to socialism while in prison. He said that he spent his time reflecting on the circumstances that brought him there. In jail he read the ideas of Karl Marx through the popular interpretations of Karl Kautsky, and got both a copy of Marx's three-volume *Capital* and a memorable lecture about socialism from Victor Berger, both of which, he later said, "set the wires humming in my system" (quoted in Salvatore, 1982, p. 150). And, public hostility toward railroads and banks continued to build a Populist - Labor political coalition that reached a peak in 1896.

Labor and Populism

The depression added fuel to the fiery successes of the People's Party or Populist movement. Wage cuts, bankruptcies, and falling farm prices of the depression combined with the growing political discontent among workers to encourage independent political action. The two major parties seemed to be losing their influence. Anger over the cautious or nonpolitical stance of the AFL led dissidents to challenge the leadership of Gompers in the AFL in the fall of 1894. A dispute inside the leadership of the AFL over the adoption of the English labor movement's openly socialist "Political Programme" divided the organization in 1894. The opposition, made up primarily of eastern socialists and western populists in the AFL, and joined by the highly sectarian Daniel DeLeon of the Socialist Labor Party, succeeded in electing John McBride president of the AFL, displacing Gompers for the first and only one-year term in his long career. DeLeon was enjoying the rising tide of socialist sentiment among workers. A year earlier he had helped depose Powderly from the leadership of the remnants of the Knights of Labor. John McBride, the president of the United Mineworkers of America, led a union that had been moving toward independent political action for several years.

Almost simultaneously with the Pullman Strike/Boycott, McBride led 180,000 coal miners in their first nationwide coal strike. The issues were falling coal prices and falling pay. State courts and governors throughout the coal region brought forth injunctions and national guard units to break the strike. Governor William McKinley sent so many troops into the coal fields he nearly broke the Ohio state budget. Private bankers with ties to the coal operators made emergency loans to the state to meet military payrolls. After the strike was broken, McBride, like Debs with whom he worked in support of the Pullman strikers, became convinced that state and local governments were simply tools of business. McBride cut his ties to the Ohio Democratic Party and went to work with Jacob Coxey and other local populists to merge his labor platform with that of the People's Party. Ohio farmers never supported the coalition, and the AFL leadership shifted back to Gompers in the next election. Labor radicals and socialists, however, joined with populists in a third-party movement that called for nationalizing the railroads and telegraph and telephone systems, abolishing the injunction in labor disputes, and setting the eight-hour day by law. McBride and many of the labor/populists added calls for the municipal takeover of streetcars as well as gas, water, and electric plants from private ownership (*American Federationist*, 144–45).

Both the rhetorical thunder and the political lightning were taken away from the labor side of the Populist movement in the actual election campaign of 1896. The issue that dominated the election grew out of monetary policy that originated in the financing of the Civil War. Printing of an unsupported currency called greenbacks had contributed to inflation that caused prices for goods to rise. The gradual retirement of that debt by increasing the nation's gold reserve was, most farmers believed, deflationary and ruinous. The answer to millions of farmers and businessmen was in bimetalism, a standard of gold and silver together. Populists called for the free and unlimited coinage of silver against a fixed standard of value with gold; they wanted sixteen ounces of silver to equal one once of gold, regardless of the quantities of silver available. Western miners favored it. There were huge new silver deposits they hoped to mine. Farmers made it a crusade. Falling farm prices, they were convinced, would be reversed by a controlled inflationary policy. Debts would be easier to repay.

When the Democrats nominated the evangelical and Populist hero, William Jennings Bryan, for the presidency they dropped or sidelined many of labor's planks from the platform. Bryan's "Cross of Gold" speech rocked the convention the day before his nomination and became the centerpiece of his unsuccessful campaign. Democrats still held onto the support of Debs and McBride, but ran badly everywhere the industrial and commercial workforce lived. AFL leaders around the country campaigned for Bryan, and put pressure on President Gompers to endorse him. Gompers reiterated his "pure and simple unionism" message. He privately supported Bryan, and said he favored the idea of sixteen to one silver. But he always thought of farmers as small businessmen, stayed true to his principles, and kept the AFL officially out of it.

As in so many elections before and since 1896, workers either voted their own specific local interests, or chose the candidate who seemed least worse. The People's Party, after its absorption by the Democrats, was finished and faded quickly even in the areas where it had previously won elections. At the state level, especially in the South, newly institutionalized racism destroyed fragile populist coalitions of black and white farmers. Tom Watson, the fiery Georgia populist congressman, turned his back on the black and white farmers he had once bravely helped to lead. Watson scalded racism: "You," he told his black and white listeners, "are made to hate each other because upon that hatred is rested the keystone of the arch of financial despotism which enslaves you both." Now he flipped to become a staunch advocate of segregation and race baiting. Republicans no longer threatened his power base and he could read the political future correctly.

In 1898 the Supreme Court closed the door on the possibility of racial unity in politics. The Court, in *Williams v. Mississippi,* upheld the legality of Mississippi's scheme to deny black citizens the right to vote. If black citizens were going to be largely disenfranchised, there would be no gain for any candidate in defending their interests. Watson, like the other remaining Populists, became a vigorous public racist. The same general process repeated itself elsewhere, and was only reversed after federal intervention restored the franchise to black voters with enforcement of the Voting Rights Act (1965). Not too long after that, many public racists became enlightened integrationists for similar reasons.

Governor William McKinley's Republican campaign took votes away from Bryan among workers in the cities of the North and East. McKinley's campaign, under the direction of the able millionaire industrialist, Marcus A. Hannah, raised the enormous sum of $19 million, an unheard of amount until then in any election. The campaign and the deliberate program of large employers was aimed at assuring workers that Republicans were the party of prosperity, and that a Bryan victory would mean lost jobs and shut-down industries. The depression, workers were reminded, had taken place during the presidency of a Democrat, Grover Cleveland. Promising a better future, and blaming the ills of the present on the incumbents worked among workers in 1896 and has worked in most elections since.

Labor in the Age of the New Empire

As soon as McKinley took office he was surrounded by men convinced of the need for a more aggressive foreign policy, a "Large" or "Expansionist" program. The United States had grown internally, continentally while at the same time the other great industrial powers had extended their colonial dominions around the world. The old empires of England and France were enhanced and enlarged by new conquests in Asia, Africa, and the Middle East. The great nations were combing the earth in competition for mineral resources, markets, new areas of protected investment opportunity, and the labor sources that were required by their newly modernized productive capacities. Rapidly modernizing Japan had just gained a military victory over China (1894), and Germany was becoming a colonial power in Africa, where even tiny Belgium's King Leopold was carving out a rich kingdom in the Congo River region.

McKinley was pressed by his political allies to appoint young Theodore Roosevelt as assistant secretary of the Navy, a post made more important by the weak health of the secretary. TR was an avid fan of USN Captain Alfred T. Mahan, the author of *The Influence of Sea Power in History*. No great power, Mahan argued, had ever existed without a great naval force to protect its trade. In the age of coal-fired steam engines the United States needed, at the least, naval bases and coaling stations throughout the world. Within three months of the election, TR, Senator Henry Cabot Lodge of Massachusetts, and a group of political and military leaders were hard at work preparing for war with a fading power fast losing its grip on its remaining colonial possessions, Spain. No members of the working class were included in this close group later known as the "Expansionists of 1898." Among their favorite meeting places was the elite and private Metropolitan Club in Washington, D.C. (Nicholson, 1999, pp. 214–27). Their work had enormous consequences for both labor and capital.

The Spanish-American War of 1898 was only the first step, the debut of the United States as an independent force in world affairs. The secretary of state, John Hay, called it a "splendid little war," because so much was gained at so little cost to the nation. Hay's Open Door policy was announced to the other powers even before the Treaty of Paris that ended the war with Spain was signed (December 1898). In just the next few years the United States established its place among nations as a great power. The bitter and costly Philippine-American war was brought to a successful conclusion (1903). Hawaii, Puerto Rico, Guam, and Midway became national colonial possessions. Cuba was made a protectorate. The Boxer Rebellion in China was crushed (1900) with U.S. military participation. The Panama Canal was taken over from France and built by the United States (1903–13). President Theodore Roosevelt's Big Stick and Corollary to the Monroe Doctrine, and President William H. Taft's Dollar Diplomacy were put forward (1906–9) as assertive foreign policy positions. The Russo-Japanese War was ended with the intervention of TR in the Treaty of Portsmouth (1905), the "Great White Fleet" was sent on a global cruise (1906), and President Woodrow Wilson's military interventions in Mexico, Hispaniola, Nicaragua, and the Great War (1913–17) were all military or diplomatic interventions of the United States launched by the war with Spain.

Rapid expansion in military technology and methodology of production were required to continue the new policies. New scientific heights had to be scaled, and reached quickly. A secretive naval building program was undertaken in 1903 that sought to make the United States "second to none" among the world's naval powers. The completed building plan was quietly announced in the annual report of the secretary of the Navy in 1913.

Public education at every level had to be expanded to train workers and create a larger pool from which to draw more engineers and technicians. A more technically demanding military similarly required better educated recruits. Vocational and manual training schools proliferated in the opening years of the new century. Where once public education had been the demand of workers to offset the advantages of the wealthy in a democracy, now education served the need of capital to enhance the productive capabilities and military power of the nation, and drove the reform.

Every aspect of social and economic life was altered by the newly aggressive foreign policy, not least of which was the place of labor. From the invigorated and growing middle class, social and political reformers were heartened by the modern and scientific advances, and added goals that named the era a Progressive one. Both major political parties embraced what at least one prominent historian, Gabriel Kolko, has titled, "The Triumph of Conservatism." Every institution in the capitalist structure emerged stronger as the result of the reforms of this period (1898–1914). Unions, on board with the program, enjoyed temporary gains as well.

Loyal armies of soldiers and production workers had to be secured, waste and inefficiencies curtailed. In order to prevent breakdowns in transportation services from railroad strikes, the Erdman Act was passed into law in 1898. In future disputes the parties (railroad corporations and those unions covered under the law) could make use of mediation and arbitration services provided by government. The right of certain railroad workers, switchmen, and telegraphers to join unions and to be free of having to sign yellow dog contracts was protected by the new law, at least for a few years.

In 1908, in *Adair v. US*, the Supreme Court threw out the federal ban on yellow dog contracts in the Erdman Law. The Court said such contracts were strictly private matters freely entered into by the parties and therefore protected by the U.S. Constitution. Similar state laws, inspired by Erdman, were done in by the same Court in *Coppage v. Kansas* in 1915. Finally, private yellow dog contracts were also reaffirmed as legal by the Supreme Court in *Hitchman Coal v. Mitchell* (1917). That last Court action halted the organizing of coal miners in West Virginia who had been forced to sign such agreements as a condition of employment.

Labor's Choices

The AFL, in spite of Gompers's initial opposition to the Spanish-American War, patriotically rallied behind the government as soon as war was declared. Most of the skilled trades and millions of workers followed the lead of the press and accepted the position of the government about the war. The press declared it a war on behalf of oppressed and freedom-loving Cubans against a tyrannical colonial power. Most people had never heard of the Philippine Islands where the first battle of the war took place. Debs spoke out against the war for his newly organizing Social Democracy movement:

> There are thousands who are not swept from their feet by the war craze. They realize that war is national murder, that the poor furnish the victims and that whatever the outcome may be, the effect is always the same upon the toiling class.
>
> In 1894 the press denounced us for the alleged reason that we were murderous and bloodthirsty, and now the same press opposes us because we are not.
>
> We are opposed to war, but if it ever becomes necessary for us to enlist in the murderous business, it will be to wipe out capitalism, the common enemy of the oppressed and downtrodden of all nations. (quoted in Ginger, 1949, p. 203)

Wartime wages went up, prices went up, and union membership soared, especially in AFL trades. In 1897 there were 447,000 union members. By 1903 the number more than quadrupled to 1,913,900. During the same period the AFL grew from 264,825 to 1,465,800 (Perlman and Taft, 1966, p. 13). After 1904 the expansion of the AFL flattened or declined from a height reached that year of about 1.7 million. The growth of general union membership also ended at about 2 million and a slight decline set in until the end of the decade. War and imperial expansion once again had the effect of increasing material benefits for at least some of the nation's workers. War increased their ability to organize unions, and pushed ahead educational and technological opportunities for their children. But the numbers only tell a part of the story.

The National Civic Federation

Samuel Gompers and the AFL were enjoying the social status and respectability their brand of patriotic unionism favored. Gompers always loved the praise and flattery he received from businessmen. The building trades were emerging as a larger and more powerful bloc in the AFL, and the conservative Carpenters Union was an increasingly powerful force among the city centrals of the AFL. Indeed, many of the building trades' union leaders were, or became, contractors themselves. Concentrated in large cities, craft union leaders also enjoyed close ties to the political machines that were infamously common at the time. Though never implicated himself in charges of personal corruption or gangsterism, Gompers kept a consistent general silence when AFL leaders were so charged. His brand of "business unionism"—that the union was an enterprise to protect the interests of workers from those of business—by its very definition invited corruption, self-seeking, and opportunism. Since an important object of the union was to bring personal gain to its leaders, it was inevitable that many of them would engage in deceptive practices to exaggerate their accomplishments and minimize their failings to their members. Like business executives they often emulated, AFL officers frequently used their positions to betray workers, pillage union treasuries, and loot benefit and welfare funds. Huge public and private building construction projects brought fat pay envelopes or other rewards to everyone involved in the city centrals where AFL leaders typically enjoyed close contacts with government and business leaders. Gompers always maintained, nonetheless, that AFL leaders were, with only a few exceptions, men of integrity who were devoted to their members.

Gompers was delighted to join the National Civic Federation (NCF) when it was organized in 1900 as a national version of the seven-year-old Chicago Civic Federation. The goals of the organization, composed of the most prominent and powerful business leaders in the country, didn't trouble Gompers at all. He certainly wanted industrial peace and was an outspoken opponent of socialism's rising influence among workers, two objectives mentioned in the preamble of the new organization in 1900. Gompers and John Mitchell, the new president of the United Mineworkers, and the leaders of the Railroad Brotherhoods were among the explicitly nonsocialist union leaders invited to form one-third of the participants. Business leaders and public figures were to comprise the other two-thirds. The NCF really was a new kind of employers' association though, since both the business and public figures all shared a business outlook, served on boards of corporations, were heads of institutions funded by corporate wealth, or, like former President Cleveland, had been elected to government positions with business endorsements. The NCF was formed as much to secure the loyalty of these labor leaders and the workforce they represented as it was to achieve anything else. Gompers became the first vice president and Mark Hannah, the Ohio industrialist and man most responsible for making William McKinley president in 1896, became the president of the new body.

The NCF, during the period of its greatest influence, 1900–1905, intervened in the settlement of several major clashes, most notably a strike against subsidiary companies of U.S. Steel in 1901, the great anthracite coal strike of 1902, a bituminous coal strike in 1904, and a brief strike of New York transit workers against the Interborough Rapid Transit Company in 1905. In several cases its intervention and the services of its Committee on Conciliation averted strikes, as in a threatened strike of teamsters in New York in 1904. The role of the NCF, however, was hardly neutral. In all of the strike situations the NCF either weakened or destroyed the union goal of recognition by the company. The NCF consistently prevented an expansion of the strike action to other unions, or it brought an end to the strike without the achievement of the wage or hour goals sought by the action. The information and publicity services provided by the NCF countered socialist attacks on the class system with examples of cooperation and constructive settlements that were referred to as "welfare capitalism."

Many progressive leaders hailed the organization as an alternative to the disruptive and costly conflicts between labor and capital that were so commonplace. But, in the aftermath of every major dispute the NCF was bitterly attacked by those workers at the forefront of the struggle. Debs scoffed that the object of the NCF was to guide labor "into harmless channels." The socialist lawyer, Morris Hillquit, brilliantly criticized what may have been only the beginning of the neutralization of labor independence in the twentieth century:

> The game played by the Civic Federation is the shrewdest yet devised by the employers of any country. It takes nothing from capital, it gives nothing to labor and does it all with such an appearance of generosity, that some of the guileless diplomats of the labor movement are actually overwhelmed by it. To the organized labor movement the policy of the Civic Federation is the most subtle and insidious poison. It robs it of its independence, virility, and militant enthusiasm, it hypnotizes and corrupts its leaders, weakens its ranks and demoralizes its fight. (Hillquit to Easley, June 6, 1911, *NCFA*)

Many AFL leaders also criticized Gompers and Mitchell for their participation. Resolutions were regularly advanced (and defeated) at AFL conventions condemning the NCF.

The NCF established an important precedent in labor relations, and there was nothing really comparable to it in other industrial nations. It was the foundation and model for the formation of subsequent wartime government-labor-business boards and various other national and international cooperative agencies. It was one of the first liberal responses of business to the challenge of labor militancy and radicalism. It was liberal because it affirmed the inherent value of labor and expressed the legitimacy of labor organizations, their right to exist within a boundary carefully marked out by the interests of capital. Supreme Court Justices Louis D. Brandeis (appointed to the Court by President Woodrow Wilson) and Felix Frankfurter (appointed by President Franklin D. Roosevelt), among several others, expanded on the concept of union recognition and helped to give it institutional authority in legal decisions several decades later.

Gompers, Mitchell, and the other labor representatives defended the lavish dinners and social contact they enjoyed with powerful men of corporate and government institutions. They probably did bring some real benefits back to their own organizations and members as a result of their open collaboration. Businessmen had always been willing to pay a premium wage to a small number of highly skilled and particularly loyal workers. Now many of the union representatives of workers in important crafts or industries gained information about investment opportunities, frequently got simple stock tips, and advanced their own fortunes from the relationships they made on the NCF. At least some of them happily accepted gifts offered by businessmen. Michell, for example, received a $1,000 diamond ring as a gift after the 1902 coal strike was brought to an end. It was hardly surprising to hear him trumpeting the virtues of labor's collaboration with the capitalist state thereafter. In 1903, for example Mitchell observed: "The Trade union movement in this country can make progress only by identifying itself with the state"(quoted in Dubofsky, 1994, p. 39). Miners' wages were soon reduced to prestrike levels and most other gains given back, but the NMU under Mitchell's leadership continued to thrive.

Gompers and the other labor leaders consistently defended their social relationships with men of power and wealth as realistic and practical responses to the actual world they were in. Their critics, they always sneered, were dreamers, utopians, or fools. If Gompers and the others owed anybody anything for what they received from the tables of the rich, it was probably the growing radicalism and socialism of the workers they ridiculed. Without the increasing menace of the labor left it is doubtful that Gompers and his business-oriented counterparts would have gotten anything at all. Of course, business leaders found other responses that were not so liberal to the challenges of labor militancy and radicalism.

The National Association of Manufactures

The National Association of Manufacturers (NAM) was originally set up in 1895 to advance trade and commercial interests. Once organized, these representatives of industry quickly realized that one of their most important common interests was in stopping the spread of industrial labor organizations, and breaking those they currently faced. The NAM soon became a national employers' association, very similar to the local and regional organizations that had been formed previously. It brought most of the active employer associations together under one roof. By 1902 the NAM was actively lobbying against all of labor's legislative goals, such as anti-injunction legislation and the eight-hour workday. A year later the organization devoted itself almost exclusively to serving as the center for a nationwide antilabor crusade. The NAM created the Citizen's Industrial Association of America (CIAA), and for their first couple of years shared the presidential services of David M. Parry. The two groups were always highly interlocked. Indeed, both organizations included many prominent members of the NCF, and many of the same people were also prominent in the new American Anti-Boycott Association. The boycotts that the latter was formed to combat were against products that unions urged their members not to purchase because of the antilabor practices of their manufacturers.

Unlike the NCF, the NAM and its offshoots had no liberal pretensions, espoused no liberal goals, and were absolutely opposed to unionism of any kind. To the NAM unions were un-American, Gomperism was socialism, and socialism was a threat to the very foundations of the nation. One of the NAM's longest-lasting and continuous programs was the battle for the open shop, the right of an employer to hire anyone without regard to union status, and the right of any worker to refuse to join a union, no matter its status within a factory or industry. The NAM was at the forefront of a national drive against union shops where employees had to be, or become, union members as a condition of employment, or closed shops where only union members could be hired.

For most of its history the NAM raised enormous amounts of money, sponsored speakers, published thousands of tracts and pamphlets in millions of copies, held conferences and meetings in every town or city in the nation, fought endless and numberless legal battles, and lobbied at every level of government to equate unionism of any kind with a threat to the nation. If liberty meant anything at all to the NAM, it meant liberty to capital, the right of the owners of property to have complete authority over everything their wealth controlled. Labor, many of their tracts and materials contended, was no different from any other commodity, something that was to be freely bought or sold in the marketplace. Whatever labor might do to interfere with the absolute rights of property had to be stopped by law. The first big victory of the NAM was against the use of the labor boycott.

Danbury Hatters and the Buck's Stove and Range Company

Business and industry were clearly becoming national entities. Markets were made national because of the increased scale of production and transportation. Corporate consolidation and trusts brought national managerial unity to business organizations. The process had been going on since the Civil War. Labor organizations and actions, like the ARU in the Pullman conflict, were moving in the same direction. One favored tactic used by opponents of the powerful, with roots in the American Revolutionary era, was the boycott, the refusal to purchase or use products made or sold by the foe. A boycott is a nonviolent strike by purchasers or users. The boycott was frequently used by local and regional labor groups to bring pressure to bear on manufacturers.

Since the passage of the Sherman Anti-Trust Act in 1890, and the use of that law against labor in the New Orleans and Pullman cases, the question arose about the legality of advocacy of an interstate boycott of manufactured products by labor organizations. Because it was a national federation of autonomous member unions, the boycott was one of the most effective tactics at the disposal of the AFL. Indeed, it was the only forceful action the AFL could take aside from a general or sympathetic strike to aid a union in a conflict with an employer. With over 1.5 million member-readers of its newspaper, *The American Federationist*, the AFL maintained an effective "We Don't Purchase" list. The two cases that settled the matter (for a time) against labor involved boycotts of Danbury Hats and Buck's Stove and Range Company products.

The two cases started their journeys through the courts a year apart. The boycott against the Danbury, Connecticut hat maker, E. W. Loewe, by the United Hatters' Union was challenged by the company as a violation the Sherman Act and an injunction was sought in federal court in 1906 to stop the union action. When the company lost, it appealed the case to the U.S. Supreme Court, where it prevailed. The union, after fruitless appeals, was subject to huge fines with triple damages, and its assets, and those of its Danbury members were subject to seizure.

Other unionists nationwide assisted the Danbury workers by contributing to the payment of the fines after the final 1913 decision. The loss contributed to the growing socialist argument that the legal power of the nation was in the hands of business, and that neither major political party could or would protect the interests of labor against capital. Prior to these two cases, trade unions enjoyed a distinct advantage over their industry-wide counterparts. Craft union strikes and AFL affiliate labor actions were mainly local, and not broken as routinely by injunctions as industrial conflicts. With the loss of the power of the boycott, the power of the AFL would be reduced to almost nothing.

James W. Van Cleve was the president of the Buck's Stove and Range Company of St. Louis, Missouri. In 1907 he was also president of the NAM and a member of the American Anti-Boycott Association. He was also active in his own industry's antiunion Stove Founders National Defense Association, and he was determined to break his own workers' union, the Iron Workers International. When the company's products were placed on the "We Don't Purchase" list of the *American Federationist*, Van Cleve won a federal injunction against the AFL under the Sherman Act. Gompers's refusal to honor the injunction, like Debs before him, subjected Gompers to charges of contempt. The AFL leader defended himself and the union newspaper based on the U.S. Constitution's protection of freedom of speech and freedom of the press. The Supreme Court upheld the claim of the stove company. After the constitutional case was lost, Gompers was able to appeal the fines and jail terms that he and other AFL leaders faced.

So, while employers could boycott union members with yellow dog contracts and concerted use of the open shop, and use the press and their own media resources against labor freely, the unions could take no meaningful actions against the products made by the labor of those same employers. The legal rights of property seemed to overwhelm the rights of labor. These losses forced Gompers to revise his "pure and simple" unionism. He concluded that he would have to become more involved in the politics of the nation. In 1908 Gompers openly took the side of the Democratic Party when he endorsed its candidate, William Jennings Bryan, for the presidency. All of labor was involved in politics, whether it liked it or not, and whether it knew it or not. With the exception of the leadership of the AFL, most of labor, not there already, began turning toward socialism.

The Political Challenge of Labor

At no other time in the history of the United States did the independently formed political outlook of labor loom so large as it did in the decade before World War I, in spite of its continuing divisions of race, gender, ethnicity, religion, region, and ideology. President Roosevelt was not misguided (or alone) in his fears for capital posed by the rising influence of socialism and other expressions of radical labor militancy among workers. TR's close advisor, Senator Henry Cabot Lodge, warned that the stubbornness of businessmen, especially coal operators in the 1902 conflict, was "breeding socialism at a rate which it is hard to contemplate" (Lodge to TR, October, 6, 1902,

Selections from Correspondence, 1925). The older socialist movements had been more marginal in their appeal. Utopian social experiments, almost by definition, lacked connection to the real world, the one in which most people found themselves. Socialism previously seemed tied to European working-class debates, or was regarded by most workers as highly sectarian and ideologically rigid. Practical people with access to the vote and to local government were not easily attracted to the theories and rhetoric that many reformers, often from other social stratum, brought to them.

Eugene V. Debs and the newly formed Socialist Party (1901) were something different. So were the conditions of life and the circumstances that most workers faced every day in the early years of the new century. The autocratic order found in the factory, mine, mill, and business establishment was regarded by more and more workers as oppressive and totalitarian. Workplace tyranny was out of step with the increasing democratic rhetoric of progressive reformers and civic leaders. The accident and injury rate was as high as it was because of the greed of employers, workers argued. Progressive journalists like Upton Sinclair and Ida Tarbell exposed the ruthless greed of wealthy industrialists in popular magazines and books. It seemed obvious that safer mines, mills, and factories were possible, but might cost more to set up. Whether in terms of "industrial democracy" or "workplace control" workers' newspapers and pamphlets raised the attack on the arbitrary authority they experienced every day. The Socialist Party newspaper, *Appeal to Reason,* was founded in 1894 by J. A. Wayland, with the assistance of Mother Jones. *Appeal to Reason* increased its circulation to over 50,000 a week by 1904. By 1908 it had 250,000 regular readers and was the first journal to publish Upton Sinclair's novel, *The Jungle.* By 1912 *Appeal to Reason* reached over half a million subscribers at a cost of twenty-five cents a year.

Increasingly, on the picket lines and at the ballot boxes, masses of workers throughout the nation were looking for a fundamental change in the conditions of life. Most of the western Populists, especially among those who had not left the party for Bryan in 1896, became Socialists in the early years of the new century. The extreme contrasts between the social lives of the wealthy and the impoverished, whose labor created that wealth, was a challenge to the ideals of the nation itself. Class and consciousness of class became harsh realities, not abstract concepts, for most workers, many farmers, professionals, and a large number of small or independent business owners.

At the center of Debs's radicalism was the democratic experience of the nation, not the ideology of Marx and Engels. Debs never really became of student of Marx. Most of what he learned about socialism came from more popular writers on the subject or his own observations. What is so striking in retrospect is not how wrong or erroneous Debs and the Socialists undoubtedly were about socialism's realistic chances in the United States, but how many of the critical observations and fears of the Socialists were realized or came true in subsequent decades. The popular author, Jack London, wrote a serious novel in his own brief socialist phase called *The Iron Heel* (1908). In this story, London reflected the widespread views of many Socialists when he anticipated the totalitarian dangers that severe economic crisis and international war could unleash from an endangered capitalist nation, no matter how democratic its pretensions. London did not live to see his prophetic fears played out in World War I, the Great Depression, and Nazi Germany, or in the destruction of democracy by the military in Franco's Spain (1936–38), Arbenz's Guatemala (1954), Mossadeq's Iran (1953), Allende's Chile (1973), or in so many other situations and places.

Debs was a midwesterner, born in Terre Haute, Indiana. Like so many labor leaders before him, he always linked his radical views to those of Jefferson and Paine as much as to those of Marx or other Socialists. Like the Workies of 1830, the National Labor Union of William Sylvis, the Knights of Labor, his own contemporaries of the Industrial Workers of the World (IWW), and future radicals in the Congress of Industrial Organizations of the Depression and war years, and the civil rights activists and new leftists of the 1960s to 1970s, Debs's Socialist Party was a radical democratic movement deeply rooted in domestic reality. All of these groups and mass movements shared a naive optimism that brought forth tremendous courage and willingness to make sacrifices for worthy goals. Their legal standing was uncertain, tentative at best, and they were willing to test the limits of the democracy. All of these popular groups, including the various socialist organizations of this period, were "big tent" movements that contained a broad spectrum of ideas, and a multiplicity of positions on specific issues and tactics. When internal disputes led to splits and mass defections to other groups, the original organizations usually folded, but the poetry and songs they all left behind are an unmatched heritage of the continuity in ideas their struggles stood for.

Socialism was never more influential and powerful a force in the life of the United States than it was from about 1908 to 1914. Socialism had the quality of a secular faith for hundreds of thousands of workers ground down by long hours of hard labor, little reward, and less hope. Debs ran for the presidency four times in elections starting in 1904 and ending in 1920, when he campaigned from his jail cell in the federal penitentiary in Atlanta, Georgia. For personal and health reasons he chose not to run in 1916. His best showing came in the election of 1912 with almost 900,000 votes or 6 percent of the total vote cast, more than twice his previous vote of just under 425,000. Twelve hundred Socialists were elected to state and local offices that year, including seventy-nine mayors in twenty-four states. After the election of 1912 Debs said: "It is entirely possible that in four years more the Socialist Party may sweep the nation" (quoted in Ginger, 1949, p. 334). Nobody else was attracting more votes as quickly as the Socialist Party. The Socialists reached their peak of success in state legislatures in 1914 when thirty-three were elected nationwide.

Because of the strength of socialism in the labor organizations, the National Civic Federation lapsed into insignificance in this period. The United Mineworkers, for example, at its convention in 1911, made service on the NCF grounds for automatic expulsion from the union. John Mitchell promptly resigned from the NCF. Socialist influence was rising in the AFL as well, though Samuel Gompers was able to defeat a resolution similar to the NMU's in the same year. Working with the NCF and the newly formed (1912) antisocialist Militia of Christ, an AFL-sponsored Catholic and conservative labor organization, Sam Gompers hoped to combat socialist influences among Catholic workers with leaflets, newsletters, and speakers.

Though still relatively small in numbers, Socialists forced the other candidates in 1912, Woodrow Wilson (Democract), William Howard Taft (Republican), and Theodore Roosevelt (Progressive or Bull Moose), to take up the issues they raised and respond to the challenge they made. Every organization that sought to represent working people or was engaged in a struggle to advance the rights of black Americans, women, children, or native Americans, either included Socialists in their leadership or was engaged in the discourse raised by Socialists in these years.

Organizations and People: The Labor Side

While the AFL was the largest labor organization in the United States, it had almost no desire to bring unionism to unskilled labor or to organize workers in the emerging mass industries. In spite of its generally conservative views, at least one-third of the members of the AFL thought of themselves as Socialists. Some quite revolutionary Socialists worked within the AFL with the goal of educating and turning the rest of the organization in their direction someday, a practice called "boring from within." It was impossible to attend an AFL convention and not become a partisan on one or another of the many resolutions either advanced by the Socialists, or by those opposed to the Socialists. Immigrants, many of them familiar with the arguments of Socialists from their homelands, most black and native-born workers in unskilled jobs or mass industries, were forced to look elsewhere, though, if they wished to organize.

The Western Federation of Miners

The largest and most important of the industrial unions in the western states was the Western Federation of Miners (WFM). Originally organized among the hard rock metal miners who had fought the battles at Couer d'Alenes and elsewhere in the 1890s, the WFM was affiliated with the AFL until 1900. In spite of continuous and concerted efforts by absentee employers that included some of the largest trusts in the nation, the WFM grew from a few thousand members in fifteen locals in 1900 when it left the AFL, to almost 45,000 members in 177 locals in thirteen states, Canada, Alaska, and British Columbia by the end of the decade. As an industrial union it was open to anyone who was employed in any of the mines, mills, or smelters where it sought recognition. The union actively tried to recruit native American mine workers and Spanish-speaking residents of the Southwest, the latter sometimes incorrectly referred to as Mexicans.

Class warfare is the most succinct way to describe accurately the conflicts of the WFM with employers, state militia, hired gunmen, and vigilante gangs. The radicalism of western miners grew from their stark living and working conditions, and the violence that was brought against them. Familiarity with dynamite, a penchant toward train derailings, and a willingness to use firearms set them apart from most other unions. Mining camps and company towns offered few of the amenities and none of the distractions of traditional towns and cities. In some of the older towns of the West, the WFM gained the (sometimes temporary) support of local shopkeepers and businessmen who were opposed to the arrogant power of giant corporations that had recently moved in. Stark social class lines were formed under the absolute authority of the mining companies and the compliant state governments that openly served them. The newspaper of the WFM, *Miners' Magazine,* reflected the union's militant devotion to advancing the cause of socialism. Their secretary-treasurer, William D. ("Big Bill") Haywood, was a principal organizer of the revolutionary union, the Industrial Workers of the World (IWW), when it was formed in 1905.

The IWW

The IWW never became a large organization comparable in size to the earlier Knights of Labor or later CIO, but it gained an unusual prominence because of its unique revolutionary ideology, the creative and colorful personalities of many of its leading figures, and its prominent role in some of the important labor battles during the decade of its most brazen existence. The biting, off-the-cuff humor of IWW broadsides, its *Little Red Songbook,* its cartoon heroes and villains, its bravery, and its hip caustic slogans have earned Wobblies, as members of the IWW were called, a permanent place in the folklore of national life. The black cat became their symbol for industrial sabotage, a technique they recommended only in the unlikely circumstance of an employer refusing to recognize or negotiate with the union. Wobblies were militantly antiracist and urged black workers to cross the picket lines of striking unions that refused to allow them to join. The IWW disdainfully called unions that would exclude any honest worker "social clubs." In some circles the IWW was said to be the most dangerous and fearsome domestic threat to the United States in its history. Wobblies certainly were the most hounded and deliberately destroyed labor activists in that history. Their constitutional rights were put aside when federal, state, local, and vigilante assaults wrecked the union and sent most of its leaders, who weren't lynched or murdered, to jail or into exile during World War I.

The IWW was established in Chicago at a meeting of just over 200 of the nation's most prominent Socialists and militant labor leaders. Haywood presided. Debs was on hand, and so was Mother Jones, at age seventy-five, the "miners' angel," and, to her critics, "the most dangerous woman in America"(Fethering, 1974, p. 85). Daniel DeLeon, the contentious leader of the Socialist Labor Party, was also among the founders of the IWW. De Leon coined the phrase "labor fakir" to describe Gompers, and DeLeon briefly gained control of the new organization a year later. In 1905 he and Debs were seeking to reconcile some of their differences in forming the new IWW, but the Western Federation of Miners was the most forceful influence present.

There never was a clear-cut IWW ideology. Though often referred to as anarcho-syndicalists, the Wobblies were not really either, though they borrowed heavily from both anarchism and syndicalism. They were the first union of workers in the United States that was truly internationalist in its loyalties and ambitions. Their primary objective was "One Big Union" of all workers that would culminate in a general strike big enough to bring the capitalist or corporate order to a halt. Workers, organized democratically on an industry-wide basis, the IWW contended, could then take up the task of setting production goals for human use rather than private profit. According to most IWW arguments, government, as it was formerly known, would fade away, as "wage slavery" and the need for coercion also passed into oblivion. Material abundance, democratically available, would, according to Wobbly ideology, end the need for traditional forms of government. One of the favorite IWW songs of the day was "Big Rock Candy Mountain," which includes the lines, "Where they hung the jerk, That invented work," and where, the lyric promises, all the good things in life were freely available, "At the lemonade springs, where the bluebird sings," to all, all the time.

In the meantime, the IWW showed no respect for the institutions or the authority of what it called the exploiters. The IWW accepted anyone who worked into its membership, except social parasites, as they called bankers, lawyers, and professional gamblers. Wobblies actively opposed racial and gender discrimination among workers. After 1910 they aggressively sought to recruit black workers in the United States and, when a small group of Wobbly seamen were in South Africa, they urged the Industrial Workers Union there to build racial solidarity in their struggle. The IWW's western newspaper, the *Industrial Worker* conveyed some of the assertive evangelism of the IWW: "The IWW organizes without regard to color. The Only Negro we fight is he who employs labor. There is no color line in the furnace hells of the steel trust and there will be none in the *One Big Union*. White, black, or yellow, the workers of the world must unite!" (quoted in P. Foner, 1978, p. 111).

Membership in the IWW was never large, but every member seemed to add intensity and fervor to the loose-jointed organization. There were usually no more than a few thousand active members at any given time. At the height of its national reputation after the tremendous notoriety gained from the successful "Bread and Roses" strike in Lawrence in 1912, the IWW reached its maximum size, with only about 18,000 dues-paying members.

A banking panic and economic slump in 1907 crimped all of labor organizing for a couple of years, and when the recovery came the IWW was more prominent than ever, especially among black workers, migratory agricultural workers, lumber workers in the Northwest, and hard rock miners. The IWW red card and encoded signals in railroad yards all over the country brought protection, solace, comradeship, and traveling tips to thousands of itinerant workers, especially in the trans-Mississippi West. Audacity was another attractive Wobbly feature, especially when it was expressed eloquently from the lips of what looked like a bindlestiff (hobo) who had just arrived by "side-door coach" (boxcar) from a remote mining, lumbering, or agricultural work camp. Wobbly leaders included no pacifists. Many were accustomed to carrying pistols. Frequently in court on various serious charges, including murder and conspiracy to commit murder, Haywood and other leaders narrowly escaped conviction numerous times. Joe Hill, born in Sweden and named Joel Hagglund, and also known in the United States as Joe Hillstrum, the best known Wobbly songwriter, was not as fortunate. The composer of "Rebel Girl" and dozens of other radical tunes was executed by a Utah firing squad after an unsuccessful protest movement that reached international proportions in 1915. Hill was found guilty of a robbery/murder charge after a trial made infamous for its lack of due process. His name was added to the list of those figures unfairly killed by the state for their association with the cause of labor. His telegram to Haywood on the eve of his execution continues to be quoted (and misquoted) by labor activists: "Goodbye, Bill. I will die like a true blue rebel. Don't waste any time in mourning. *Organize.*" His last will conveys the Wobbly whimsy that touched so many hearts:

> My will is easy to decide,
> For there is nothing to divide.
> My kin don't need to fuss and moan-
> "moss does not cling to a rolling stone."
> My body? Ah, if I could choose,
> I would to ashes it reduce,
> And let the merry breezes blow
> My dust to where some flowers grow.
> Perhaps some fading flower then
> Would come to life and bloom again.
> This is my last and final will,
> Good luck to all of you.

The IWW was consistently attacked by the press, religious leaders, and most established institutions for its revolutionary fervor and its acceptance of violent class conflict. Ironically, in their greatest victory, as leaders of the Lawrence, Massachusetts textile workers' strike in 1912, their emphasis was on nonviolence. Haywood and the other Wobs came in to help the strikers when their own leaders were jailed. From prison, the Wobbly leader, Joe Ettor, cautioned against any form of violence in Lawrence: "In the last analysis," he warned, "all the blood spilled will be your own." To prevent violent retaliation in Lawrence after the death of a young woman striker, Bill Haywood also urged nonviolence. The unified strike could be broken, he warned, only if violence or arson against property gave the mill owners the opportunity to employ force.

The IWW was never patriotic, or racist. Women and recent immigrants played decisive leadership roles in all of their actions. When they spoke of One Big Union, they meant it. Most unions and union leaders, they said, were "pork chop" unionists looking out for their own advantage first, workers second. Union welfare benefits were condemned by the IWW as "coffin benefits." No political party claimed the allegiance of the IWW, and none was worth it in their minds.

Governments, to the IWW, were simply the organized repressive agencies of the capitalist class. Yet, if the IWW is to be remembered for making a lasting contribution to labor in the United States, it is their "free speech" campaigns that strengthened the First Amendment to the Constitution that stand out the most. When some Wobbly activists were arrested for handing out leaflets or making public speeches, others soon arrived to take up the same tasks. They quickly filled the jails and their supporters took to the streets in demonstrations for the release of their wrongly jailed comrades. They won more of these contests than they lost.

The eventual destruction of the IWW by federal, state, and local governments, abetted by vigilante violence, corporate thuggery, and lynching, during World War I, is also a testament to how greatly feared they were. Most of the leaders of the IWW were jailed for their antiwar speeches, or on other charges. Hundreds of Wobblies were deported without any hearings or due process, all their offices were ransacked by police agencies, and their labor organizers were beaten and killed by mobs using the cover of patriotism in a time of wartime danger.

As a union the IWW was never truly effective, and it was not a political party at all. It was more of a revolutionary workers' association. The IWW fought to protect workers who were the most vulnerable, most obviously subjected to abuse and exploitation, and furthest removed from the protection of established political or social authorities.

In Lawrence, Massachusetts, they joined and helped to win the fight of immigrant women workers against powerful textile manufacturers. Their own "Rebel Girl," Elizabeth Gurley Flynn, was a leading Wobbly agitator in a victorious free speech fight in Spokane, Washington, in the strikes in Lawrence, Kansas, Paterson, New Jersey, and Everett, Washington. She was also a Socialist and a co-founder of the American Civil Liberties Union (which, hypocritically, drove her out because of her later Communist Party association), and she was sent to jail for alleged subversive activities in the McCarthy period.

Whenever they won a strike, Wobblies usually refused to enter into written agreements with employers. Capitalists, they argued, had no legitimacy and none should be provided by making formal contracts with them. Naturally, many of their verbal agreements fell apart or were easily undermined soon after they were made. The size and longevity of their union organizations varied from solitary individuals to short-lived unions of thousands of members. Most industrial centers and most cities had an IWW office. When their organization was smashed and most of their leaders exiled, jailed, or killed, many remaining Wobblies joined the newly formed Communist Party USA in the early 1920s. Others came back to work as union organizers with the Congress of Industrial Organizations (CIO) during the New Deal era of the 1930s. A small group of stalwarts kept the IWW itself going for decades by maintaining an office and bookstore in Chicago. From there they preserved many of their materials and kept the songbook in print. The New Left of the 1960s, though almost completely disconnected to labor, discovered an inspirational democratic and revolutionary irreverence in the heritage of the IWW.

If the IWW was the most radical expression of worker socialism in the first two decades of the twentieth century, and the AFL was the most conservative in its criticism of the wage labor system of capitalism, the garment workers, the newest group of workers to form large and permanent labor organizations, were in between.

Socialist Unions in the Needle Trades

While the Wobblies and the Socialist Party were growing fast in the aftermath of the economic slump of 1907, the AFL saw rapid growth in two areas, mining and clothing manufacture, the latter called the "needle trades." The two leading organizations that emerged among textile workers were the International Ladies Garment Workers Union (ILGWU) and, after 1913, the Amalgamated Clothing Workers of America (ACWA). Both were organized and led by moderate or mainstream Socialists. The ILGWU formed out of the women's wear branch of the immigrant labor sweatshops of the garment industry in New York and several other cities in 1900. They included former Knights of Labor workers, members of the United Hebrew Trades of New York, and groups from the United Garment Workers of America. The separate men's organization at the time included locals of the United Garment Workers. Both were AFL-affiliated, though, unlike typical AFL locals, many skills and tasks were represented among their members. In this respect they were similar to the United Mine Workers, which included a multitude of work responsibilities and tasks within one AFL union.

Hours were long in the needle trades, ten- to twelve-hour days the standard, fourteen to sixteen hours during the so-called busy season. The conditions of work were deplorable, even for this benighted time. The loosely defined term *sweatshop* became the commonplace description for work in these shops. A better definition of the term is that it is a place where the subcontracting of work allows completely unregulated circumstances, and workers are paid per item completed. Often women and children were literally sweated for endless hours for a pittance by unregulated and unaccountable employers. Strikes in the growing garment industry were commonplace, mean, and filled with bitterness. Workers wanted union recognition, a reduction in hours, better pay, and an improvement in working conditions. Few gains were made in the early years of the new century. The New York, Chicago, and St. Louis locals of the United Garment Workers all suffered disastrous strike losses in 1904 to a well-organized National Clothiers' Association.

So many of these garment workers were immigrants that they brought to the workplace both an ethnic and a European class consciousness that mixed easily with the progressive and democratic critique in the United States of the excesses of capitalism of the time. Among the various ethnic groups in the needle trades, socialism became a common unifying language and faith. Unlike the Wobblies, who were convinced that it was the imminent destiny of workers to become the dominant force and class in history, most of the women garment workers and their leaders, mostly male at the time, translated their socialism into a desire for a good, secure, and dignified life for workers in exchange for a fair share of the wealth that their labor made. Perhaps eventually, down the line somewhere in the future, enlightened workers in a democratic setting would become real political majorities and play a leading role in social and economic decision making. For now, socialism meant an end to abuse and exploitation by arrogant and autocratic bosses, and a chance at a safe and decent life as a worker in an imperfect world.

A long and bitter strike took place over the winter of 1909–10, begun by about 15,000 of the mostly Italian and Jewish young women of the Ladies' Waist Makers Union, Local 25 of the ILGWU in New York. The strike attracted the attention of progressive reformers, especially the National Women's Trade Union Association, religious leaders, other unionists, Socialist Party speakers, and even a few sympathetic women members of the city's wealthy elite. Eventually over 30,000 workers in New York's garment industry were idled before the strike came to an end in February 1910. John Mitchell and the National Civic Federation failed to bring the sides together early in the strike when manufacturers refused to recognize the legitimacy of the union. The police and courts were especially harsh on the pickets and protests. During the course of the conflict, more than 700 women were arrested. Many of them were cruelly beaten, and most given little defense before arbitrary sentences kept them in squalid prisons for varying terms. Some women were held for a few hours while others served sentences of many months. The union sought arbitration in early January 1910, but again employers refused. Public sympathy sided with the women. Extreme poverty and frigid temperatures forced many strikers back to work and across the picket lines of other workers. Hundreds of other strikebreakers crossed the picket lines, many of whom were black women excluded from the trades and the union. Finally, after a sympathetic garment workers' strike in Philadelphia was settled on February 8, the union put all of its efforts into winning agreements one by one with the employers.

The results were mixed. The New York strike was the largest and longest strike by women in the nation's history. It gained fame in legend and song as the "Uprising of the Twenty Thousand." It was industry-wide and, in spite of police, court actions, and strikebreakers, had public sympathy and was never really broken, though the gains were modest and inconsistent from shop to shop. More, and bigger, strikes would soon follow, and, abetted by tragedy, greater public attention would be paid to workplace health and safety issues for all workers.

In June 1910 the New York Cloakmakers, mostly male members of the ILGWU, went out on an even larger strike than its predecessor. More than 50,000 struck this time over similar issues of workday, union rights, wages, and shop conditions. The strike went on through the summer. A sweeping injunction declared the strike an illegal conspiracy because one of the union's demands was a closed shop. Workers refused to honor the injunction and almost a hundred were jailed. Finally, and once again with the intervention of progressive reformers who won public sympathy for the workers, an agreement was reached. The settlement was known thereafter as the "Protocols of Peace." The union achieved almost all of its wage, hour, workday, and overtime goals, and even gained what appeared to be a reasonable compromise on the question of union security. Instead of the closed shop, the union got a hybrid called a "preferential shop." Employers could hire nonunion workers only if no union workers could be found. A Joint Board for Sanitary Control was established to do inspections. A Board of Arbitration was also set up to review and make final decisions on grievances. The board was to be composed of three members: one selected by the union, one by the employers, and one a neutral to be acceptable to both parties. A lower-level Committee of Grievances with two representatives from each side was created to hear minor disputes.

No labor agreement in the nation's history had been so comprehensive. It appeared to create a form of industrial government, and it put the ILGWU and its mostly immigrant female labor force at the vanguard of organized labor in the United States. The union was also at the forefront in the development of what later came to be called "fringe benefits." The ILGWU encouraged its members to participate in its mutual benefit society, the Arbiter Ring (AR), or Workman's Circle. The AR, with its socialist orientation, provided low-cost disability and life insurance and gained a charter from New York State in 1905. If the term *industrial democracy* soon came into widespread use, it could truly be said that it came to life in the initiatives of the ILGWU. The union, now an institution of consequence itself, had as much at stake in contract administration as management.

Chicago Garment Workers Follow New York

Encouraged by the New York garment workers' settlement of 1910, almost the same number of Chicago garment workers shut down their industry in September. Planned by socialist and anarchist Jewish and Italian workers in advance, the immediate issue was over a one-quarter-cent rate cut. Eventually, the strike took up goals similar to those in New York. The center of the strike was against the shops of Hart, Shaffner, and Marx where the rate cut took place, but the walkout soon spread throughout the garment industry of the nation's second largest city. Approximately nine ethnic or national groups of men and women of almost every age were on strike. Reformers once again sought to mediate and assuage the rising class animosities that this strike, like almost all of the others of this era, were bringing to the foreground. The strike lasted over four months. Almost a thousand workers were jailed, and seven people, including one "private detective," were killed before it was over.

In Chicago, as in New York, the Women's Trade Union League played a leading role in mobilizing prominent progressive leaders, social workers, and university professors on behalf of an agreement. Here too the final settlements varied from shop to shop and were somewhat inconclusive. Only the Hart, Shaffner, and Marx workers, represented by the United Garment Workers, actually made a contract that estab-lished the right to collective bargaining. Both the company and the union accepted the creation of a Grievance Board. The union chose Clarence Darrow as its repre-sentative, and the company appointed its attorney, Max Meyer, to the new board. A subsequent agreement in 1913 added the same preferential shop concept won by the ILGWU in the New York Cloakmakers' strike of 1910. When the workers covered under this agreement broke away from the United Garment Workers and affiliated with the new Amalgamated Clothing Workers of America (ACWA), the agreement continued unaffected by the change.

Sidney Hillman, an apprentice cloth cutter at the time of the Chicago strike, became president of the new organization in 1914. Though an outspoken Socialist himself, Hillman had gained prominence as a moderating influence by preventing radicals and IWW dissidents from defeating the 1910 agreement in a final vote. Hillman was soon the leading advocate for what he called the "new unionism" of the time. This new model for industrial union and management relations was set by the New York and Chicago agreements. It is the model that advocates of "industrial democracy" point to as the beginning of workplace due process and worker rights. Hillman broad-ened his associations with prominent manufacturers, Progressives, and government leaders during World War I. He continued to expand on the idea of industrial democ-racy during the postwar era, and was there to bring it into the discussion of labor relations in the New Deal period.

Strikes and labor battles continued in the needle trades and textile industry until World War I. The most notable of these was in Lawrence, Massachusetts, in the frigid early months of 1912. The IWW reached a pinnacle of prestige for its contribution to the tremendous victory in the "Bread and Roses" strike, so named for the poem by James Oppenheim and the song that came out of it. In Lawrence the strike was won by ethnic solidarity and industrial unity combined with public outrage.

Cold and hunger forced strikers to copy the European workers' practice of seek-ing refuge for children in nearby cities. When police attacked and beat women and children bound for temporary care in Philadelphia, a national public outcry followed. Lawrence was immediately filled with reporters and sympathetic observers, includ-ing Mrs. William Howard Taft, the wife of the president. A highly publicized congres-sional investigation exposed the poverty and abuse heaped on the mostly women and children workers of Lawrence. The photographs of children mill workers by Lewis Hine touched the hearts of the public and strengthened the arguments of reformers.

A victory for the workers soon followed when a contract was ratified with raises up to 21 percent, overtime rates at time-and-a-quarter, and a standard fifty-four-hour-week. Similar benefits quickly were extended to a quarter million textile workers throughout New England, but not every textile or garment worker strike was victo-rious. In Paterson, New Jersey, in 1913, a silkworkers' strike inspired by the outcome at Lawrence, and led by some of the same Wobblies, was defeated.

The Triangle Shirtwaist Fire, 1911

If public sentiment had helped workers in strikes in New York, Chicago, and Lawrence, it reached near overwhelming proportions after a fire took the lives of 146 mostly young Italian and Jewish women workers at the Triangle Shirtwaist Company on March 25, 1911. The fire spread through the top three floors of the ten-storied Asch Building. The rear exit door of the eighth floor shop, where the fire started, was customarily locked shut until the twelve-hour shift was over. Other doors opened inward so that the crowd trying to get out of the conflagration couldn't open the hot doors into themselves. Fire hoses were cracked and couldn't be used. A fire escape loaded with girls collapsed. A small elevator was driven to the basement under the weight of girls on its top so that it couldn't be used again. Workers, their clothing in flames, began to climb onto the thin window ledges to escape the inferno. The new net brought to the scene by the Fire Department failed and the girl who fell into it was killed. More jumpers followed, some in groups of two and three holding hands as a gathering crowd watched in horror. Some fell onto an iron fence and were impaled, others onto the street.

The city was stunned. Rose Schneiderman, a leader of the ILGWU, rose to the stage of the Metropolitan Opera House several days later, the setting chosen to commemorate those killed, and put her socialist challenge before the somber crowd: "The life of women and men is so cheap and property so sacred," she intoned, "I can't talk fellowship to you who are gathered here, too much blood has been spilled" (quoted in Baxandall, Gordon, and Reverby, 1995, pp. 203–4). The audience and the city responded in much the same way as the nation had reacted to many of the criticisms of capitalism's brutal disregard for the human consequences of the relentless pursuit of profit. Repairs were undertaken of the most flagrant physical abuses in the workplace in the judgment of outsiders, but no actions were taken to address the systemic problems experienced by workers inside the industry and depicted by Schneiderman and socialist critics.

New York State Senator Robert F. Wagner Sr. and Assemblyman Alfred E. Smith set up a Factory Investigating Committee filled with reformers that included Smith, Rose Schneiderman, and Frances Perkins (who later became the first woman cabinet member as secretary of labor in the first New Deal administration). The committee recommended legislation that protected women and children workers. Hours were restricted, women could not be made to work until four weeks after a childbirth, doors in shops and factories had to open outward, sprinklers had to be installed and red lights placed to indicate exits. Businessmen hated all of it. Government, they cried, should not interfere with the marketplace except when injunctions and militia were needed to protect property. Worker organizations gained nothing from these measures. The right to join a union was not protected by law. Workplace democracy was unaffected as well. Protected workers were now more dependent on the state than on their own organizations or political parties. Nonetheless, the reforms brought about a welcome change. No one can tell how many lives were saved by these simple measures, and from these labor struggles and sacrifices, a new age was dawning in labor relations in the United States.

Black Protest and Black Labor

Not every advocate for worker reform was equally successful in the Progressive era. Lynching still took the lives of more than a hundred black men and women a year. Tens of thousands more black workers suffered horrific conditions in almost every state of the former Confederacy in convict leasing and brutal prison labor practices. To its credit, the IWW kept up a constant critical attack on lynching, Jim Crow, and convict leasing that was carried on by ex-Wobblies, Communists, and some Socialists in the decades that followed. Abolition of the convict leasing system was also attacked by progressive journalists and in some state legislatures. These efforts did finally begin to get results. However, as the convict leasing system ended, according to one authority, it did so "uncertainly, ambiguously" (Ayers, 1984, p. 222). Chain gangs and labor camps persisted, and from 1981 to the present prison privatization schemes have maintained some of the for-profit exploitative aspects of the old system, if not all of its horrific brutality.

Socialists and progressive reformers also started new organizations to fight racial discrimination. W.E.B. DuBois, now broadly identified as a Socialist himself, spoke sharply about the need for racial unity among workers in a speech in Atlanta in 1907: "It is only a question of time when white working men and black working men will see their common cause against the aggressions of exploiting capitalists" (quoted in P. Foner and Lewis, 1978, p. 80). Du Bois, frustrated with the accommodation practices of Booker T. Washington, joined a group that founded the Niagara movement in 1905, the organization that became the National Association for the Advancement of Colored People in 1909. Employers and labor unions were both criticized for their racial practices, the former for using black workers as strikebreakers and then tossing them aside, the latter for proscribing them from membership. The Niagara movement's Declaration of Principles warned in 1905 that discriminatory racial practices "will accentuate the war of labor and capital, and they are disgraceful to both sides." The radical black Socialist, Hubert Henry Harrison, in a 1912 speech, was even more explicit about the benefits of racism:

> It pays the capitalist to keep the workers divided. So he creates and keeps alive these prejudices. He gets them to believe that their interests are different. Then he uses one half of them to club the other half with. In Russia when the working men demand reform, the capitalists sick them on the Jews. In America they sick them on the Negroes. That makes them forget their own condition; as long as they can be made to look down upon another class. (quoted in Marable and Mullings, 1999, pp. 228, 232–33)

Race and Labor Organizations

There were several important exceptions to the standardized government and AFL racial discrimination practices among workers of this period. We have noted the inclusiveness sought by the IWW. In Philadelphia, for example, the IWW successfully overcame ethnic and racial divisions that had frustrated previous attempts to organize longshoremen and dockworkers. Two successful IWW strikes in 1913 of longshoremen and boatmen led to further organizing and more victories for the radical union. By 1916 the wages of more than 3,000 black and white Philadelphia waterfront workers had increased from $1.25 to $4.00 per day.

The United Mine Workers included locals in both the North and South where interracial cooperation and strike solidarity were well established during the early years of the century. Black workers mined coal in the South as slaves, and after the Civil War under the convict leasing system, and as free laborers. Northern mining companies brought thousands of black miners into the coal fields of Appalachia, Pennsylvania, and Ohio as strikebreakers and as low-cost labor in the strife-filled decades of the late nineteenth century. As a practical matter, the union signed up every miner it could, though ethnic and racial conflicts were common. By the turn of the new century the UMW included the largest number of black workers of any of the national unions. Nationally, the UMW was an exception in the ranks of the AFL in its call for equal pay for equal work, regardless of race. Similar circumstances on a smaller scale occasionally united black and white workers in other industries. The lack of greater interaction was due to racial exclusion and discrimination in hiring practices. More than two-thirds of all black workers on the eve of World War I were employed in either agriculture or personal or domestic service, the vast majority of whom were in the South. The most dramatic example of labor unity continued to be among black and white workers in New Orleans.

The New Orleans Dock and Cotton Council Strike, 1907

Socialism and radicalism among workers in the early years of the twentieth century were not restricted to western miners or northeastern immigrant workers. Covington Hall was the popular and well-known adjutant-general of the United Sons of Confederate Veterans, and was the Socialist Party candidate for mayor of New Orleans in 1904 and for Congress in 1906. Hall's father was a Confederate veteran and Presbyterian minister, his mother a wealthy southern socialite. In 1905, when the IWW came to town, Hall gave up his white supremacy stand, which he had previously maintained was consistent with socialism. Hall became involved in a conflict between the AFL and local brewery workers in New Orleans. The Brewery Workers Local No. 215 came under AFL attack for not releasing some of its members for separate affiliation with unions that were part of the city Central Trades and Labor Council of the AFL, especially the Teamsters Local No. 701. The Teamsters wanted to represent the men who loaded and drove the beer wagons. Hall and the prominent socialist editor and journalist, Oscar Ameringer, became part of a group that included the popular white brewery and cotton workers unionist Thomas Gannon, the black cotton worker teamster president Joseph Coats, and local Wobbly journalist Peter Molyneaux. Radicalism was no stranger in New Orleans or rural Louisiana, where radical Populists had won elections in some of the upland parishes (similar to county governments elsewhere).

The AFL model was to organize separate crafts into autonomous locals, sometimes several in the same workplace. The AFL was constantly engaged in hundreds of disputes with the IWW, Socialists, and independent union activists, along with large numbers of AFL unionists who objected to the narrow craft model for organizing. In New Orleans, the general practice was along industrial lines. Everyone, regardless of specific job or task, who worked in the same industry tended toward organization in one union, but this became increasingly unacceptable to the Central Trades and Labor Council, AFL, of the city. The powerful biracial Dock and Cotton Council of waterfront unions in New Orleans and the black workers Central Labor Union, also led by levee leaders, all backed the industrial model of the brewery workers when their charter was revoked by the AFL, and, at the same time, they went on strike. The dispute over support for the striking brewery workers split the unions in the city, with the biracial and socialist/IWW side dominant. The AFL actually encouraged strike-breaking for a while, which led to bloodshed and libel suits. A new city central United Labor Council, opposed to the AFL, was created by the dissidents. The jurisdictional battle continued for almost a year, during which the general levee strike of more than 10,000 workers closed the entire port of New Orleans to commerce for twenty days.

The strike of the levee workers was brought on by a lockout of employers that turned into a general waterfront and railroad strike. The shipping companies and their agents were intent on breaking the racial solidarity that had led to the half-and-half rule and had set the best, and only nondiscriminatory workload rates among the workers on the entire Gulf coast waterfront. What was so remarkable about the levee strike was not only the victory the workers achieved, but how solidly they all stood together, black and white, skilled and unskilled, immigrant and native-born.

All of the local commercial newspapers attacked the strikers and used racial smears. Steamship Company agents put forward plans for the creation of a new "White League," a Klanlike organization that had led a murderous uprising against the Reconstruction government of Louisiana in 1874. False rumors of black assaults on whites and the threat of lost jobs could not break the unity of the workers. Mayor Martin Behrman tried to play a neutral role in the strike. His efforts kept out the state militia. He tried to end the strike, but could not convince the striking workers to send an all-white committee to sit down with management representatives. The half-and-half rule was unanimously defended by the assemblies of workers, even to include negotiators, or representatives to labor-management committees.

After the strike, when the Louisiana General Assembly established a Port Investigation Commission to study the matter, its 1908 report concluded: "One of the greatest drawbacks to New Orleans is the working of the white and negro races on terms of equality" (quoted in Rosenberg, 1988, p. 142). New Orleans dockworkers maintained that unity and their workload advantages until after World War I, when racism and the open shop finally broke them down.

Strikes as Class Warfare, 1894–1914

Those workers who lived through the strikes of these years remembered them for the rest of their lives. They remembered the privations, the cold and hunger, the look in the eyes of children, and the fear. The strikes commonly took on the aspect of class warfare when strikers battled strikebreakers, police, vigilantes, company gunmen, and militia, and where strikers had no institutional authority to rely on but their own solidarity. Labor activists, including some IWW members, openly advocated and some carried out acts of sabotage, arson, and, as in the case of the bombing of the *Los Angeles Times* building in 1910, even murder.

Western mining strikes were the most warlike, with militia units or paramilitary police regularly employed against strikers. At Cripple Creek, Colorado, in 1894, miners were subjected to a "reign of terror" by a sheriff's army of 1,200 (Perlman and Taft, 1966, 4:176). At Telluride, Colorado, in 1901, more than 250 workers armed with Winchester rifles drove out strikebreakers, and won the eight-hour day when the governor refused to send in the national guard.

Two years later open warfare resumed in Colorado, with a governor, James H. Peabody, firmly in the antilabor camp. Peabody, who called himself a "law and order" governor, refused to carry out court orders favorable to unions, and allowed vigilante and military groups complete latitude in the abuse of the rights of miners. The Western Federation of Miners was attacked, its leaders imprisoned, its locals defeated, open opposition crushed by militia. The state government was completely under employer control.

In McKee's Rock, Pennsylvania, hundreds of armed state constables and deputized sheriffs battled a crowd of 4,000 rock-throwing striking workers in July 1909. More than a dozen were killed before the successful strike against the Pressed Steel Car Company came to an end in late August.

Of the many public embarrassments to the Rockefeller family, the worst was probably its role as owners of the mines in the "Ludlow Massacre" in 1914. A tent colony, the temporary residence of striking coal miners and their families was swept by machine gun fire in Ludlow, Colorado. Some of the people had fled the tents, others had dug pits inside them. When the camp was captured it was set on fire. The result was the burning to death of eleven women and children by the Colorado militia. The nation was shocked. Workers organized themselves into military units and began to take reprisals. Federal troops, sent by President Woodrow Wilson, finally suppressed the conflict.

Radicalism and class conflict weren't the only problems for employers. Because of the size and magnitude of industry, every large strike had consequences beyond its own immediate boundaries. Tons of bananas rotted on the docks of New Orleans while cotton piled up on the wharves during the strike. Railroad strikes tied up everything else. President Roosevelt knew that factories and cities were dependent on coal for electricity and heat when he intervened in the coal strike of 1902. Throughout the country progressive critics and efficiency experts were questioning the long- and short-term economic waste that such struggles inevitably produced. Market factors alone, or "voluntarism" in labor-management relations would cause too much waste, generate too large a negative economic ripple effect. So, while businessmen and government maintained all of their historic willingness and determination to use force and the power of law against labor, they were also awakening to new concepts of scientific management and worker representation that might actually enhance their hegemony at a lower cost.

Modernism in the Workplace and the Culture

The application of science and practical technologies for increasing the productivity of industry, developing new products, and expanding markets was well established by the end of the nineteenth century. Now these scientific efficiencies were applied to the workplace itself, to workers, to their work, and to the world in which workers lived. Frederick Winslow Taylor, known derisively as "Stopwatch" Taylor because of the time-and-motion studies carried out under his aegis, helped to change the workplace. Taylor was an engineer, a graduate of Stevens Institute of Technology, and is often credited with being the founder of the concept of scientific management because of the title of his book, *The Principles of Scientific Management* (1911). Taylor was actually enlarging a process that had begun at least a hundred years earlier, the deliberate application of science and mathematics to economic productivity. Taylor's studies complemented the development of moving assembly lines and the breaking down of labor tasks into smaller units, processes already well underway. Worker resistance to Taylorism has been hilariously represented in film and television depictions of assembly lines overwhelming hapless workers. Charlie Chaplin's worker in "Modern Times," Lucille Ball's "Lucy," and Jackie Gleason's "Poor Soul" all grappled unsuccessfully with a fast-moving technology beyond their control. Millions of workers understood the situation all too well.

Modernism meant more than just deskilling the workforce or increasing production. Techniques for adding efficiency and strengthening managerial controls went to every aspect of labor processes. Differential pay scales and premium and bonus plans were introduced into mass production industries. New categories of workers, usually called employees, were paid salaries by the week, month, or year to differentiate and separate them from hourly workers. The number of office workers, retail clerks, teachers and social service workers, and government employees was growing rapidly, though they were still less than 5 percent of the nonfarm workforce in the Progressive era. Some of these employees were known as professionals because the specializations for which they were trained were certified outside of the workplace by universities or government licensing agencies. Naturally, their salaries and work autonomy were usually, but not always, superior to those of other workers without the same credentials. Credentialing agencies maintained controls and organizational relationships with these workers throughout their careers, as their worklife came to be called. Licensing practices and renewals, association memberships, journal subscriptions, education, and social status separated these new professional workers from their industrial and craft counterparts. Many professional employees found entry into the middle class from royalties paid for their published work or from their business associations. Taylor was one of these, along with other engineers, and white-collar professional employees.

Just as some workers were to be rewarded for the efficiencies they added to the workplace, others were expected to be culturally prepared to accept less. Taylor himself observed: "One of the very first requirements for a man who is fit to handle pig iron as a regular occupation is that he shall be so stupid and phlegmatic that he more nearly resembles an ox than any other type animal" (quoted in Stone, 1973, p. 37). The same logic required that every worker/employee have the appropriate temperament, intelligence, and attitude for her or his job. Taylor actually thought of himself as a Progressive, an expert whose work would help rationalize and improve both the workplace and the society. Had he lived longer (he died in 1915), he might have gone on to become a technocrat, part of a movement, begun during the 1920s by men like himself, which advocated the entire management of society along scientifically engineered lines. In the meantime, social scientists were taking up some of the challenges raised by workplace radicalism and conflict.

Social science had the tools to deal with what industrial managers were calling a "crisis of social control." The goal was to make an "antagonistic workforce behave stably and predictably" (Ewen, 1976, p. 13). The French sociologist Gustave Le Bon published two enormously influential books that were quickly translated into English, *The Crowd; A Study of the Popular Mind* (tr. 1897) and *The Psychology of Socialism* (tr. 1899). Le Bon didn't mince words: "To act on the crowd one must know how to work on their sentiments, and especially on their unconscious sentiments; and one must never appeal to their reason, for they have none. One must accordingly be familiar with their sentiments in order to manipulate them" (Le Bon, 1899, p. 412). On the eve of World War I, the American Academy of Political and Social Science devoted two issues of its journal, *Annals,* to the broad social challenge of managing employees.

Good Citizenship, Patriotism, Militarism

Like Taylorism, professional approaches to workplace and social control were scientific refinements of processes that were already underway. In 1910 William D. Boyce, a Chicago publisher, met Lord Robert Baden-Powell in London. Baden-Powell was the founder of the English scouting movement. Boyce brought the idea back to the United

States and established the Boy Scouts of America in 1910 as an organization with a clear ideological purpose. The object of scouting was to promote patriotism, militarism, and training in citizenship among working-class boys. Rotary Clubs and Kiwanis Clubs among businesspeople in almost every town or city were established to advance a similar, patriotic, if less militaristic, message. Social service projects carried out by businessmen (no women were members of either Rotary or Kiwanis organizations until 1987) were expected to improve their otherwise selfish image. Settlement houses were seeking to assist immigrants in developing good citizenship practices in the crowded working-class slums of large cities. The Pledge of Allegiance was introduced into the public schools in October 1892. The Pledge was originally part of the Columbus Day celebration; its regular use spread quickly throughout this era.

Progressive labor reformers were advocating the achievement of similar patriotic and good-citizenship goals. A sharing of some of the increased productivity of industry with workers would curb their appetite for radicalism. Advertising was rapidly becoming more sophisticated in seeking to manipulate popular sentiment. Moving pictures showed their enormous potential to both reflect and promote mythologies, none more powerfully perhaps, than D. W. Griffith's popular affirmation of racism, *The Birth of a Nation* (1915).

Conclusion

The responses of capital to the challenges of labor had always been varied. In this era the horizons for both the domestic and global expansion of capital were drastically increased, and so were the challenges and the conflicts. Manufacturing technologies led directly to mass production that increased the competition for global markets and resources among capitalists. World war was one outcome of that competition. The need for skilled workers meant that they were always better rewarded by masters and employers than the less skilled or unskilled. Samuel Gompers and Booker T. Washington understood these simple economic formulations, and both made some real gains for themselves and the outlook they represented. Gompers enlarged his organization, its bureaucracy, and his own importance by embracing the outlook of business. Booker T. Washington became known as a responsible Negro educator, gained large financial contributions for his Tuskeegee Institute, and was similarly praised by corporate leaders for his realistic understanding of the existing racial codes. The Socialist Party and the IWW posed a different kind of challenge.

The danger of socialism went beyond the workplace. A new battleground was forming for both labor and capital. The traditional conservative approaches of crude repression and ethnic, gender, and racial division were now being augmented by social engineering that sought to manipulate the entire society and to shape the culture itself. The historic liberal tradition to gain social stability in the present by encouraging hope for a better future turned from the agricultural frontier to the urban and industrial center. Progressives worked in every area of national institutional life to sanitize, improve, and rationalize existing class relationships.

Workers historically formed loyalties and structures that brought protection or solace from the abuses they experienced. Socialism reached its highest level of credibility among workers in this era. Ethnic unity maintained itself for working people by adapting to the new nation in neighborhoods and around religious and cultural practices that were buffers to some of the harsh realities of the workplace world. Some of that ethnic unity was transferred to labor solidarity and fierce conflicts. The IWW was neither a political party nor a traditional labor union, yet it briefly became a cultural force of national significance. Part of the IWW's success was its appeal to unassimilated groups of immigrant workers.

The extreme severity of the loss experienced by black workers following the *Plessy* case had powerful cultural consequences. Blues music was born in this era of crushed hopes, lynch law, and fading possibilities. Popular self-created music was a terrain of liberty where every human sentiment could be freely expressed. Just as spirituals contained veiled messages of escape and freedom beyond the world of slavery, the blues was a flowering of irony, humor, and warmth in a cruel and oppressive world. Blues music was a poetic and soulful response to the nation's racism. It stands in sharp authentic contrast to the dominating culture's commercially successful blackface minstrelsy of the same era.

Mass circulating newspapers, the "yellow press," sensationalized events and manipulated readers, most famously by stimulating popular endorsement of the Spanish-American War. The same press cooperated with government censorship of the ugly Philippine-American War that immediately ensued, and generally, with some important exceptions, attacked unions and defended corporate interests. Local big city manufacturers sponsored baseball teams and other cultural diversions to promote their products and provide new heroes and profit-making distracting activities for working-class audiences. Coney Island was very popular. Electricity made amusement parks possible in or near every great urban or industrial center.

In spite of all its divisions and diversion, the height of working-class influence in national life was reached in this era. In its many and varied union organizations and their well-known leaders, in the Socialist Party of Eugene V. Debs, in the hundreds of labor and radical newspapers that were read by millions of workers, in the independent militancy of garment workers, metal workers, miners, transit workers, dockworkers, and longshoremen, and in the revolutionary credibility of the IWW, workers throughout the United States were a powerful, though weakly connected force in the life of the country. Though greater material gains were still ahead, as were huge increases in union membership and political potential in World War I, the New Deal, and the World War II era, nowhere in the future did labor enjoy the independent power and voice that it had achieved on the eve of the Great War.

This woman is shown operating a punch press at the Frankford Arsenal in Frankford, Pennsylvania, during World War I, a generation before "Rosie the Riverter" was made famous for being a woman doing a traditionally man's job (in wartime). (Library of Congress, Prints and Photographs Division, Reproduction No. LC-USZ62-59157)

CHAPTER 6

Bang, Boom, and Bust: The Great War, Jazz Age, and Great Crash, 1914–1932

Once I built a railroad
Made it run,
Made it race against time.
Once I built a railroad
Now it's done,
Buddy can you spare a dime.
—E. Y. "Yip" Harburg

Fast Forward

Too much of consequence happened in the United States in these years to allow a casual summation. Like the silent films of this era, events seemed to move in quick step. From the outbreak of the most destructive war yet in human history, to the onset of the worst economic catastrophe in the modern industrial world, those who lived through this brief era were forced to turn toward government authority more than ever for protection and relief from the dangers and turmoil around them. They were also drawn to more exciting distractions and commercial entertainment than ever.

Every large urban center in the Midwest and Northeast had a professional baseball team and a group of locally worthy heroes and celebrities who happily performed their skills as extraordinarily well paid workers. Millions of people were willingly entranced by a new, nearly universal and popular celebrity culture that was made easily available by the electronic communication wonders of radio and film. It was also easy for workers to start small businesses that required very little capital. Those that succeeded encouraged both the illusion and the reality that, as President Calvin Coolidge proudly claimed, "the business of America is business." Worker organizations soared to new highs and crashed to new lows in astonishingly short sequences of time. The speed of labor's forward motion was only equaled by that of its reverses.

Success

Success, or at least the perception of success, is a sure-fire way to build confidence and credibility. When leaders are successful, their popularity swells. Winning a war, or a strike, is obviously far better for prestige building for those in the leadership than losing one. From the beginning of Woodrow Wilson's presidency in March 1913 until the Great Crash of 1929, the harmonious relationship of business and government in the United States appeared, with but a few small setbacks, to lead the nation through a string of successes that built the prestige and cultural hegemony of capitalist culture to new levels of credibility and power. Those worker organizations that joined this happy coalition also briefly prospered, even if their members did not. Wages fell sharply against wartime inflation rates and no-strike agreements. Union membership, on the other hand, nearly doubled during the military crisis of World War I.

Ethnic, regional, class, and folk cultures diminished proportionately to the increasing hegemony of the dominant national trends, or were turned into commercially standardized products. Wartime patriotism and the choking off of immigration further solidified the national culture. Racism knitted white citizens together in a conservative harmony of undemocratic privileges. The most popular radio program of the 1920s (perhaps of all time) was "Amos 'n Andy," a humorous caricature of racially degrading stereotypes.

Technological achievements and production efficiencies that were made possible by the intellectual and scientific labor of engineers and technicians offered real and practical benefits to everyone. From mass-produced innovations like the bicycle and radio, indoor plumbing, and electrical appliances that entered everyday life, to big singular projects like the successful opening of the Panama Canal by the United States in 1913 (where France had failed earlier at a cost of 25,000 workers' lives), national life seemed to be changing for the better. For the United States, the victorious experience of World War I was relatively brief (1917–18) and military losses relatively minimal, at just over 50,000 dead. Compared to any of the other powers, which lost millions of young men, the cost of war to the United States was by far the least. The French army was mutinous by 1918, the British severely demoralized. In Russia, the czar's huge military losses and economic disorder brought down his family's Romanov dynasty, and helped to install the first communist government in the world. Germany's trauma fueled the rise of Hitler.

The productivity of the economy of the United States began to appear as an un-limited cornucopia in the 1920s. Advertising stimulated otherwise nonexistent needs for mass production technology to satisfy. Or, as several social scientists have argued, it was the other way around: mass production created the need for advertising to help promote the sale and consumption of abundant goods. Giant department stores flourished in cathedral-like splendor in every great city. The *Sears Catalogue* served the imaginations and consumer appetites of small town and rural shoppers. It had other practical uses as well. Henry Ford, an autocratic tyrant to his workers, and an ardent supporter of the emerging fascist movements in Italy and Germany, became one of the most popular postwar heroes in the country. His moving assembly lines were turning out cars so fast and at such low prices, they came within the reach of millions of workers. Skyscraper architecture, like the medieval towers they exceeded, enthralled everyone who saw them. External events far beyond the control of work-ers or their organizations began to shape their thinking, their culture, and their very existence.

The old battleground between labor and capital began to shift. Once there had been a contentious social and political mix, with neither side completely or permanently in charge of the culture itself. Cultural bonds formed in the workplace, among work-ers in company towns, and in the working-class or ethnically solid neighborhoods of cities were giving way to, or absorbing, a public and commercial culture that cel-ebrated and reinforced a business outlook on everything. Advertising and the mass communication of the commercial press were augmented by radio and film images. Babe Ruth reportedly said that he deserved a higher salary than Calvin Coolidge in 1927 because he had had a better year than the president. Most workers probably agreed. The marketplace for labor in the business economy was each against all.

The AFL played a leading role in recognizing the historic power of capital, and capitulating to it for the respectability and place at the table Gompers hoped to gain for both labor and himself. Gompers lived long enough (d. 1924) to see his services scorned when, in the postwar years, they were no longer needed. Of course, no one can see the future as well as one can see the past. The troubling question that must be raised about Gompers is, was he right or wrong to capitulate so completely to capital when the struggle for economic democracy and social justice was still worthwhile? He, and the other craft union leaders, put themselves and their members first. Social issues like the battles for racial justice and women's rights were not on the craft union leaders' agenda, except insofar as they opposed the independent and democratic rad-icalism that brought them forward from other workers.

American Democracy on the Eve of War

Following the election of 1912, no single master plan or grand conspiracy guided the thinking of all of capital or all of labor. Nor did the governments of any of the Great Powers (the nations with global empires) have a singular plan or scheme for the future, except to advance their national interests in the world. It was in the thousands of large and small day-to-day decisions that the events of war, economic boom and bust, were played out. Some of the players held more and better cards than their rivals, and some made judgments that brought them great advantages, often unknowingly.

The success of the United States was partly due to its having the most flexibility and the least rigid restraints among nations on its responses to any of the circumstances that arose. The limited democratic practices of the United States were ahead of most of the nation's rivals, but criticized by many Europeans as slow and awkward. Too much contentiousness, critics argued, accompanied decision making in the United States, and the political inclusion of the propertyless was disruptive and not conducive to bringing the nation into war. Europeans argued that a democratic nation could never become a great world power. Workers, it was believed, would never vote themselves into a great war where they would bear the heaviest burden of the fighting and enjoy the least benefit of the outcome. The critics and skeptics were wrong.

The enormous productive capacities of the nation and its delayed entry finally allowed the United States to tip the balance and decisively end the war. The real problem for the United States, prior to its entry, was that this terrible war wouldn't end itself, and its stalemated continuation, like a long strike in a vital industry, was bringing harm to all, politically and economically. To the progressive way of thinking, this kind of waste was not acceptable. To President Wilson, that which was not conducive to an orderly expansion of capitalist objectives was also morally repugnant, whether in Mexico, Central America, Europe, or at home.

Woodrow Wilson, the AFL's Man in Office

Woodrow Wilson was elected as a progressive Democrat with the support of Samuel Gompers and the AFL, the single largest workers' organization in the country. Gompers and the AFL had moved beyond earlier "unionism, pure and simple," and "voluntarism" concepts in the wake of the legal defeats suffered by labor on boycotts, injunctions, and yellow dog contracts (see chapter 5). The Socialist Party of Eugene Debs was the largest independent working-class political organization at the time, and seemed to be at the beginning of a serious challenge to the established parties. War, and plans for war, were not any part of the election campaign in 1912, though the United States and all of the other Great Powers were engaged in a massive naval arms race, and all of those Powers had prepared elaborate war plans. Wilson's opponents (Taft, Roosevelt, and Debs) all claimed progressive credentials similar to his. All expressed a willingness to make use of government as the agency of power to correct or adjust the social problems and economic abuses of the industrial nation. None spoke of war.

The IWW, at the crest of its influence in 1912, officially stayed out of the election just as they refused to make binding written contracts with employers. Few Wobs were registered voters anyway. Government itself, the Wobblies claimed, was an instrument of social control on behalf of property owners. No simple electoral victory would allow for the kind of historic transfer of wealth and power they had in mind. The IWW expected little from a Wilson presidency. Wilson's victory meant that, politically, he owed something to Gompers, could not casually disregard the votes that went to his opponents, and owed nothing to the IWW. In the war that was coming, Gompers would be rewarded for his loyalty, Eugene Debs imprisoned for his opposition, and the IWW crushed.

As soon as he took office in March 1913, President Wilson created the Department of Labor as a cabinet-level post. Wilson appointed Congressman William B. Wilson of Pennsylvania as the nation's first secretary of labor. William was not related to Woodrow, but he was a Democrat and chairman of the House Labor Committee. W. B. Wilson served as the United Mine Workers' secretary-treasurer from 1900 to 1908, and had gone to jail once for defiance of an injunction. President Wilson gave in to pressure against the appointment of Louis D. Brandeis as attorney general or as secretary of commerce. Brandeis was known as "the people's lawyer" for his legal efforts on behalf of workers, and was a favorite of many Progressives and moderate labor advocates, including President Wilson. But, Brandeis was a Jew, and the country wasn't ready for that barrier to be broken yet. He broke another barrier instead when he was appointed to the Supreme Court in 1916.

President Wilson was a disappointment to women who sought the vote, and to black and white civil rights advocates too. Though personally in favor of women's suffrage, Wilson, in office, said the matter of the vote was best left to the states. Racial segregation of federal employment was extended throughout the federal bureaucracy by the new administration. Black workers were dismissed, downgraded, and excluded from areas of employment they formerly held, a clear betrayal by Wilson of W.E.B. DuBois and other NAACP leaders who had endorsed his election. Southern Democrats from states that barred black people from voting held positions of leadership in Congress that they had not enjoyed since before the Civil War. Wilson needed the political loyalty and shared the prejudices of his southern allies. To the dismay of Booker T. Washington, whose electoral support he had also courted, President Wilson publicly defended the idea of white supremacy and the practice of racial segregation. The two Wilsons did finally accommodate the AFL, for a time, and a serious inroad against socialist claims on the loyalties of industrial workers was attempted.

Progressive Labor Reform: The Seamen's Act

One of the leftover pieces of unfinished progressive legislation from the administration of President William H. Taft was the Seamen's Act. This measure was aimed at curbing the crude and outdated abuses suffered by crew members of merchant vessels. The bill set minimum standards for maritime safety and ended bondage-like contracts for seamen. Andrew Furuseth, the president of the Seamen's Union, had been fighting for protective legislation for years, and after finding a sponsor for it, saw it pass through both Houses of Congress in 1912. Taft killed it with a pocket veto. After some delays due to questions raised about the measure's conflict with international treaties, it was finally signed into law by President Wilson in 1915.

The Clayton Act

The Clayton Anti-Trust Act of 1914 was intended to strengthen the federal government's ability to take action against monopolies and correct the deficiencies of the Sherman Act. All of labor wanted the law to exclude unions from antitrust prosecution. The Clayton Act was hailed (prematurely, as it turned out) by Gompers as labor's Magna Carta because it appeared to limit the use of injunctions against unions. However, it did not make unions totally exempt from the law, the objective originally sought by the AFL. The phrase from the new legislation that Gompers hailed in the *American Federationist*, "The labor of human beings is not a commodity or article of commerce," was tacked on to the bill, but did nothing to protect labor from the law. The Clayton Act's total worthlessness to labor was made clear by the Supreme Court in two cases: *Duplex Printing v. Deering* in 1921, and, conclusively, in the *Bedford Cut Stone* case in 1927.

Child Labor

The Keating-Owen Child Labor Act of 1916 was hailed by some observers as the key piece of progressive legislation of the Wilson years. Most industrial states had imposed legal controls on the use of child labor, but many states, especially in the South, had no such restrictions. The National Association of Manufacturers said it opposed the idea, as did almost all its critics, not because they favored the exploitation of children in mines, mills, and factories, but because the new law increased the power of the federal government over the discretion of the states. It was unconstitutional, they claimed, because it enlarged the police power of the federal government, a power properly given to the states by the U.S. Constitution. In 1918 the Supreme Court agreed with the critics when it overruled the Child Labor Law. The Court held that the law was not a matter of commerce, over which federal power might be constitutionally exercised, but about labor, over which the states were solely responsible.

Workman's Compensation

Congress passed and Wilson signed the Kern-McGillicuddy Act in 1916 to provide compensation for federal employees injured or disabled on the job. This law was modeled after those that had been put into practice by several industrial states and represented a catching up by the federal government, not a completely new initiative on behalf of workers. Wilson, of course, accepted credit for this positive step for labor.

The Adamson Act

To prevent a national railroad strike set by the four railroad brotherhoods for September 4, 1916, Wilson hurried the Adamson Act through Congress. The United States Board of Mediation, a public body set up to carry on the efforts of the National Civic Federation, had failed to bring the disputing parties to an agreement. The union would not give up its demand for an eight-hour day with no reduction in wages, and time-and-a-half for overtime. Wilson's original compromise proposal included the eight-hour day, but took out punitive overtime conditions. The company mangers rejected Wilson's plan. A strike vote of 400,000 railroad workers passed overwhelmingly with 94 percent in favor in August. Wilson called 15,000 federal troops from the Mexican border to be ready in the event of a strike and urged Congress to act quickly. The bill that Wilson signed on September 2 set an eight-hour day for railroad workers with no pay loss, and came from the House Interstate Commerce Committee. The new law also established a commission to study the problem of preventing further conflict that might bring harm to business or national security. War clouds were on the horizon. The railroad companies refused to accept the law, and tested its constitutionality in the Supreme Court. A 5–4 decision by the Court upheld the Adamson Act on March, 17, 1917, just a few weeks prior to the nation's entry into World War I.

The Commission on Industrial Relations, 1912–1915

To investigate the dangers posed by violent clashes between industrial workers and their employers and the rising credibility of Socialists and other radicals, or, as its progressive advocates said, to "solve the problems of democracy in its industrial relationships," Congress established the United States Commission on Industrial Relations (USCIR) in 1912. President Taft nominated the original members, and included three union officials among the first nine commissioners, with three more to come from business, and three from the public. Taft could not get his nominees approved, even with the help of Gompers and the antilabor National Association of Manufacturers lobbying together for them. Gompers and the NAM became bedfellows because both were afraid that President Wilson would be guided by Louis D. Brandeis and appoint a Wobbly or Socialist to the commission. Politics confounded their plans as the Taft nominees were blocked by congressional Democrats who wanted to name their own business and public commissioners. This left the appointment process to Wilson, who named Frank P. Walsh, a labor lawyer from Kansas City, as chairman. Wilson kept the three labor nominees, and filled the other positions with people known as strong Progressives and good Democratic Party stalwarts. The prominent labor economist and historian from the University of Wisconsin, John R. Commons, joined the well-known Democratic Party fund-raiser, Florence ("Daisy") Harriman, and Walsh to represent the public.

The USCIR, led (or driven) by Walsh's independent style and determination, carried out a wide ranging and comprehensive investigation from the fall 1913 to spring 1915. Every industrial hot spot drew the attention of the commission's hearings, from the Paterson, New Jersey silkworkers to the lumbering camps of the Pacific Northwest. Public hearings made headlines, especially when such prominent figures as John D. Rockefeller Jr. were on the stand, and rigorously questioned. Rockefeller was grilled for three days in the aftermath of the brutal outcome in the Ludlow, Colorado strike of his Colorado Fuel and Iron company (see chapter 5). His proposal to the commission, known thereafter as the Rockefeller Plan, was no surprise. He called for managerial grievance procedures to handle workplace disputes without the recognition or presence of a union. To the delight of labor advocates everywhere, Walsh treated Rockefeller as a hostile witness.

Statistical data publicized by the USCIR portrayed a nation in which wealth was narrowly controlled by a tiny minority of the population. The commissioners heard that the richest 2 percent owned 60 percent of the wealth of the nation, while almost two-thirds of the people owned but 2 percent. Squalid working and living conditions were the norm for millions of industrial and agricultural workers and their families. The hearings brought attention to oppressive work rules, arbitrary dismissals, and cruel punishments that were commonplace in the nation's mines, mills, factories, and agricultural workplaces. Though Walsh was privately a critic of racial segregation, and the investigation and public hearings were supposed to be comprehensive and all-inclusive, the USCIR studiously avoided inquiry or comment on the state of black workers in the South. By omission their degradation was accepted by the USCIR.

The USCIR concluded its work in a controversial report that focused mainly on managerial autocracy and made the goal of "industrial democracy" the key to achieving harmony in the workplace and stability in the society. The commission was divided three ways among the members. The three business representatives took a predictable course in a written dissent that favored moderation and enlightened management, reasonableness on the part of workers and their unions, and the open shop. Walsh, joined by the three labor votes, called for the legal protection of the right of workers to form unions of their own choosing. This was the dramatic highlight, the first time any federally funded agency of the government ever advocated such a step. The remaining public representatives disagreed with the Walsh-led conclusion and issued their own statements. Commons called for a larger role for government in the mediation of industrial disputes. Harriman echoed the opinion of business and conservative critics when she called the report "incendiary and revolutionary" (Harriman, 1923, p. 175).

Labor cheered. The May 1915 report momentarily united Gompers of the AFL, Haywood of the IWW, and Debs of the Socialist Party. In the hearings Haywood expressed doubt that any legislation would ever be allowed to pass that might alter the class-dominated economy, but he joined the other labor leaders in upholding the absolute right of workers to unionize without employer interference. Gompers, still professing "voluntarism," also had some reservations, and never accepted all of Walsh's recommendations.

The Walsh recommendations included an array of social proposals for workers and their families that most labor leaders and the labor press enthusiastically favored. Federal tax policy should redistribute wealth more equitably, unemployment protection and compensation should be provided to workers, and retirement pensions should be guaranteed by law. Walsh urged Democrats to protect workers in their struggle to "control their share in industry through the power of collective bargaining," and condemned "militarism, Taylorism and the concentration of wealth" (McCartin, 1997, p. 35).

Republicans used Walsh as a campaign foil to attack the Wilson administration. Wilson accepted the report without comment. He took no public stand on its contents, but, despite a massive strike upsurge and ultimately tepid labor legislation in his first term of office, scored a tremendous public relations victory among workers and Progressives everywhere. Wilson wasn't hunting for votes among Republican businessmen. Though little came from it in the short term, the conclusions of the USCIR were the foundation for the legislation of the New Deal a generation later (see chapter 7). The report of the USCIR might not be a bad place to start as an international program for labor in the twenty-first century.

The Federal Conciliation Service

One concrete labor agency to emerge in the first year of the Wilson presidency was the Federal Conciliation Service, established in 1913 to mediate labor-management disputes. The new agency was very similar to the private National Civic Federation, but enjoyed greater credibility as a result of its public stature. The service became involved in 1,780 cases from 1915 to 1919, a tremendous increase in comparison to the NCF, which only heard 274 cases during its most active years, 1902–5.

The resolution of industrial conflict through mediation and arbitration has often been resisted by both sides, since both must be willing to accept the authority of the arbitrator or mediator for the process to work. Such conflict resolution takes some power away from labor and management and gives it to a supposedly neutral or external third party. Conflicts resolved this way usually bring little glory to either labor or management. On the other hand, outside intervention frees labor leaders and managers from appearing to their constituents as too conciliatory when there are serious conflicts. Contract grievance procedures that involve a third party accomplish a similar result. Mediation is the voluntary acceptance of a compromise or negotiated settlement as offered by the mediator. Arbitration is the making of a settlement by the third party, the arbitrator, and may be voluntary or binding, depending on the circumstances or contract language.

Labor Anger and Action

Part of the reason for seeking more conciliatory intervention was the increase in labor-management disputes. Strike activity and labor militancy reached a new high in the nation's history in 1916–17. The war in Europe increased demand for goods made or grown in the United States and choked off immigration of new workers into the United States. Prices were rising and unemployment was falling off to almost nothing. Worker activism went beyond the bounds of the AFL, or the Socialist Party and IWW, during this brief period. Riots in New York and Philadelphia over high food prices took place in March and April 1917. Communities and block organizations, or sometimes single tenement building residents, organized rent strikes against landlords.

Nontraditional allies and advocates for labor appeared. The National Association for the Advancement of Colored People began its determined struggle for full citizenship rights for everyone, regardless of race. It was not going to be easy, but the color bar was under serious legal attack that would not let up. The *Messenger,* a magazine described by its editor, A. Philip Randolph, as the only black journal of "scientific radicalism" in the world, reached a circulation of over 40,000 in the United States by World War I. Women were on the way to winning the right to vote, and began to make inroads into professions and occupations in the world of work that had previously excluded them. Wartime demand for goods opened up new jobs for hundreds of thousands of women and black workers, and this heightened the desire for full equality. Women workers were at the forefront of prewar labor struggles, especially the movement for the eight-hour day, and almost every large city now had a prominent Women's Trade Union League. Religious reformers from every major faith were turning their sentiments to the cause of labor. Settlement house workers in large cities took up the cause of labor. The remarkable Helen Keller overcame more than her physical disabilities when she became a socialist critic of the heartless exploitation of labor by capital. The poet, Carl Sandburg, celebrated the social idealism of the Walsh Commission Report. Harvard-educated journalist Jack Reed covered the rising of the working class wherever he found it; in the Mexican Revolution 1911–13, the United States in 1912–17, and the Russian Revolution covered in his *Ten Days That Shook The World* (1919).

The Issues

Of the nearly 4,000 strikes and lockouts in 1916, and the more than 4,300 in 1917, more of them than ever before were about the workplace; fewer were based solely on wage demands. Anger at Taylorism, or "scientific management," turned out work- ers in nearly all of the metal working trades where the introduction of new machin- ery was drastically taking autonomy away from skilled workers. Engineering design and technological innovations set quality standards, determined the pace of work, and established production quotas. Battles over union rights, union recognition, ar- bitrary firings, and the authority of management over workplace rules and regula- tions became more commonplace. In their songs and poetry workers condemned the monotony, repetitiousness, and gloom of mass production industries.

No consideration was given by managers to worker comfort, safety, or health. Deaf- ening noise, choking dust and lint, contamination from poisonous chemicals, and waste products were everywhere. The death toll from workplace hazards was highest in mining and railroad employment in these years, but of little concern to employ- ers. Altogether, tens of thousands of workers died every year in the United States in what employers continued to call "accidents," a significant number of which were preventable, but where prevention would add cost to the production process. Mining and railroad work were among the most dangerous, with 4,334 workers killed on rail lines and 3,242 dead in mining in 1907 alone. No industrial workplace was free of hazards. Life expectancy rates for industrial workers were actually falling during the years 1902–17, at the same time as public and consumer health and safety im- provements were adding longevity to other social groups. Why was the workplace so dangerous, so lethal?

Once again, it was the sharp contrasts between what might be possible and what was real that contributed to the anger of workers. The brutish hazards of industrial life and labor began to appear in stark contrast to the urbanizing world that offered new comforts and amenities to workers, though at a price. Advertising emphasized the convenience and ease that new appliances brought into the home. Why was the workplace still so brutal? Progressive reformers brought new attention to public san- itation issues, personal hygiene, drug and alcohol abuse. Why was the workplace so foul?

The civil and physical differences between the world of the office and the factory separated white-collar "employees" from their industrial counterparts. Soft hands and clean clothing were admired and resented by men and women with calluses and work-stained garments. Why was the workplace so coarse? Educational and language differences added to the contrasts seen and felt by workers. Unions have never really succeeded in bridging the social and cultural gap between these workers, even when they have organized both groups. Why were some workers so lucky? Why did some workers have those advantages?

The Progressive era was reviving the historic ideals of democracy itself, and these too were in marked contrast to the absence of any rights in the workplace. Politi- cal bossism and corruption were under attack by reformers across the country. Sen- ators were to be elected directly, according to the Seventeenth Amendment to the Constitution (1913). States, bowing to the efforts of a new generation of women's rights advocates that included more working-class activists, were granting the right to vote to women. Rose Schneiderman of the ILGWU was also vice president of the Women's Trade Union Unity League and one of these new women's rights advocates. The Nineteenth Amendment to the Constitution finally secured the right of citizenship to women just in time for the national election in 1920. The widespread introduction of the referendum and recall gave ordinary citizens direct participation in political decision making. None of these democratic notions had made progress in the industrial workplace. Women were subject to physical and sexual abuse by managers and employers (and sometimes other workers) with almost no recourse to action or protection, except for the scorn and possible scandal that might result from disclosure. Embarrassment and threats of dismissal, or worse, directed at the victim protected assailants. Workers were fired, promoted, or reassigned at the whim of managers and supervisors. The workplace was becoming the last bastion of tyranny and absolute power in a nation about to go to war, as Wilson said, "to make the world safe for democracy." It is no wonder that so many workers were angry and on strike. What is remarkable is how many so willingly went off to fight in that war.

The War at Home

The nation was quite uneasy about entry into the Great War. All of the labor organizations and socialist groups were originally against intervention. So was most of the population. Secretary of State William Jennings Bryan was adamantly against it, and resigned from office when the decision to enter it was made. Wilson campaigned for votes in 1916 with the popular slogan, "He kept us out of war." Irish and German American organizations were actively opposed to any form of U.S. support for Great Britain. Many people could not understand the need for entering a conflict so far away. Neutrality rights meant little to most citizens. Wilson's idealized explanations seemed vague. The nation was under no imminent danger of attack. Some critics blamed bankers and munitions makers for the war since they seemed the only ones to profit from it. Others, like Professor Scott Nearing of the University of Pennsylvania, Eugene Debs, and most Socialists, agreed with the English economist John Hobson's prophetic book, *Imperialism* (1902), that the war was a conflict over the division of the colonial world, a battle to control the earth's finite resources, markets, and labor sources among the imperialist powers. Workers, those critics said, would bear the brunt of the fighting and, regardless of the outcome, enjoy none of the fruits of victory. Nonetheless, the nation declared war on April 7, 1917, and, as in every former war, called on its labor force for extraordinary service at home and on the front lines. Scott Nearing at Penn, along with a pacifist professor at the University of Virginia, and three University of Nebraska war critics were all fired. The great historian, Charles Beard, though he favored the war, resigned from Columbia University in 1917 in protest over the firing of three of its faculty war critics. Teachers in the nation's schools were fired for any expression of criticism of the war. Most kept their opinions to themselves.

Conscientious objectors (COs), those who refused military service because of their ideological or religious beliefs, were treated more severely in the United States than in other countries at war. In the United States, seventeen COs were sentenced to death, 142 to life terms, and 345 to average prison terms of over sixteen years. At the end of the war most of the severe sentences were commuted (Sexton, 1991, p. 129). Debs, in spite of illness, age, and a lengthy nationwide amnesty movement on his behalf, was not released from federal prison until Christmas Day, 1921.

The big challenge for industry and government was how to bring the working class in line with the war program. The strike wave showed no sign of letting up. It actually reached a record high during the first six months of the war, from April 6 to October 5, 1917. During those six months 6,285,519 workdays were lost to strikes, according to the National Industrial Conference Board. Business and government leaders faced an enemy abroad with Imperial Germany and its allies, and at home in the form of a truculent and rebellious working class. An effective armed force of four million soldiers and sailors had to be raised, provisioned, trained, and transported to the battlefront. Obedience, if not outright support from labor, was essential. Opposition to the military and industrial goals of capital would have to be overcome or crushed.

Samuel Gompers and the AFL rallied around the flag. The AFL leader reversed his position on the war in the fall of 1916, just in time to be named by President Wilson as a civilian advisor to the newly formed Council of National Defense (CND). Gompers was ready to help his country prepare for war on both fronts. He was eager to assist the government in the suppression of the Socialist Party and the outright destruction of the IWW, his two main rivals for the leadership of labor. The CND was only the first of many such government agencies on which Gompers served.

Unlike their European counterparts who quickly rallied behind nationalist leaders, the industrial working class in the United States had little interest in the Great War. So many were recent immigrants, they had not yet developed emotional loyalties to their new nation. Most of the Socialist Party and the entire IWW opposed the war, or worse, from the perspective of business, proposed turning it into a class war. West Coast radical labor leaders Tom Mooney and Warren Billings were convicted of murder for a bombing attack on a business-sponsored pro-war Preparedness Parade in San Francisco in July 1916 that left eight dead and forty injured. The Mooney–Billings trial lacked any semblance of due process, and was a precursor to the disregard of the constitutional rights of independent labor organizations and war critics that began less than a year later. Mooney was finally released from prison in 1939.

When the question of whatever happened to labor militancy and socialism in the United States is asked, the beginning of the answer can be found in the entry of the nation into the Great War. With the declaration of war, President Wilson made Gompers the official spokesman for all of labor, and the two set out to break or destroy opposition to the goals of capital at home and abroad.

It wasn't only the direct actions of Wilson or Gompers that crushed industrial labor activism and the labor left in World War I. Their leadership provided the context and the cover for what actually happened. Broad federal policy, embodied in wartime leg-islation, government agencies, directives, and economic activity set the tone for state, local, and private actions, including vigilante mob attacks and unpunished lynchings. The Espionage Act that Wilson quickly signed in June 1917, for example, made it a crime to hinder the national war effort by criticizing it. Every antiwar publication, magazine, or newspaper was banned or suspended from the use of the U.S. Postal Service. The postmaster general withdrew second-class mailing privileges for anti-war labor and socialist organizations. Some were prohibited from sending or receiv-ing first-class mail even though nothing in the law granted the postmaster general that right. No one stopped him either. Taking their cue from the federal government, vigilante mobs, sometimes calling themselves citizens' committees, and organized by local business-sponsored groups, destroyed local labor or socialist newspaper offices and presses. By the end of the year the only labor or left press still in existence was pro-war. Without a media voice, the seventy-four socialist mayors elected in 1911 were cut, unsurprisingly, to eighteen in 1917. Small town and rural socialism in the United States was virtually wiped out when approximately 1,500 offices of such groups were destroyed by vigilante mobs. No independent working-class organizations emerged to take the place of the Socialists.

In Jerome, Arizona, the local copper mining companies formed a special vigilante posse, which called itself the Jerome Loyalty League, to break a miners' strike in July 1917. Their success and support from the Arizona governor inspired a more massive and concerted arrest of over 1,200 striking miners and their supporters in the town of Bisbee, Arizona. The Bisbee miners, on strike since June 28, were rounded up by a sheriff who had "deputized" a vigilante army of 2,000 for the task. The workers, and every local labor advocate, IWW member, and sympathizer (including several local businessmen), were packed into railroad cattle cars with minimal provisions and stranded in the midst of the New Mexico desert. The "deportees" gained refuge at a nearby U.S. military base in Columbus, New Mexico, where they were detained until September.

A few days after the Bisbee "deportations," mine operators in Butte, Montana, be-gan planning a union busting program of their own. The well-known IWW organizer and war critic, Frank Little, was made the target of a business-sponsored vigilante attack that left his tortured and mutilated body hanging from a railroad trestle bridge in the middle of the night of August 1, 1917. No action was taken by state or local authorities to capture his murderers. In spite of demands for federal intervention by labor advocates, none was undertaken since, opponents argued, no federal statute had been violated. Once again property rights, which frequently provoked a federal intervention when challenged by labor, exceeded labor rights when violated by prop-erty owners. Most of the press around the country cheered the murderous vigilante action. So did many elected officials.

The strike wave continued, nonetheless, at record levels. Gompers, the federal gov-ernment, and the leaders of the United Mineworkers (AFL) worked diligently to reach an acceptable wartime accord that would reduce or eliminate strikes. The UMW

model, known as the Washington Agreement of October 1917, guaranteed coal production increases, set high wage rates (for the time), and granted union protection.
Severe penalties could be imposed on wildcat or unauthorized strike actions during
the wartime life of the agreement. The coal operators got what they wanted: stability,
production, and high profits. So did the union: membership doubled to over half a
million by the end of the war. John L. Lewis, the budding leader of the UMW, told
the 1918 convention, "In no two year period of our organization has equal progress
been accomplished" (quoted in Zeiger, 1999, p. 26). The same pattern was followed in
nonunion wartime industries and crafts. Employee Representation Plans (ERPs), or
company-sponsored worker organizations (known simply as company unions), were
permitted by all of the wartime agencies and labor boards, but real union growth
was strong throughout the war. Only the workers suffered. Inflation sharply cut into
wages, especially in the company towns where most miners lived, and where there
was no real retail competition to the company-owned stores. Prices went up but wages
stayed flat, or rose at a lower rate. The no-strike feature allowed mining companies to
get away with lax health and safety measures without reprisals. Even the Armistice
that ended the fighting in November 1918 was not considered cause to make necessary wage adjustments, since, technically, the war wasn't officially over and the
Washington Agreement was kept in place for another inflationary year.

The Expansion of the Labor Force

The war brought forth a similar mixture of union gains, high profits for business,
and plenty of work and inflationary wage losses for labor throughout the country.
Households made up for the flat wages by sending more members into a larger labor
force, and by working longer hours, especially in wartime industries. Five hundred
thousand black workers and as many women entered areas of employment formerly
closed off to them, though typically at the bottom end of the scale or in entry-level
positions. Black workers were subjected to abuse and discrimination at work. They
were given the least desirable jobs and restricted from upward mobility by Jim Crow
factory codes. Black workers suffered white racist taunts and were frequent victims
of assaults in their attempt to find housing in northern cities. In several cities white
mobs attacked black people or stormed into their communities, and when the assailed resisted or fought back, these incidents were called "race riots" by the press.
The worst of these wartime conflicts took the lives of thirty-nine black people, eight
whites, and two policemen in East St. Louis, Illinois, in July 1917. The AFL was little
help to black workers. At its 1917 convention the AFL, according to W.E.B. Du Bois,
"grudgingly, unwillingly, and almost insultingly," voted in favor of the unionization
of black workers, but said nothing critical about the racial discrimination that was
common everywhere in the organization and the nation (quoted in Green, 1980, p. 98).
    The Department of Labor Women's Bureau issued a bulletin (no. 12) entitled *The
New Position of Women in American Labor* in 1920. The government reported that

women were at work in a vast array of jobs previously deemed suitable only for men. Women worked in blast furnaces, in copper and brass smelters, in oil refineries, in making steel, chemicals, explosives, machine tools, electrical apparatus, railway, automobile, and airplane parts. Thousands of women left farms and households where they were not counted as part of the labor force to enter jobs in textile manufacturing, laundries, nursing, and offices. Women served in government agencies connected with the war effort, as, for example, the Women's Committee of the Council for National Defense. It was their wartime service that ultimately won women the right to vote. Between 1915 and 1918, fifty-six of the men who had first voted against the women's suffrage amendment changed their vote and enabled the measure to gain the two-thirds majority it needed to pass in the House of Representatives.

Some industries, like shipbuilding, soared under wartime orders. The Emergency Fleet Corporation, for example, increased its payroll from 88,000 to 385,000 in one year. Strikes in shipbuilding followed almost proportionately, from a total of 26 in 1916, to 101 in 1917, to 138 in 1918 (Jacoby, 1985, p. 143). The same kind of increased labor activism carried into almost every industry. Munitions workers struck in Bridgeport, Connecticut, the nation's most vital production facility, and against the orders of their own national union and directives from the National War Labor Board. The government reaction was to seek to accommodate patriotic unions and break down militancy and strike activity. Instead of curbing the legal abuses of the Espionage Act, the federal government increased its punitive qualities with a stronger Sedition Act, signed into law by President Wilson in early 1918.

Censorship and Repression

Any form of criticism of the government or of the war, or any advocacy of cutting war effort or production was made illegal. This repressive measure struck especially at workers in industry where immigrant, black, and female labor was most concentrated and AFL organization least present. The organizations to which these workers turned, and which did not turn them away, were least likely to favor the war or any strike moratorium because of the war. Recent arrivals to the nation, women, and black workers gained the least and gave the most to the wartime prosperity. The IWW and the Socialist Party, which sought to represent some of these workers, were turned into outlaws by statute. So were strikes in most industries. State governments enacted their own, even more severe laws against labor militants, strikes, and war critics. Over 2,000 indictments were brought against labor union leaders and worker advocates during the war, and more than 1,000 convictions resulted, including the sentencing of sixty-four-year-old Eugene Debs to a ten-year prison term. Debs's crime was a speech in Canton, Ohio, that criticized businessmen for opportunistically using patriotism as a cover for their real desire to silence labor critics. Those who still identified themselves as IWW were forced underground in 1918. Hundreds of vigilante attacks, beatings, and lynchings continued with tacit government sanction. Some of the virulence of these attacks came from the approval and, in many cases, the participation of established local authorities, including police and business leaders.

A privately funded volunteer group, known as the American Protective League (APL), enjoyed the assistance of the Justice Department and built "a national spy network" of about 350,000 members (Sexton, 1991, p.128). The Federal Bureau of Investigation (FBI), founded a few years later, picked up where the APL left off. The main work of the APL was to conduct secret investigations of the loyalty of soldiers, government employees, and people who applied for passports. APL activities included wiretapping, burglary, opening mail, and acting as provocateurs to disrupt "unpatriotic" group meetings and organizations. Its volunteers passed the information they gathered to police agencies. With the information from APL sources, police made raids and large-scale arrests. During the course of about a year approximately 400,000 people were detained and questioned on suspicion based on the work of the APL and local police. In three days in Chicago, 150,000 people were questioned, 16,000 arrested. Labor activists, political radicals, the IWW, and black workers were especially targeted.

The War, Craft Unions, and the AFL

Gompers and conservative union leaders enjoyed membership on various government- and business-sponsored labor and industrial boards and commissions throughout the war. Their union membership was growing, and they imagined that a new age of industrial relations was dawning. Never known for understatement, Gompers called the war the "most wonderful crusade ever entered upon in the whole history of the world" (quoted in Larson, 1975, p. 25). The sixteen separate railroad brotherhoods, under government administration, prospered as well during the war. Their leaders enjoyed big salaries and even bigger opportunities for institutional growth. They invested union funds in banks, real estate, and other ventures. Gompers and the other patriotic union leaders were looking forward to the postwar world with the expectation that a new age of labor-management cooperation would continue to unfold. Union recognition and legitimacy also gave these craft leaders the social approval and respect they believed they deserved.

Another token of appreciation that Gompers won from his wartime loyalty and economic conservatism was a role in the expansion of his kind of business unionism. Wherever the United States extended its power, particularly in the Philippine Islands and Puerto Rico, Gompers and the AFL were present. The AFL staff worked both openly and secretly with government agencies to block the formation of independent or socialist unions in places that were "wards" (really colonies or economic dependencies) of the United States. Unions were growing up throughout the Americas too, and Gompers, secretly aided by government funds, was working to set up his brand of conservative unionism throughout the hemisphere (Buhle, 1999, pp. 77–78). Here too Gompers joined businessmen and government leaders in a common hostility to socialism and labor radicalism that, to all of them, justified illegal and undemocratic measures.

Class Warfare, at Home and Abroad

The war at home continued for almost five years after the end of fighting in Europe in November 1918. The secretive agencies founded in wartime continued, or took on new and permanent structures. The attorney general, A. Mitchell Palmer, set up an antired squad after the Bolshevik Revolution and hired a youthful J. Edgar Hoover to head the team. Every militant or independent union, socialist, or working-class radical organization came under their surveillance, manipulation, or attack. Labor organizations of all kinds, including—much to his chagrin and surprise, Gomper's AFL—were either destroyed or reduced to near impotence by 1923. Few observers, then or even now, appreciated the full historic force of organized capital and its global nature. Abroad, the United States openly joined the other Great Powers in a failed attempt to overthrow the Bolshevik Revolution in Russia during 1919–21, and in the more successful suppression of anticolonial uprisings in Africa and Asia. Mussolini's March on Rome and the Fascist Party seizure of power over Italy in 1922 were cheered and subsidized by business and government leaders in the United States as a welcome alternative to the possibility of a democratic and popular left-wing labor government. Adolf Hitler enjoyed the same kind of enthusiastic approval and financial assistance from global business leaders in the 1920s until it became obvious that his and Germany's plans were a threat to the national capital of England, France, and the United States. The revival of the KKK and its spread to northern cities was maintained until scandal broke it up in 1924. The battle at home between labor and capital reached a crescendo of intensity in the year after the fighting ended in Europe.

Labor's War

Not all workers were as compliant or as well-paid as Gompers and his craft unionists during World War I. No completely accurate score card exists to tell of the wins and losses for labor in its strikes and job actions in the period of prewar and wartime struggle. Most strikes before the end of the war were to extend job rights and to gain wage, hour, and other material benefits. Skilled workers fared best, though the advances in Taylorism continued to erode their workplace control. The idea of industrial democracy, or of contracts with due process protection against arbitrary firings, seniority, and other rights, was temporarily extended. Company unions flourished. Businessmen hated the idea of relinquishing any control. Property rights, they believed, entitled them to the control of all decision making within their domains, a carryover from the feudal and landlord eras to the age of business and industry. The idea of a union shop or closed shop was bitterly resisted, and made little progress for labor in the war. Gompers was angrily attacked for his wartime acceptance of the open shop by such otherwise conservative AFL leaders as William L. Hutcheson of the Carpenters Union.

The Great Strike Wave of 1919–1920

Real income for workers actually fell as prices nearly doubled between 1915 and 1919. Flat or slowly rising wages against fast-rising prices were only partly made up by workers through the availability of abundant overtime or second jobs. Women and black workers previously excluded from industrial work added new income to their households and experienced a generally higher standard of living than before the war. Postwar feminism and a flowering of black literary and artistic expression in several northern cities are only two immediate consequences of that material gain. More work and more workers meant more pay, but the crunch of inflation and the sacrifices of wartime led to the explosive labor rebellion of 1919. That rebellion was also a consequence of the unmet desires of the prewar and wartime eras combined with a worldwide uprising of exploited workers and oppressed colonials.

Rebellious anger was rising against the owners of property, their managers, and governments everywhere at the end of World War I. The collapse of the Russian Empire brought a revolutionary socialist government to power in what was to be called for seventy years the Union of Soviet Socialist Republics, or, simply, the Soviet Union. The Irish Republic was proclaimed in an uprising in 1919. Germany, Italy, and Hungary seemed on, or over, the brink of socialist revolutions. In India, Africa, the Middle East, and China, nationalist movements were mobilizing against European colonial domination. Massive strikes and revolutionary movements of industrial and agricultural workers were underway in every major nation and throughout the colonial world.

In the United States there was no revolutionary uprising in 1919, but the strike wave was enormous. This outbreak took place in spite of the near destruction of the IWW and the weakness of the Socialist Party, with Debs in prison and most of the radical labor leadership broken or reeling from wartime repression. Nonetheless, every major industry was struck in 1919–20, most notably steel, coal, textiles, telephones, construction, metalwork, meatpacking, and shipbuilding. Freight handlers in New Orleans struck in 1920 with the support of the biracial longshoremen and screwmen of the Dock and Cotton Council. During the week of July 4, 1919, strikes took place throughout the country to protest the continued imprisonment of Tom Mooney.

The steel strike of 1919 alone idled more than 300,000 workers, skilled and unskilled, those in and those outside the twenty-four separate AFL craft unions in the industry. Steelworkers were led by an ex-Wobbly and now a communist activist, William Z. Foster, who demanded an end to the twelve-hour day and seven-day week. (For many categories of work in steel mills, a day off was only available after working a swing shift of twenty-four hours every thirteen days.) The steel strike was finally defeated with the use of more than 30,000 black strikebreakers and a reign of terror in central Pennsylvania, the center of the industry. Public meetings were banned in Allegheny County. Police indiscriminately beat and arrested strikers, who were then held in prison indefinitely on vague charges and high bail. State police prevented public gatherings by driving people off the streets with clubs. Federal troops were sent to bolster national guard units, and Attorney General A. Mitchell Palmer, warning of the threat of "bolshevism," carried out antisubversive raids and deportations of striking noncitizens.

There was a general strike in Seattle, Washington, that was brought on by rank-and-file members as a sympathy strike on behalf of striking shipyard workers. Seattle was under the control of a General Strike Committee of the city's Central Labor Council for six days in early February 1919. Workers served up over 30,000 meals a day from twenty-one dining halls set up throughout the city. Finally, union leaders, including left-wing radicals, convinced the membership to call it off. Seattle Mayor Ole Hansen called the strike "an attempted revolution," despite the absence of any seizure of property or class violence (quoted in Brecher, 1997, p. 111). In Boston, Massachusetts, the police went on a strike, which was only broken with the intervention of national guard units sent in by Governor Calvin Coolidge. The pennant-winning Chicago White Sox threw the World Series in 1919 as a labor action in protest against team owner Charles Comisky's broken promises on pay and bonuses. The players involved accepted money from gamblers to trim their play enough to lose the series.

There were never as many men involved in the mining of coal in the United States as in 1919 when they numbered almost 800,000, about half of whom were represented by the United Mine Workers of America (UMWA). Miners were a varied mix of every national, racial, ethnic, and religious group in the nation, usually housed in homogeneous (unmixed) mining towns, though frequently in contact with one another in their grim work and as fellow unionists. Their strike that year was the first in a series of battles that stretched over the next four years and left their organization in near ruin. To gain a settlement in 1919 the federal government won a court order to force the UMWA to call off the strike. Union President John L. Lewis and his executive board complied but, as expected, the workers refused to go back into the mines. The government then made plans to bring 100,000 troops into the coal fields, placed taps on every union office phone, flooded the coal area with federal agents, brought contempt citations against eighty-four union officers, and rounded up for deportation any alien activists they could identify. Finally, a settlement was negotiated, but no real labor peace was achieved. Ferocious strikes marked by murderous violence on all sides, both union-authorized and -unauthorized wildcats, continued in the coal fields until 1923.

As in the courageous actions of Manyunk, Lowell, and Lawrence women and children, or in the massive outpouring of rage in the Great Uprisings of 1877 and 1886, or in the determined unity of black and white workers in the New Orleans Dock and Cotton Council strikes, the strike wave of 1919–20 was not the result of the work of a few militant leaders, or simply a fight for higher pay. It wasn't the product of good or bad leadership. Nor was it a revolutionary movement, though it was an expression of genuine and deep discontent. The postwar strike wave was another massive democratic expression of the anger of workers who used the only tool they had, their unified labor power, to confront their adversaries. Most business and government leaders, however, didn't agree.

Business Reacts

Newspaper editorial writers joined businessmen in accepting Mayor Hansen's view that linked the postwar strike wave to the Russian Revolution. To most businessmen, the very concept of organized labor, of the unionization of workers, had always been regarded as un-American and dangerous. Businessmen had no interest in "industrial democracy." Any obstacle put in the way of the expansion of capital, or any infringement on the absolute rights of property, had to be thrust aside or crushed, especially now that the wartime emergency had passed. Democracy itself would not be permitted to inhibit that process.

When business leaders organized the American Legion in 1919, it was for the stated purpose of combating radicalism, especially as it manifested itself in the labor goal of the closed or union shop. The American Legion was created, and incorporated by an act of Congress on September 16, 1919, as an action arm of the National Association of Manufacturers after the Russian Revolution. The NAM president, John Kirby, could not have made his position any clearer when, in 1914, three years before the communist victory, he said that the trade union movement itself was "an un-American, illegal, and infamous conspiracy" (quoted in Boyer, 1955, p. 211). Before 1919 was over, Legionnaires had helped to break a streetcar workers' strike in Denver, Colorado (August), and attacked the IWW meeting hall in Centralia, Washington (November). When they were met with armed Wobbly resistance in Centralia, Legionnaires captured, castrated, and lynched the IWW leader, Wesley Everett, a decorated World War I veteran. The patriotic vigilantes of the American Legion made no secret of their political ideals. The featured guest speaker at the American Legion Convention in San Francisco in 1923 was one of their heroes, the Italian Fascist dictator, Benito Mussolini.

The Palmer Raids

Attorney General A. Mitchell Palmer agreed with the hard-line approach, and 1920 was an election year. Palmer hoped to win the Democratic Party nomination for the presidency. Blaming radicals for the strike wave would not diminish his political support from the AFL, as it had never hurt any political aspirant in the past. An assault on labor would set Palmer apart from the wartime Democratic Party attempts to secure labor peace by promoting labor-management cooperation schemes. The threat of

communism was an old workhorse of an antilabor excuse anyway, even when no socialist or communist government existed in the world. The red menace was part of the
business and government justification for severe measures against labor in the Uprising of 1877, the Eight-Hour-Day Movement of 1886, and in hundreds of smaller, more
isolated labor conflicts with capital. In reality, the recently hatched and divided Communist Party was tiny, and, aside from some exceptional individuals like William Z.
Foster, played no significant role as an organized force in the strike wave that was underway. The two quarreling groups, the Communist Labor Party and the Communist
Party USA, with no more than a few thousand adherents altogether, were made up
of ex-Socialists and Wobblies, a handful of labor and intellectual idealists inspired by
the Bolshevik success, and government agents who, it was rumored, were the only
ones who paid their dues on time. The threat of communist influence would serve as
a convenient scapegoat. There was no dissent from the AFL.

Using the federal intervention in the steel and coal strikes as warm-ups, beginning
on the evening of January 2, 1920, Palmer, with his young assistant, J. Edgar Hoover,
launched a series of sensational raids and attacks on radical working-class organizations across the country. Palmer said he was going after "alien filth" with typically
"sly and crafty eyes." More than 10,000 suspected subversives were arrested in seventy cities as simultaneous sweeps were carried out in twenty-three states. Very few
of those arrested were ever charged with any crime, but most were held without counsel or bail in temporary prisons. In Detroit, 800 people were detained for six days in
the corridor of the federal building. Only one toilet was available, and no food was
provided until the second day. In several cities the captives were displayed in chains
marching through city streets to detention centers, or, in the case of a few hundred
not-yet-naturalized aliens, dramatically deported to the Soviet Union, whether that
was their place of origin or not. Most workers, ironically, for all of their workplace militancy, and in spite of the revolutionary fire and rhetoric of a number of their leaders,
were broadly patriotic in the United States.

State and local governments followed the lead of Palmer and the federal government. Criminal syndicalist and sedition laws were passed by states that made radical
or revolutionary speech illegal. Thirty-two states banned the flying of a red flag. New
York State made the Socialist Party illegal in 1920 by statute, and refused to allow five
Socialists their seats in the legislature, even after all five were reelected. Seventy-seven
major cities still had bans on street meetings in 1921. Labor radicalism and strikes were
portrayed as due to foreign influences, the result of an open immigration policy.

Racism Redux

Vigilante-led attacks on labor were accompanied by a revival of lynch law and violence directed against black citizens. Service in combat and industry brought about a
vast migration from the rural South to urban and industrial communities for millions
of black workers who experienced an unprotected vulnerability to attacks from white

workers. With wage and union setbacks threatening all, white workers in many cities clung to racial privileges that they believed their patriotism and citizenship granted them. The most murderous attack on a black community in the nation's history was the total destruction of the Greenwood section of the city of Tulsa, Oklahoma, in 1921 by a white mob that included units of the Oklahoma national guard. Approximately 300 black people were killed, their entire community devastated, and 10,000 people made homeless; no one was punished or criminally charged for the deed. The Ku Klux Klan's nationwide revival added antilabor, antiforeign, anti-Catholic, and anti-Semitic sentiments to its traditional racism. Many racist lynchings, said to be the result of sexual advances, were actually the result of wage disputes or conflicts over jobs.

The new Klan reached a national peak of influence in 1924, and a national membership estimated at four and a half million, before fading quickly under various charges of scandal and corruption. As if to answer both the constant appeal of Gompers for immigration restriction and the antiforeign bigotry of the Klan, new federal immigration restriction acts of 1921 and 1924 set quotas on newcomers to the nation based on national origins. Immigration from eastern, southern, and central Europe was cut sharply, and stopped altogether from Asia.

Normalcy, Sacco and Vanzetti, Fordism, and the American Plan

Warren G. Harding summed up the postwar goal of business leaders, and many citizens disillusioned with the smoky idealism of the war, when he misread the word *normality* from his March 1921 presidential inaugural notes and created a new word, *normalcy*. To business leaders, the Progressive era itself, particularly its prewar and wartime accommodations to labor, was an abnormality, an unwanted expansion of federal authority on behalf of consumers, the wilderness, and the rights of women and children. Too many democratic hopes and aspirations had been raised too high. Too many immigrants with alien practices had entered the country. Now, with conservative businessmen like Andrew Mellon as secretary of the Treasury for most of the decade, an age of democratic reform was over. For labor, organized and unorganized, the power shift was clear.

Open and nearly unlimited European immigration, which had been the mainstay of industrial labor since the 1840s, was shutting down. Good citizens were expected to assimilate and express prevailing views, not like those radicals, Nicolo Sacco and Bartolomeo Vanzetti, who were on trial in Massachusetts as much for their unassimilated antiwar and pro-labor views as they were for a payroll robbery and murder. The arrest of Sacco and Vanzetti in 1920, their openly biased judge, unfair trial, unsuccessful appeals, and the massive national and international protest on their behalf reached a conclusion with their execution in 1927. They joined fellow immigrants, the Molly Maguires and Joe Hill, as martyrs, made victims of the state for their labor advocacy in cases whose outcomes were built on strong prejudices and weak criminal evidence.

By far the most popular man of the decade was Henry Ford, with Babe Ruth a close second. Ford was the hero of the newest phase of mass production, the use of the moving assembly line. His product, the inexpensive automobile, became increasingly available to ordinary workers as production efficiencies allowed price reductions in the postwar era. In 1925 a worker could buy a new two-seat Model T Ford for $250, down from $860 in 1908. The soaring corporate skyscraper and the pleasure car were real and symbolic representations of success in the 1920s, joined briefly in the closing years of the decade by the stock market boom on Wall Street.

Ford's workplace ideas were not new, but they were summarized as "Fordism," one tenet of which was ethnic and religious intolerance. Most of Ford's employees were immigrants, and 900 of them were fired for missing work to honor their Eastern Orthodox Christmas in 1914. A Ford company spokesman said simply that workers who lived in America "should observe American holidays" (quoted in Montgomery, 1987, p. 236). Some European ideas were embraced by Ford. He was an open fan of the labor crushing policies of Mussolini and Hitler, in both of whose nations Ford began to invest heavily in automobile and truck production. Ford's openly anti-Semitic newspaper, the *Dearborn Independent*, waxed enthusiastic about Hitler until lawsuits and politics caused him to shut it down.

The open shop, widely publicized as the "American Plan," was another fixed belief of Fordism. Americans, the argument went, were free individuals, whereas unions were collective and foreign entities that imposed limits on personal autonomy and choice. No union represented Ford workers until 1941. Ford hired what he called "sociologists," or what were later called personnel managers to boost morale, cut absenteeism, and minister a kind of "welfare capitalism." Other business leaders recognized the importance of some accommodation of workers' needs to counter criticism of exploitation and to bolster consumption. The new paternalism included the widespread creation of company unions, still known as Employee Representation Plans (ERPs), and some salary improvements. Throughout the decade, a constant barrage of antiunion literature flowed from the National Association of Manufacturers and filled company and institutional newsletters. Workers in the United States, the business propaganda argued, had no need to sacrifice their individual liberties for the alleged gains of collective bargaining, a foreign notion of little value in the land of the free and home of the brave. Enlightened capitalists, according to this line of reasoning, would secure the well-being of their workers. The steel industry did away with the two twelve-hour shifts per day, and put in three eight-hour shifts with no loss in pay for workers in 1923.

Nonetheless, even after the recovery from the postwar business slump of 1920–21, wages for workers in the United States remained flat through most of the 1920s, and unemployment stayed high, at about 10 percent or more of those actively seeking work. Union membership slumped after the war to just about 3.5 million and never recovered despite the economic expansion of the mid and later years of the decade and the growth of the labor force. Women and black workers lost ground, were more isolated in gender- and race-specific areas of employment, and were less likely to enjoy any form of union representation, company or independent.

The Changing Nature of Work

Business itself was creating new tiers, or levels, of workers. The number of specialized technicians and engineers increased sharply during the decade. Office equipment like typewriters and adding machines needed maintenance and repair, as well as constant redesign and improvement. Office staffs, accounting, and advertising work increased enormously as well. Every major university in the nation added or enlarged a business school during these years to prepare professionals for the new specializations required by business, not least important of which was personnel management. Clerical work, teaching, and sales positions also increased. The children of mine, mill, factory, and sweatshop workers sought many of these new jobs, or "careers," as a way to escape the hard physical labor and lower pay of their parents. Different work rules, educational requirements, dress habits or codes, and weekly, monthly, or yearly salaries—not hourly wage rates—separated these new workers from their industrial counterparts, and from the labor organizations and ideas of their parents. As in the past, workers also continued to seek refuge from jobs that led nowhere by starting small business ventures that might grow into large ones. Whether from pushcarts, out of small shops, or in the provision of services to their larger communities, workers found new things to offer or sell, some legal and some illegal.

The Jazz Age

Prohibition turned out to be a boon to labor, but not because it cut down on the consumption of alcohol. Making, selling, and transporting the bulky product required hundreds of thousands of willing hands and backs. Farmers had a long tradition of making whiskey and dodging tax collectors. Now they were joined by urban brewers and distillers, smugglers, truckers (some scholars say the influence of the mob among drivers started here), and night club operators of speakeasies in a business that, instead of declining because of its illegality, grew rapidly. A popular renegade culture was formed by bad law.

The music they all listened to was jazz, the sounds and sentiments that came from the lives and work of black labor as it translated itself, and was translated, into popular culture. No undemocratic restrictions were artificially imposed on musical talents, except, of course, those that restricted entrance into formal musical conservatories. From slavery times, nonclassical musical performance genius among workers was permitted by masters to flourish. Children with musical talents were encouraged by their elders, since performance abilities might offer youngsters some material advantages in later life. The radio and record player expanded the audience nationwide.

Like the Gothic cathedrals of Europe and Italian opera, jazz music was a gift to human civilization from the United States, but not everyone who labored in it was fairly compensated for their creative work. Only a few individual artists, composers, singers, and bandleaders did well. Record companies, copyright holders, producers, and agents did better. Labor, as usual, created wealth for a market by the conversion of artistry into commodity. The laborer-artists were easily separated from what they produced by the simple necessity of selling it. The tune, "Happy Birthday," for example, was originally composed in 1859, but various legal and corporate interventions have been able to prevent its becoming a public property until at least the year 2010 for its current owner, the Time-Warner Corporation. The *Wall Street Journal* reported (August 21, 2001) that the nine-year copyright extension won in 2001 was worth an estimated $20 million for Time-Warner. For every successful artist of the postwar era, like the great Louis Armstrong, there were hundreds of other talented musicians who scraped by, hoping for a breakthrough, and thousands more whose musical energies never brought them any material reward. Every musical artist, from road house to concert hall, contributed to a buoyant popular culture in a nation that, for all its limits and shortcomings, was "sittin' on top of the world."

Until World War I there was no truly universal national culture in the United States. There were many regional, ethnic, national, and religious subcultures. White supremacy, embraced uncritically by Thomas Jefferson, Abraham Lincoln, and Theodore Roosevelt, was the only commonly shared national creed. Workers, nonetheless, continued to construct their own subcultures by blending dominant influences with local habits and traditions. Now, with film and radio joining print, there was an extension of the mass media. The children of immigrants and the children of the native-born cheered equally for Babe Ruth. They all danced to jazz music and swooned or gasped at the same film heroes and villains. They heard the same advertising and began to buy the same or similar products from giant corporate producers. Sports, film, and musical celebrities became household heroes to working-class adults and children alike.

New or updated images of success entered everyday working-class life that did not come from the workplace, or specific ethnic, national, or regional tradition. The dandy, often a professional gambler, hustler, or successful criminal, was a slick and well-dressed urban figure well-known in every working-class pool hall or speakeasy. His cool independence set him apart from other workers, many of whom imitated aspects of his style. In virtually every workplace small-time gambling activities, petty theft, and other forms of economic redistribution provided extra income to ambitious workers willing to take on the risk.

Part renegade, part establishment imitator, the gangster with political influence became a folk hero in many communities, especially when some of his wealth was spread around. While there was not much new about crime, the enormous profits from illegal alcohol led to organizational structures with local political influence that were comparable to legitimate businesses. What is called "organized crime" is illegal business with the covert protection of local government. Hence, only federal intervention could topple Al Capone from his power base in Chicago. State and local authorities easily came under the sway of their own local businessmen, and still do. The image of the Prohibition era gangster, a pro-capitalist outlaw, remains part of the national folklore because it is no contradiction to the capitalist worldview. Like the legitimate businessman, the hoodlum or thief is out for himself, with no concern for social or economic justice whatsoever. No union officer, or great strike leader, not even Gompers, let alone Eugene Debs or Mother Jones, enjoyed the media-endowed popular status of Capone and the various murderous godfathers, bank robbers, and gangsters who followed. It is hardly a coincidence that the romantic hero of the great American novel of the 1920s, *The Great Gatsby*, by F. Scott Fitzgerald, lived opulently in a shadowy criminal world and ultimately had his fate determined by an automobile.

Working Women in the 1920s

Women's rights advocates were divided among themselves between the battle for more protective legislation for working women, or the struggle for an equal rights amendment to the Constitution. Few women favored both, but neither approach made any progress in the 1920s. The Supreme Court undermined the protection position when it ruled in *Atkins v. Children's Hospital* (1923) that minimum wage legislation for women was unconstitutional. In the same year an Equal Rights Amendment that lacked the support of the Women's Trade Union League and its leader, Mary Anderson, failed in Congress. The women's rights movement remained divided over seeking protection or fighting for equal rights for years.

In a contrast that was typical for the time, the beauty pageant to name Miss America was started in 1921 in Atlantic City, New Jersey. The superficial standards by which these women were selected were hardly any tribute to the kind of women who had fought at the front lines of labor, or on behalf of the equal rights for women for almost a century. A year after winning the right to vote, adult women were paraded in bathing suits before male judges for the amusement of the nation. It is impossible to know how many young women have chosen to emulate the beauty pageant standard promoted in Atlantic City, rather than the one established on the front lines of labor and equal rights battles set by women like Mother Jones, Emma Goldman, Elizabeth Gurley Flynn, or Rose Schneiderman.

The State and Labor

Samuel Gompers died in 1924, and was replaced as president of the AFL by William Green, a lackluster figure favored by the craft union barons. The AFL maintained its close association with government leaders through the decade in spite of sharply declining union influence and membership. Green advocated a Christian cooperative spirit instead of confrontational tactics with management. He was an ardent anticommunist, and never failed to accuse any of his opponents of playing into the hands of the "red menace." The AFL continued to participate in open and secretive labor activities with the State Department in the Americas and elsewhere. Their common objective was to counter independent socialist or communist influences among workers wherever the interests of the business community of the United States might be affected. Every secretary of labor until 1930 came from the executive ranks of the AFL. President Hoover broke the tradition when he named William N. Doak, of the unaffiliated Brotherhood of Railway Trainmen, to the post.

In spite of this close collaboration, old victories for labor were overturned in the 1920s. Labor's presumed exemption from injunctions in the Clayton Anti-Trust Act was blasted by the Supreme Court twice, first in 1921 in *Duplex Printing Press v. Deering*, then in 1927 in *Bedford Cut Stone*. In the first case an injunction was allowed to stop a union picket line that, the Court said, constituted a "conspiracy in restraint of trade." In the second, an injunction was upheld against stonecutters who refused to work on stone cut in quarries blacklisted by their Stone Cutters Association. The Court considered this refusal similar to a monopoly acting "in restraint of trade." In his dissent, Justice Louis Brandeis contrasted with deliberate irony the warm willingness of the Court to interpret the Sherman and Clayton antitrust laws in order to permit U.S. Steel and the United Shoe Company the right to completely dominate their industries, to their cold unwillingness to grant stone cutters the right to refuse to cut stone. More than twice as many court-ordered injunctions were used against labor organizations in the 1920s than in any other comparable period. In the *Coronado Coal Case* of 1922, the Court rubbed salt in the deep wounds of mining unions, as well as other unions for whom the decision might apply, when it held that unions could be sued for acts of their officers.

Another loss of a Progressive-era accomplishment for labor was the above-noted Supreme Court ruling in *Adkins v. Children's Hospital* in 1923. Minimum wage laws passed by state or local governments were declared unconstitutional violations of the protection of liberty of contract. To the Court majority there was no difference between labor and any other commodity in the marketplace. The dissenters in this case would eventually be vindicated by the Fair Labor Standards Act of 1938. This act included a federal minimum wage, and when it was upheld by the Court, the decision in *Adkins* was overturned.

For one group of labor organizations there was a little light in the governmental gloom of the decade. Four hundred thousand striking railroad shopmen in six craft unions refused to accept their leaders' deal with employers and stayed out in 1922. The nation's rail system was a mess because the workers were more militant than their union. The union was prepared to give up overtime pay for work on Sundays and holidays, but the workers were not. The employers went to the Railroad Labor Board, a leftover wartime agency, to get relief. The board complied by calling the workers' action an "outlaw strike," and the attorney general, Harry Daugherty (not yet scandalized for his part in the corruption of the Harding administration), brought a federal injunction against the workers under the Sherman Act, and supported by the decision the year before in *Duplex Printing Press v. Deering*.

Reluctantly, the railroad workers returned to their jobs, but something needed to be done. All of business was united against the disruption to commerce of national railroad strikes. Railroads were still the most economical means of bringing natural resources to manufacturers and manufactured goods to markets. By necessity they were often monopolies. Progressive business leaders and labor activists from the Trade Union Educational League continued to call for the nationalization of the railroads, an argument originally brought forward by Populists in the 1890s, and one that was gaining ground, or already in place, in most of Europe. In the AFL convention of 1920 delegates went so far as to override President Gompers, by voting 3–1 in favor of the Plumb Plan to nationalize the nation's rail system. A wide spectrum of political moderates and Progressives, workers, farmers, and small business owners were coalescing around the proposal of Glenn E. Plumb to place the operation of the nation's rail system under the three-way control of its employees, users, and bond holders.

Railroad industry leaders and conservative unionists accepted the Railroad Labor Act of 1926 instead. The new law broadened the legal authority of the railroad unions and granted workers in the industry the right to collective bargaining, a peacetime precedent. The federal government extended its protection to railroad workers who wished to have union representation. Rules were set, and no arbitrary firings, coercion, or discriminatory practices against unionists were allowed. Procedures were established for conciliation, mediation, and arbitration of disputes. Conservative union leaders were given more power over their members, who were now legally obliged to adhere to the contracts they made. The union became stronger at the expense of the shop-floor militancy of railroad workers. When the New Deal arrived seven years later, this concept would be attempted on a national scale. Meanwhile, if all railroad workers could be unionized, one important, previously excluded group was ready to sign up.

A. Philip Randolph and the Brotherhood of Sleeping Car Porters

Racial discrimination and relatively open immigration placed most black workers into service jobs, or on the bottom rung of the industrial labor ladder. On the railroads black workers were waiters in dining cars, carried baggage, and tended to all of the various chores associated with sleeping cars, club cars, and specialty cars. One such worker was A. Philip Randolph, the son of a preacher and a graduate of the City College of New York. Randolph was a well-known labor activist, and had been fired from his job as a porter for attempting to organize his co-workers in 1917. He went on to organize elevator operators and became nationally known as the outspoken socialist editor of the monthly journal of hotel and restaurant workers, *The Hotel and Restaurant Messenger*.

In 1925 Randolph accepted the offer of a group of porters, led by Ashley L. Totten, to take on the job of organizing black railroad workers. The journal's name was changed to *The Messenger,* and became the organizational voice of the new union. The porters' union quickly expanded from its Harlem, New York origins, though winning new members was never easy. Decent jobs for black workers were scarce. Many porters, like Randolph, were college graduates, some held professional or advanced degrees but could find no other work. The Pullman Company stubbornly resisted and used all of the traditional methods to stop the unionization drive: firings (estimated at between 500 and 1,000), beatings, infiltration of company agents into the budding local, and the creation of a company union. The wives, mothers, and sisters of workers carried on the organizational struggle in a Ladies' Auxiliary while men were working the lines. Women ran small offices, printed and distributed leaflets, and kept up networks of correspondence in semi-secretive circles. Some said (and a few continue to say) that it was the women who organized the union. Still unsuccessful with Pullman in 1928, Randolph took his emerging union, soon to be the largest union of black workers in the country, into the AFL over the objections of many of his colleagues, who criticized the racism of the national organization. From this platform, Randolph became one of the most important national leaders in the struggle for racial justice for almost the next half century. But first he would have to live with the complacent racism of the AFL.

John L. Lewis, the UMW, and the Decline of Industrial Unionism

As much as the decade that followed the war was a success for national business, commerce, and culture, it was a disaster for the largest group of organized industrial workers. Coal was still the primary fuel for homes, industries, and institutions, though the shift to fuel oil was already beginning to make some inroads. Naval vessels, built after 1903, for example, were designed to burn oil, but coal was cheap and abundant for most other purposes for decades to come. More than half of the nation's coal miners were represented by the United Mine Workers of America, led by the big bushy-eyebrowed, and, when he needed to be, dictatorial, John L. Lewis.

By their concerted efforts employers almost completely destroyed the coal miners' union in just a few years. State and local police were used continuously to enforce injunctions or protect private property. Private security agencies and vigilante violence were used without respite against strikers, union organizers, or worker advocates. Armed conflict in towns such as Matewan, West Virginia (1921), resulted in substantial losses among miners, and the defeat or destruction of labor organizations, primarily the UMWA, that represented them. By 1928 Lewis represented barely 80,000 workers. Four years later in the midst of depression, that dismal number was cut by half among those miners still working. Industrial unions were taking a similar beating everywhere.

New Orleans

In New Orleans, the racial unity of the Dock and Cotton Council continued throughout World War I, but was broken afterward by the combined efforts of employers and civil authorities. Jobs on the New Orleans waterfront were more specifically assigned on racial terms during the war. By the end of the wartime boom most members of the longshoremen's union and most waterfront workers were black men. White workers were channeled into other areas of employment as machine operators, office workers, and foremen or supervisors. The old half-and-half rule for assigning work or setting up work crews could no longer be maintained without being an obvious form of discrimination against black workers. The city's Jim Crow laws were extended to every aspect of public life, and the local laws were enforced by police. Every public facility and civic event was racially exclusive, or segregated. In 1911, for example, New Orleans banned black people from any further participation in the annual Mardi Gras festivities.

Organizational unity persisted, nonetheless, among black and white union leaders until the end, one that arrived after a series of failed strikes that began in 1921. The United Fruit Company and the Southern Pacific Railroad took the lead in abandoning union contracts in 1922. They were soon joined by other companies in New Orleans in establishing the open shop, and a year later the last of the great "levee wars" came to an end with the destruction of the old unions and the creation of company unions in their place. Finally, by 1931, black workers were excluded from waterfront work almost altogether by a union-imposed resolution, one that soon became a city ordinance that required only "certified registered voters be employed in loading and unloading" the ships, trains, and trucks within the city's limits (Rosenberg, 1988, p. 174). Black waterfront work now became white waterfront work as black citizens were disenfranchised in the city.

Coal miners and New Orleans dockworkers had been among the strongest and most highly organized of the nation's industrial labor force. Both seemed finished by the onset of the Great Depression. With the exception of what was left of the craft unions of the AFL and the Railroad Brotherhoods, organized labor seemed to be passing from the scene in the United States.

Crash, Bust

The question of "agency," of the active role of workers or their organizations in influencing or determining events, is much debated among labor historians. In at least one area there is no debate. The stock market crash of 1929 and the Great Depression that followed it were not caused by workers, their unions, or their political organizations, no matter their radical, militant, or even revolutionary objectives. Nonetheless, it was among the nation's workers that the Depression of 1929–40 had its most severe consequences and took its greatest toll in suffering, impoverishment, starvation, homelessness, and death. For every publicized suicide of a failed businessman or stock speculator, thousands of innocent workers, women, and children died of starvation, malnutrition, or exposure. No one will ever know for sure how many working-class women died of botched abortions, or how many infants were killed or died because of the effects of the Depression. No laboring family was untouched. Everyone who depended on their labor for survival lived in fear, since no job was completely safe, no pay envelope secure. By the terribly cold winter of 1932–33 a full third of the labor force was unemployed and without regular income. In large cities and industrial centers the unemployment rate was 40 to 50 percent. Almost half of those still employed could not count on regular work. Most large industries were at or near a standstill. Public revenues declined so sharply that many state and local governments were bankrupt and could not pay their own public employees or provide adequate relief to the unemployed. Some local governments printed their own script or deferred civil service, teacher, police, and firemen salaries. Private pension systems fell apart or went bankrupt and left millions of elderly workers without any source of income.

The word *capitalism* lost the glamour it had enjoyed during the so-called roaring twenties, but the Republican administration of President Herbert Hoover (1929–33) saw little need to take any action on behalf of the nation's workers. "Prosperity," Hoover repeated, "was just around the corner." In response, homeless workers named their shantytowns "Hoovervilles," and spoke of "hooverizing" on milk and eggs and other basic needs when they did without them.

Hoover did sign one piece of legislation that marked a new direction for government policy and labor. He signed a bill authored by two progressive Republicans, Senator Frank Norris of Nebraska and Congressman Fiorello LaGuardia of New York City. The Norris–LaGuardia Act of 1932 outlawed yellow dog contracts and imposed restrictions on the use of injunctions by federal courts in labor-management disputes. Now that there were few jobs, workers who were still holding onto them by their fingertips had the right to freedom of association partially affirmed. The concept of federal protection of the right of workers to form collective organizations for representation, however, would soon become one of the foundations of the rapid expansion of unions during the New Deal. That right is usually credited to the new president, Franklin Delano Roosevelt, but actually began its advance in the administration of Herbert Hoover.

Protests, Unemployment Marches, Strikes

Unemployed workers did more than scavenge city dumps and try to learn to do without the basic necessities of life. Few of them accepted the Depression as an act of nature, or as some kind of historic inevitability. They found or improvised ways to help each other in their families and communities. Workers shared meager resources, and doubled or tripled up in apartments and houses. Families were disrupted and reformed as workers set out in search of jobs in faraway towns. Hobo jungles were encampments formed in railroad yards in or near every major industrial center. The unemployed achieved a true equality among black and white workers in most parts of the country. Outside the civic codes of the dominant society Jim Crowism quickly faded. Men, women, and children of every color and description huddled around campfires in temporary shelters. They shared their meager goods as they moved around the country in search of jobs in the midst of a catastrophe they knew they had no part in making. Workers had once been legally and politically dependent on their masters. Now they enjoyed political liberty, but were dependent for survival on their unwanted labor, the same labor that had created the wealth that could no longer sustain them.

As in prior industrial depressions, workers turned out to protest their impoverishment and unemployment. Every large city in the country hosted such rallies and demonstrations. More than a million workers gathered at the Trade Union Unity League and Communist Party sponsored protest on March 6, 1930. The police clubbed demonstrators in Union Square, New York, where over 100,00 marched. Observers compared it to the severe brutality of the Tompkins Square beatings in 1874. Police gave the same explanation for their severity: they were fighting communism. Huge crowds turned out at the same time to protest in Detroit, Chicago, Pittsburgh, Milwaukee, San Francisco, Los Angeles, Seattle, Denver, and Philadelphia. There were rent strikes and mass protests to prevent or block evictions in New York, Chicago, and Philadelphia. Leaders of these actions came from left-wing organizations and the ranks of independent labor organizations, not from the top ranks of the AFL. In these popular protests there were no dues to collect, no respectable status to be gained, and no political goals to be won that the AFL wanted.

As late as November 1932, the complacent AFL still expressed opposition to federal unemployment compensation and stayed out of the presidential election. Workers had no official or institutionally sanctioned voice to express their feelings. There was no numerically significant political party for them, and no organizational vehicle to represent their interests. Workers were better organized as workers in 1830, or 1870, or 1916 than they were in 1932. Lacking organization, millions of workers were, nonetheless, angry, frustrated, fearful, and ready to do something.

The Communist Party, with no more than about 12,000 members nationwide in 1932, was still minuscule in comparison to the former strength of the Socialist Party. Nonetheless, the CP took the lead in breaching the color bar in its part in all of the rent strikes, unemployment councils, hunger marches, union organizing drives, and mass protests that took place, north and south. No other group included black workers, writers, and unionists so prominently in the leadership of battles for labor than the Communists. Whenever Communists were not in the lead of such protests, they were blamed or tagged for it anyway, and that only increased their temporarily growing popularity among workers in the early years of the Depression. It was frequently pointed out that there was no comparable depression or unemployment problem in the Soviet Union, and reports of Stalinist purges, political tyranny, or prison gulags had not yet come forth.

The Government Response to Labor in the Great Depression

Neither major political party strayed from the conventional wisdom of the time. The mainstream press and most political leaders agreed that economic problems of the nation would be best left to take care of themselves. They all agreed that only private business could be the proper engine for the revival of economy. Until the banking crisis of 1933, and the first hundred days of the New Deal, the government did not intervene on behalf of people in the same way as it responded to demands for help on behalf of business. Helping to relieve the distress of business was accepted as a legitimate course of government action, whereas helping impoverished people was not.

The Reconstruction Finance Corporation (RFC) was established by the federal government in 1932 to make $2 billion in loans available to banks, railroads, and insurance companies. In the same year a Federal Home Loan Bank System put $500 million at the disposal of savings and loan banks to try to revive the construction industry, and the Glass-Steagall Banking Act sought to expand credit through the Federal Reserve System to stimulate business activity. But nothing was done for labor. No federal relief was provided to unemployed workers. Private charity, some state and local relief measures, and soup kitchens were all that was available. Government leaders believed that the national recovery, when it came, would depend exclusively on private business. The AFL accepted the same viewpoint. The Democratic Party campaigned on a platform similar to that of the Republicans in 1932, though FDR spoke vaguely of a "new deal for Americans" and pledged support for limited unemployment compensation. Neither party took issue with the harsh clearing of about 15,000 unemployed Bonus Army marchers from Washington, D.C., by U.S. Army units, using tanks and tear gas, under the command of General Douglas MacArthur in the summer of 1932.

Conclusion

The response of working-class voters to the Depression was to look for an alternative, any alternative, after more than a decade of Republican leadership in government. In 1930 Republicans lost majority control of Congress for the first time in a decade, and extended their losses in both Houses in 1932. Voter turnout in 1932 was greater than it had been in a generation. The Socialist Party candidate for the presidency in 1932, Norman Thomas, won 880,000 votes, and the Communist Party candidate drew just over 100,000, up from less than 300,000 combined Socialist and Communist Party ballots cast four years earlier. FDR captured twenty-three million votes, almost 90 percent of the electoral vote. A new political coalition was beginning to form among ethnic groups alienated from Republicans by Prohibition, unemployed and underemployed industrial and urban workers, small business people hurt by the Depression, and old Progressives with nowhere else to turn. The votes of labor in search of some protection in the hostile environment of depression was the foundation of this new political structure. The gloss was gone from the shining capitalist aura of the previous decade, but most workers weren't looking for a revolutionary transformation of their nation. What they wanted was a government that took their interests as seriously as it did those of the companies that employed them. Now they were numerous and strong enough to demand that kind of radical change.

The business community in the United States faced a threatening world as well. The Depression was not a local problem. It was a crisis of capitalism itself, and political instability brought forth new challenges. Japan, long regarded as a potential military rival, was launched on a path that was bringing it into direct conflict with the national goals of the United States and the Open Door policy. The Japanese seized Manchuria in 1931 and turned it into a colony called Manchuko. Foreign investors in Manchurian railroads and mining and lumber industries now had to deal with tough Japanese administrators and new restrictions. Adolf Hitler pledged to destroy, among other things, the Treaty of Versailles and rebuild German military might. The United States would once again require the loyalty and service of its working people on the front lines and in the factories to defeat its enemies. As in the past, efforts to secure those loyalties would include the expansion of political rights as well as material benefits for all of labor. With the immigration supply choked off, the greatest gains would be made by those at or near the bottom, by black workers, by women, and by all industrial workers. Nothing would ever be quite the same again.

Flint sit-down strikers. Automobile seats are put to alternative use as workers in Fisher Body Plant No. 3 relax in early 1937. (Library of Congress, Prints and Photographs Division, Reproduction No. LC-USZ62-131617)

CHAPTER 7

Labor Valued: The New Deal and War, 1933–1945

What I want to do—what I want to help to do—is to make America an industrial democracy.
——John L. Lewis (quoted in the *Catholic Worker*, August 1936, pp. 1–2)

Democracy Rising

The collapse of venerable institutions in the Great Depression and the global threat of the Axis Powers to the Open Door foreign policy of the United States upset the superficial stability of the 1920s. Unlike Germany, Italy, and Japan, where authoritarian traditions were revived to meet the economic crisis, the United States reacted to the crisis with an expansion of democracy. FDR and the New Deal replaced fear with hope, labor alienation with institutional legitimacy, and the reality of poverty and inequality with the possibility of abundance and greater economic equity. Hitler, Mussolini, and Hirohito called on nondemocratic cultural foundations and on arrogant nationalism to unite their working classes and prepare for war. FDR relied on the democratic strength of the heritage of the United States and won out. Working people of the United States saved the nation so that it could fulfill its promises to them.

Federal authority increased in the crisis while state and local authority dimmed in contrast. Federal power was the only possible way to respond to an international threat. The federal government was also forced to bail out bankrupt or stymied state governments that were unable to deal with the economic collapse. The private sector, on its knees, also had to give way to greater public authority in the economy in exchange for protection of the banking system and billions of public dollars in new infrastructure investment.

The New Deal approach to the crisis was to draw on the effective traditions from the past to enlarge democratic standards for labor, and raise the legal status and material expectations of millions of working people. The pump-priming ideas of British economist John Maynard Keynes were congenial with the already established notions of the worker as a consumer-generator of economic growth. Labor power on the military front lines and in the mines, mills, offices, fields, and factories ultimately won the war against fascism and militarism, and made the United States the foremost world power in human history. Industrial labor moved from an undeserved periphery to the center of domestic policy and politics during the Depression and war years. The left-wing democratic slogan of meat packing workers, "Negro and White, Unite and Fight," was central to advancing the labor struggle at home and winning the military battle abroad.

Democracy is messy, inherently radical, and almost always perceived as dangerous to the owners of capital and the elite institutions capital creates. Even though the New Deal prescribed a medicine that was ultimately good for them, businessmen hated the New Deal and the democracy that it harnessed for the good of the nation. Business fought unionization and ultimately undermined and eliminated the radical democracy that was briefly legitimized by the New Deal. Businessmen despised the social security system begun in 1935 and the Fair Labor Standards Act of 1938. The democratic universalism of both these measures contributed to raised expectations for millions of workers. Businessmen resented federal power itself when it was directed at their prerogatives, even when it was for their own good. Business leaders prefer the more malleable authority of state governments and their ability to manipulate one state against the other for the purposes of investment activity and control of the workforce.

Democracy is also inherently contentious. Disputation can paralyze action or propel conflict to extreme limits, to potentially uncontrollable consequences. Nowhere was this contentiousness and ferment more evident than among workers themselves. In their unions, their politics, and their varied cultural and ideological formations, workers battled each other endlessly, at times heroically, at other times cynically, and, on some occasions, brilliantly. Union leaders fought ferocious ideological and political battles among themselves, just as they contended for the dues of millions of new members. Labor leaders confronted their external adversaries during the Depression and war years with the confidence and solidarity of their best traditions. The stakes were, or seemed, higher than ever. Fascism, militarism, socialism, and communism were available and lively possible options to labor, given the extreme circumstances faced by millions of desperate people in 1933. Instead of any one of those, workers in the United States drew their radicalism from the democratic traditions and promises of the nation itself.

As in the past, organization and political accomplishments for labor followed popular and democratic upheavals. That's what happened among the early women workers of Manyunk and Lowell and in the first worker political parties of the late 1820s. Democratic accomplishments accompanied the rise of the National Labor Union in the era of Reconstruction. The Great Uprising of 1877 preceded a decade of growth of the Knights of Labor, and a general strike preceded the successes of the New Orleans Dock and Cotton Council. The burgeoning mass organizations of miners and textile workers and the radical appeal of the IWW and Socialist Party helped to fuel the democratic reforms of the Progressive era.

Prior to the mass union organizing drives of the 1930s workers were beginning to mobilize on a broad variety of fronts, often with socialist and communist assistance, sometimes without it. Most of the left accepted the Marxist notion that industrial labor was forming a new class, a proletariat comparable in historic importance to the middle-class businessmen who had previously overthrown royal and aristocratic power. Helping to organize and mobilize that class was the job, many believed, of modern radicals now inspired as much by Debs and Lenin as by Jefferson and Paine. Hunger marches, rent strikes, blockage of household evictions, relief demonstrations, the formation of unemployment councils (especially the nationwide Unemployed Citizens' League), and sit-down demonstrations in state welfare offices were common in every large city and most smaller ones.

Twenty thousand unemployed and dispossessed coal miners dug "bootleg" coal. These illegal "coal leggers" built up an industry that brought an estimated five million tons of coal to market by 1934 (Brecher, 1997, pp. 146–47). With no help from government or leadership from the AFL, and in the depths of the worst economic collapse in the nation's history, workplace militancy and union organizing drives began to increase sharply over the bitter winter of 1932–33. Without a union, 15,000 autoworkers in Detroit struck for the right to organize in January 1933. A democratic upheaval was well underway in the United States before the inauguration of Franklin Delano Roosevelt in March 1933.

The Making of a New Deal for Labor

Critical events and past experience, not ideology, and certainly not any commitment to or preference for labor drove the policies of President Franklin D. Roosevelt. Like Herbert Hoover, FDR rejected all of the AFL's suggestions for a secretary of labor. Instead, he selected Frances Perkins, the New York State industrial commissioner, for the position, and she became the first woman member of a president's cabinet.

The banking system's collapse was the first order of business. By simply declaring a "bank holiday," and closing up the nation's banks a day after his inauguration, FDR allowed a pause that brought temporary psychological relief to the shattered industry. Roosevelt's first "fireside chat" was broadcast on Sunday, March 12, and inaugurated a series of radio broadcasts aimed at reassuring a frightened and insecure public. Sixty million people listened to his assertions that banks were now safe places for people's savings. When presumably certified banks opened the next day, people lined up to make deposits.

An Economy Act was quickly proposed and passed before the end of March. The law was aimed at balancing the federal budget by cutting veterans' benefits and the salaries of government workers. A Federal Emergency Relief Act was also passed that brought immediate help, mostly food, to the hungry. Organized labor still had to wait a few months.

It wasn't until May that a complex rescue program for industry, called the National Industrial Recovery Act (NIRA), was signed into law. Labor, which had made the difference in the election, now had something in return. The new law was formed along the lines of the War Industries Board of World War I. In exchange for lifting federal antitrust and price fixing regulations, and the provision of a vast multibillion-dollar public spending program under a Public Works Administration, business was expected to set up trade associations and "codes of fair competition."

Labor advocates like John L. Lewis, a lobbyist for the AFL, pressed their congressional allies for something in the law as well. In spite of strenuous business efforts to stop it, the NIRA included a protection clause for union rights similar to the Railway Labor Act of 1926. Section 7a of the new law required that all industry codes include minimum wage and maximum hour regulations and restrictions on the use of child labor, and, most significantly, said that "employees shall have the right to organize and bargain collectively through representatives of their own choosing, and shall be free from the interference, restraint or coercion of employers" (Rauch, 1944, pp. 72–80). Conservative and patriotic union leaders, it was argued, would take away the growing influence of leftist radicals among the working class. It had worked in the railroad industry, why shouldn't it work now?

Labor and the Blue Eagle

Lewis was thrilled. He and his United Mine Workers of America (UMWA) were off and running. "President Roosevelt," his organizers proclaimed in their leaflets to miners, "wants you to join the union." Lewis hoped to harness the rising tide of democratic radicalism among mineworkers to build his own organization. He reversed his former exclusionary practices toward leftists and put them to work among his organizers. In response to critics who charged that there were Communists in his UMWA, and later in the Congress of Industrial Organizations (CIO), Lewis roared: "Who gets the bird, the hunter or the dog?" He was out for the big gains in membership—and dues—that the new law could bring him, and he was prepared to use every means at his disposal. In the big organizing drives of 1936–37 he brought back dissident UMWA critics of his own leadership, Socialists and anarchists to work as CIO staff in the rubber, steel, and automobile industries.

It certainly looked as though Lewis was right. Using the law, strikes, and the threat of strikes for union recognition, his own union membership increased spectacularly, from about 50,000 to over 300,000 in the first year of the New Deal. The atmosphere was exhilarating and spread throughout industry. The "Code of Fair Competition" Lewis won from the coal companies in September 1933 included most of the things that miners had been fighting for throughout their history: a wage increase, the eight-hour day, the five-day week, the end of payment in company script, a prohibition on the use of child labor, and on-the-job rights that included a grievance procedure. Less than a year later Lewis won further improvements to the code that ended discriminatory and substandard wages and working conditions for black miners.

Textile workers led by Sidney Hillman's Amalgamated Clothing Workers (ACW) and David Dubinsky's International Ladies Garment Workers Union (ILGWU) made similar gains in the first year of the National Recovery Administration (NRA), the federal body established to administer the law. Together the two unions quickly enrolled more than 200,000 new members. Both unions had maintained their socialist orientation from the pre–World War I era with an important political alteration. Both had purged or driven out of their leadership antiwar Socialists or, later, Communists. They were now patriotic unions that confined most of their socialist objectives to the benefits that might be won by the union and extended to their members. Health and welfare programs, pension funds, summer camps, housing, insurance, credit, and recreational activities administered under union auspices were taking the place of plans for transforming capitalism itself.

Along with the success of coal miners and garment workers, the AFL reversed its membership decline as well, though not because of any organizing skill or leadership initiatives of its own. Workers all over the country organized in mass production industries and applied for AFL charters. Rubber, electrical, steel, and automotive workers were organizing themselves by the hundreds of thousands. The atmosphere was compared to a religious revival, and indeed, many old familiar church hymns were converted with new lyrics into union organizing songs. On the picket lines they sang: "Just like a rock that's standing by the river, We shall not be moved."

The AFL national organization was caught short. It was neither accustomed to nor interested in industrywide organization, and had no desire to organize unskilled or most semiskilled labor. As a concession to Lewis and Hillman, the best the AFL could offer to these rowdy newcomers were federal charters that established "federal locals" or "amalgamated craft associations." A federal local could not elect its own officers. The leaders were hand-picked by the AFL national executive committee. Worse yet, as soon as they came into the AFL, the federal locals were raided by AFL craft unions who signed up their skilled members into existing or new AFL unions. In some cases federal locals were raided by dozens of AFL unions, their membership almost completely depleted. Federal locals frequently fought these raids, but many were picked clean of all but the least skilled workers. Many unions, like the United Auto Workers, protected the independence of their leadership, survived the raids, and, later, went on their own way.

Workplace militancy and democratic mass movement activism, growing rapidly since 1930, increased sharply under the New Deal's NRA. The Blue Eagle, the NRA symbol that was used by participating industries, combined a patriotic attack on the Depression with at least the nominal protection of the rights of workers to organize unions. The number of strikes tripled from 1932 to 1933, most for recognition under the NRA. Federal locals in the AFL increased from just over 300 in 1932 to almost 1,800 by 1934. AFL membership soared by 500,000 new members in 1933, and 400,000 more were added in 1934, but the numbers tell only the smallest part of the exhilarating story.

The industrial workforce was taking over the center of national life. Workers used sound trucks, radio and newspaper advertising, billboards, slowdowns, sit-downs, mass picket lines, and flying squadrons of automobile units to mobilize their communities and organize unions. Workers organized public forums, meetings, and debates, and started choral groups to carry on the radical cultural traditions of Wobbly and socialist organizers. Women were an increasing part of the workforce (growing from 20 percent to 25 percent of the total in the Depression years), and returned to positions of labor leadership from the margins to which they had been assigned after World War I. Every large-scale industry organizing drive included a "Women's Auxiliary" to back up picket lines and sit-downs, and to bolster the morale and courage of the men.

Blue Eagle Blues

The NRA was clearly showing its limitations before the end of its first year in practice. Workers battled hundreds of hastily organized company unions for recognition. Outside of coal and textiles, the AFL provided no leadership for the massive rise in labor populism, anger, and militancy. Lewis and the textile union leaders began to see the AFL craft unions and President William Green as a hindrance to their goals. Black workers brought complaints to NRA officials of wage differentials allowed under the more than 700 industry codes, especially throughout the South. Because the new minimum wage codes were often higher than customary for black workers, thousands were fired to make way for white workers. Black critics called the NRA the "Negro Removal Act." Other critics said the codes favored only the large corporations that wrote them. The renowned attorney, Clarence Darrow, now seventy-seven, was appointed to chair a National Industrial Recovery Review Board. He attacked the monopolistic advantages garnered by large industries at the expense of smaller competitors in the codes they wrote.

The law had other problems. It provided no effective enforcement mechanism. Industry codes under the law were drafted by business leaders, and the provisions were interpreted and implemented arbitrarily and inconsistently, but always to the disadvantage of workers. As in its wartime precedent, an enormous bureaucracy of almost 5,000 federal employees was created to administer the law and sort through the codes. Altogether, the weaknesses of the law seemed to generate more conflict and more bloodshed than existed without it.

Most business leaders wanted none of it, and used their full arsenal of devices to block or destroy independent unionization efforts in spite of the law. Workers were not simply fighting for the right to organize company or company-styled unions, or even unions within the narrow confines of the NRA or AFL. They wanted solutions to real problems in the workplace, and a real voice and vote in the management of their new organizations. The battles of 1934 showed a labor force moving beyond the control of government and established union authorities.

1934

The West Coast

A West Coast uprising among dockworkers in May spread from San Diego to Seattle. Led by longshoremen, the strike shut down every West Coast port. Workers were incensed over bribery and corruption in "shape-up" hiring practices. To get work, payoffs to foremen or supervisors were common. Workers were enraged as well at the AFL's willingness to accept company unions. In San Francisco alone more than 130,000 workers of all kinds paralyzed the entire city for four days in July. The general strike was provoked by police and national guard attacks on striking dockworkers that left two dead and over 100 hospitalized. Conflict between Bay area AFL craft and transit unions and the International Association of Longshoremen, the latter led by the fiery radical and open Communist, Harry Bridges, ended the general strike inconclusively. One accomplishment was the ending of the bribe-riddled shape-up, but the entire area seethed with class hatred in the aftermath. Senator Hiram Johnson of California sent a note to President Roosevelt reporting on the situation: "Here is revolution not only in the making but with the initial actualities" (quoted in Bernstein, 1970, p. 287).

The Midwest

In Toledo, Ohio, the picket lines of striking workers at the Electric Auto-Lite plant were joined by members of the Lucas County Unemployed League. The joining of the unemployed with striking workers was an unprecedented class-conscious action. When the national guard fired into the picket lines, both workers and their unemployed supporters were among the killed (two) and injured (fifteen). Leadership in this struggle was shared between the union and A. J. Muste's American Workers Party, a socialist-led organization that had brought out the unemployed. The city was on the brink of a general strike on June 1, when an agreement was reached that granted union recognition at Auto-Lite and Toledo Edison. The massive rally that was planned to launch the strike action was turned into a huge victory celebration for all of labor.

Minneapolis

Minneapolis General Drivers Local #574 defied their national union, the Teamsters, and federal mediators in a series of strikes from May through July that mobilized the unemployed councils, local construction workers, and the entire community. Thousands of workers joined with local 574 in opposition to the national guard, police, and "special deputies" brought in to break the strikes. The Women's Auxiliary set up a food service capable of providing 10,000 meals a day that worked on a twenty-four-hour basis. Union leaders handed out baseball bats and lengths of iron pipe to arm strikers. Flying squadrons of union cars patrolled the city to block nonunion truckers. A union motorcycle squad of five units patrolled the city streets twenty-four hours a day. Over just a few days, bloody confrontations with police left three dead and almost a hundred injured. The strike went on after the arrest of several of the union leaders, and the issuance of warrants for the arrest of others, including the Dunne brothers, Ray, Grant, and Miles, all well known as Trotskyists. The workers of the city stood firm, even after the seizure of the strike headquarters by the national guard and the imposition of martial law in the city. The governor of Minnesota, Floyd B. Olsen, elected with farmer-labor and socialist support, was forced to free the jailed unionists, and the employers finally gave in to the demands of the workers. The Dunne brothers gave Trotskyists their biggest labor victory in the United States.

Left Rising

Workers and their independent or left-wing leaders in dozens of other cities turned their federal locals into citywide labor councils and began broad-scale organizing campaigns that included labor clubs, political groups, drama societies, consumer cooperatives, and drum and bugle corps. In the absence of AFL leadership, workers found their own, and accepted the help of willing Socialists, former Wobblies, and Communists.

The actual number of Communists (to outsiders, Stalinists and Trotskyists were not differentiated) and Socialists was not as great in this labor upsurge as their influence made it appear. Actual party members never reached more than about 55,000 in the United States at the peak of Communist Party influence by the middle of the decade. Socialists were a little more numerous, but the Socialist Party organization was weak in comparison. It was the energy, discipline, and devotion to the cause of labor that brought Communists and other radical critics of capitalism into the leadership of unions and put them at the forefront of the union organizing battles of the era of the Blue Eagle and beyond.

Aside from a handful of their leaders, few Communist Party members had any contact with the Soviet Union or Joseph Stalin, though everyone who joined accepted some level of the authoritarian discipline the organization required. Communists were both credited with and blamed for opening up the reviving labor movement to full inclusion, including leadership, for black workers. Because the party line condemned racial discrimination, members could be, and were, expelled for racism. No church, synagogue, or mosque had ever done the same. When, in 1932, the NAACP dropped it, or lost control of it, the Communist Party took up the nearly impossible legal defense of the Scottsboro Boys, a group of nine young black men and boys falsely accused of raping two white girls in Alabama. Communists may have been naive, or worse, about the ideology they embraced, but they were the only organization among the working class to combat racism actively. They forced the issue to the foreground of the labor movement and the nation when no other group outside of the black community would take it up.

Textile Workers, North and South

The largest single strike in the nation's history began in early September 1934. In nine states, from Maine to Alabama, 500,000 textile workers in cotton, woolens, silk, and related industries walked off the job, nearly half of them in the South. Working conditions in the mills were abysmal. The "stretch-out" (more work demanded for the same pay) was common in the industry. Outsiders were shocked by the illness and malnutrition rampant among southern workers. Depressed wage rates were so low everywhere that children were ragged and shoeless, living conditions terrible. New Deal photographers like Walker Evans and Dorothea Lange preserved some of the pathos and terror in the faces of millworkers, migrant workers, dispossessed farmers, and their children.

The work stoppage in textiles, which began during the Labor Day weekend, was more of a revolt than a strike. Twenty-five thousand workers shut down Hazelton, Pennsylvania, in a one-day general strike in solidarity with the textile workers. In Rhode Island, where 50,000 workers were on strike, Governor T. H. Green sent national guard units to several peaceful towns to put down what he described as a communist threat. His troops provoked angry crowds, and tear gas, bayonets, and rifle fire soon claimed several lives. Before the strike was over, fourteen strikers were killed. Governors of all of the textile states came to the aid of the employers by the second week. National guard units and special militia were used to keep the mills open. Strikers were evicted from company houses, and state relief agencies cut aid to unionists, striking or not.

The machinery of the NRA resulted in a report that satisfied neither side but forced a conclusion to the strike. The United Textile Workers failed to gain the union recognition it sought. Employers, aided by the National Association of Manufacturers, found ways of firing or not rehiring strike leaders and union members. Wage and stretch-out issues were to be the subject of further studies. Eventually, when these reports were completed they were, like industry codes, unenforceable and worthless.

Alternatives

Before the year was over, national guard units had been called out to break strikes in twelve states with Democratic governors. Workers were soon referring to the NRA as the "national run-around." In Louisiana, the radical-populist governor, Huey Long, was boosting his national political ambitions as a possible rival to FDR in 1936 amid the statewide creation of "Share the Wealth Clubs." Upton Sinclair's "End Poverty in California" was a popular Socialist Party challenge to Democrats put forward by the well-known author-candidate for governor. On the extreme right, the Catholic priest,

Father Coughlin, was stoking the flames of fascist, racist, and anti-Semitic explanations for the continuing hard times in radio broadcasts that won massive audiences in urban neighborhoods nationwide. At the AFL convention in 1934 one of the leaders of the United Textile Workers put forward a proposal that the organization abandon the Democratic Party and join with Socialists, Communists, and industrial workers to create an independent labor party. Though there were not enough votes to carry the measure, it was clear that the program of FDR was in trouble among industrial workers. Win or lose for labor under the Blue Eagle, radical critics of all stripes were gaining ground. Business leaders, of course, continued to smolder and rage against the New Deal.

NRA Ends; NLRB, Fair Labor Standards, and Social Security Begin

The National Association of Manufacturers was determined to continue its fight against union organizing despite the NRA. So were most businessmen, who were convinced that the new law was unconstitutional and should be destroyed. The Supreme Court, not yet in accord with FDR, agreed in May 1935. The Blue Eagle of the NIRA was dead, along with several other early pieces of New Deal legislation. The three main component parts for labor of the NIRA—the protection of workers' right to organize unions, protective codes regarding minimum wage and child labor, and federal oversight of the collective bargaining process—were all given new life in new legislation.

The National Labor Relations Act, popularly known as the Wagner Act for its principal advocate, Senator Robert F. Wagner of New York, was, after initial resistance by FDR, signed into law by the president in July. The law reaffirmed the right of workers to organize in its Section 7. A National Labor Relations Board (NLRB) was established with greater authority than under the former law to mediate, arbitrate, or conciliate conflicts. The NLRB was given the authority to oversee collective bargaining elections, and could bring legal action against employers for "unfair practices" against workers. For the first time courts could be used to enforce a law on behalf of labor's right to organize and engage in collective bargaining. In spite of this power, it should be noted that throughout its entire history no businessman has ever been jailed for violation of the National Labor Relations Law, no matter how serious or flagrant the violation. Businessmen and their lawyers, however, were sure that the new law would be thrown out by the Supreme Court, and meet the same fate as the NIRA. Until it was upheld by the Supreme Court in 1937, the Wagner Act piled up a mountain of unsettled litigation. Once it was upheld business leaders looked for other means of resisting or fighting back.

Instead of unenforceable industry codes, or the inconsistencies inherent in thousands of separate collective bargaining contracts, uniform standards of minimum wage, maximum hours, and child labor restrictions were first established in law with the passage of the Walsh-Healy Government Contracts Act of 1936. The law required all government contractors to adhere to a minimum wage set by the secretary of labor, an eight-hour day, a forty-hour week, and prohibited the use of child labor or convict labor. The provisions of Walsh-Healy were applied to all businesses engaged in interstate commerce by the Fair Labor Standards Act in 1938, the last New Deal measure enacted for labor. Minimum wage was to be adjusted by law.

The Social Security Act of 1935 guaranteed federal pension protection for workers through a payroll tax matched equally by employer and employees. Business groups attacked the measure as socialistic and continue to hate the social security law because they must match the payments, hence their continuing desire to "save," "privatize," or "reform" it. Too many voters soon enjoyed its benefits, so its critics had to mute or transform their objections. At first the social security system accepted a racist differential in payments that reduced benefits to nonwhites as demanded by southern Democrats. Wartime service ended that injustice.

The Wagner Act protected the right of workers as individuals to form collective associations, not the right of union organizations to enter into agreements with employers for the purpose of achieving collective bargaining. The AFL fought the concept of individual worker rights unsuccessfully in court actions for several years. The law blocked the federation from reaching private agreements with employers without the democratic participation of workers, a well-established practice the AFL bitterly hated giving up.

The protective legislation of 1933–38, and the union organizing drive that accompanied it, won the political loyalty and the votes of industrial workers for the Democrats for the next thirty years. Only a few critics noted that all of this protective legislation might make labor more dependent on and more vulnerable than ever to the power of government, and that what was gained by law could just as easily be lost or taken away in the same manner.

There was a distinct upturn in the economy in 1935–36 that added to the popularity of the New Deal and spurred the union organizing drive. Millions of households put food on their tables because of federal relief, reform, or reconstruction programs. FDR won labor's gratitude in his overwhelming electoral sweep in 1936 when he carried every state but Vermont and Maine. Democrats were elected to 331 seats in Congress, their greatest majority in the century. Lewis and his associates formed Labor's Nonpartisan League, a poorly named body devoted to the reelection of FDR, and the predecessor of the later Political Action Committee (PAC), formed by the CIO during the war to support pro-labor candidates, and the Committee on Political Education (COPE), a similar postwar organization. Labor votes on the side of Democrats made the difference in added congressional seats, in several governors' races, and in dozens of mayoralty and local contests. The 1936–37 period was the high point of labor's political clout, and the time in which black voters decisively left the party of Lincoln for FDR and the Democrats. If FDR and the Democrats were enjoying the votes of labor, it was John L. Lewis who set out to win their organizational loyalty and collect their dues.

The CIO

Bad law, no law, or new law, labor activism in politics, on the streets, and in the factories was continuing with a fury never seen before. The challenge for government and for Lewis was to try to harness that fury, and to bring it under control. Once the Wagner Act was passed and labor's right to organize was reaffirmed, Lewis was determined to push ahead with a strategy that would place him in a position to wrest control of the result.

David Dubinsky, president of the International Ladies Garment Workers Union (ILGWU), and Sidney Hillman, president of the Amalgamated Clothing Workers of America (ACWA), shared Lewis's frustration watching their radical rivals on the left gain prestige and power among industrial workers while the AFL did nothing, or worse than nothing. To these ambitious moderate Socialists and conservative union leaders, the power vacuum in organizing was handing the left, especially the Communists, the command of the battle to unionize industrial workers. Even worse from their perspective, the radicals were collecting the dues and building the new institutional and political structures for potentially millions of workers. Lewis was frustrated as well by the failure of the AFL to organize the steel industry, which controlled almost 10 percent of the nation's coal production in company-owned, or "captive mines." If Lewis was kept from organizing the "captive mines" he was in danger of losing those miners he already had.

At the AFL convention in Atlantic City in October 1935 Lewis was the most prominent advocate on behalf of the remaining federal locals and the younger activists, though he gained neither the support nor the votes for proposals to engage in industry-wide organizing campaigns. Angered by the stubborn arrogance of the old guard, Lewis was on his way to the podium to speak in defense of some young rubber tire workers when his journey took a detour. Bill Hutcheson, the powerful president of the Carpenter's union, and, like Lewis, a former Hoover Republican, had raised technical objections in order to stop the debate on industrial unionization. As he passed near Big Bill's hearing, Lewis muttered something about the technicalities as nothing but "small potatoes." Hutcheson called Lewis a "bastard." Lewis, then fifty-five years old, almost six feet tall, and about 200 pounds, clambered over some chairs, reached back, and flattened the sixty-one-year-old, and bigger, Hutcheson with a punch that signaled the break that was soon to divide organized labor itself. Hutcheson was helped out of the hall to repair his bloody face while Lewis calmly relit his cigar and continued to the podium.

The next morning at a breakfast meeting of industrial union supporters, Lewis made plans to take the organizational matter into his own hands. Three weeks later, with pledges of financial backing from Sidney Hillman, David Dubinsky, and five other AFL labor leaders, the Committee for Industrial Organization (CIO) was formed. Lewis had big game in his sights.

Instead of attending the AFL executive council meeting in balmy Florida in January, which denounced his independent and unauthorized action, Lewis was out in the freezing streets of Akron, Ohio, thundering his support for striking workers who had taken over the city's giant rubber tire plants in massive, well-planned sit-downs. He sent his top organizers, including some of his own former radical critics, John Brophy, Powers Hapgood, Adolph Germer, and Rose Perotta, into the industrial heartland of the Midwest to make contacts and lay the foundation for future organizing drives.

Lewis tried to keep the door open for a reconciliation with the AFL until June, when he set up the Steel Workers Organizing Committee (SWOC) under the leadership of his popular and charismatic UMWA vice president, Philip Murray. That step brought the AFL to the breaking point. Accusing the renegade CIO national unions of "dual unionism," they were all expelled from the AFL. The formal division came with the establishment, and name but not acronym change, of the Congress of Industrial Organizations at a convention of its own in November 1938.

The two years from the bust-up in Atlantic city to the fall of 1937 were surely the high-water mark in labor union organizing in the history of the United States. It is hardly a coincidence that it was also one of the most democratic periods in the nation's history, one that business, social, and institutional elites would spend the rest of the century seeking to undo. Working-class people elected more candidates to public office, gained more favorable legislation, and, for the first time, were able to look to the courts for positive rulings in their conflicts with employers.

The most dramatic expression of the democratic daring of industrial workers was their willingness to engage in illegal, some said revolutionary, means to achieve rather modest objectives: they seized the property of their employers and held it hostage until they gained recognition for their collective and legal right to organize democratic associations to advance their common interests. To unionize, they simply sat down together.

The Sit-Downs

The IWW had used the sit-down as a tactic in a strike against the newly formed General Electric Company early in the century. Aside from some European union actions it remained little used in the United States until 1933, when meatpackers employed by Hormel in Austin, Minnesota, employed it to win a strike for union recognition. To prevent scabs from breaking picket lines with the protection of military or police forces, workers stopped production and remained in place. Electrical power, moving assembly lines, and the interconnected nature of industrial processes gave this tactic unique practical advantages, especially in bad weather. Basic necessities in the form of food and other supplies could usually be brought in by outside supporters, other workers. In most cases there were deliberately organized women's groups or auxiliaries to back up the striking men.

Success, as we have seen, encourages imitation. In Akron, Ohio, the plants of Firestone, Goodyear, and Goodrich were forced to accept collective bargaining agreements after sit-down strikes in early 1936. After their victory the rubber workers turned their backs on the AFL, reorganized themselves as the United Rubber Workers, and joined with Lewis and the new CIO. Along with prompting Lewis to form the Steel Workers Organizing Committee (SWOC), the victory inspired a string of sit-downs in factories throughout the Midwest. In June, Wyndham Mortimer of the United Auto Workers (UAW) led a group of radical organizers in a planning project of almost six months that, according to one labor scholar, sparked "the most important single strike confrontation of the century," the great Flint, Michigan sit-down against General Motors from December 1936 to February 1937 (Green, 1980, p. 155).

Flint

Excessive noise, constant danger, speed-ups, wage cutbacks, arbitrary layoffs, favoritism, and an atmosphere of dictatorial authority prevailed in the auto industry. The General Motors Corporation was the largest manufacturing corporation in the world, and the builder of almost half the automobiles in the nation. Communists and other radical unionists made plans for disciplined actions patterned along military lines to win union recognition in Flint, the main assembly plant for GM.

Workers throughout the industry, however, were way ahead of those who would become their leaders. Hastily organized sit-downs, small and large, were breaking out on their own. The Atlanta local of the UAW called a sit-down in November 1936 over cuts in piecerates. A week later, a UAW local stopped the Bendix Corporation in South Bend, Indiana, with a nine-day sit-down that resulted in a contract for the workers there. Sit-downs at the Midland Steel Frame and Kelsey Hayes Wheel companies in Detroit in early December won wage increases, seniority rights, union recognition, and time-and-a-half for overtime. When the workers at General Motors in Cleveland, Ohio, sat down on December 28, 1936, it took the radical UAW Flint leaders by surprise. Mortimer quickly sped from Flint to Cleveland (his hometown), where he urged the workers to settle for nothing less than an industry-wide agreement.

Two days later in Flint, the largest GM Fisher Body plants in the nation were seized the same way. With two plants stopped in Flint and a third struck in Cleveland, auto production at GM quickly ground to a nationwide halt. Other GM facilities joined in the sit-down or were struck in the conventional manner. Women workers left the occupied plants and formed Women's Emergency Brigades, which, along with Ladies Auxiliaries, mobilized community support. Auto workers came from other cities to buttress the Flint sit-downers. Food and other provisions were hoisted in through windows. An internal democracy among the workers set up a government structure, including tribunals to deal with slackers or other infringements of civil order inside the seized plants. Street confrontations took place with police and special deputies. One "Battle of Running Bulls" became a legend among workers who scattered sheriff deputies sent to break the strike. For thousands of men and women, this was the turning point in their lives. It was the same for their country. Workers vowed to die rather than give in to defeat.

The Flint sit-down turned into more than a strike; it was a struggle for the future of the industrial workplace itself. The exhilaration of fighting for something that the government had deemed legitimate and that workers had struggled for more than a century to obtain was extraordinary. In Flint it nearly coincided (or was planned to coincide) with the inauguration of a new Democratic governor of Michigan, Frank Murphy. In their elections almost two months earlier Murphy and FDR enjoyed the overwhelming support of labor. As the new governor, Murphy resisted pressure to break the strike in spite of his own misgivings and tremendous pressure from the automaker. No military forces were used to displace the strikers. Murphy used the national guard solely to maintain order.

Lee Pressman was a savvy thirty-one-year-old Harvard law school graduate. He was an articulate radical (according to his own account, a recent ex-Communist), and the general legal counsel for the CIO. Pressman blocked a court-ordered injunction to vacate the plants. He discovered that the judge in the case owned some GM stock and was therefore acting in conflict of interest. Crucial weeks passed until another injunction could be obtained. GM and the UAW signed their historic agreement, formulated by Lewis and drafted by Pressman, on February 11, 1937. Some grumblers questioned the extent of a victory that only gave the union six months with the exclusive right to represent GM workers, and little else after this monumental fight. But, victory was real, there was no going back. The UAW, originally organized by the AFL, about a year earlier, was now firmly established in the rival CIO, and became the cornerstone for the national industrial organizing drive led by the CIO that immediately followed. "Victory Is Ours" read the sign placed on the roof of the huge No.1 Fisher Body plant by the workers at the end of the celebration in Flint on the night of the 11th.

Big Steel Signs On without a Fight

Lewis bagged one of his greatest victories three weeks later. Without the shop-floor mobilization of the workers, but firm in the use of the threat of such disruption as likely, he negotiated an agreement that gave his SWOC a contract with United States Steel, the world's largest steel producer. This was a secretive deal made at the top between the labor baron and his corporate counterpart, Myron P. Taylor, the chairman of U.S. Steel. One can only imagine the conversations between the two powerful men. Neither of them wanted to go through the shop-floor upheaval that brought GM to accept union recognition. Both were accustomed to autocratic control, and shared an abhorrence to any form of worker or workplace democracy. Pressman, once again with essentials provided by Lewis, put the finishing touches on what became another historic contract. This one included recognition of the SWOC as bargaining agent, a 10 percent wage increase, and a five-day, forty-hour workweek. Just a couple of weeks later, in mid-April, the Supreme Court upheld the constitutionality of the Wagner Act in all respects.

Union

Now the floodgates began to open to union mobilization under the banner of the CIO. For a brief historical moment, under the protection of federal law, and with state and local leaders elected with their votes, the servants appeared to be gaining on their masters. With political protection, workers seized the initiative won by their bold actions. Chrysler autoworkers in Detroit, who had been in a sit-down since early March, reached an agreement for 100,000 workers in April similar to the one for GM workers. This settlement was also negotiated by Lewis, with Homer Martin, the UAW president, Pressman, and officials from the company present, including Walter Chrysler himself, as the head of his company's team.

The fury of the struggle, especially the working-class audacity of the sit-downs, is why people remembered this time as a union movement, not simply an organizing drive. Millions of workers engaged in strikes and sit-downs. They walked picket lines, slowed down, and protested for recognition of their unions under the law during the next several months. No industrial workplace was without an activist presence, strike, sit-down, or organizing drive. Every sort of worker, including sanitation workers, sales clerks, stockboys, laundry workers, engineers, blind (sightless) workers, and gravediggers, took part in sit-downs over the course of the next year. People sat down in protest in relief offices, in employment agencies, against police in eviction demonstrations. Prisoners adopted the tactic in jails in Joliet, Illinois, and Philadelphia, Pennsylvania. Children did the same in movie theaters to protest program cuts. General Motors required the assistance of the UAW to end the outbreak of approximately 170 small- and large-scale sit-downs that took place at its various plants during the three months that followed the Flint agreement. By late summer 1937, the CIO had 3.4 million members and was larger than the AFL.

Dave Beck, the Seattle Teamster leader, used the momentum of the sit-downs to expand his organization's membership along the West Coast. According to Beck, "When we first went into LA (in 1937) we had 400 members, when we finished organizing, we had over 100,000" (quoted in McCallum, 1978, p. 74). It was a nationwide phenomenon.

On August 25, 1937, twelve years after its founding, and after hundreds of firings, threats, and beatings, the Brotherhood of Sleeping Car Porters, led by A. Philip Randolph, with the assistance of federal mediators and the serious threat of a nationwide strike, forced the Pullman Company into recognition of the union and a contract agreement. His union became the foundation on which Randolph built the subsequent struggle for civil rights and full racial equality in the United States. Risking arrest for sitting down for racial equality had its origins when Randolph and his associates made their union the most important legal institution on behalf of black workers in the nation. Sit-downs for union recognition were declared to be illegal in court in 1938. A generation later the tactic was successfully revived by civil rights activists guided by Randolph.

Randolph and several other prominent black labor leaders formed the National Negro Congress (NNC) a year earlier because the mainly middle-class NAACP opposed the CIO. At the first convention of the NNC Randolph linked the struggle for industrial unionism and full civil rights. No one realized it then, but the great surge of democratic union building was reaching a peak with his BSCP-Pullman agreement. Opposition forces, both within the unions and outside, were determined to contain, control, or destroy the militant democracy unleashed by labor during the previous five years.

Government and Labor

By the end of 1936 the federal government and FDR had won the loyalty of labor. Even the radical left gave the New Deal and the Democrats their votes and their devotion. The rise of fascism and the growing threat of war made uneasy and temporary political bedfellows out of the Soviet Union and the United States. Franklin Roosevelt became the first president of the Untied States to recognize the Soviet Union when the two nations exchanged ambassadors for the first time in 1933. The U.S. Communist Party line on most matters, with some notable twists and turns, coincided with that of the Democratic Party from 1935 to 1946. The CP called its embrace of the New Deal its Popular Front period, and actually dissolved itself temporarily in the United States in 1944 as an act of wartime solidarity. Those Socialists who were led by Hillman, Dubinsky, and Schneiderman were also firmly in the camp of the Democratic Party.

Besides protective legislation, FDR's appointments to the NLRB, the courts, his cabinet, and federal agencies and boards earned his administration the reputation of fairness and sensitivity to issues of importance to most working people. After 1938, when the Democratic majority in Congress decreased, and actually was outnumbered on domestic issues by the coalition of southern Democrats and conservative Republicans, the New Deal actually came to an end. The increasingly dark clouds of impending war overtook the news and public thinking, and obliterated further legislative initiatives for labor. When FDR turned, as he said, from "Dr. New Deal" to "Dr. Win-The-War," he carried the nation's workers with him. Certainly, the New Deal was an effective preparation for the war. Unlike Wilson, FDR led a unified labor force into war.

The ultimately conservative political success of FDR and the New Deal came from preventing the emergence of a real or independent labor party, and his maintaining the loyalty of workers to the existing two-party system of the United States. The rambunctious hundred-year-old democracy of labor was put in harness on the cheap, too. While many industrial workers were achieving some representation and protection, many millions more never won union rights, and most others were not protected under the law at all. At their peak in the postwar era, unions never represented more than about one-third of the labor force. Nonetheless, workers everywhere in the nation, union and nonunion, industrial, service, and professional, black and white, men and women, looked mainly to the CIO and the Democratic Party for political leadership and direction. But, what was good for many Democratic candidates, occasionally some Republicans, and two generations of comfortably well-connected labor bureaucrats, ultimately faded as a democratic expression of the sentiments of labor, as an entity, itself. The CIO and the Democratic Party were unable to sustain the democratic initiatives of this era into the next, the period known as the cold war.

On the state and local levels of politics, labor votes determined the outcomes in hundreds of elections by 1936, and continued as a significant factor thereafter. Labor's political strength continued to be a factor, though continually on the defensive, for the next thirty years and helps account for the relative prosperity of labor unions and the success of the Democratic Party at the polls. Republicans in industrial states like New York, Pennsylvania, New Jersey, and Michigan were forced to accept the gains of organized labor as well in order to be elected. No one can openly attack social security without serious political risk.

Nonetheless, by 1937, at the peak of labor's political influence, a new coalition of conservative and outspoken racist Democrats (elected in states that barred black citizens from voting rights) began to join forces with antiunion Republicans to put an end to any further New Deal legislation. The new coalition was intent on curbing the dangerous democracy an independent labor movement represented. Their "Conservative Manifesto," issued at the end of 1937, condemned the sit-downs, called for reduced taxes and a balanced federal budget, and favored a reduction of the power of the federal government and a return to states' rights. The "Manifesto" was critical of public economic activities and welfare assistance to stimulate the economy. Government encouragement of private enterprise was the only means of economic stimulation they could accept. The "Manifesto" was a broad attack on the New Deal and a plea for a return to the previous era. That it would become the program for a revived conservative offensive three decades later is hardly surprising.

The AFL was no less vigorous in combating the victories of the rest of labor. President Green and his minions put most of their organizing energy into jurisdictional battles against the CIO; their legal efforts all went into attempts at overturning the authority of the NLRB. The AFL presented itself to employers as a safer, more compliant alternative to the more militant CIO. Thousands of "sweetheart" agreements in contracts and union recognition were made between AFL and business leaders after both were forced to live with the legality of the NLRB. When a CIO group secured the opportunity to hold a collective bargaining election, the AFL was on the spot seeking to challenge their rival, or to separate out craft workers for their own organization. A virtual civil war between the AFL and the CIO raged over 1937–38. FDR sought in vain to broker a peace between the rival organizations for his own political reasons in 1939. Realistic talk of a reconciliation would have to wait until after the major leaders, Lewis, Murray, and Green, were dead.

Lewis had internal troubles as well. His CIO, carrying on in the inclusive and democratic tradition of the Knights of Labor and the IWW, was rife with fractious and volatile forces. Dubinsky brought his 200,000-member ILGWU back into affiliation with the AFL in 1940. By then the AFL had overtaken and surpassed the CIO in membership.

Despite the political prominence of many union leaders, there would be nothing more in the way of positive national legislation for labor after the passage of the Fair Labor Standards Act in 1938. Women and black workers were the least protected by the Fair Labor Standards Act because of their greater employment in non-interstate-commerce-related work. States rights advocates knew the difference then and still do.

In contrast to the structural power of the more unified English Trade Union Council (TUC) in the English Labour Party, and its achievement of a national healthcare system, labor in the United States held no formal institutional place in the Democratic Party and gained no healthcare legislation for all workers. All forms of healthcare services would soon be lumped with "fringe" benefits, things that workers presumably could do without, or would have to win through separately negotiated agreements with individual employers. The Fair Labor Standards Act, with its provision of a minimum wage, infuriated southerners, and drove more congressmen and some senators from that region into the anti-New Deal camp led by Republicans.

On the state and local levels, political victories continued to bring some further results for labor in the form of disability and unemployment insurance. States varied with inconsistent child labor restrictions, workplace health and safety requirements, and protective legislation for women. Powerful city labor councils, or "city centrals," led by AFL craft unions and augmented by new CIO unions, continued to exert considerable influence for their members. In dozens of cities, the most popular mayors were elected with labor votes. Before the Depression was over, Fiorello LaGuardia became the most successful and best-loved mayor in the history of the city of New York. He was a progressive Republican and a fusion candidate with the endorsement of the city's powerful Labor Party.

With almost no foreign immigration, the fastest-growing group among industrial workers were black men and women drawn from rural poverty to the urban possibilities of employment and New Deal relief. Racism and gender discrimination were set back by the universalism of the federal New Deal programs, not any specific protection of human or civil rights. Every industrial worker, regardless of race or gender, was eligible for social security. Labor law took in all nonagricultural workers in interstate commerce related employment. Relief measures helped all of those in need.

In contrast to the democratic gains for workers of the New Deal, racial segregation and gender-specific labor prevailed in the industrial workplace, and in almost every other place of employment in spite of remarkable efforts to internally desegregate many CIO unions, and the CIO's expressed commitment to equal pay for equal work. Indeed, the CIO was, by 1938, the largest, most important national voice for racial equity, a federal antilynching law, and opposition to the racially discriminatory poll tax. It was wartime necessity, and the threat of a massive march on Washington planned by A. Philip Randolph in 1941, that opened up millions of jobs to black workers. State and local codes and ordinances in the South and nearly insurmountable social practices in housing, education, and employment practices maintained a color bar everywhere else. The military forces of the United States and most areas of civil service work were strictly segregated by race until 1948.

Business Reacts on Its Own

No large employer was without a plan to stop, destroy, or wrest control away from mobilizing workers throughout the New Deal era and beyond it. The American Legion actually approached Marine Commandant General Smedley Butler, according to his later testimony to Congress, with an offer to lead a fascist overthrow of the Roosevelt administration in 1934. A so-called Liberty League was formed in 1934 by wealthy business leaders to restore the open shop and attack the New Deal. A northern version of the KKK, called the Black Legion, was formed to kidnap, beat, and torture union organizers. At least ten were killed by this group, funded, according to the governor of Pennsylvania, George H. Earle, by members of the DuPont family, corporate leaders of General Motors, and the financial backers of the Liberty League (Boyer, 1955, p. 281).

At the end of 1937 a U.S. Senate investigation of violations of workers' civil liberties, led by Senator Robert M. LaFollette of Wisconsin, disclosed some of the extravagant and illegal ends to which business went to thwart labor's organizing drive. Tens of millions of dollars a year were spent on industrial espionage, goon squads, and bribes. Millions more went for propaganda on behalf of company unions, but money wasn't the only price that business was prepared to pay. Corporations were prepared to sacrifice the nation's laws, even the protection of the Constitution itself, if necessary, in this battle. Some business antiunion practices became almost as legendary as the union sit-down tactics of the time.

One of these was the quite deliberately illegal Mohawk Valley Formula, designed by the Remington Rand Company of New York, and disclosed after an inquiry by the NLRB in 1937. The use of threats to close plants, false criminal accusations against unionists, red-baiting, intimidation by police, vigilantes, "special deputies," and company agents, were all old hat, but were now newly packaged and carefully arranged with staged back-to-work rallies and the formation of so-called Citizens' Committees in a nine-part program that was enthusiastically promoted by the National Association of Manufactures (NAM) and the American Iron and Steel Institute. The immediate goal of the Mohawk Valley Formula was to stop what the law allowed, and what Lewis and Taylor agreed to: collective bargaining for industrial workers. The rest of the steel industry, known as "Little Steel" and comprised of companies like Bethlehem, Republic, Youngstown Sheet and Tube, and others, were led by men who were "violently antiunion" (Bernstein, 1970, p. 480). These businessmen were determined to halt the organizing drive, despite its nominal legality. If they could no longer count on government to do the job for them, they were quite prepared to take matters into their own hands. There were thousands just like them.

Corporate Terror

Henry Ford wasn't having any of it. His so-called Service Department included men recruited directly from prison cells with the aid of cooperative parole boards for the sole purpose of brutalizing workers who might dare to build an organization of their own. This hoodlum gang was led by Harry Bennet, a former member of the Michigan parole board. Under Bennet's direction workers were terrorized inside Ford plants all over the country, where they could be beaten for simply talking to one another on the assembly line. In one notorious event, Bennet's thugs viciously beat UAW leaders, women leafletters, reporters, and photographers on an overpass near the large River Rouge plant in May 1937. Eventually, Ford was found to be in violation of the rights of the workers by the NLRB, but no one was ever jailed for the deliberate assaults, and it was not until the brink of war in 1941 that Ford was forced to relent, allow a collective bargaining election, and sign on with the UAW.

One of the most brutal acts of violence ever carried out against organizing workers was the Memorial Day Massacre at Republic Steel on May 30, 1937. Little Steel's determination to resist the CIO brought on strikes at several companies in the heartland of the industry. Violent confrontations between staged "back-to-work-movements" in Pennsylvania and the Midwest left eight steel workers dead, dozens injured, and scores arrested. On the south side of Chicago, members of the SWOC gathered in a holiday picnic and protest demonstration at a Republic Steel plant. The company, according to the La Follette Committee, provided machine guns, rifles, revolvers, tear gas, and bombs to a blue-coated mixture of police and company security forces.

With no provocation, the police opened fire at the crowd, driving into the frightened picketers with clubs swinging. Many of the ten killed that day were shot in the back. The wounded were clubbed as they huddled on the ground; at least one was beaten to death. Women and children were among the scores treated for injuries. The carnage at Republic stands out because it was so well captured on newsreel film and in photographs. Though a Paramount News cameraman carefully recorded the event, his employer suppressed its showing. It remained for other news sources to describe the ugly film footage in print until it became more widely accessible years later. Photographs appeared in *Life* magazine over captions that falsely claimed the police were acting in self-defense.

Physical intimidation, threats, and an economic downturn allowed Little Steel, Ford, and a host of other corporate employers, large and small, to remain nonunion until 1941. Many of them remained nonunion indefinitely if they did not need to rely on federal defense contracts. Corporate acts of violent intimidation, illegal conspiracy, and brutality against workers were usually, as Adam Smith observed more than 150 years earlier, carried out covertly, or through deniable surrogates like the Liberty League or Black Legion. At Ford and Republic the gloves and the masks were off.

Curbing the Power of Labor

Shaping an angry antilabor public sentiment was another deliberate business objective. During 1937–38 the National Association of Manufacturers circulated over two million copies of a pamphlet entitled "Join the CIO and Help Build a Soviet America." Appeals to patriotism and the alleged danger of a red menace were effective antilabor devices after World War I. Now, in the spring of 1938, in the aftermath of the great wave of sit-downs and the rise of the CIO, the conservative and white supremacist coalition in Congress formed a House Committee on Un-American Activities (later known as HUAC) to "investigate" the threat to national life posed by foreign subversive influences.

The new committee had no interest in Germany or Japan. The first witness called was John Frey, an AFL official, who termed the CIO a "seminary of Communist sedition" (quoted in Kennedy, 1999, p. 316). The AFL provided scores of names of CIO leaders thought to be Communists to the committee, chaired by Texas Democrat Martin Dies. Though formally only an investigative body, the committee was sensationalized by the press's coverage of its hearings. The first HUAC victim was Governor Murphy of Michigan, who was publicly pilloried for his failure to use force to break the Flint strike the previous year. Murphy lost his bid for reelection in November to his predecessor, Frank Fitzgerald, a Republican under whom Harry Bennet, Ford's notorious Service Department chief, had served on the state parole board.

No law made association with the Communist Party a crime, and no one could say with certainty that the sit-downs were a left-wing tactic. In none of the big strike actions of 1934–37 were socialist, communist, or political programs or demands of any kind advanced. It is more accurate to conclude that all of the organized labor groups, including the Communists, that were seeking control or influence amid the rising turmoil among industrial workers ultimately did more to stop sit-downs than provoke them. Prejudice, however, not facts, meant everything to the committee. To these worthies the worst offense of the CP-USA, aside from its labor militancy, was its uncompromising stand on racial equality.

Many middle-class citizens, small business owners, and professionals agreed. They reacted against the gains of the most oppressed sections of the working class, people they had contact with every day. The New Deal benefits of jobs, unions, or relief that went to the unemployed, to service workers and manual laborers, especially to women and black workers, were resented by many in more privileged or advantaged social groups.

Even in the depths of the Depression and an era of militant labor activism, polls showed that more citizens thought themselves to be members of the middle class than any other. Unlike their European counterparts, most craft and industrial workers in the United States, including the unemployed, identified themselves as middle class, and patriotism and racism were core sentiments of the respectability associated with this group's outlook. Few candidates for public office in the United States through nearly all of its history have been harmed by appeals to patriotism or racism. This political and social backlash, and a sharp economic downturn in 1938, were reflected in the congressional elections that year. Republicans gained seventy-five seats in the House of Representatives, and seven in the Senate, their first gains since the beginning of the Depression. Together with their southern allies in the Democratic Party and support from the AFL and the NAM, this new coalition was determined to turn back the tide of organized labor. Their first target was the NLRB.

For the first four months of 1939 a series of bills or amendments to change the NLRB to favor the AFL, or to abolish the board altogether, were put before Congress. Senator Robert Wagner defended the law that created it, now commonly referred to as the Wagner Act. Wagner pointed out that there were fewer strikes, and the trend was continuing downward since the law had been upheld by the Supreme Court, than in prior years. The law was doing what it was supposed to do: it was reducing industrial conflict. FDR defensively responded to the congressional threat by appointing more moderate, less labor identified, figures to the board. Not satisfied, Congress established a special committee, known as the Smith Committee for its chair, Howard Smith, an anti-New Deal Virginia Democrat, to investigate the NLRB.

For two months of highly publicized hearings, beginning in December 1939, the NLRB was blasted. The antilabor majority on the Smith committee provided a forum for every kind of attack. The committee called the kind of witnesses they knew would bolster their case. The press gave prominence to the attacks, nearly ignoring the more friendly hearings going on simultaneously in the House and Senate labor committees. The CIO, the CP, and the NLRB were, it was alleged, in bed together. The labor board should be abolished or the law drastically changed. Smith proposed a long list of amendments to the law with the general concurrence of President William Green of the AFL. Green still favored the AFL tradition of voluntarism, and the modifications to the proposed law emphatically favored AFL unions over the CIO. The Senate, still led by its labor committee, buried the amendments, but FDR was put further on the defensive. He named more conservative and pro-business figures who tipped the majority of the NLRB away from labor. The House also cut the budget appropriations to the NLRB.

The Smith Act

Another of the actions of the enhanced congressional majority against labor was the passage in 1940 of the Smith Act (Alien Registration Act), named for its principal author, Congressman Howard Smith. With fears stemming from the outbreak of war in Europe in September 1939, the law made it a crime to "teach and advocate the overthrow and destruction of the Government of the United States by force and violence." Obviously, to be a member of a group with that goal put one in legal jeopardy. The attorney general of the United States was expected to assemble a list of groups and organizations that fit that description, and the federal courts were to hear charges.

Once again German and Japanese groups and individuals had little to fear. Most pro-Hitler or pro-Imperial Japan groups dissolved themselves or were underground by this time. Labor, once again, was the real target. Farrell Dobbs, the Dunne brothers, and about two dozen of their fellow unionists were all Trotskyist leaders of the recently reorganized Local 544 of the AFL-affiliated Teamsters Union. The tiny Socialist Workers Party (SWP) was their political organization and the only political group prosecuted under the Smith Act in the prewar period. The SWP favored the idea of a labor party and was the only left-wing organization that had not embraced the New Deal. By 1938 the energetic Dobbs and the Dunne brothers organized a North Central District Drivers Council that represented forty-six Teamster locals spread over eleven states. They led a quarter of a million men. Altogether eighteen of these union leaders were found guilty of violating the Smith Act and sent to federal prison, though no criminal act, other than "teaching" or "advocacy" was ever charged. The AFL cheered the destruction of the radical Teamster leadership, and Dan Tobin of the AFL, with the help of streetwise toughs willing to get a little blood on their hands, men like young Detroit warehouseman Jimmy Hoffa, moved in to gain control of the broken organization. The pro-Stalin CP cheered the destruction of the Trots as well, in the same year that Stalin actually arranged the assassination of his notorious critic, Leon Trotsky.

The Socialist Workers' Party had almost no friends at all in the Smith Act case. The American Civil Liberties Union was the sole dissenter of any prominence, and the solicitor general, Francis Biddle, who approved the original criminal prosecution, later expressed regret at his part in it. The ACLU and Biddle (eventually) found no "clear and present danger" in the SWP that justified the infringement of the U.S. Constitution's protection of freedom of speech. A precedent was set, however, and the same law was used to jail CP leaders after the war. Hoffa went on to take over the Central Conference of Teamsters and used it as a base for extending his national leadership over the union. In an ABC television interview less than a year before Hoffa's disappearance (November 30, 1974), Farrell Dobbs credited Hoffa's rise to Teamster power to the help he received from numerous sources, including the Minneapolis Police Department, the courts, the mayor, the governor, a state antilabor law, the FBI, and the United States Department of Justice. Said Dobbs, "Under those circumstances you got to admit Hoffa had just a little help, didn't he?" (quoted in Sloane, 1991, p. 30).

This Land Is Your Land: Labor Confidence at the End of the Depression

Despite corporate intransigence, propaganda, and the use of terror to block unionization, the power and prestige of labor in the United States was nearing a cultural pinnacle. There were real tangible accomplishments. The Tennessee Valley Authority put tens of thousands of people to work and brought inexpensive and renewable hydroelectric power to millions of people in towns, cities, and rural communities all over the South. Businessmen may have bristled with rage at having to deal with labor unions, but they welcomed the more than $11 billion in construction contracts provided by the New Deal. Cheap electricity also fueled a business revival in the South and Northwest that has continued to support prosperity in those areas for more than half a century.

The planning and construction of 8,000 national and local parks, 500,000 miles of highways, almost 100,000 bridges, as many libraries, post offices, courthouses, and other public buildings put almost nine million people to work on projects of inestimable public value, while pouring billions of dollars into the stagnant economy (Kennedy, 1999, pp. 149, 253). Government spending was actually making a stronger and better nation while it was putting people to work.

The skills of the people were improved as well by the New Deal. Though racially segregated and restricted by quotas, approximately 250,000 young black men were employed by the Civilian Conservation Corps (CCC), where many of them were instructed in the use of machinery like bulldozers and typewriters. The use of that kind of equipment and the development of the skills their use required were denied black workers by most private employers, but would prove to be a valuable asset in the war effort that was coming (Jones, 1998, p. 343). Theaters and recreational lodges were built by government programs. Artistic, literary, musical, photographic, and historical preservation projects put thousands of creative minds and hands to work when they had nowhere else to turn. Work itself, not simply profits or money making, was honored for its social value and its contribution to human enrichment. The artistic work of photographers like W. Eugene Smith and filmmakers shifted from their depictions of the despair and misery of the early years of the Depression to the excitement and confidence inspired by the accomplishments of labor by the end of the decade. Woody Guthrie's bleak "Dust Bowl Ballad" was soon eclipsed by songs heralding the bountiful wonders of the Bonneville and Grand Coulee dams. Massive European orders for steel and other war materiel and agricultural goods in 1939 only added to the central role of labor in the future of the nation. Gearing the nation itself up for war a year later only added confidence, swagger, and a sense of social solidarity throughout the expanding ranks of labor.

Toward War

Once again the nation moved toward war without much public discussion or understanding by workers of any of the issues that had brought the conflict about. After the outbreak of war in Europe in September 1939, FDR tilted the nation toward a cautious interventionism on the side of England and France with little opposition from most of his fellow Americans. Only the little Communist Party and the big John L. Lewis held to a rigid position of nonintervention. The CP was following the direction of the Soviet Union after the Stalin–Hitler Pact that was made only a month before the German invasion of Poland. Once the Soviet Union was invaded in June 1941, six months before the attack on Pearl Harbor, the CP reversed itself and became an active proponent of war against Hitler.

The power and confidence of labor was reflected in the audacity of the CIO leader. Lewis initially joined the isolationist opposition to intervention, and then resumed his Republican loyalties after FDR rejected him as vice presidential candidate in 1940. Lewis was enraged at FDR over other things as well, especially the president's preference for dealing with Sidney Hillman on labor matters. Lewis was furious at the awarding of fat defense contracts to companies like Ford and Little Steel that remained defiant of NLRB rulings and the Wagner Act in general. Lewis and FDR were an impossible personal or political match-up anyway. After FDR's third-term victory in 1940, Lewis left the leadership of the CIO to Philip Murray, and withdrew to his presidency of the United Mineworkers of America.

The Good War

This was a war that only began to look good the farther one got away from it. World War II was the most destructive and horrific conflagration of human violence ever carried out. Most of the estimated fifty-five million people killed by military power were civilians, and most of those were workers with very limited or no political capability to influence the war's causation. That number does not include the workers who were killed in industrial incidents, typically called accidents, but when predictably caused by wartime speedups and safety lapses, should better be known as collateral losses. In the United States there were over 88,000 workers killed in various industries, more than eleven million seriously maimed or injured from 1941 to 1945, according to the U.S. Bureau of Labor Statistics (*Handbook*, 1947, no. 916, p. 164).

Few citizens had ever heard of Pearl Harbor until the day it was attacked. When FDR explained where it was and what had happened, the public listened and rallied in a display of national unity that had never been seen before. Rank-and-file labor militancy faded quickly as dangerous foreign enemies replaced exploitative employers as enemies. Union leaders, for the most part, and with the exception of a few Trotskyists and John L. Lewis, were quick to accept a No-Strike-Pledge (NSP) almost immediately after the attack. In exchange for giving up their only real bargaining weapon, the unions got to participate once again on a War Labor Board, the federal body that would oversee presumably reasonable wage settlements in the absence of strikes. The unions also received "maintenance of membership" protection. Since the unions pledged not to strike, it was argued that workers would be less inclined to pay union dues. Maintenance of membership was a government union shop guarantee. All workers in the industry were required to become union members. The enormous increase in defense work contributed to the over 40 percent increase in union size during the war with no organizing expenses for the unions. The dues check-off was allowed as well for the collection of union dues as a payroll deduction by the employer, saving the union the trouble and expense of collecting its own dues. Government, union, and management came to share a community of interest in stable labor relations.

A Price Control Act, passed in January 1942, was the first step in curbing wartime inflation by law. The law established an Office of Price Administration, and, together with the rationing of many consumer items, sought to stabilize prices while assuring a fair distribution of goods. The two measures held wartime inflation to just below 30 percent, far less than had been the case in the prior war. Nutritional standards in the United States actually increased due to full employment and rationing. Giving up the strike weapon, accepting wage and price controls, rationing, speedups in assembly and production, and lapses in workplace safety were all considered reasonable sacrifices for workers to make while their sons, brothers, neighbors, and friends were putting their lives on the line in combat.

Wartime unity and full employment also brought about declines in crime rates, suicide, and divorce. The birth rate stayed almost as low as it had been in the Depression years as housing was in short supply, and young people who were unsure of their futures delayed marriage or limited the size of their families. Wage restrictions were overcome by plentiful overtime and the entry into the workforce of previously uncounted millions, especially that well-established reserve army of labor comprised of women and black workers. Household incomes rose, along with savings rates, even though strict hourly wages failed to keep pace with inflation. People had money in their pockets, more than ever. Interviews with workers confirm the statistical data: the standard of living improved significantly and universally in the United States during the war. World War II gave working people positive feelings. In spite of the dangers and sacrifices, most people were bonded to the established authorities enough to accept their outlook. Government, business, and union leaders enjoyed extraordinarily high levels of credibility. The war, too, after the first few uncertain months, went well, according to news and government statements. Reports of victories soon far outnumbered defeats. The entire nation was mobilized. This was no "rich man's war and poor man's fight," even though business profits were never as sternly controlled or regulated as wages.

Wage and workplace disputes were settled by conciliators, mediators, and arbitrators provided by the NLRB. A civilian army of tens of thousands of industrial relations specialists from government, business, and labor were given the responsibility of hammering out fair agreements without disruptions in war production. Labor leaders learned to accommodate their social vision and goals to those of business and government. There was immediate and rapid inflation in the first year of war that forced the issue of wages to the foreground. At the same time, Little Steel, the companies that had violently resisted unionization, and that reluctantly accepted collective bargaining and the defense contracts that went with it was stalled in reaching a wage settlement. The first major act of the War Labor Board was a "Little Steel Formula" for wage agreements. The formula was based on inflation rates calculated over the period January 1941 to May 1942. It set a baseline of a 15 percent cost-of-living increase for that time period, and that became the standard for countless other settlements. The formula was not as precise as it seemed because there were so many other variables, such as regional and baseline differences, but it was used by the parties to explain to their constituents why they had to accept something they might otherwise have wished to reject—or fight.

Strikes didn't come to an end, in spite of the pledge, though they did dramatically decline in 1942, the most dangerous year of the war for the United States. When there were strikes, they were usually very brief, the average being four days, or less than half the previous peacetime duration. Most strikes were not over wages, but were caused by conflicts over discipline, workplace justice, or health and safety issues. John L. Lewis led his coal miners on three highly contentious strikes in 1943 over money, and concluded with a clear victory. Wartime strikes gradually increased nationwide, from a low of about 3,000 in 1942, to over 3,700 in 1943, then, as the outcome became more certain, to almost 5,000 in 1944 with a militancy that rivaled the sit-down era of 1937. The Communists, with prominence in the leadership of nearly one-third of the CIO national unions, were among the staunchest opponents of wildcat strikes, and were often the most conservative voice on other issues. The CP approved wartime speedups, piecework, and safety lapses that were usually anathema to unionists. *Business Week* magazine was positively rhapsodic about the Communists: "Today they have perhaps the best no-strike record of any section of organized labor; they are the most vigorous proponents of labor-management cooperation; they are the only serious labor advocates of incentive wages. . . . employers with whom they deal now have the most peaceful labor relations in industry" (March 18, 1944, pp. 83–84). Walter Reuther actually increased his stature as a leader over his CP rivals in the UAW because he was more militant than they were during and right after the war.

Union leaders were not as directly involved in government wartime agencies as they had been in World War I. They played almost no role in the Office of War Mobilization, the Office of War Production, or the War Manpower Commission. The agency that counted for labor was the National War Labor Board (NWLB), established in January 1942. The original NLRB included four members each from labor, business, and government, and was charged with resolving disputes and reaching wage agreements. The demand for the services of the NLRB was so great that twelve regional boards were set up in 1943. An extensive body of law and precedent setting standards built up. Court and NLRB rulings set standards and precedents for thousands of other settlements, and unions became administrative agencies that were quasi-governmental themselves. The need for expertise in these matters created specialists, and more elaborate administrative organization by business and unions. Negotiations took on fixed stylistic practices, becoming almost ritualistic. A bargaining table decorum set in as the law increasingly set the parameters for collective bargaining.

With dues pouring in fast for both AFL and CIO affiliates, and expenses stable or in decline because of fewer strikes and declining costs associated with organizing, unions became powerful entities. Their leaders were taken seriously in the press. Big city newspapers all had at least one regular reporter on full assignment to labor issues. The term *labor statesman* came into use, usually to describe a conciliatory agreement one of them had made. The CIO bought property and built a huge office building in Washington, D.C., in 1942 for $300,000. Sidney Hillman's political importance expanded accordingly.

In late 1943 the CIO stepped up its political activities after the passage of the regressive War Labor Disputes Act (also known as the Smith-Connolly Act for its sponsors) by a stronger Republican–conservative Democrat congressional coalition. The wartime law required a strike vote be taken thirty days or more before a strike action, and allowed the government to nationalize a struck industry. It placed new restrictions on union funds used in political campaigns. In preparation for the 1944 elections Sidney Hillman set up the second badly named union means of supporting (mainly) Democratic Party candidates for office, the Political Action Committee (PAC). The PAC produced some outstanding educational materials and pamphlets in support of pro-labor candidates and labor issues. To its credit, PAC publications continued the strong CIO commitment to gender and racial equality.

Structural relationships were being built that would last. Unions became elaborate administrative entities with their own hierarchies and practices. Internal democracy was not one of them. Devices like "iron clad caucuses" that controlled voting blocs, open delegate balloting for officers instead of membership voting with secret ballots, and absolute control of committees and budgets assured incumbents complete control of unions. The law and the actions of the War Labor Board, especially the "maintenance of membership" rule, protected the unions and the leaders formed in this war, and made them at least, as Alan Brinkley said, "wards of the state" (Brinkely, 1995, p. 200).

Though their unions and contracts were highly dependent on government protection, tens of thousands of individual organizers, local leaders, shop stewards, and democratically inspired individuals continued the struggle for economic and social justice throughout the labor movement. Labor organizations once had been independent democratic forces that posed a challenge to the social and economic order. Though weak, they offered an alternative vision of a good society based on the democratic virtues of organized labor, but the law and the institutional prosperity union leaders enjoyed under it turned them into instruments of control and stability. The AFL accepted that role in World War I. Now the industrial workers were brought aboard as well via the CIO. The grassroots mobilization of millions of workers that were first harnessed by independent radicals in the midst of depression were transformed by law and war into autocratic and patriotic organizations dependent on the state, and subservient to it. That relationship, though modified significantly, endured for more than a generation afterward, or at least until the cold war loyalty of workers to business and the nation was completely secure, or was no longer needed. Lewis knew, and many others suspected, that the state can be a fickle friend. Two other groups of workers enjoyed the dubious intervention of the federal government on their behalf.

Black Workers and Soldiers

Racial division prevailed in the United States during the Depression and war years as a consequence of both law and custom. Though a legal attack in the courts on racial segregation was beginning to undermine it, racial discrimination prevailed in public and private life. Neither the radical unions that attacked racism as divisive of working-class solidarity nor the near universality of New Deal programs made a major difference in altering the status of the approximately fifteen million black citizens. The law that protected a worker's right to join a union did not guarantee equal protection of the law to all citizens. NLRB rulings on labor disputes and wartime protection of collective bargaining rights did not contradict Jim Crow practices of segregation in the workplace or the society at large. The destiny of black citizens was only altered (once again) by the urgent necessities of war. It was on the front lines of combat and in the workplace that black labor brought black people closer to long denied social and political rights.

Every war, as we have seen, demanded an extra measure of devotion from the nation's workers, and every war repaid that devotion with some increases in democratic opportunities, usually withdrawn or curbed afterward. The War Labor Board put it succinctly in 1943: "Whether as vigorous fighting men or for production of food and munitions, America needs the Negro; the Negro needs the equal opportunity to work and fight. The Negro is necessary for winning the war, and at the same time, is a test of our sincerity in the cause for which we are fighting." Under pressure from civil rights advocates and wartime necessity, the Fair Employment Practices Commission (FEPC) was set up, with very limited enforcement power, to end discrimination against black workers in defense industries. Nonetheless, in those industries millions of black workers endured segregated work assignments and customarily did the most physically demanding jobs. Black workers were restricted from various skills and promotion opportunities, almost never gained supervisory authority over white workers no matter how deserving of it, and experienced segregated eating and washroom facilities nearly everywhere. Major league baseball stayed segregated until 1947.

With little wartime help from the federal government or their unions, black workers carried out a massive second migration from rural areas to large cities and industrial employment. In seeking housing in northern and southern cities, they found discrimination and violence, always called "race riots" by the press. Big "hate strikes" took place in several cities, North and South, when tens of thousands of white workers sought to block the entry of black workers into previously restricted jobs or residential areas. A Detroit antiblack riot left thirty-four dead in June 1943, and a similar riot in Philadelphia a year later required the intervention of 5,000 federal troops to restore order. In Philadelphia, the CIO, in marked contrast to the indifference of the AFL, courageously defended the desegregation of transit work that had precipitated the riot.

Until the Battle of the Bulge late in 1944, black soldiers saw very little front-line combat in their racially segregated companies. They were confined to some of the hardest and most dangerous physical labor. Black soldiers and sailors loaded and unloaded munitions, drove trucks under fire, and were service personnel to white officers. Only after white U.S. troops suffered heavy casualties against the Germans during the last year of the war did enlightenment dawn on the General Staff. All-black platoons were joined with white platoons in semi-desegregated combat companies. The military forces of the United States remained racially segregated officially until

1948, though the Navy, facing manpower shortages, quietly undertook some deliberate desegregation practices in 1945.

Women at Work and at War

As in the previous war, patriotism reaffirmed established patriarchal institutions, but placed new demands upon women. Women kept up all of their domestic duties, worked in industry, and served in every branch of the military. They found jobs in places few had ever thought about. Millions of women in the United States joined black workers and colonized peoples in Africa and Asia in the broadly democratic struggle to defeat the Axis powers. One of the most popular female wartime images was of "Rosie the Riveter," pictured as the muscular equal of any man by the popular artist, Norman Rockwell, on a cover of the *Saturday Evening Post*. In defiance of widespread prejudices about a "weaker sex," women not only drove rivets, they worked in shipyards, aircraft factories, and electrical assembly plants, and drove buses and trolley cars. As in the prior war, there were few jobs from which they were excluded.

The Bureau of Labor Statistics said the need for workers "literally forced employers to try out women in all industries and almost all jobs" (P. Foner, 1980, 2:343). Prejudice and discrimination in job assignments, promotion opportunities, and supervisory positions continued to limit or restrict women, nonetheless. Black women found their situation compounded by racism and sexism. In industry black women were assigned the dirtiest and meanest work. The first report of the FEPC showed that more than 25 percent of all discrimination cases were filed by black women. Wartime wages went up, but women still trailed behind men in the same or comparably skilled jobs, in spite of an NLRB General Order that allowed, but did not require, equalization of pay. Equally lacking, due to loopholes and vagueness, were several state "equal pay for equal work" laws. Government looked equitable on the issue and gave a great deal of publicity to the importance of women in industry, but lack of enforcement teeth in federal codes and state laws, custom, and inconsistency among the member unions of the AFL and CIO prevented much progress.

The important role of women in unions was likewise more talk than walk, though CIO unions did include and advance more women into union membership and leadership than the AFL. There were no women officers at the top of either the AFL or CIO. As it did on race, the national office of the CIO kept up a steady stream of educational information that urged member unions to combat discrimination against women. One of the biggest breakthroughs for women came from the federal funding of child day care services provided by some private employers. Shipbuilding and aircraft manufacturing employed a higher percentage of women than other industries because of federally supported child care. Companies like Curtiss-Wright (aircraft) and Kaiser Industries (ships) outbid rival companies for women workers by providing low-cost federally funded child care centers. That the companies actually gained a net financial profit from these services did not take anything away from the positive way they were regarded by workers.

The end of the war wiped out many of the gains for women along with many of the jobs, but some permanent changes were present as well. Kaiser, for example, kept up child care services, though nationwide more than four million women lost wartime jobs, and were much less likely to find new employment in comparison to men similarly laid off from defense work. Black women were the most fired and least rehired, unless they sought work in traditional service areas. Unions, both AFL and CIO, allowed discriminatory seniority provisions to protect the jobs of men. Women who remained in many companies were reassigned to gender-specific work, for example, as seamstresses or clerks. But, the number of women in the workforce remained higher a year after the war than it was the year before, and women were now more universally accepted as members of labor organizations, if not as leaders, than ever. They still had a long way to go.

Conclusion

Historians remain divided on the question of the radical, liberal, or conservative nature of the New Deal and wartime era. All of those elements were certainly present. Government shifted from its customary role as the protector of one business or industry in a labor struggle, to a more general role as protector of all of the nation's industry and business. Traditional structures were inadequate. Private business was crippled and humbled somewhat by the Depression; state and local governments were unsuitable agencies for resolving either national or international crises. The medicines prescribed by FDR, and accepted as necessary by some corporate leaders, were not as easy to swallow for others. President Roosevelt's liberalism bonded the loyalty of workers to the destiny of the nation's owners of wealth more than any other national leader in the century. In that respect FDR could also be considered the most successful conservative president of the century. Laws carefully structured labor relations for fewer than a third of the nation's workers by allowing them to form unions. The others, in service employment, wearing white collars, or in agricultural or other nonprotected jobs, remained nonunion but were touched as well by the industrial and democratic upsurge. The universal nature of social security and the Fair Labor Standards Act were liberal extensions of rights and benefits to every household.

The radicalism of the Depression and war years was the democratic power felt by workers themselves on the job, in politics where they had real advocates, and in their organization of unions. There had never been anything quite like it before. Real tangible victories came to labor. Big strikes were won. Important court decisions favored workers. Union recognition came from hostile and reluctant adversaries. At the end of this era there really was a progressive income tax, social security, a minimum wage that meant something, and an end to sweatshops. Prejudices and restrictions on women workers and black workers were diluted by material gains, new opportunities, and social and political achievements.

Labor gained cultural power as well. In films, photographs, music, literature, and art, workers were portrayed sympathetically and with nobility. All of labor earned the dignity it had always deserved but rarely enjoyed in the popular imagination. This was the age of big industrial power and mass production in the United States, and workers won credit for their role in making every ton of coal and steel, every battleship and airplane. In the life and death labor of war, the work of soldiers and sailors added to that glory.

At the end of the war no one knew for certain what the future would hold. Most serious analysts erroneously feared a return to depression conditions. Wartime economic sacrifices by labor indicated that big postwar demands were coming. On the other hand, a business reaction against the power of organized labor, likewise held in check by war, was almost certain. In the uneven historic struggle between labor and capital in the United States an unusual equilibrium was reached, with the government holding the balance of power. For a moment, in early August 1945, all of labor stood proud of its accomplishments, and powerful in the life of the United States.

But then, we know by now what happens to labor when the war is over, don't we?

AFL-CIO executive council. These were the "new men of power" at the time of the merger of the AFL and CIO in 1955. Cleansed of radicals and devoid of women, they enjoyed almost twenty years of comfortable influence and status in Washington, D.C., though no reform of Taft-Hartley or other favorable labor legislation was achieved by them. (The George Meany Memorial Archives)

CHAPTER 8

Constructing Consensus: Labor in the Cold War, 1945–1968

Labor did it!
—Harry S Truman, 1948 (*New York Times*, November 4, 1948)

The Fruits of Victory for Labor, the Bitter and the Sweet

At the end of the war, unions and unionization, and the history of labor reached an odd place. Unions were rich in dues and glowing with patriotic prestige, but more dependent than ever on law and government allies for their institutional legitimacy. The prosperity and power of the unions was now going to be tied to their relationship with government, not their ability to serve their members. Rambunctious labor democracy, as fragile and limited as it was in the large national unions, gave way to near permanent bureaucracies, organizational stagnation, and elitism. In several cases this new power took the form of outright gangsterism; in others it imitated the top-down and autocratic corporate model, not so different from gangsterism itself, but legal. Radicals were either expelled from leadership, forced into subordinate positions, or their weakened national unions were driven out of the AFL and CIO. New law, or changes in old law, further narrowed the scope of the institutional power of labor, but the actual numbers and the percentage of the unionized labor force continued to grow from just over one-fifth to nearly one-third of the national workforce over the twenty years that followed World War II.

Unions and the State

Though they won few new battles and endured major legislative setbacks, labor union leaders enjoyed unprecedented public status and access to the corridors of power. Many of them mistook their marginal inclusion for the real thing, as they also became more dominant than ever over their own members. The sociologist, C. Wright Mills, described the accession of status of union leaders in the title and substance of his book, *The New Men of Power* (1948). In a subsequent essay, "The Labor Leaders and the Political Elite," Mills began to express skepticism about the capability of labor leaders to have any significant social or economic influence: "These unions are less levers for change of that general framework (the present political economy) than they are instruments for more advantageous integration with it" (Mills, 1963, p. 108). Three years later, in a new book, *White Collar: The American Middle Classes*, Mills was more emphatic about the conservative nature of the emerging labor relations system: "Trade unions are the most reliable instruments to date for taming and channeling lower-class aspirations, for lining up the workers without internal violence during time of war, and for controlling their insurgency during times of peace and depression" (1951, p. 318). Other academic and journalistic observers believed that a new arrangement of power was reached during these years between labor and business, with government as a balancing force or referee. However, what looked liked integration with power, walked with the swagger of power, and talked as if it had real power, was an indulged and comfortable labor elite, not the independent power of labor.

Unions and Labor

Historians once portrayed the history of unions and the history of labor as the same thing because of the long uphill struggle to create permanent organizations of workers. During the 1945–68 period, it looked as though that goal had been achieved by the AFL- and CIO-affiliated unions. It certainly seemed as if the impact of the large labor unions on the rest of labor in this period established them as the guardians or model for all of labor, including public employees who began to join the ranks of the organized by the millions in the 1960s. As a part of the institutional life of the nation, the history of labor unions and the study of labor law and labor-management relations were now included in the curricula of major colleges and universities. That it was also a period of tremendous economic expansion and a rising standard of living added to the overall impression that unions were exerting a powerful influence on behalf of workers and the democratic nature of the nation. The achievement of the five-day, forty-hour workweek coupled with a rising standard of living led many observers to believe that so much wealth and leisure might create new and unforeseen social problems for workers. A book by John Kenneth Gailbraith, *The Affluent Society* (1958), brought national attention to the question of what the nation's goals ought to be once it met all of its own material needs. Despite their apparent power, the unions were vulnerable. The battle for internal control put the unions at the forefront of the nation's undemocratic purge of the left. When the internal battle was over, the left was defeated, and the unions had lost the fiery independence and broad social vision that had stirred millions of workers. As unions withdrew from labor and human rights issues outside of their legal sanction, they also secretly joined forces with government agencies in nefarious undemocratic adventures abroad.

Shortly after the end of the war, the two large union federations surrendered their independent social vision by broadly accepting the political outlook of their employers. AFL and CIO leaders drove out dissenters, and went to work for the CIA and the State Department to advance corporate interests abroad. The large national unions, with the important exception of A. Philip Randolph and the Brotherhood of Sleeping Car Porters, took no part in building the civil rights activism of this age, and continued to trail behind or resist the struggles for gender equality, human rights, and environmentalism that followed. The AFL-CIO was a bulwark of support for the government pursuit of the war in Vietnam, even when that war became massively unpopular, and when most workers were increasingly critical of its continuance. AFL-CIO leaders lagged so far behind critics of the racially repressive apartheid government of South Africa that their only company in this position were the most conservative and antilabor business and political groups in the United States. Cold war prosperity and institutional power brought the CIO completely into the "pure and simple" unionist fold. Unification of the AFL and CIO in 1955 was really a friendly takeover of the weakened CIO by the stronger AFL once the former abandoned or purged the more radical qualities and leaders that caused their separation.

The Immediate Impact of World War II

Wartime inflation meant that hourly wage rates were off by about 30 percent, and, with the abrupt end to most overtime, all of labor was soon feeling the pinch. Almost fourteen million members of the armed services expected to be demobilized and returned to the civilian workforce. Fear of a return to Depression-era unemployment rates stirred up a strong sense of job insecurity. White male workers were the principal beneficiaries of union agreements to protect seniority rights. The Fair Employment Practices Commission (FEPC) was shut down a few months after the war, and traditional racial, gender, and ethnic discriminatory practices returned in force. Women and black workers, especially black women workers, were the first to be let go from wartime manufacturing jobs.

Feminism and Labor

Popular culture resurrected, then reconstructed, a vision of household domesticity based on a traditional and small town model that coincided with the emerging suburban setting as the idealized place for women. Religious and other cultural authorities all proclaimed that women belonged at home, or in workplace nurturing roles that reflected their historic subservience to men. Women continued to find jobs in the gender-specific areas of nursing, textiles, offices, and food processing. Movies, music, magazines, radio, then television—all commercial media—portrayed happy women in child care and housekeeping labor. The mass media assigned women the role of consumer-shoppers in its advertising, or portrayed them as romantic or sexual objects of male fantasy. There was a brief postwar decline in the number of women workers, but by 1947 more women were employed in the wage and salaried labor force than ever before in peacetime, and their total numbers in the workforce continued to grow. There they faced gender-specific work assignments, discrimination in promotion and mobility, sexual harassment, and near complete exclusion from the leadership of those unions to which they were permitted membership. For the same or similar work, women were paid much less than men. Government statistical data found that the median income for women workers in 1948 was less than half that of men, and for black women it was half of that. The obvious conflict between the idealized depiction of women workers and their real participation in the economic life of the nation helped to propel a new struggle for the rights of women by the end of this era. The unions, as powerful as they seemed to be, and in spite of their long association with women workers, exerted no leadership in the renewed feminist movement. By 1946 the CIO was aligning itself with the national reaction against the wartime gains made by women. The revived struggle for women's rights would come mainly from women in professions, or working women outside of labor unions.

Union Goals at the End of the War

Union membership growth during the war was driven by law and the huge expansion of the defense industry, while large segments of the rest of the workforce remained little or nonunionized. In the South, especially in the huge textile industry, neither the AFL nor the CIO had much strength. Only the left-led industrial unions and some AFL craft unions had any significant presence in the South. Philip Murray knew that failure to organize the South would hurt the CIO organizationally and politically. Industry would relocate there to escape collective bargaining elsewhere. Antiunion politicians from weakly organized states would hammer away at labor's legal victories unless they faced the threat of a politically mobilized and unionized population.

A counteroffensive from business had been building continuously since 1937 to amend or abolish the Wagner Act. A majority of states (about thirty) had, by 1945, already passed laws curbing some of the rights of labor within their borders, and more antiunion legislation was anticipated at the state and federal levels. Both sides were mobilizing for new battles over old issues.

A massive strike wave, building up momentum in 1944, reached a new record high level in the months that followed the surrender of the Japanese in August 1945. No period in all of the nation's history, not 1877, not 1886, and not even 1919, matched the number of strikes for lost work-hours, or the average duration of the work stoppages that took place from November 1945 to the end of 1946. Local unions with their own elected leaders had the autonomy to make contracts. Many of these locals now represented hundreds of thousands of workers. Close to the rank-and-file membership, leaders had to be willing to risk strike action or be replaced. The year-long outbreak of militancy once again came from workers themselves, not their union leaders, as it had in almost every similar period in the past.

The Communist Party, the only labor group or disciplined faction of any significance that was not under AFL or CIO control, held the leadership of about a dozen national unions, nearly a third of the total. But the CP at the end of the war was not inclined toward militant confrontation with the owners of capital. These radicals even proposed that the No Strike Pledge (NSP) continue after the war came to an end, though they quickly abandoned that stance in the weeks that followed the surrender of Germany in May 1945. A common temporary enmity toward fascism had made the CP odd bedfellows with business and government. Only the wartime alliance with the Soviet Union allowed that fragile relationship to last.

Now, in the immediate aftermath of war, some AFL and a select few CIO leaders were secretly participating with the State Department and various espionage agencies (the CIA wasn't set up until 1950) in European and Latin American operations in an enlargement of the similar role they had played in the 1920s. Several CIO leaders were actively at work in Germany in the spring of 1947 assisting in the business- and government-sponsored work of stopping the German Communist Party from winning control of labor in West Germany and West Berlin (Eisenberg, 1983, p. 295). The United States was forced by the weakness of the other powers to take the lead in postwar political and economic reconstruction plans. Foremost among the goals of the United States was its traditional Open Door policy, the removal of impediments to its businesses interests abroad. Now that policy aimed at stopping left-wing labor groups from increasing their political control in the power vacuum caused by the collapse of antilabor fascist and collaborationist national governments in Europe. The place of a radical left in labor, and in the nation itself, was becoming more of an obstacle to respectable labor goals as the cold war set in, despite the CP's patriotic participation on the front lines of combat and industry and the deep democratic roots of radicalism in labor itself.

The Strike Wave, 1945–1946

The last great eruption of workplace activism by labor in the United States was driven by the inflationary sacrifices of war, and the even sharper price increases that immediately followed the war as rationing and price controls were ended. Workers still enjoyed the self-confidence they had won for themselves prior to the war, and felt an extra measure of self-assurance from knowing the part they had played in winning it. While some national union leaders opposed confrontation, they knew that big wage increases were due, and that they would not come without concerted action. Now was the time.

Every large industry—steel, coal, automobiles, electrical products, meatpacking, railroads, and thousands of small producers—were struck within the year. Thousands of soldiers and sailors, though nonunionized, also went on strike, demonstrated, or took part in riotous protests, mostly in the Far East, over delays in discharge procedures. Their killing work done, they wanted to go home. Though nonunion, they too took concerted action to press their demands.

Autoworkers Lead the Way

Once again it was the shop floor militancy of the autoworkers that forced the wage issue on a divided and uncertain union leadership and a hostile business community. Nearly a hundred separate unauthorized work stoppages rattled automakers and some union leaders from late August to November 1945. CIO President Philip Murray, UAW President R. J. Thomas, and a portion of the Communist Party labor leadership were among those distressed by the spontaneous workplace actions. The leaders were hoping to achieve a new kind of industrial relationship, one they envisioned would allow the resolution of conflicts without the disruption, waste, and rancor of strikes. The CP naively expected the wartime alliance with the Soviet Union to continue. The labor chiefs were all misreading the major players. Rank-and-file labor was confident and unafraid. Labor won the war, unions were legitimate, money was the issue, and workers were impatient with their leaders and ready for action.

The mood of business was changed as well. Businessmen did not expect the profitable wartime contracts with government that included low and controlled labor costs to continue. Corporate leaders were also determined to roll back the power labor had won in the Depression and war, but were not inclined to revive the wasteful and confrontational hostilities of the past. President Harry S. Truman was not FDR (who died in April 1945), and his closest advisors included men with uniformly conservative views about labor.

So much had changed in the country and in the world as a result of the Depression and war that no one had a completely accurate picture of what to expect. Economists were predicting a return to Depression-era conditions of high unemployment and low factory utilization. The union leaders wanted to avoid the nightmare losses of 1919, but many, including Walter Reuther, wanted to press ahead further with shared governance between union and management over production issues, investment decisions, and profit sharing. Murray made frequent use of the concept of "industrial democracy" to describe his goals.

The UAW struck General Motors in November 1945 in the first big postwar test of wills. Reuther took the lead in the strike when he borrowed an argument from the Trotskyists that called for opening up the corporation's books. Reuther hoped to prove that the company could provide a 30 percent wage increase without raising the prices of its products. The strike lasted for over three months. By the end of January, GM workers were joined by over 400,000 striking workers in electrical manufacturing and meatpacking and 800,000 steelworkers led by Murray. Soon workers in the manufacture of farm equipment and 60,000 oil workers were out. By early February 25 percent of the entire CIO was on strike.

Reuther's militancy was an accurate assessment of the sentiments of the membership, and helped him to take over the leadership of the union. On the other hand, he misread the management at GM, and his ambitious goals came to nothing. He was also undercut by a United Electrical (UE) workers agreement with GM, and separate UAW agreements at Ford and Chrysler that granted eighteen-and-a-half-cent-an-hour increases, a pay raise of about 17.5 percent, as recommended by government fact finders. GM refused to open its books. The UAW actually lost some ground in management rights issues in the Ford settlement. Other large industrial strikes were concluded along similar lines. Reuther held out for a few weeks for a face-saving extra penny an hour, then finally settled without it.

It really did appear as if a new era was dawning. There were no scabs, no attempts at replacing striking workers or breaking picket lines. There was no disorder, vandalism, or violence on the picket lines. The work stoppages were massive and highly disciplined. No police, vigilantes, national guard units, or private security forces intervened. Nor was there any cooperation, plan, or coordination among the CIO unions.

The Strikes and the Government

The government acted more as a disciplinarian than a referee in 1945–46. After a failed Labor-Management Conference called by Truman in November 1945, the president asked Congress for power to stop or forestall strikes that might harm the "public interest." Truman wanted authority to bar a strike for thirty days to allow time for federal fact finders to make nonbinding recommendations, a variation on the sixty-day provision in the original Railroad Labor Act of 1926. Congress stood pat as union leaders thundered out against the idea. Truman appointed fact-finding boards anyway, first for the GM strike, then steel and meatpacking. While the wage increases seemed large, the government gave manufacturers a green light to go ahead with price increases to pay for them. No one knew it then, but prosperity and inflation would pay for labor peace for a generation to come.

Truman's troubles weren't over. In April 1946 John L. Lewis led all of his coal miners out on strike, and a national rail strike was also threatened. Lewis wanted a health and welfare fund paid for by a surcharge or royalty of $.05/ton. Over a century, mining accidents and disease had claimed the lives of more miners (400,000) than U.S. military losses in World War II. Lewis demanded medical care and family benefits for those still doing the deadly work. With no coal coming, steel mills began banking their fires, electricity cuts were ordered by utility companies in big cities, industries began to slow production. Truman despised Lewis personally, thought him arrogant and theatrical, and carried bitter resentments toward him from the wartime coal strikes. He liked the railroad leaders better, but had no more luck holding them off than he had with Lewis.

A rail strike staggered the nation on May 22, a day after Truman ordered the military seizure of the nation's coal mines. Perishable food began to rot as trains stood at sidings, passengers were stranded all over the country, European relief supplies were halted, and personal heartbreaking stories were reported in all the papers the next day. Unlike the Great Uprising of 1877 or the Pullman strike of 1894, this strike was nearly total; virtually all freight, passenger, and commuter trains were at a standstill. Two days later, in a special 8:00 P.M. radio address to the nation, Truman threatened to call out the military if the strike was not ended by 4:00 the next afternoon. Negotiations were continuing throughout the strike action. Truman stood before the House of Representatives as the deadline passed and requested "temporary emergency" legislation to draft the striking workers into the U.S. Army. That would put them under his authority as commander-in-chief. The House gave him a 306–13 vote in favor of conscripting the strikers, but a few days later wary conservatives joined liberals in the Senate to defeat the measure 70–13. Government was powerful enough, they agreed, memories of Mussolini and Hitler too fresh. In the interim the railroad strike was settled along the lines of earlier agreements. Lewis signed with the coal companies on May 29, and got everything he wanted: the $.05/ton royalty, a five-day week, vacation pay, and the now standard $.185/hour increase.

Truman won no new friends among labor (except for Lewis) or business leaders from his boldness, though his actions added to his no-nonsense, bantam-rooster image, and strengthened the emerging concept of the government as the final arbiter of labor-management disputes. The press touted Truman for his toughness, and the public ate it up. Labor leaders were castigated by the same journalists for their lack of concern for the public welfare, a deficiency linked to their questionable patriotism in the face of an emerging new threat to the nation. Some unionists who were angry at Truman began to think and speak about the formation of a third-party movement for 1948.

The year-long failure to reach an agreement with the Soviet Union on the future of Germany coincided with the strike wave and meant that the wartime alliance was over. Communists were losing whatever goodwill their patriotic service had won them during the war. The strikes added fuel to the reaction against labor that had been held in check by war. Business groups, racially exclusive southern Democrats (soon to be called "Dixiecrats"), and conservative Republicans (from districts or states where labor votes were insufficient to challenge them) attacked in full force in the wake of the strike wave. The CP, with prominence or leadership in almost a third of the CIO unions (mostly achieved before there was a CIO), was the politically sensitive target for all of labor's enemies, and some of its friends. Oddly enough, the United Steelworkers of America (USWA), led by its president, Philip Murray, indirectly aided this reaction by accepting one of its premises in a resolution at its May convention:

unions, the delegates agreed, should not come under the sway of foreign influences in the guise of the Communist Party, USA.

Operation Dixie

In the same month of May as the steelworkers' resolution, and while the great strike wave was still underway, the CIO launched one of the most massive organizing drives in its history, a Southern Organizing Campaign (SOC), popularly known as "Operation Dixie." It had to do it. The South was the least organized part of the nation. Workers there had not recovered from the terrible defeats endured in the great textile strike of 1934. Only the left-led industrial unions, the Food and Tobacco Workers of America, the International Longshoremen's Union, and the Mine Mill and Smelter Workers, had been able to establish collective bargaining rights of any consequence for mass production workers in the South. Because these left-led unions put racial solidarity at the foreground of unionism, they were either excluded or sidelined from this drive by the CIO, which concentrated its efforts on the nearly all-white textile industry. Alfred Van Bittner, the master strategist for the SOC, was no racist, but he sought not to irritate local prejudices on the subject. Organizers were to stress "purely an organizational campaign," around strictly "bread and butter issues." There were to be "no extra-curricular activities—no politics—no PAC—no FEPC, etc." The "etc." meant that race was to be kept on the margins (Zieger, 1995, p. 233). The CIO was returning to the "pure and simple" unionism of Gompers.

More than a million dollars was raised from the largest national unions, and over 200 full-time organizers were put to work in the campaign. It was to be a highly centralized drive with its headquarters in Atlanta, Georgia. George Baldanzi, Van Bittner's deputy, was in charge of the day-to-day work, and he supervised the state directors. Staff positions were filled with outspoken anticommunists. Volunteers with left-wing backgrounds were excluded from the campaign. Organizers were mostly white war veterans and were expected to wear neat clothing, go to local churches on Sunday, and avoid politics and social issues, especially the question of race or civil rights. They were red-baited, race-baited, Jew-baited, and Yankee-baited in billboard ads, posters, leaflets, newspapers; by radio commentaries, chambers of commerce statements, sheriffs, AFL rivals; and from the pulpit. The CIO, according to southern critics, stood for "Christ Is Out."

Here and there minor victories were won, some very temporarily. People signed union cards, then voted against the union. Most of the victories were outside of textiles among the somewhat more autonomous wood products workers, food and tobacco processors, and in the CIO defeat of the AFL in an election to represent chemical workers in Oak Ridge, Tennessee. After six months the dimensions of the disaster were becoming clear, but the drive continued to sputter and stumble along for more than a year. By 1949, the embattled president of the Textile Workers Union of America

(TWUA) admitted, "We are worse off today in the South than we have been" (quoted in Griffith, 1988, p. 162).

No careful analysis was done afterward to evaluate the reasons for the failure of the SOC. There were, however, plenty of critics on the scene at the time who blasted the SOC for its timidity, its lack of militancy, its defensiveness on race, and its unwillingness to tap the pro-union energy of black workers and put them into the front lines of the organizing campaign. Operation Dixie could have been the opening drive of the modern civil rights movement, one that might have been led by labor, not by major league baseball a year later, or Truman's executive order to desegregate the military a year after that.

In every previous era of successful organizing, workers were inspired to join unions by the courage and audacity of idealists and radicals, even when they didn't share the same political outlook. Leftists brought an appealing idealism to the project of unionism that could not be matched by the hard pragmatism now favored by the SOC. No successful large-scale labor organizing drive ever took place without the expression of a larger and more democratic vision of the nation than the current one. This one tucked it in, lost out, and started labor on the slide to the sidelines of democratic reform in the nation. As one thoughtful observer concluded over forty years later: "For American labor, Operation Dixie was, quite simply, a moment of high tragedy from which it has yet to fully recover" (Griffith, 1988, p. 176).

Reaction

Antilabor and antidemocratic forces were mobilizing at the same time as Operation Dixie was faltering. Older progressive corporations that once led the way on union recognition and worker rights were taking a new direction. The General Electric Corporation, under the early leadership of Gerard Swope in the 1920s, started out as a pacesetter in modern labor relations. The "welfare capitalism" of the 1920s was a GE objective. In October 1946, after strikes that brought improved union security clauses and pay raises ($.185/hour) to its workers, GE President Charles E. ("Electric Charley") Wilson declared that "the problems of the United States can be captiously summed up in two words: Russia abroad, labor at home" (quoted in Boyer, 1955, p. 345).

GE's subsequent approach to bargaining was known as Boulwarism, named for its new vice president for labor and community relations, Lemuel Boulware. His job was to break the considerable power of the huge 600,000-member and CP-led United Electrical (UE) workers, a union that dared to charge GE with wage discrimination against women at the War Labor Board. Boulwarism was take-it-or-leave-it bargaining, with no room for discussion or negotiations. It usually resulted in the intervention of federal mediators or arbitrators, or in charges brought before the NLRB of failure to negotiate in good faith. Boulwarism was the new hard line. It pushed the limits of the law until it was finally ruled an unfair labor practice by the NLRB in 1964.

GE was so impressed with the Screen Actors Guild's cooperation with the House Committee on Un-American Activities (HUAC) investigation into communist influences in Hollywood in 1947 that they put the union's president, actor Ronald Reagan, on a nationwide speaking tour. In his testimony before the congressional committee, Reagan confirmed the red menace that HUAC sought to expose. Secretly, he turned over his union files and provided information to investigators that aided the committee's hunt for Communists. GE helped to launch Reagan's political career after it subsidized him as a host and in occasional acting jobs on its televised "GE Theater" during the 1950s. Clearly, one way for GE to deal with the problem of "labor at home" was to link it to the other problem, "Russia abroad."

Both Operation Dixie's exclusion of leftist organizers and the Steelworkers anticommunist resolution followed Winston Churchill's announcement of the beginning of the cold war in his famous "iron curtain" speech delivered at Fulton, Missouri, in March 1946. If the United States faced a new enemy in the Soviet Union, and if the CP-USA maintained any lingering identification or association with that new enemy, then those organizations and individuals associated with the CP were going to be regarded as either disloyal or potentially disloyal to the United States. Loyalty and disloyalty were never precisely defined by law. Criminal actions like espionage could always be prosecuted. This was something new. Could the political ideas of U.S. citizens be deemed disloyal? If so, what actions could legally be taken against them? The first formal action taken against workers was the creation by the House of Representatives Civil Service Committee of a subcommittee to look into the loyalty of federal employees in early July 1946.

The CIO acted at its November convention. Ironically, given the roles they soon would play, both Philip Murray and Walter Reuther had condemned red-baiting in the past as a cheap tactic aimed at dividing workers and breaking union organizing drives. Nonetheless, Reuther himself used it as a tactic to win a narrow election victory to the presidency of the UAW in March 1946. Reuther said his anticommunism was based on the CP's undemocratic qualities, and its reflexive obedience to its own centralized authority. Murray brought the USWA's anticommunist sentiment to the entire CIO in November. The delegates, the new resolution stated, "resent and reject efforts of the Communist Party or other political parties . . . to interfere in the affairs of the CIO" (Zieger, 1995, p. 259). Clearly, the resolution did not reject the influence of the Democrats, the Catholic Church, or even some Republicans.

Richard Nixon successfully used red-baiting against his New Deal Democratic congressional opponent, the incumbent, Jerry Voorhis, when he ran for Congress from California in November 1946. The election, according to the Republican Party National Committee Chairman, B. Carroll Reece, offered voters a choice between "Communism and Republicanism" (Caute, 1978, p. 26). That year the Republican Party, with many of its candidates using this appeal, gained a majority of seats in the House (246–188), a loss of fifty-four for the Democrats. Joseph McCarthy used the same smear against his opponent to win a race for the Senate in Wisconsin that year. In the Senate as well as the House anticommunism was a winning political formula.

Republicans outnumbered Democrats in the Senate, 51 to 45. (There were still only forty-eight states.) Anticommunist hysteria soon reached into every institution in national life, but the main item on the agenda of the Eightieth Congress when it convened in January wasn't the real or imagined danger of communism, it was the power of organized labor. Abroad, there was no threat coming from the Soviet Union, only a barrier to the traditional Open Door goals of U.S. foreign policy.

Democratic and left-wing forces were threatening to fill the power vacuum left by the defeated Axis powers and their conservative business collaborators. Throughout Africa, Asia, and the Middle East colonized people were rising up to overthrow imperial powers, many of them allies of the United States. AFL and CIO leaders were hard at work, both openly and secretively, for the State Department in Germany, France, and the decolonizing world to make sure that labor organizations in those countries did not come under the control of Communists or leaders unfriendly to the postwar reconstruction or postcolonial installation of capitalist institutions.

The Soviet Union really was an impediment to the Open Door. So too were CP-led unions in Europe, and anticapitalist nationalist revolutionaries in the decolonizing world. A powerful and independent domestic labor movement was the same kind of obstacle to the power of capital at home, communist or not. Capping the power of labor at home and expanding the Open Door abroad were two sides of the same coin.

Taft-Hartley and the Truman Doctrine

Containment, not direct confrontation, was the new government program for both the domestic problem of labor and the foreign problem of the Soviet Union. Abroad, the new policy was presented diplomatically in March 1947 as the Truman Doctrine. The United States, the president declared, would assume the right to intervene anywhere in the world to prevent the Soviet Union or (this "or" would be most important) left-led (called "communist" whether connected to the Soviet Union or not) nationalist movements that threatened the interests of private capital. The term *Free World* was used to describe any place where capital was free to do as it chose without interference. Governments, no matter how tyrannical, that provided unrestricted access to labor, natural resources, markets, and opportunities for investment were to be protected by the United States and its allies. A National Security Act was passed in June to build a global military force and secret services to carry out the new policy. Secretary of State George C. Marshall recommended a multibillion-dollar plan to subsidize the reconstruction of western European capitalism. The Marshall Plan, adopted a year later, was, according to Truman, the other half of the "same walnut" as the Truman Doctrine.

A similar approach to the labor left at home was taken with the passage of the Taft-Hartley Act. Just before that law was passed, Truman's executive order 9835 set up a Loyalty-Security Program to screen government and defense industry employees. Loyalty oaths were required and security checks against an attorney general's list of "subversive organizations" were in place before Congress took similar action against the rest of labor in the new law.

The Taft-Hartley Act did not throw out the National Labor Relations Law as many legislators favored, but it did thoroughly revise it according to the desires of the National Association of Manufacturers, labor's historic antagonist for nearly half a century. The proposed measure was large and complex with nothing in it helpful to labor. Everything was designed to curb, contain, or constrain independent labor action or organizational autonomy.

There were eight principal parts to the law: (1) Unions could now be charged with unfair labor practices, and employers' rights to "free speech" were enlarged to permit vigorous antiunion campaigns. Mass picketing, secondary boycotts, or strikes to win jurisdiction were barred. Conventional union organizing became much more difficult, if not altogether impossible. (2) Work supervisors, or foremen, were no longer given the protection of the labor law if they chose to unionize. Big companies, like Ford, began to fire unionized foremen as soon as the law was passed. (3) Restrictions were placed on the use of dues for political purposes, and union books and accounting practices were opened to government scrutiny. (4) The closed shop (the employer must hire only union members) was made illegal, though union shop rights (workers must join the union or pay dues to it as a condition of continued employment) could be established by a majority vote. States were given the right to pass laws banning compulsory membership in unions where a union shop had been achieved in negotiations. Dues would be harder to collect, union organizing drives easier to stop. So-called right-to-work laws soon passed in seventeen southern and western states. (By 2003, twenty-two states had passed such measures.) (5) A strike deemed harmful to the "national interest" could be halted by the president through a federal injunction that could impose an eighty-day "cooling-off" period while mediation sought a resolution to the dispute. (6) Strikes were still legal, but mediation and arbitration were established as preferable by courts as methods of grievance and conflict resolution, no matter how long the process took. The number of strikes declined. (7) Unions could be subjected to lawsuits for unauthorized strikes, or other forms of "breach of contract." Labor organizations were now responsible for the policing of their own members, or risk being sued. (8) All union officers had to sign an affidavit or oath stating that they were not members of the Communist Party, "nor affiliated with such party, and that he does not believe in, and is not a member of or supports any organization that believes in or teaches, the overthrow of the United States Government by force or by any illegal or unconstitutional means." (The attorney general would define what that last part meant, but it was generally understood that it referred to groups or organizations allegedly under the influence of the CP, or "front groups.") Officers or unions that did not comply were, like foremen, denied protection under the law. Union democracy itself was put aside by this provision until the Supreme Court ruled it unconstitutional in 1965 and threw it out. Belief, not action, was proscribed by law for union officers. Radical critics of capitalism, including non-Communists, found it almost impossible to be elected to union offices. Only a business-friendly leadership, or a certified government-friendly anti-communist-left would be permitted to be elected to union offices for nearly a generation.

Labor Reacts to Taft-Hartley

There was an immediate uproar. Union leaders were enraged. They called it a "slave labor" bill. John L. Lewis said it was "the first ugly savage thrust of fascism in the United States" (Boyer, 1955, p. 347). Massive rallies and letter writing protested the measure. When Truman received the Taft-Hartley Act near the end of June he vetoed it, and ultimately won back the political support of millions of workers for his stand. Truman's Council of Economic Advisors accurately warned that the law would "inject the Government into almost innumerable details in the internal affairs of labor organizations of all sizes and in the collective bargaining process" (McLure, 1969, p. 173). Front-line labor relations specialists condemned the new law almost universally. But it was clear that Congress had the votes to override Truman's veto, and did so quickly, with more votes in favor the second time around. More Democrats joined Republicans in voting for the bill and the override than voted against it.

Following some posturing and complaint, the unions went into a period of internal conflict over compliance with the anticommunist affidavits. Most went along with it. For some critics it was infuriating to single out labor for a political purge. Management had no obligation to screen its officers, legal staff, or labor specialists under the law. Lewis stormed out of the AFL over the conservative federation's compliance. He favored a return to "voluntarism" and the repeal of both Taft-Hartley and the National Labor Relations Law. Lewis felt secure enough among his coal miners without the protection of the NLRB. In marked contrast, Walter Reuther accepted the purge. Reuther compared the need to get rid of the Communists to cutting out cancerous cells to save a life.

After a little more than a year 81,000 union officers filed as non-Communists, including the leaders of 89 of 102 AFL unions, 30 of 41 CIO affiliates, and 45 independents. The nonsigning unions were expelled from the AFL and CIO in 1949–50, and competing unions were set up by the AFL and CIO to win back members from the ousted organizations. Some officers signed and remained secret Communists, and some of those were exposed and sent to jail a few years later in 1952 as "Smith Act" Communists for failing to register as "enemy agents." The bitterness and resentment from those internal battles left a permanent residue in the unions. In many unions the best leaders were sacrificed, and some outstanding unions were split and broken by expulsion and raids on their membership.

The Taft-Hartley Act crippled the political independence of labor and stripped it of some of its most powerful tactics, but the big unions eventually learned to live with it. Strikes represented expensive losses of revenue to unions. Getting rid of the reds opened up opportunities for control of the organizations by more conservative unionists, their longtime adversaries. The "national emergency" provision was invoked seven times by Truman and four eighty-day injunctions were issued to stop strikes in the first year of the new law. Once the weapon to stop strikes was in place and used a few times, it did not have to be employed as often. The number and severity of strikes declined sharply, and never again approached the 1945–46 level. With rare exceptions, unions and union leaders withdrew completely from leadership roles in civil and human rights battles. They confined themselves narrowly to that which the law allowed.

The Progressive Party and Labor, 1948

The union left was divided about what to do. Socialists didn't like Taft-Hartley, but were not unhappy about the grief it was bringing to their hated red rivals. Communists, and those who defended their constitutional and democratic rights, had nowhere to turn for support in either major political party. U.S. policy toward the Soviet Union provoked criticism from just a few independent thinkers and political figures, but only rarely did congressional Democrats or Republicans dare to challenge this foreign policy. Old-fashioned isolationists, like Republican Senator Arthur Vandenberg, were completely on board. Only the more extreme right wing, which clamored for a confrontational approach with the Soviet Union, was acceptable in dissent in this debate. Republican critics, like Richard Nixon and Joseph McCarthy, only wailed that Truman and the Democrats were too "soft" on communism for not taking a more aggressive stand against the Soviet Union, and for their greater willingness to seek accommodations with big labor. There was no room for opposition to the cold war in the two major parties.

Henry Wallace, the former vice president (1941–45) and Truman's secretary of commerce, was forced to leave the cabinet because of his opposition to U.S. belligerence toward its former ally. Wallace also criticized the increasing attacks on domestic radicals. In a radio talk in March 1948, Wallace warned: "The men who speak of reigns of terror in Europe, are fast introducing a reign of terror here at home" (quoted in Caute, 1978, p. 31). Wallace and the CP found themselves in an odd embrace when they formed the Progressive Party to challenge Truman in 1948.

The campaign for Wallace was the last gasp of the independent spirit that had flourished in the sit-down and wartime eras, but once again the CP had misread the mood of workers. Lee Pressman called it a "miscalculation." This time a patriotic hegemony was sweeping through the country. The public had little or no reason to doubt the foreign policy pronouncements of their government. Neither Wallace nor the Progressive Party could claim any real leadership of labor, even with the active participation of Pressman of the CIO. The Progressive Party was not a labor party. The Progressive campaign was critical of the emerging cold war and it was antiracist, but despite the wonderful voice of Paul Robeson and the music of Pete Seeger, Woody Guthrie, and the Almanac Singers at rallies, Wallace carried no states and drew only a little more than 2 percent of the vote cast. A racist Dixiecrat splinter off the Democratic

Party carried four southern states with about the same total vote as Wallace won nationwide.

The government that Harry Truman led had real credibility with the public, and he defied all the odds makers in his remarkable election. On his victory, Truman said: "Labor did it" (*New York Times,* November 4, 1948). Though Truman lost the key Democratic and strong labor states of Pennsylvania, New York, New Jersey, and Michigan to his Republican rival, Thomas E. Dewey, it was not because of defections to the Progressive Party. The war was won under Democratic Party leadership. The enemies of the nation were soundly defeated, and the return of the Depression was thwarted. The social security system was in place for a decade and was putting regular checks into the hands of millions of grateful citizens. The GI Bill of Rights was providing veterans' benefits to millions more. FHA and VA mortgages made millions of workers homeowners. Returning soldiers were realizing plans to start small businesses, attend college, and enter professions. The class-conscious anger of 1932–37 was being replaced by aspirations of upward social mobility and patriotic loyalty.

The radical left was defenseless. Pressman was forced out of his job at the CIO by Philip Murray. The purge of labor and the sensational Hollywood hearings of HUAC were followed by state and local purges, or the censorious repression of dissenting teachers, journalists, radio commentators, and public employees. Over the next decade more than a hundred congressional committee hearings investigated communist influences among workers. More than 15,000 federal employees lost their jobs because of their political ideas, or the beliefs of family members, during the 1947–56 period. Even those on the left who were hard critics of the CP in labor, the media, and education, were in for a "reign of terror." This reign was soon to be known as McCarthyism, for the senator whose abuses exceeded what was needed to do the job. Those who defended the constitutional rights of those under fire were regarded as "pink" or "soft on communism," and were also vulnerable to firing. Upward mobility required a right-leaning disposition. Anything else led the other way or nowhere. Labor was forced to adjust or suffer the consequences.

Cold War in Labor

For most of the next decade unions spent more of their energies and money in internal battles against each other for control of membership than they devoted to either organizing the unorganized or in their struggles with management. They got almost nothing from government. Remaining New Deal labor objectives such as a national healthcare program were shelved. So was the prospect of increasing shop floor governance or workplace democracy. The once popular term *industrial democracy* all but disappeared from use. In driving out eleven unions that showed a "sympathetic pattern of pro-Soviet behavior," the CIO expelled about 20 percent of its total membership, or almost 250,000 workers (Zieger, 1995, p. 287). Two of the largest unions that left the CIO, the United Electrical Workers (UE) and the International Longshoremen's and Warehousemen's Union (ILWU), maintained themselves with some strength as independents. The CIO set up a rival International Union of Electrical, Radio, and Machine Workers (IUE) with the blessings of business, the Catholic Church, the media, and government. Over the next several years the CIO spent almost a million dollars to help IUE battle with UE for members and jurisdictional control. The main beneficiaries of the long-running struggle were General Electric, Westinghouse, and other large corporations who were able to play the two rivals against one another in contract negotiations. UE, though sharply depleted of members, eventually stabilized and enjoyed a revival in the 1960s because of its positive association with civil rights, the antiwar movement, and women's rights. When UE and IEU leaders reached an accord to work together in bargaining to defeat the remnants of Boulwarism at GE in 1969, it looked as if a new era in cooperation might be dawning for labor.

The rest of the expelled unions were smaller and more vulnerable and were either destroyed, replaced, or reabsorbed back into the AFL-CIO after they were purged of left-wing leaders. Thousands of local union leaders, shop stewards, and organizers "trimmed their red wings" or withdrew from labor activism altogether after the jailing of twenty-eight "Smith Act" Communists in 1952. Ronald Reagan's Screen Actor's Guild accepted a Hollywood blacklist that barred members of his union from jobs because of their political associations. Reagan required the signing of a loyalty oath for new members of the Screen Actor's Guild in 1953. Without an independent or autonomous left, what was called the "Labor Movement" was finished, and the age of institutionalized industrial relations was underway.

The linking of domestic radicalism with a foreign threat was carried forward in Congress by Congressman Richard Nixon, who shifted attention away from labor to the alleged betrayals of the nation by well-educated professionals, like Alger Hiss. Nixon, the most successful political figure of the next twenty-five years, manipulated the communist threat more deftly than McCarthy, and went on to two terms in the vice presidency and two successful elections to the presidency. Ironically, when he resigned from the presidency in disgrace in 1974, Nixon probably enjoyed more support from organized labor than when he took office in 1969. Union households gave him more votes in his reelection campaign in 1972 than they gave to his Democratic Party rival, Senator George McGovern.

One problem for the future of labor was the absence of an independent left, or radical democratic voice or presence. The unions expelled in these early years of the cold war were the most alert to the broad shifts taking place in the nature of work itself. The unions that led white-collar workers, professionals, public employees, and workers in the newest technological areas, like UE, had the most progressive nontraditional union activists and were hardest hit by the purge. Among the smaller CIO unions charged with following the CP line were the United Public Workers, Office and Professional Workers, and the American Communications Association. The leaders of these unions were the most forthright in calling for more energy and resources for organizing the neglected and growing workforce in banking and insurance, among public employees, clerical workers, engineers, and technicians of all kinds. When their unions were broken or taken over by the old guard, their forward-looking views were also replaced by the traditional manufacturing and craft outlook for organizing.

The purged unionists were also the most aggressive about putting the issues of racial equality and women's rights at the top of labor's agenda. For the first time in the nation's history, the largest union organizations were no longer leaders in efforts to advance democracy itself. The cold war neutralized or silenced independent voices on behalf of human rights and gender equity for decades in the highest councils of the AFL-CIO. The number of women activists actually declined in the CIO over the next several years in spite of the increasing importance of women as a growing part of the wage and salaried labor force. Organizing itself came to a near standstill. The CIO's research department reported in 1953 that "no significant industry or service which was not organized before 1945–1946 has been organized since then" (Zieger, 1995, p. 344).

The CIO voices that were loudest were those that cheered the cold war foreign policy of Truman and his successors. They began to move closer to the AFL in vigorous support for NATO, the war in Korea, and every anticommunist international intervention. CIO leaders were now so firmly ensconced in the anticommunist spirit that no dictator, no matter how corrupt and no matter how cruelly repressive to his own labor force, was unacceptable or unworthy of their endorsement in the great struggle with the Soviet Union and, beginning in 1949, Red China. At the same time, no leftist government, no matter how democratically elected or constitutionally legitimate, would be allowed to exist. Secretly, CIO leaders stepped up their work for the CIA after 1950. They dispensed hundreds of millions of dollars to finance anticommunist unions in Europe, Asia, Africa, and Latin America. Under the cover of the Free Trade Union Committee (FTUC), George Meany, the AFL secretary-treasurer, helped promote the activities of Jay Lovestone, the FTUC's secretary at the end of the war. Lovestone worked closely with Irving Brown, who channeled CIA money to ex-fascists, heroin dealers, hoodlums, and assassins to prevent Communists, independent Socialists, or democratic radicals from gaining influence in unions in Europe, Latin America, and the new nations emerging from colonialism. Labor leaders became so completely devoted to the objectives of the State Department that Victor Reuther, Walter's brother, referred to it as "trade union colonialism" (quoted in Cochran, 1977, p. 320).

The Life of Riley

The unions took undeserved credit for the rising standard of living of workers. It was government action, not business or labor, that drove the prosperity and provided the base for a high wage policy. Success in war was followed by European economic reconstruction, the Korean War, and cold war military expansion; all were driven by the United States. The burgeoning military-industrial complex paid union and nonunion workers well, and set a standard for related industries. Patriotism paid off, and never before in the nation's history had a wartime economy and military establishment been maintained on such a permanent basis.

This was no free market boom, or laissez-faire success story. The Marshall Plan gave nations friendly to the foreign policy objectives of the United States a line of credit for purchases worth approximately $14 billion at the time. That meant subsidizing a huge European shopping expedition for goods manufactured mainly by American corporations and paid for by U.S. tax dollars. The United Nations' approved military action in Korea from 1950 to 1953 was fought and paid for principally by the United States. "Electric Charlie" left GE to head the government production program for the duration of the war. His counterpart at General Motors, also—coincidentally—named Charles E. Wilson (known as "Engine Charley") left his corporate job to become President Eisenhower's secretary of defense. The latter is well known for putting aside criticism about any conflict of interest by saying, in essence, that what was good for General Motors was good for the nation, and vice-versa. The Marshall Plan and Asian war were both powerful stimulants to the domestic economy. An arms race and space race with the Soviet Union led to a moon landing in the summer of 1969 for the United States and contributed to the bankruptcy of the state-driven multinational empire of the USSR a generation after that. Millions of workers in the United States found good jobs financed by huge federal deficits and the expanding global power of the nation. The federal highway building program that went into high gear during the Eisenhower administration (1953–61) and continued until 1975, was another massive publicly funded economic stimulant. No public works project in human history could match the interstate highway system constructed in these years. The nuclear power industry was a direct federally funded spin-off of the defense program. Social security benefits were expanded and minimum wage kept pace with, or briefly, exceeded the increase in the consumer price index during these years as well.

Levittown got underway in 1947, and soon there were hundreds, then thousands of low-density residential communities like it all over the country. Suburbanization was just what the auto-industrial lobby wanted. It was subsidized by government highway, bridge, and tunnel building that eclipsed public expenditures on much needed public transit systems in cities. Federal tax exemption for suburban home-owner interest and local tax payments was likewise not matched for urban renters. Racial segregation in the booming suburbs was underwritten by the Federal Housing Administration and Veteran's Administration, the two most important federal mortgage insurance programs. The federal courts allowed racially exclusive covenants in titles to new homes in securing all-white suburbs. Private home ownership for white workers quickly came to exceed that of any other industrial nation, and ultimately was attained by more than 70 percent of them. Community colleges, federal student loans, state colleges and universities, and tuition subsidies put postsecondary education within the grasp of nearly every suburban household's offspring. Just about every white worker would describe his family's social status as having achieved entry into the "middle class" by the end of this era. Suburban neighbors were no longer shopmates or close relatives, but economic and social peers in this newly imagined middle class. Nonwhites or immigrants were thought to belong to the "working class," or, more commonly, the "lower class." Class consciousness was based on what people thought or bought, not on what they objectively were.

Television brought the news of the well-being of the country to millions of homes almost before the technology was capable of doing the job. Most people had to replace their tiny-screened-snowy-first TV set if it was purchased before about 1950. By then most households had one and were enthralled with its wonders. News, sports, music, and public affairs had a fresh and profitable appeal as folk, ethnic, and regional cultural life gave way to a more nationalized corporate version. As radio had done in the 1920s, and movies in the 1930s and 1940s, television was expanding the very definition of mass media. Cultural life itself became big business similar to agri-business or steel. The film and music business came to be called the "movie industry" or "music industry" and took on the structural forms of corporate and, later, conglomerate organization. So did television and, after that, the Internet. Live events, like sports, were one of the new medium's most exciting distractions from the ordinary routine of earning a living. Workers were portrayed by sympathetic figures dealing with the details of everyday life in serialized dramas and comedies. The domestic and foreign enemies to that tranquillity were likewise carefully presented by the emerging corporate communications and entertainment industry.

The corporate media, entertainment, and new communications industries would more effectively resist labor union organizing efforts than manufacturing, mining, and the basic industries that preceded them. Corporate enterprises invested billions of dollars a year advertising their products on the new media. In the early years some corporations advertised themselves as "G.E. Theater," "The U.S. Steel Hour," "Westinghouse Playhouse," and "The Texaco Star Theater."

Organized labor never had a voice or presented a noncorporate vision of labor to the nation on a medium whose airwaves were leased by the government for no charge for commercial and profitable purposes to business interests. Unions were pleased to tend the contracts the law allowed and accepted the political and social vision of reality that was conveyed to workers by their employers.

Contract Unionism

The efficiencies of a systematic workplace were nothing new to managers. By refining the law in 1947 and maintaining an atmosphere of patriotic national emergency, an expansion of managerial hegemony was achieved by business over labor and labor unions over workers. Capital had gotten the better of labor before, but not until this era did they do so by convincing workers that they had won something. Patriotism and racism bonded workers to their employers at the expense of their own liberties. Just as the AFL-CIO had gone to work for corporate goals abroad by helping to build a labor movement bonded to private profit seeking goals, the organization became an extension of managerial objectives in dealing with the labor force at home.

Employers want workplace discipline. Labor law made the union responsible for work under the contract, or risk loss of the right of representation. The Supreme Court in the *Sands* case in 1939 held that violation of the contract meant loss of legal protection under the National Labor Relations Law. There would be no more union-sanctioned sit-downs. That action was declared illegal by the Supreme Court in 1938. Taft-Hartley toughened union responsibility for discipline by making unions vulnerable to lawsuits for damages resulting from contract violations. Wildcat strikes, or other independent job actions, became anathema to union leaders.

Employers want conflicts resolved easily and cheaply. The grievance machinery of the contract gained the force of law when arbitration awards were made legally binding by the courts. Unions and employers were establishing a system of workplace governance in the contract. The Supreme Court held in 1960 that the collective bargaining agreement was "more than a contract," it was "an effort to erect a system of industrial self-government" (Brody, 1993, p. 237). Instead of comprehensive labor law that protected all workers, thousands of separate contract agreements exhibited a wide range of workplace governance from the highest levels of due process and fairness to the lowest. Collective bargaining established grievance procedures, salary schedules, benefit packages, and everything else the law allowed in the contract, all of which could be improved or weakened in the give and take of negotiations.

In almost all cases, unions, not their individual members, made the final determination as to whether or not a managerial action was in violation of the contract and could be subject to a grievance action. Union officers decided these matters. As important as workplace governance can be, the requirements of democracy were not stringently required of either party by the courts. Unions were free under the law to be nearly as arbitrary and autocratic as managers. Secret ballot elections for national union officers, for example, have never been mandated by federal labor law. At the state level union officers are typically elected at conventions by delegates (on union paid expense accounts) in signed, not secret, ballots. The message is: vote the wrong way and your hotel and air fare check may not be forthcoming, and this may be your last convention. The term *union election* came jokingly to mean one slate, one party, no contest.

Employers want legitimacy for workplace inequalities and power relationships. The contract provisions for seniority, promotion opportunities, work assignment practices, fringe benefit provisions, and overtime are often contentious. Unhappy workers are directed to turn their complaints about these matters to the contract, not the employer. The union has the burden of defending the contract or bringing a grievance action if it believes the contract has been violated by management. The federal courts made unions legally liable to their own members in a decision in 1967. If workers believe that the union has not acted to protect their rights, or has failed to handle a legitimate grievance, they can take legal action against the union for failure to provide its "duty of fair representation," an option unheard of in European or Japanese labor law.

Employers also like saving money and curbing waste. Contract unionism reduced supervisory expenses as shop stewards and other unionists enforced contractual work obligations over the workforce. Work quotas, speed of assembly lines, and productivity requirements might now be in the contract, not left as the arbitrary assignments of bosses or managers. Nonetheless, the UAW lost out on control of assembly line speed in the early years, and a four-month-long steel strike was waged in 1959 over job assignment practices. Contracts continued to vary widely on these issues. Quality control and production standards could also be made contractual obligations with disciplinary provisions imposed if they were not met. Fewer supervisors, foremen, and inspectors meant big savings for employers. Theft, vandalism, and the destruction of equipment and tools are markedly reduced in union workplaces.

Contract unionism, or "workplace contractualism," as it has also been called, was a double-edged sword for workers and unions in the United States for many reasons. For millions of workers it was the mainstay of workplace rights and fairness when they were faced with arbitrary employers and supervisors. Every union developed a thick book or case history of grievance decisions that augmented the meaning of the contract and brought resolution to individual disputes. The profession of industrial relations flourished around the arbitration, mediation, and conciliation services of federal, state, and local labor boards. Lawyers, at least from the time of Lee Pressman forward, played an increasingly important role.

For unions, their organizational function narrowed. They were turned into legal collaborators with management, and constructed elaborate, near-permanent bureaucracies in their leadership. The traditional AFL goals of "unionism, pure and simple," seemed vindicated and the organization grew while its rival CIO was broken up and began a gradual long-term decline. The cooling fires of workplace democracy were barely kept alive on the union front lines by the dedication of tens of thousands of shop stewards and elected local leaders who still battled to protect the rights of their members under the contract. Some of the bitterest local battles were with their own state or national union officers, not their employers.

Contract unionism meant little to the workplace rights of nonunion members. Nonunion employers in comparable industries were free to match or even exceed union wages and benefits, but could maintain rigid and autocratic workplace control, something they were often willing to trade for. The more political unionism of European and Japanese workers sought the greater security of law, not individually negotiated contracts, in the protection of workplace rights, for retraining programs, national healthcare, and sometimes even vacation and other benefits. In those places strikes are far fewer, and when they do occur are brief and frequently aimed at government itself, not at individual employers.

Strikes

Though sharply curtailed in their frequency, scale, and duration, strikes continued during the era of contract unionism and beyond. Several illustrating the changed nature of industrial-labor relations stand out. There were real opportunities for union leaders here. When the Supreme Court held in 1949 that benefits like health insurance and pension funds were legitimate items for collective bargaining, they gave unions another incentive on the road to contract unionism with a double edge. A steel strike in 1949 gave the union control over newly won insurance and pension fund management. The UAW won the same things in strikes in 1949 and 1950. The unions were free to invest these funds in real estate, stocks, and bonds. Strikes lost political or social focus and took on purely economic or organizational objectives.

Steelworkers struck for 116 days in 1959 in the largest single industrial stoppage in the nation's history. But this was largely a defensive labor action, taken to prevent losses, especially over work rules and the size of work crews. A federal injunction finally forced workers back into the mills, and brought about a settlement. Nothing new was won, nor much lost. The term *industrial democracy* all but disappeared from use thereafter.

Autoworkers struck GM for "justice on the job" in September 1964. The bumper stickers on UAW cars read "Humanize Working Conditions." Reuther, nominally in charge of the action, was unenthusiastic. He pressured several dozen locals to remain on the job to prevent a more complete nationwide disruption of auto production. Reuther told the press that workers wanted yearly salaries, not hourly wages, no compulsory overtime, longer work breaks. They got very little of those things. A series of separate settlements were made under pressure from Reuther. He urged militants among the ninety striking locals to get the job done (end the strike) before the November election. They did, but little was changed in the industrial relationship. The monetary settlement was patterned after an agreement with Chrysler on September 10, and included higher wages, more vacation time, and an early retirement incentive. A year earlier a famous essay entitled, "The UAW—Over the Top or Over the Hill," by labor-journalist and author Harvey Swados had accurately prophesied the outcome. Swados acidly complained that the UAW "no longer takes its own demands seriously" (Swados, 1963, pp. 321–43).

Strikes increased in numbers in the later 1960s, but they never attained the length or frequency of those in 1945–46, and the goals were narrowly circumscribed. Organized labor was no longer an engine or center for social or democratic change in the country. That role had been traded in for institutional legitimacy, stability, and security.

The Merger of the AFL and the CIO, 1955

The AFL and CIO, though separated and in vigorous conflict since 1937, were unified in 1955, three years after the deaths of Philip Murray and William Green. At the time of the merger unions reached the peak of their representation of the workforce at more than 33 percent. George Meany followed Green to head the AFL. Meany was Green's secretary-treasurer and the AFL's primary CIA contact in various open and secretive foreign operations. The energetic Walter Reuther took over the leadership of the smaller and declining CIO after Murray's death, but David J. McDonald of

Murray's powerful United Steelworkers Union played the main role in the actual merger agreement.

Meany and Reuther both believed that consolidation was the only way to revive the stagnant labor movement, and they set up a unity committee that produced a "no-raiding" agreement at the end of 1953 and made plans for the merger. Reuther accepted the traditional and conservative AFL position of local autonomy on race, in spite of its emergence as the foremost social challenge of the time. The CIO had at one time been a national leader in the fight against racial discrimination, and Reuther's leadership of the UAW kept that issue prominent. Now the newly merged federation was intent on leaving the sensitive matter to the discretion of individual locals. The merged organization could expel unions from membership, and did so for various reasons, including electing Communists to their leadership or for charges of corruption. Locals that excluded black workers, however, remained free to do so. Mike Quill, the fiery head of the Transport Workers Union of the CIO, condemned the merger as giving in to the AFL's "three R's," racism, raiding, and racketeerism.

Reuther defended the concession on racism as a worthwhile compromise in the interest of unity and the hope of union revival that it represented. It was said that he also hoped to succeed Meany one day. No racist locals were expelled from the AFL-CIO. It wasn't until 1960 that Reuther and the UAW began to take serious action against racism in their own autoworkers' locals.

Walter Reuther

By the early 1960s Reuther helped to fund civil rights activists and was prominent as the lone white labor leader alongside Martin Luther King Jr. at the March on Washington in August 1963. Nonetheless, a year later Reuther helped President Lyndon Johnson to force an unwelcome compromise on the seating of the Mississippi Freedom Democratic Party at the Democratic Party Convention in Atlantic City. Fannie Lou Hamer remains the great figure from that encounter. She was unwilling to compromise with the ruthless brutality of the regular Mississippi delegation, and could not accept the skimpy deal imposed by Reuther on behalf of President Johnson. "We didn't come all this way for no two seats," she said after eloquently describing the beatings and bloody ordeal she and others endured in Mississippi in pursuit of the right to vote.

Reuther's idealism was always mixed with practicality and ambition. As an effective unionist he appreciated tangible results. At the same time he contributed to the birth of the New Left by encouraging youthful activists, and he favored the election of a woman to the International Executive Board of the UAW beginning in 1964, a project that was successful in 1966. The Port Huron Statement of Students for a Democratic Society (SDS) was done with Reuther's patronage at the education center and woodland retreat of the UAW, just north of Detroit, in 1962. Reuther couldn't keep up with the pace of his young protégés, however. Unlike SDS, which called the first massive protest rally in Washington in April 1965, Reuther stayed loyal to President Johnson's Vietnam War policy through 1968. Reuther eventually joined the open opposition to the war, but only after Richard Nixon's defeat of Hubert Humphrey for the presidency. By then it made little difference, though the foreign policy dispute within the AFL-CIO between the hawkish Meany and the more moderate Reuther led to the disaffiliation of the UAW during the summer of 1968, a few months before the contentious national election. By 1969 returning veterans were among the leaders of the antiwar movement, and it was no problem for Reuther to criticize Nixon.

Reuther fell behind the curve once again on race when he condemned the revolutionary black militancy of the Dodge Revolutionary Union Movement (DRUM). He called their wildcat actions and election challenges in his own UAW during 1968–69 the acts of "extremists" and "terrorists." Though still youthful and ambitious at sixty-two, Reuther didn't get to see his star rise or fall farther. He and his wife were killed, along with his bodyguard and crew, when his twin-engine Lear jet crashed in May 1970.

In effect, the AFL swallowed the remains of the CIO, including Walter Reuther, in 1955. The goal was to increase the respectable political clout and public presence of organized labor, not to win new members or advance any social goals. Meany became the chief of the merged AFL-CIO, and no organizing drive or leadership on any social issue ever took place on his watch (1955–79), or that of his successor, Lane Kirkland (1979–95). The two leaders favored clandestine interventions in foreign social and labor politics, "covert operations," "intrigues and payoffs," with the Central Intelligence Agency (Buhle, 1999, p. 145). Much Meany–Kirkland rhetoric continued to espouse organizing images and New Deal concepts, but no money or energy went into them in comparison to that which was expended on political campaigns or their own elaborate administrative structures.

George Meany's Leadership

Meany boasted that he was never on strike, never walked a picket line in the few years when he worked as a plumber and served as a union officer. He recoiled at spending money on organizing campaigns. He was businesslike. If people wanted to buy what he had to sell, they would come to him, not the other way around. Practical businessmen, like Meany, knew they needed friends in government, and spent freely to get them. But, despite their big political budgets, PACs, committees on political education (COPEs), and lobbying, the AFL-CIO was unable to secure any significant legislation or policy shifts on behalf of labor unions, even in those few years (1961–69) when Congress and the White House were firmly in the hands of Democrats.

The Johnson victory over conservative Republican candidate Barry Goldwater in 1964 brought the largest Democratic Party majorities to power in both Houses of Congress since the elections of 1936. That Congress, on the threshold of the escalation of the war in Vietnam, established the "War on Poverty," instituted Medicare, extended social security benefits, and increased the minimum wage. Voting rights for black citizens were aggressively protected from state and local racial discrimination by federal law (1965) for the first time in a century. Meany and the AFL-CIO had nothing to do with any of it, nor could Meany gain any revisions in the restrictive features of the Taft-Hartley Act.

The merger of the AFL-CIO failed for the same reasons as Operation Dixie. Neither ambitious program was undertaken in harmony with the popular democratic impulses current at the time. Meany and the AFL, consistent with their combined past, chose to sit out the sit-down militancy of the 1930s, and left it to Communists and other radicals to mobilize the popular unrest that was sweeping through the industrial heartland. Just as timidity on race and radicalism undermined Operation Dixie, it made the merger in 1955 more corporate than populist, and took the unions out of the leadership of the struggle for gender equality and human rights for more than the next generation.

Unity itself, despite the merger, remained elusive for labor as jurisdictional disputes continued to consume more resources than anything else. Internal union democracy fared no better with the merger, and its absence allowed autocratic abuses and flagrantly corrupt union practices to flourish. The International Brotherhood of Teamsters (IBT) was expelled from the AFL-CIO after internal hearings in 1957, not for their undemocratic, near feudal arrogance toward their own members, or their cynical and conservative endorsement of a host of state and local Republican Party politicians, but for corruption charges against their leaders.

Teamsters

The IBT wasn't troubled at all by the expulsion. They actually seemed to fare better outside the hollow walls of big labor than within them. The federal highway building program and the public and private disinvestment (taking resources out, and failing to maintain existing levels of investment) in the nation's rail system helped to make the IBT the fastest-growing labor organization at the time, not old-fashioned organizing tactics. Trucks, not trains, were carrying the preponderance of the nation's freight. The old local tradition of wagon drivers allied with conservative urban craft union workers was giving way to huge regional and nearly national Teamster contracts.

Trucking companies in the Prohibition era carried most of the illegal alcohol of that time, and drivers and owners of trucks built profitable relationships with huge criminal syndicates that included politicians and judges on their payrolls. Lots of illegal wartime black market and untaxed cargoes continued the lucrative relationships in the years that followed. Once the radical Trotskyists were cleared out (see chapter 7), the next best organized group were "pure and simple" business unionists with mob connections in an industry that was growing quickly.

Dave Beck

Under Dave Beck, the IBT added 500,000 to its dues paying ranks in the five years of his presidency (1952–57). Beck was the epitome of a business unionist. He hated strikes, always defended "free enterprise," became personally very rich on real estate and other investments, was an Exalted Ruler of his Elks Lodge, and was an honorary member of the American Legion for over fifty years. He served as president of the board of regents of the University of Washington (his home state) and as a member of the Washington State Parole Board. He was loyal to Meany, critical of Reuther during the merger, and no great friend of union principles, generally. He loved making money, watching television, and reading about Napoleon Bonaparte. Under his orders, he boasted, "Teamsters went through picket lines many times" (quoted in McCallum, 1978, p. 75).

Democratic elections to establish collective bargaining rights were never a favored Teamster option. The IBT was especially adept at organizing the bosses, not the workers. Teamsters preferred threats and intimidation of employers over conventional organizing drives among workers, and became the nation's single largest labor organization with over two million members by 1969. Outside the labor federation, they were not constrained by jurisdictional agreements or rules, and were soon bringing in a vast array of neglected groups of workers that included clerks and agricultural workers, as well as drivers, warehouse employees, and related workers in transportation industries.

Jimmy Hoffa

The last labor leader whose name was well known in every household in the country was Jimmy Hoffa. Hoffa gained prominence as the president of the IBT when he assumed the leadership of the union after federal investigators began closing in on his predecessor, Dave Beck, in 1957. Beck was finally sent to prison for thirty months, beginning in 1962. Hoffa, on his own, became notorious for two things: (1) His contracts set the pace for all of industrial labor. No group of workers with comparable skills did better than Teamsters. Hoffa was close to constructing a national contract in 1964 when he reached an agreement that covered almost 400,000 workers. (2) His own and inherited criminal associations and activities finally caught up with him. Hoffa's long-running battle with the Justice Department, led by Attorney General Robert Kennedy in the early 1960s, resulted in his imprisonment in 1967. He was released in 1971, then disappeared in 1975. Beck and others noted that Hoffa's disappearance meant that his silence was now assured forever. Beck received a full pardon that restored all of his citizenship rights from President Gerald Ford in 1976. The IBT was an ardent supporter of Republican candidates for public office, and Hoffa's release by Nixon owed something to that, along with an agreement not to resume his old job.

Image

Corruption charges against Beck and Hoffa were not the only image problem for unions in the age of contract unionism and corporate mass media. Hollywood was the first prominent victim of the ideological purges of the cold war and no longer celebrated the virtues of shipyard workers heroically turning out ships to win wars. The sensitive and appealing actor, Marlon Brando, played a working-class motorcycle roughneck in *The Wild Ones* (1951), another working-class brute in the film adaptation of Tennessee Williams's play, *Streetcar Named Desire* (1953), and a union goon who turns on his murderously corrupt dockworkers' union and-mobbed up brother, Charley, in *On the Waterfront* (1954). Lawmen and other authority figures took the place of working-class renegades and popular democratic heroes in most of the films of this more buttoned-down era. There would be no more movies like *Salt of the Earth,* the story of the Empire Zinc Strike that was made by blacklisted director Herbert Biberman in 1954. That labor battle and prophetic feminist film was banned and prevented from entering normal circulation. Discontent was personalized, internalized, and made strictly an individual's unique issue in the great films of this era. James Dean played appealingly quirky intense loners in films until his all too personal death in his Porsche in 1955. Marilyn Monroe led the parade of female images in films. No movie was made in these years about Emma Goldman, Elizabeth Gurley Flynn, Harriet Tubman, or any woman like them. The play, then film, *The Miracle Worker,* about Helen Keller featured her remarkable teacher Annie Sullivan. Keller's mature espousal of socialism was completely exorcised from the story.

McCarthyism and advertising revenue combined to mute an independent labor viewpoint in the press. George Seldes's fiery progressive newsletter, *In Fact,* with a significant circulation of about 175,000 weekly readers, was driven out of business in 1950. *In Fact* was the first national media outlet for the story of tobacco as a major killer of smokers, and consistently showed antilabor linkages of major corporations to pro-fascist organizations and the State Department. No other print source wished to compromise advertising revenue or alienate corporate board members with articles inconsistent with cold war dogma. Seldes was no Communist, but he did accept financial help from red sources. The progressive New York daily newspaper, *PM,* closed down in 1948. As in the aftermath of World War I, every leftist critical voice in media was silenced, exiled, or heavily infiltrated with police or FBI agents and informers that compromised its ability to continue.

Another example of the suppression of democratic dissent is W.E.B. DuBois. One of the founders of the National Association for the Advancement of Colored People (NAACP), and the brilliant scholar-editor of the journal, *The Crisis,* Du Bois lost his passport in 1950, was all but silenced in mainstream media, and finally departed for Ghana in 1961, where he died two years later on the eve of the August 1963 March on Washington. If an independent labor voice was hard to find in the information-rich United States, it was not because there was nothing to say. The nation was experiencing the dramatic expansion of a new industry, the manufacture and construction of consciousness.

Television, a more commercially controlled medium in the United States than anywhere else in the world, was not friendly to labor either. No images sympathetic to specific labor interests or unfriendly to the imperatives of business could be found in the regular weekly dramas and comedies or in the various specials and spectaculars that regularly appeared.

Candidates for public office, along with incumbents, were learning to take advantage of the small screen for their own purposes. Senator John McClellan of Arkansas chaired the Senate's Select Committee on Improper Activities in the Labor and Management Field, formed in 1957. The televised public hearings focused almost exclusively on labor leaders, especially Beck and Hoffa. Reuther was included as well but came away personally unharmed, though he was lumped unfairly in the public impression with the others.

The Republican-dominated McClellan Committee was stacked against labor. Most of its members came from states that had passed "right-to-work" (open shop) laws, though the young attorney from Massachusetts, Robert Kennedy, the brother of Democratic Senator Jack Kennedy, served as its counsel. A Gallup Poll showed public approval of unions fell from 76 percent prior to the hearings to under 64 percent right afterward. The approval numbers continued to drift lower in the polls until they stabilized at around 56 percent a few years later. This last number is of interest because union membership began a sharp decline over a decade later while still generally favored by workers and the public (see chapter 9).

The problem for anyone called before these committees was the absence of any form of due process as required in court, though witnesses could be prosecuted for perjury if they made false statements. No cross-examination was permitted, nor were there discovery requirements that let witnesses and their attorneys know what was coming. Witnesses who refused to testify under their Fifth Amendment right were pilloried by news commentators as hiding incriminating information. Witnesses could be carefully selected to give maximum emphasis to the hostile impressions about unions the committee majority sought to advance. There was little recourse for those called to defend themselves.

The Landrum-Griffin Act

Besides its antiunion influence on public opinion, the McClellan Committee recommended a change in the federal labor law to further weaken the power of unions. The resulting Landrum-Griffin Act of 1959 did three things: (1) It imposed greater restrictions on union financial practices and increased Department of Labor oversight of union records. The law actually had the cumbersome name, Labor-Management Reporting and Disclosure Act. (2) The law enlarged the definition of illegal secondary boycotts, which made it virtually impossible for one union to take action in solidarity with another that was on strike. (3) To weaken internal union solidarity, the law provided a "bill of rights" to ostensibly protect union members from the undemocratic power of their leaders. Little in the way of real democracy was required of unions by the law, but individual membership rights were enlarged. The outcome of elections remained as predictable as ever, convention practices stayed as they were, no elite or bureaucratic structures were disturbed, but union discipline was weakened.

The powerful coalition of conservative Republicans and right-to-work-state Democrats was manipulated and outflanked by Senate Majority Leader Lyndon Johnson to pass monumental civil rights legislation in 1957, but was unstoppable when it came to adding new restrictions to organized labor. Nonetheless, the degree of union political dissonance was no greater than that of the two dominant parties, with nearly everyone comfortably under the cold war umbrella. Meany continued the rhetoric of the New Deal era and complained about Taft-Hartley and Landrum-Griffin, while many of the conservative AFL craft leaders stayed close to Republicans. What remained of the CIO and its domesticated Socialists was tucked behind the leadership of Reuther and bonded to the Democrats.

Popular democratic vitality nearly disappeared from union leadership. The rank and file stopped singing at union meetings. Class conflict and worker consciousness were replaced by civic responsibility and patriotic loyalty. Cold war patriotism and good citizenship gave union workers clear benefits as their former identity dissolved and was replaced by a suburban middle-class imagined unity with their employers.

Landrum-Griffin continued the reformation of unions as legally sanctioned labor agents with business interests of their own. Management of pension fund investments in real estate, in stock portfolios that included nonunion and antiunion corporations, in racially segregated housing developments, and in gambling casinos took up more of the time and energy of most union officers, and was more profitable than organizing the unorganized or fighting to enlarge the liberties of those without them. Despite Landrum-Griffin and periodic recessions, the national consensus seemed secure. Indeed, it was working so well that the federal government soon invited more workers to join in.

Public Employees and Contract Unionism

The legal model for collective bargaining set in place by the Wagner Act, Taft-Hartley, and Landrum-Griffin was so effective in bringing order, discipline, and accountability at a lower cost to the workplace that President Kennedy adopted it as a right for all federal employees in his executive order 109988 in 1962. As a Democrat, he knew that his party reaped the bulk of the political reward from union leader endorsements and campaign contributions. Most large industrialized states followed Kennedy's action with similar enabling legislation for public employee collective bargaining rights by the end of the decade. Contract unionism for public employees carried more restrictions than the law provided in the private sector. Strike actions were either illegal or narrowly circumscribed by elaborate stages of mediation, arbitration, and fact finding.

Government employment increased from over five million workers in 1947 to almost twelve million by 1969. About one-third of these workers, or more than four million, won or were granted collective bargaining agreements by the early 1970s. For a decade after Kennedy's action, public employee unionism under the law kept the total number of union members rising and the percentage of the unionized workforce at nearly the same level, despite the beginning of sharp declines in manufacturing and other sectors. Meatpacking and coal mining, for example, were losing unionized members by tens of thousands a year due to mechanization and industry reorganization. Black workers were particularly hard hit by job losses in mining, meatpacking, and other physically brutal but unionized jobs that were eliminated by technological or organizational innovation. Union jobs were also lost because of the shift of the textile industry to the nonunion South, and the movement of the electronics industry abroad. Women workers and black workers in industry lost union representation much faster than more senior white male workers, and could not make up for the losses in the growing public and service jobs available to them. The AFL-CIO acknowledged that of the thirty-five million workers who joined the workforce from 1960 to 1970, its unions gained only two million new members.

Contract unionism also helped to dissolve the remaining political differences that had divided craft and industrial labor leaders, and now included public employees in most industrialized states. Of course, the two-thirds of the rest of the national labor force that had neither a union to represent them nor a law to provide them with any benefits, gained little from contract unionism, public or private. Minimum wage law, for example, was not required by law to match inflation rates, and did not protect workers outside of interstate commerce employment. Because each union had to make its own best deal, technological innovations, deindustrialization, and the free mobility of capital were able to undermine the power of organized workers. That grim reality only began to sink in a generation later. Unionized public employees, whose jobs could not easily be exported, and whose numbers continued to increase, played a larger role inside the AFL-CIO, but their political and social outlook stayed within the organization's mainstream.

Kennedy–Johnson, 1961–1969

Until the war in Vietnam, a real harmony was reached for labor and government in the early years of the new decade. Minimum wage and social security benefits were improved. Appointments to important federal agencies, including the Supreme Court, included many people close to organized labor and known for decidedly humanitarian and liberal views. Michael Harrington, the author of the best-selling exposé of poverty in the United States, *The Other America* (1962), was brought into government to help plan the "War on Poverty." Arthur Goldberg, a liberal labor attorney, was appointed to the Supreme Court. The Manpower Development and Training Act (1962) provided $35 million for a three-year period to retrain workers displaced by technology, an idea that has continued to expand in European social democracies, but has all but disappeared in the United States.

Of course business and industry in an age of economic expansion continued to have a need for cheap, dependent, and politically vulnerable labor. Immigration restrictions imposed in the 1920s cut back the historic flow of new workers into the United States. Hundreds of thousands of people from Puerto Rico, as U.S. citizens in one of the nation's few actual colonies, filled some of that need for some employers, especially in the steel industry in the Midwest and as service workers in New York during the twenty years that followed World War II. Immigration restrictions were waived for several thousand Hungarian anticommunist "freedom fighters" after their failed uprising in 1957. But the need was greater than those groups, or "illegals," could fill. President Johnson signed the Immigration Return Act in 1965 that ended the specific ethnic and racial restrictions of the 1920s and opened the door significantly. The quota system was replaced by fixed limits on immigration from any one country, and included inducements for increasing the number of skilled and professional immigrant workers.

Civil Rights, Women's Rights, and Native Americans

The dramatic actions taken by workers to win institutional legitimacy and a change in both the workplace and the society inspired others who were excluded or denied equity in the democracy. Civil rights activists, led, among others, by A. Philip Randolph of the Brotherhood of Sleeping Car Porters, borrowed the playbook used by labor, added Gandhi-inspired nonviolence, and Martin Luther King Jr.'s Christian appeal for brotherhood and forgiveness. Randolph launched the modern movement when he threatened a march on Washington to win the establishment of the Fair Employment Practices Commission in 1940, and told a U.S. Senate committee in 1947 that he would urge draft refusal among young black men if racial segregation was continued in the armed services. The Montgomery, Alabama bus boycott and student lunch counter sit-ins resulted in arrests but ultimately contributed to the overturning of racial segregation in public facilities nationwide. Civil rights and voting rights legislation that aimed broadly at ending all legally enforceable or institutionally sanctioned Jim Crow practices began in 1957. Civil rights laws were carried further under President Lyndon Johnson in 1964 and 1965, and replicated the legal victories won a generation earlier by labor. The laws similarly made their beneficiaries dependent on federal executive authority for enforcement, and on the courts for effective interpretation of what was really won.

The battle to end Jim Crow practices exposed other manifestations of racial injustice. There was increasing anger in ghettoized black communities in northern cities over job discrimination, bank lending practices, police brutality, public service injustices, poor schools, and racism in the craft unions that did the work for contractors on big public and private projects. Rioting against police and arson in big cities began to follow police attacks, or rumors of them, throughout the nation. Nearly every large city experienced an uprising or rebellion of its ghettoized and restricted black population during the 1963–68 period. Hundreds of people were killed, fires devastated commercial and residential districts. Revived expressions of racial nationalism, "black power," community pride, and self-help challenged the liberal reformism and desegregation goals of Martin Luther King Jr. Only a few labor leaders put themselves on the front lines of the battle for the economic and social justice that ending racism required. Contract unionism stilled most of their voices. Many prominent unionists, especially in the South, echoed the racist sentiments of their region. Labor, once at the forefront of this battle, now protected its interests from the sidelines.

Malcolm X admired some of the emerging leaders among the newly independent African nations, and publicly made the connection between racism in the United States and the racism of Europeans in their colonies when he returned from a pilgrimage to Mecca. Exploitation of labor and expropriation of property were legitimated by legal and institutional racism wherever it was found. Black Americans were not alone in feeling the destructive injustice of racism, Malcolm X declared. He was killed in February 1965, a few months after making these observations. Malcolm X was catching up to the ideas of the exiled scholar, W.E.B. Du Bois, in seeing the relationship between racism and the exploitation of labor and the expropriation of property.

Martin Luther King Jr. joined heavyweight boxing champion Muhammad Ali (formerly Cassius Clay) in connecting racism at home with the murderous intrusion into the home of the Vietnamese people. Ali was stripped of his boxing title during his athletic prime while he battled for his status as a conscientious objector in the courts. King turned his organization into a "Poor People's Movement," one that supported striking sanitation workers in Memphis, Tennessee. It was there, in Memphis, where he was helping those workers, that King was killed in April 1968. King, Ali, Malcolm X, and Du Bois were moving toward labor, or already there, but labor hardly moved at all.

It was government action through legislation, executive actions, or judicial decisions that replaced the workplace as the arena for righting social wrongs and finding justice. Workplace disputes ultimately came before government authorities as well, but were limited to arbitration decisions, court actions, injunctions, or state and federal labor board rulings on contractual issues. Black activists began to seek the election of people from their own communities to city and state offices and school boards.

The righteous successes won in the streets and in the courts for labor and civil rights activists inspired working women to move beyond the protective legislation of the Women's Bureau of the Department of Labor. That agency was added to the Department of Labor in 1920 and spent most of its history seeking to protect the health and working conditions of women. Wartime efforts to end racial job discrimination linked the goals of women workers to the goals of civil rights. By the early 1950s the Women's Bureau began to shift its emphasis from protection toward ending discrimination against women by employers and unions. Increased gender-based job segregation caused the earnings of working women to fall against those of men. By 1960 the gap had grown to .$60 for every $1.00 earned by men of comparable skills, a significant loss from wartime highs of nearly $.65. Even the newly merged AFL-CIO gave tepid encouragement at the local level to equalize pay rates after 1956, but member unions rarely fought that battle in contract negotiations or in political campaigns. Maternity leaves, social security and tax benefits, and a removal of discriminatory barriers to employment could open new opportunities to women.

The Women's Bureau, not organized labor, urged President Kennedy to set up a Commission on the Status of Women in 1961 to study discrimination against women. Similar bodies were established by state governments around the country and these groups mobilized hundreds, then thousands, of women. From these organizations came the National Organization for Women (NOW), organized in 1966, which put aside the protective approach in favor of an all-out drive to end discrimination. By 1970 the Women's Bureau joined NOW in support of an Equal Rights Amendment to the Constitution, the foundation of the reborn, or "second-wave," feminist movement.

Discrimination against workers was attacked on other fronts as well, though the lead was not taken by labor unions, despite their reaching their highest postwar influence and power in government circles during the Kennedy–Johnson years (1961–69). The Age Discrimination in Employment Act that passed in 1968 advanced the civil rights of all workers when it barred forced retirement based solely on age. A reborn American Indian Movement (AIM), also inspired by the activism of civil rights, fought in court and with direct action to redress the multitude of wrongs its people had endured.

War on Poverty

The sharpest criticism of enduring poverty in the midst of apparent abundance was made by Michael Harrington's book, *The Other America*, when it was published in 1962. Harrington, the heir to the leadership of the Socialist Party of E. V. Debs, A. J. Muste, and Norman Thomas, exposed the grim reality faced by nearly 20 percent of the people of the nation. President Johnson launched his "War on Poverty" concurrently with the rising engagement of U.S. troops in Southeast Asia.

A Head Start Program for preschool children, school lunch subsidies, food stamps, rent subsidies, federal jobs programs, increased federal funding for mass transit, public works, housing, and education followed Johnson's smashing election victory over conservative Republican Barry Goldwater in 1964. In addition, a domestic peace corps known as Volunteers In Service to America (VISTA), and community recreation and arts projects flowed into rural and urban pockets of poverty. Nothing like it had been seen since the early New Deal, and none of it was part of the political program of the AFL-CIO. Organized labor was already fully committed to the foreign policy of the corporate state, and made no specific legislative or policy gains during the Vietnam conflict. Once again the immediate benefits of federal assistance programs were felt in those working-class communities of poor white and black citizens that bore the heaviest burden of casualties on the battlefield of war. This time it was in Vietnam.

Medicare and Medicaid were created by the Medical Care Act in 1965. The two measures provided publicly funded support for the medical expenses of elderly, disabled, or impoverished citizens. These health programs both subsidized the expansion of huge private medical empires and relieved many employers of some responsibility to pay the health costs for millions of underpaid or elderly workers. Medicare and Medicaid represented far less for workers in the United States than the achievement of universal national public healthcare programs that were in place everywhere else in the modern industrial world by that time. Nonetheless, the new healthcare provision was an immediate and enormous benefit to those without it.

Countercurrents

Arbitrary authority and discriminatory practices were on the defensive everywhere. The Supreme Court under the leadership of Chief Justice Earl Warren (1953–69) broke down the wide discrepancies and inequities among states in the treatment of people accused of crimes, over censorship practices, privacy, race, and political representation. The popular media reported that a generation gap had appeared between the youthful and rebellious population of postwar baby boomers and their elders. Mario Savio, a twenty-five-year-old graduate student of philosophy at the University of California at Berkeley in 1965, drew the line with his warning: "Don't trust anybody over thirty." Some serious theologians declared in 1966 that "God is dead." Writers, filmmakers, artists, and poets took on every value and belief established by authority and subjected them to a new criticism that grew up outside the workplace. The poet Alan Ginsberg said this ferment was an "explosion in the grey room," an expansion of the consciousness of the brain itself. Songwriter Bob Dylan put conventional morality on the spot with the question, "Something is happening here and you don't know what it is, do you Mr. Jones?" Dylan bridged the former labor leadership of democratic protest with the new movement in his song "I Ain't Gonna Work on Maggie's Farm No More." Phil Ochs musically admonished labor leaders for forgetting their past in "Links on a Chain." Workers joined a massive popular opposition to the war in Vietnam as government credibility collapsed.

Most labor unions, now a legally responsible part of established authority, moved farther away from the democratic currents stirring the country, though some of the independent or expelled unions participated in the populist revival of attacks on entrenched privilege and authority. George Meany gave Richard Nixon his campaign slogan for 1968 when he proclaimed a year earlier that, in spite of the loud protests against the war by some, it had the support of the "silent majority" of Americans. Meany never wavered in his cold war loyalty to the foreign policy goals of the employers of his members.

Environmentalism, Health, and Safety

Instead of growing up as a political issue among workers, the revived movement to protect the environment was carried on in the conservationist tradition of Theodore Roosevelt. There was little more done about environmental matters until the passage of the National Wildlife Preservation Act in 1964 and the Clean Water Restoration Act of 1966. Some "Earth First" air and water pollution activists and antinuclear power critics recognized the preponderant role of business in savaging the environment, but were seldom joined by organized labor. Jobs and the dues that flowed from them put the AFL-CIO on the side of business against most "tree huggers." (This continues to be a blind spot for the AFL-CIO, which joined the oil industry in favor of oil drilling in the Arctic National Refuge in 2002, though the U.S. Senate rejected the plan.)

Only in the area of workplace health and safety did some unionists join in the rising anger toward the indifference of business leaders. Anthony Mazzochi, the youthful executive board member of the Oil, Chemical, and Atomic Workers union, almost alone among AFL-CIO leaders, fought for the establishment of federal standards to protect workers from the health and safety hazards that were revealed in the workplaces of his members. Mazzochi helped to uncover hazards and publicize sound medical evidence about unsafe levels of radiation exposure that finally forced government to take action. The federal Occupational Safety and Health Administration (OSHA) owes its founding in 1970 to Mazzochi. One astute analyst claimed: "Without his persistence and vision, it would never have seen the light of day" (Aronowitz, 1998, p. 230).

The Declining Status of Work

As prosperous and secure as the unionized and union-influenced work world became by the mid-1960s, the social status and self-respect of industrial workers began to fade. In comparison to the increasing numbers of white-collar and professional workers (all of whom were now known as "employees"), whose clean offices and yearly salaries industrial and service workers envied, manufacturing and construction labor began to seem less satisfying and less important. Technology, now called "automation," continued to replace manual skills in making goods. Human intelligence was replacing brawn in engineering, extraction industries, and manufacturing processes. Even the value of a college education was questioned if it resulted in a conventional job. A union card no longer seemed to be the ticket to a better life in an apparently expanding suburban middle class. Craftsmen plumbers and electricians became independent contractors where the law allowed, and often preferred to hire nonunion laborers to work under their supervision. There was still plenty of hard physical work, but it was left to those at the bottom of the labor chain and to immigrant newcomers, more and more of whom were outside the union orbit.

Stratification among workers increased dramatically with the best jobs, material benefits, social status, and personal satisfaction reserved for those few who were higher up, or safely protected in their positions. Most of the AFL craft unions maintained strictly controlled apprentice programs. The skilled trades offered the children of union members first choice in admission, just as privileged private universities did for the offspring of wealthy alumni. Racism played a deliberate part in many of these union locals despite AFL-CIO public statements about brotherhood and desegregation. Chronic unemployment, or underemployment in part-time or "off-the-books" work with no benefits provided, and no social security deductions, was also common among increasingly ghettoized black, immigrant, and ethnically marginalized people.

There were also plenty of unhappy workers in the world of contractual bliss. The contracts could not take into account the subjective matters of job satisfaction, boredom, or the cultural and generational alienation that led workers to take steps on their own for relief. During the 1964 confrontation, Walter Reuther called General Motors "the largest, (most) glorified, gold-plated sweatshop in the world" (quoted in Lichtenstein, 1995, p. 398). Worker absenteeism, delinquency, on-the-job drug and alcohol use, petty theft, and product sabotage were all increasing as expressions of discontent and alienation at the very time when unions and material prosperity seemed to reach historic highs for workers. When they were angry or frustrated about their condition, workers blamed what was at hand, or what was permissible. Sometimes they turned on themselves.

Conclusion

Labor leaders in this time of apparent power and prominence have often been criticized for their relative timidity on the issues of race and gender discrimination, and for their simplistic patriotic identification with their employers' interests in domestic and foreign policy. Could better leaders have led workers to a higher level of class or social consciousness, or were they actually out in front, more socially aware of the realities of power than their own rank and file? Or, were the prosperous conditions and dazzling wonders of the country too overpowering for both workers and their leaders to imagine changing? Clearly, the making of foreign policy was never a democratic debate in the history of the United States. Global war and the cold war that followed it drove nearly everyone toward patriotism for protection and a sense of security. There was virtually no alternative information to challenge effectively what was laconically called the "conventional wisdom" of the time. McCarthyism silenced or tainted most dissent as disloyal, and the mass media, schools and universities, and clergy of all faiths participated in a celebration of national virtues that was unlike any other time in history.

Objective evidence also sustained these consensual sentiments. In the aftermath of war the United States really did expand its prosperity and offer new opportunities for mostly white male workers and their children to improve on the lives and conditions of their origins. Defense industry work, unionized or not, paid well and reinforced patriotic ideology. After twenty years of maintaining the first large-scale peacetime military establishment in the nation's history (1948–68), millions of workers, as either youthful volunteers or draftees, received patriotic training and indoctrination that didn't easily wear off. No public foreign policy debate preceded the war in Vietnam. Few questions were raised at the time of the fraud-based Gulf of Tonkin Resolution in 1964 that provided the thin legal cover for the military escalation that followed. The AFL-CIO never broke ranks on the war; only the UAW disaffiliated because of it.

There were spectacular public and private achievements that bonded workers to the world of their employers as well. Towering new skyscrapers were built, astronauts circled the earth, a new interstate highway system knitted the vast nation together. Athletic, musical, and film celebrities fulfilled nearly everyone's fantasies and, for the most part, confirmed the patriotic consensus. So, in spite of all of the dissonance, dominant institutions and the authority they still claimed, including the AFL-CIO, firmly held the loyalty of most citizens and most workers. Richard Nixon intuitively knew that, and played it like a violin.

Nixon didn't get the same number of votes from workers in 1968 as his Democratic Party rival, Hubert Humphrey, but he got enough to win. White workers, North and South, gave nearly 13 percent of the total national vote to the openly racist third-party candidate, George C. Wallace, of Alabama. Nixon's appeal to a "white backlash" was carefully orchestrated to play on continuing racist sentiment. Spiro Agnew was selected as Nixon's Republican vice presidential running mate, not because of any notable accomplishments made by him as governor of Maryland, but because of his racism. He said he would order military forces to shoot looters in the event of urban ghetto rioting, even if those killed might be young teenagers pilfering clothing through broken shop windows. Law-abiding patriotic citizens, frightened by civil disorder, disregarded union endorsement of Democrats and gave Nixon–Agnew and Wallace their overwhelming support. As accurately as Truman contended in 1948, Nixon could have said of his victory twenty years later: "labor did it."

A Harris poll in 1968 confirmed the conservative and soon-to-be self-defeating ideology of union members. Of government programs that required public financing, unionists placed the war in Vietnam at the top of the list of their priorities. Next in importance came education, then law enforcement. Fighting poverty, welfare programs, and aid to cities followed far behind, or were rejected altogether by union member majorities. A majority of workers polled rejected a $32 billion plan to rebuild the cities, despite the massive employment possibilities such a program would create. More than two-thirds of those polled believed that "Negroes are already trying to move too fast toward racial equality" (Bok and Dunlop, 1970, p. 460). All workers, union and nonunion, would pay dearly for their racism and patriotism. The inauguration of President Richard Nixon in January 1969 was only the beginning.

Jimmy Hoffa. The last labor leader to enjoy national public recognition was a harsh autocrat who was assisted into his position of power by secretive forces inside and outside the government. (AP/Wide World Photos)

CHAPTER 9

Labor and the Corporate State, 1969–1992

WASHINGTON: April 10 - The labor Department has decided that it will not require farmers to provide field workers with toilet facilities or drinking water, department officials said today.
—*New York Times*, April 11, 1985

The Tide Turns

The Tet Offensive in Vietnam in early 1968 marked the beginning of the end of the twenty-year rise in the standard of living for most workers, and derailed the remains of the "War on Poverty" initiated by President Johnson. Neither policy, guns abroad, nor butter at home was getting the results that were promised. Hubert Humphry's full employment plans got nowhere. Large-scale poverty, with inadequate nutrition and housing, continued to be the fate of about one-fifth the people in the United States. Poor people were dependent on government for food and housing supplements, child welfare payments, and medical care. They served as an available reserve of controllable cheap labor and as a disciplinary model for other workers. The sons of the poor, and workers with the fewest options, once again bore a disproportionately large share of the front-line casualties in Vietnam.

President Nixon had to take responsibility for an unsuccessful war and a contentious domestic policy. He sought, he said, "peace with honor," and achieved neither. War, as we have seen, brings some rewards for those who make military and domestic sacrifices. This one continued rewarding labor in the short term, while at the same time the foundations were being laid for labor's degradation in the long term.

Reshaping Labor Relations

Through all of labor's past history a social and political state of conflict existed be-tween workers and those who profited from their labor. The tension from that conflict forced democratic concessions from the owners of great wealth that both improved the material well-being of workers and advanced their political liberties. As we have seen, both business and labor formed institutions and organizational structures to increase their leverage in the encounters they had with each other. Business always held the initiative in the creation of state power, lawmaking, and setting the direction of foreign policy, and held firm control of the courts. Slaves, servants, and workers reacted to those initiatives with actions of their own that were invariably found to be illegal until some political rights could be won to make their actions and desires legit-imate. Indentured servitude is gone. So is slavery. Unions and strikes in the private sector are nominally legal. Suffrage is universal. The construction of modern labor institutions was the result of those historic conflicts, as industrial unions followed the establishment of modern manufacturing corporations. The laws that crafted those unions, and the courts that continuously refined and defined them, however, were never controlled by labor. Walter Reuther often observed that labor's victories in bar-gaining could easily be lost in elections.

Just as labor organizations in the United States became a legal part of the estab-lished national order, the business structure became more international than ever. By patriotically embracing the historic foreign policy objectives of the United States (an Open Door for corporate enterprise disguised as a cold war, and later known as "free trade"), the AFL-CIO fell into line with the goals of business and began a long de-cline. No effective multinational unions were constructed to negotiate transnational contracts in this era or beyond it. No labor institutions were formed that could com-pare to a multinational corporation, the World Bank, or the International Monetary Fund. By accepting the structures and cultural relationships that gave them power and authority, AFL-CIO leaders also became defensive of those structures and rela-tionships. Racism bonded white workers in a false aristocracy of blood with their employers, just as anticommunism deceptively bonded them with national corporate foreign policy.

The nature and forms taken by labor were also unstable, subject to changes in tech-nology and organization, and also outside of the control of labor. Just as the Bessemer process replaced the Open Hearth in steelmaking in the nineteenth century, wire and tape recorders replaced stenography in the office, and automatic switches displaced tens of thousands of telephone switchboard operators in the twentieth. Computers continue the same process in every enterprise or service. By their firm and reward-ing grip on the craft and industrial model of labor organization, the AFL-CIO unions limited themselves to a shrinking share of the expanding, but changing, labor force. When the size of the labor force grew at a faster rate than their membership during the 1970s, many unions hardly noticed the shift because their real numbers and dues income increased anyway. Though union density fell from about 25 percent to 20 percent of the workforce from 1970 to 1980, dues paying membership actually increased slightly. Public employees made up most of the new unionists, but were not sufficient to halt the slide. From 1980 to 1990 union membership fell more dramatically to only about 14 percent of the total labor force, and plant closings and deindustrialization began to cut sharply into actual union membership. Some unions, like those representing longshoremen and typesetters, nearly disappeared altogether when technology made their traditional work obsolete. Instead of taking the lead in the continuing democratic struggles for social and political reforms to expand their own competitiveness with capital, and to increase the opportunities of those workers with limited access to good jobs and social mobility, labor unions were often perceived by workers as among the obstacles to those goals. In almost every large union (e.g., steel, mining, Teamsters) a movement for democracy emerged to battle the entrenched elites. Because established leaders narrowed the focus of the unions to what the law prescribed, unions came to be regarded by friends and enemies alike as an interest group, not as a social or political movement.

New Forms of Action and Organization

Workers were out of step with their unions on another front as well. Lawsuits were given greater power in the workplace when the Supreme Court, in *Griggs v. Duke Power* (1971), made it possible for workers to sue under Title VII of the 1964 Civil Rights Act. Unions, not corporations, were the first to be sued for acts of discrimination under Title VII. Admission to union apprentice programs, contract seniority clauses, and promotion practices came under attack by those who believed they were unfairly excluded or held back. Instead of new laws to protect the rights of workers, or stronger labor organizations with the capability to make contracts that protected those rights, more workplace disputes would be resolved in civil, not criminal, actions in court. Because monetary settlements in civil actions invariably exceeded grievance awards in contract violations, many workers chose the courthouse route to resolve disputes with employers. The courthouse and the lawyer replaced the union hall and grievance officer on matters of social justice.

With labor unions sidelined as the principal agent for social and democratic progress, unions lost their position of leadership for workers in general. Despite some continuing populist rhetoric, most unions became agents acting on behalf of their dues paying members on a shrunken field of combat. With but a few exceptions (Teamsters, ILGWU, SEIU), no great organizing drives were undertaken by major national unions or the AFL-CIO itself for decades. Public employees organized when state enabling laws allowed them to. If workers wanted representation, they would either have to form new unions on their own, as some did, or organize themselves in new ways to advance their goals.

The United Farmworkers of America, led by Caesar Chavez, was one such group that battled its way to unionism with a nationwide grape boycott that brought recognition and a contract in 1970. Chavez and the farmworkers were among the more than 50 percent of the workforce that was not legally protected by the National Labor Relations Law and its National Labor Relations Board (NLRB). Chavez and his members really did it on their own by winning public support to their cause. Health and hospital workers were also outside the umbrella of the NLRB, but, with the help of civil rights activists that included A. Philip Randolph, successfully formed Local 1199, a New York City organization to represent them. Local 1199 later became the National Union of Hospital and Health Care Employees, with organizing drives going in six states by early 1969. Their success led to an amendment to the National Labor Relations Law in 1974 to extend coverage of the law to workers in "nonprofit" hospitals.

Organizations without any union identification began to proliferate in the vacuum left by labor's retreat from the social and political front lines of democratic struggles. Women formed the National Organization for Women in 1970, and women welfare recipients and social service workers took over the National Welfare Rights Organization in 1972 when they displaced the mostly male civil rights activists who had formed it a few years earlier. ACORN, an urban poor people's movement, was formed by community activists in 1970 along the lines of the Depression-era Southern Tenant Farmer's Union. Antiwar veterans organized the Vietnam Veterans Against the War (VVAW) in 1967, and quickly became leaders in the multitude of groups that formed the surging antiwar movement from then on.

Reuther and a few other socially conscious union leaders subsidized the Student League for Industrial Democracy (SLID) that, in turn, spawned Students for a Democratic Society (SDS) in the early 1960s. SDS separated from its labor foundations specifically because the student group rejected the rigidly undemocratic anticommunism of the unions. SDS also separated itself from Michael Harrington and the Social Democrats, the remnant of the Socialist Party founded by Eugene V. Debs, for the same reason. SDS, an early leader in the campus activism of the mid-1960s, broke up into several antiwar and radical organizations with no ties to organized labor, except for a few independent forays by some activists and community organizers into workplaces and neighborhoods.

Gay and lesbian groups became more openly organized to fight job and social discrimination, especially after defiance of police at the Stonewall Inn, a gay bar in New York's Greenwich Village in 1969. Four years later there were nearly 800 gay and lesbian groups around the nation. Black, Hispanic, women, and gay workers formed caucuses and built organizations within their unions to combat discrimination on the job and in the union. In 1974, the largest of these, the Coalition of Labor Union Women (CLUW), was organized at a meeting of more than 3,000 union women in Chicago. Six long years later, their president, Joyce Miller, was named to the AFL-CIO executive board, the first female to hold such a position in the organization's history.

George Meany and most other union leaders were still enjoying gay-bashing jokes, deriding the peace and women's rights advocates, and remaining indifferent to labor organizing. These complacent unionists were comfortably awaiting the program of the Nixon–Agnew administration. The rank and file of the nation's workforce, in stark contrast to their organizations and their leaders, was building a new momentum in strike actions.

Business found new forms of organization to defeat or stop labor as well. Large corporations formed smaller units of production when they discovered that it was easier to defeat a union organizing drive in a plant with fewer than 500 workers, especially when they were located in right-to-work sunbelt states with little history of collective bargaining. Mergers, consolidations, and the formation of giant corporate conglomerates went in the other direction to dilute or undo union agreements. Courts and the NLRB were, unsurprisingly, indifferent to union claims of unfair or illegal practices due to business reorganization.

Strikes, Authorized and Wildcat

There was an increase in the number and severity of strikes that coincided with the rising democratic, antiwar, and human rights movements of the late 1960s. The new strike wave that continued through the early 1970s included more than 5,000 work stoppages a year, more than at any time since 1945–46. Strikes took on many of the same tactics and practices of other protests as well. Marches and rallies by workers at corporate headquarters highlighted abusive practices and unpunished violations of labor law. Some of the goals of strikers were similar to those of the other protests. Workers wanted their rights assured, dignity and fair treatment on the job, as well as improvements in pay, healthcare, and retirement coverage. The intense three-week strike at the new and modern Lordstown, Ohio General Motors factory in 1972 by UAW Local 1112 had all of the characteristics of a youth revolt. The fast-moving assembly line (speeded up from 60 to 100 Vegas—ask someone who owned one—an hour), forced overtime, and harsh discipline drove the workers out. The media portrayed strikers, many of them Vietnam vets, as long-haired, dope-smoking hippies who lacked the work ethic and self-discipline of their elders. That complaint was common among all centers of authority at the time. Wartime inflation also brought on enforced wage and unenforced price controls under President Nixon, and that also drove workers to act.

The rising numbers of unionized public employees were heard from as well. Teachers, librarians, police officers, firefighters, hospital workers, social service workers, and clerical workers engineered strikes, slowdowns, "blue flu" sick calls, and other collective actions to win recognition and secure workplace rights. College faculty who were organizing for collective bargaining rights slept out on the lawns of college trustees, marched, and picketed the offices of public and private officials. When they formed unions, they went on strike, whether it was legal or not. Some, like the Cook County, Chicago, College faculty union leader, Norman Swenson, led strikes on an almost annual basis in the 1970s, and went to jail more than once to win a contract. At the early meetings and national conferences of academic unionists, discussions involving strike tactics drew the largest numbers of attendees. When regular local or national union leaders were unresponsive or unwilling to take up the struggle, workers did it on their own at the local level or in the greatest number of wildcat strikes in history.

The biggest wildcat strike of them all was made by public employees. It started with a walkout of the postal workers in New York City in March 1970 and quickly spread to more than a half dozen other cities. It was a rank-and-file rebellion of workers bitter about wages that were falling behind and broken promises believed to have been made by government. More than 200,000 workers defied union and court-ordered injunctions to return to work, and effectively stopped the nation's mail system. President Nixon ordered the national guard into New York as strikebreakers to sort and deliver the mail. Their untrained efforts to do the job were reported as comical by observers. Public sympathy was with the strikers. Postal workers have a positive relationship with the public. Negotiations brought the strike to a quick conclusion with substantial pay raises and amnesty for everyone involved in the three-week-long illegal job action.

A month later, Teamsters, angry at their own union-negotiated contract, briefly stopped nearly all trucking from coast to coast. Wildcat strikes took out mineworkers, autoworkers, and telephone operators. Dissident union factions challenged the union leadership in every large organization. Sometimes the fights were murderous, as in the death of Jock Jablonsnki, the challenger of "Tough" Tony Boyle for the leadership of the UMW at the end of 1969. Boyle went to prison for hiring the gunmen who killed Jablonski, his wife, and their daughter.

The Nixon Agenda

The new administration based its appeal on cold war anticommunist patriotism and racist resentment at the ending of legally enforceable racial segregation. Anger, Nixon's advisors understood, was a more potent political force than hope. The job was to align that patriotic and racist anger to the "Conservative Manifesto" of 1937 and the undoing of the New Deal structures that either restrained, taxed, or inhibited business in its dealings with labor. Nixon always had the congressional support of anti–New Deal southern Democrats, most of whom would begin to shift to his party now that black voters could not easily or legally be kept from the polls. The terrible irony is that this virulent antilabor program attracted so large a labor constituency, and that in his reelection in 1972, even the AFL-CIO gave Nixon a tacit endorsement.

AFL-CIO President George Meany, by refusing to support the strongly pro-labor Democratic candidate, George McGovern, freed his constituent national unions to give their endorsements and contributions to the campaigns of candidates of either party. Senator McGovern, of North Dakota, had been a youthful Progressive Party supporter of Henry Wallace in 1948, and was now an outspoken critic of continuing the war in Vietnam. The years of the cold war purges removed most independent critics of the nation's foreign policy from leadership of AFL-CIO unions. Those who remained, led by construction and defense industry chiefs, never wavered in their loyalty to the corporate/government position on foreign affairs.

The Nixon domestic program was neither completely secretive, nor very candid. Deceit, or sleight of hand, are better ways of understanding the political techniques of the man once known by his critics as "Tricky Dick." His appointees to federal courts and most public agencies were clearly hostile to labor and sympathetic to business. Of course he never said so, and a distinct list of apparently protective and popular reforms also accompanied the beginning of his covert assault on labor's New Deal achievements. He named as heads of the important federal welfare and antipoverty agencies people known to be among their most ardent opponents. Among the issues eventually raised in his impeachment proceedings was Nixon's attempt to defy federal law by naming people to lead agencies they deliberately intended to destroy.

Nixon made some token appointments favorable to labor, most notably, Peter Brennan, who was awarded the post of secretary of labor in 1973. Brennan, as head of the powerful New York City Building Trades Council, AFL-CIO, helped to organize a covert and brutal hard-hat attack on antiwar demonstrators on Wall Street on May 8, 1970, and then an open peaceful and patriotic demonstration of construction workers on May 20. Nixon sought to cover all his bases.

There were six enduring parts to the old "Conservative Manifesto:" (1) Eliminate or cut taxes on business and wealth. (2) Balance the federal budget. (3) Reduce the power of the federal government in areas restrictive of business interests. (4) Restore power to the states to defeat or curb progressive restraints on business. (5) Reduce or end public economic activities and welfare programs not immediately beneficial to business. (6) Encourage private enterprises—privatization—as the only way forward for the economy. The Nixon administration was not able to achieve all of these all at once, but it made considerable progress, and all of labor, union or not, eventually paid dearly for the shift.

The Supreme Court

Nixon attacked the Supreme Court in his first election campaign for going too far in the defense of civil rights, human rights, and the rights of those accused of crimes. The Court, his conservative allies knew, also defended the federal laws that gave legal rights to labor unions, protected the rights of minorities, and weakened the discretionary power of state governments in these and other important areas. That was going to be changed.

Altogether, Nixon made six nominations to fill four Supreme Court vacancies during his stormy presidency. All of his appointees adhered to the broad goals of the conservative antilabor program. Two of Nixon's candidates were turned down because of ideological extremism in their racism, or, in one case, because he was so inept. The four who were confirmed, Warren Burger, Harry Blackmun, Lewis Powell, and

William Rhenquist, served as the foundation for an antilabor conservative majority that endured for the rest of the century and beyond. Though the Court did not come through for Nixon when he tried to stop the presses in the Pentagon Papers case, nor did it shield him from justice in the Watergate burglary and cover-up, it never failed him on labor. In a 1971 decision (*Lloyd v. Tanner*), the justices overturned a 1968 ruling (*Amalgamated Food Employees Union v. Logan Valley Plaza*) that allowed union picketing inside a private shopping center. Malls, the new centers of suburban culture, were private, according to the Court, not public, so the well-known public rights of free speech, assembly, and picketing did not apply in the same manner inside as they did outside on Main Street, USA. Retail clerks and other mall employees continue an uphill battle for unions with these restrictions on their constitutional rights. Malls proliferated while urban, small town, and even suburban public shopping districts declined.

In another hostile decision against labor, *Connell Construction Company v. Plumbers & Steamfitters Local Union #100* (1974), the Court enlarged the scope of the federal government's authority to use antitrust restrictions against unions. During the Nixon years the Court continued to make some progressive human and civil rights decisions as well, not least of which were *Roe v. Wade* (1973), which protected abortion rights, and *Furman v. Georgia* (1972), which ended (temporarily as it turned out) the practice of capital punishment. The Court, like Nixon himself, was still moving in both directions.

Legislation

As in the mixed gains and losses for labor in appointment policy and in court, the Nixon administration's legislative record also went in two directions. Before he left his office in disgrace in 1974, Nixon, with Democratic majorities in both Houses of Congress, achieved several of the most important, and final legal gains for labor, human, and civil rights in the century. Nixon signed into law the Coal Mine Safety and Health Act in 1969, the year of John L. Lewis's death. The new safety standards contributed to a sharp falloff in mining accidents, but so did the greater practice of strip (surface) mining and the introduction of new technologies. The Environmental Protection Act became law in 1970 and established the Environmental Protection Agency (EPA). Congress and Nixon also responded to the persistent arguments of labor, particularly the entreaties of Tony Mazzochi, for the creation of the Occupational Safety and Health Administration (OSHA) in 1970. More than two million workers a year still suffered significant job-related injuries, with over 14,000 killed annually on the job. The agency's purpose was to improve health and safety conditions in the workplace, though its decisions and sanctions led most labor leaders to view it as mainly pro-business. The casualty numbers have declined since then, though nearly 6,000 workers died of injuries sustained on the job, and 50,000 more died of occupation-related illnesses in the last year of the century. Disputes continued to be unresolved over the meaning and nature of accidents, injuries, and disabilities. Carpal tunnel syndrome, for example, is medically insurable and treated, but the OSHA standard for acknowledging it was not accepted by President George W. Bush as a real occupational health hazard even by 2003.

In 1974, Nixon's last year in office, Congress passed the Employee Retirement Income Security Act (ERISA) to protect pensions earned by workers, but vulnerable to bankruptcies, consolidations, or mergers. The Twenty-sixth Amendment to the Constitution extended the vote to eighteen-year-olds in 1971. Indeed, if a simple listing of legislative actions and programmatic decision about labor were made, the Nixon administration would compare (on paper) quite favorably with its predecessor, though in long-term consequences it will have to be regarded as having moved in the opposite direction.

Law and Order

While repressive violence was meted out to suppress many working-class actions during these rebellious years (Kent State U., Jackson State U., Lawrence State U., Attica), none was directed at employers who violated labor laws. Indeed, the Nixon administration accelerated a sharp reversal in enforcement of "wrongful discharge" violations of the National Labor Relations Law. Employers who illegally fired workers for union organizing enjoyed a nearly free hand as multiyear hearing delays and minimal back pay restitution awards allowed businesses to stop drives for collective bargaining rights. During the 1950s the NLRB heard and ruled with reasonable fairness and speed on hundreds of these cases a year. In President Nixon's first year there were 6,000 cases. The percentage of union victories declined, outcomes took much longer, and minimal penalties (back pay and reinstatement) were absorbed by large corporations as part of the cost of breaking a union organizing campaign. The numbers only continued to increase. By 1990 there were more than 20,000 cases a year of workers who suffered reprisals for union activities. In 1998 there were 23,580 such cases.

For a president who exploited and manipulated popular fears about crime and disorder to his political advantage, Nixon's boldest move when it came to labor was his action on behalf of Jimmy Hoffa in 1971. Nixon told a reporter, William Loeb, of the *Manchester Union Leader* in 1968 that he would release Hoffa from prison in exchange for a Teamster political endorsement. Though three parole boards were unanimous in turning Hoffa's appeals down, Nixon commuted his sentence in 1971 on the condition that he not return to union office. The president spoke at the Teamsters' convention that year and enjoyed their endorsement when he ran for reelection in 1972. The union, in spite of its consistency in endorsing successful Republican presidential candidates (1980, 1984, 1988), was finally placed under a federal trusteeship in 1989, but criminal charges continued to haunt the organization and its leadership long into the future.

Nixon himself was finally forced to resign from office rather than face impeachment charges for "high crimes and misdemeanors." No administration until his sent so many of its highest officials, including its attorney general, John Mitchell, to prison.

Affirmative Action, Black Colleges, Black Business

Richard Nixon will be remembered for many things. For labor and civil rights his legacy is affirmative action. His first secretary of labor, George P. Schultz, convinced Nixon of the virtues of the "Philadelphia Plan," a proposal for increasing the number of minority jobs based on the percentage of minority people in a city's population. The idea of affirmative action, and this particular plan, had been around, but dormant, for about two years. Racial quotas on city construction crews involved in federally funded projects were appealing to Nixon. He would have something to offer urban black protesters and the NAACP. The plan would enlarge the pool of skilled workers and possibly drive their cost down, and it could weaken the tough big city craft unions by cracking open their closed apprentice training programs. Nixon's advisors also noted that it would "drive a dandy wedge between organized labor and the civil rights organizations" (Friedman and Levantrosser, 1991, p. 167).

Neither Congress nor the courts supported the Philadelphia Plan, but it was the foundation for affirmative action policies that successfully followed it, and was the only civil rights legacy of the Nixon administration. In 1971 the plan was enlarged to include women workers. A few years later the charge of sexual harassment would be found to be an actionable workplace form of discrimination as well. The Rehabilitation Act of 1973 required affirmative action by federal contractors and subcontractors.

Highly contentious legal battles among workers over restricted college admission policies for their children and over job rights soon followed. In *Regents of the University of California v. Bakke* (1978) the Court opposed affirmative action in a medical school admission case. In the case of *Weber* (1979) it upheld affirmative action in job assignments. In 2003 the court partially reversed *Bakke* in upholding affirmative action at the University of Michigan. The three cases are among the permanent remnants of this wedge driving technique. Oddly enough, most of the angry white (male) workers who continued to express their resentment over perceived affirmative action losses to themselves supported Republicans, the political party that brought it into actual practice. Democrats and liberals who defended affirmative action were blamed for it, even though Schultz and Nixon, along with Republican Supreme Court appointees, are most responsible for it. Helping a few select individuals to get ahead has never been a problem for conservative or liberal business interests when labor is concerned. Indeed, it is a welcome and regular practice that invariably assures the loyalty and faithful service of the recipient.

Nixon-era philanthropy reflected the same approach, as contributions to historically black colleges doubled during these years. Generous federal support for black business ventures, called "black capitalism," was another Nixon-era initiative consistent with generally big multibillion-dollar increases in government subsidies, grants, and tariff protection to business. Highly visible token appointments to office are another way of artfully crafting a nondiscriminatory appearance, but were more characteristic of the Reagan–Bush–Bush, not Nixon, years. By every measurable material or political standard, for the vast majority of workers in the United States, black and white, men and women, union and nonunion, white collar and blue collar, the Nixon presidency offered nothing affirmative. The few beneficiaries of jobs, appointments, or school openings were more than offset by the massive and regressive declines experienced by millions of others that were a direct result of the policies launched in these years. But Nixon's term was interrupted, so the burgeoning conservative program was continued under his hand-picked successor, Gerald Ford.

Not Much Future for Labor in Ford

The new president was somewhat unfairly depicted in the media as clumsy. Stumbling down an airplane stairway or stunning a companion with a golf club compounded the public's perception of a leader who was not in complete control. With far less publicity, business groups were more gracefully building new structural forms and organizational bodies to move their foreign and domestic program along. The Business Roundtable got started in 1972 as an expansion of the Construction Users Anti-Inflation Roundtable (CUAIR) that formed a few years earlier to break the power of the big city construction unions. The Business Roundtable was a bigger legislative lobbying organization formed by the largest corporations in the country. To help their candidates win office, corporate-sponsored political action committees increased from under a hundred in 1974 to over 800 by 1978. Financial support for their favored candidates increased proportionately. The nation would soon have the best government money could buy. President Ford himself would feel their more direct intervention in labor policy.

"An Excess of Democracy"

Samuel P. Huntington, a Harvard University social scientist, was given the task by the newly formed Tri-Lateral Commission to study the problem of the instability of the social order in the United States. His findings were part of a larger report published in 1975 entitled *The Crisis of Democracy: Report on the Governability of Democracies to the Tri-Lateral Commission*. The problem, Huntington found, was democracy itself; there was too much of it, "an excess of democracy," which called for "a greater degree of moderation in democracy" (p. 113). People were too involved in public life as individuals and as groups, Huntington explained. The result of increased democratic involvement was that the public wanted more from government, while at the same time were less willing to accept the absolute authority of government. The public would have to be taught to expect less from government, while at the same time accepting its absolute power uncritically (pp. 59–64). How to get there was not spelled out, but the concept was in harmony with the "Conservative Manifesto" of 1937. Democratic reforms favored by all or part of labor that were currently on the table for action were about to receive unexpected setbacks. The corporate state was marching to the right. Those who controlled the wealth that counted most politically wanted to unshackle themselves from the restraints imposed on them by democracy. In the three areas of labor law reform, women's rights, and capital punishment, anticipated progress was met with defeat, no action, or reversal.

Reform of Taft-Hartley

President Ford named as his secretary of labor a Harvard economist, John Dunlop. Both men were committed to finding a remedy for an old problem that labor leaders, especially the conservative and Republican inclined construction trade unionists, wanted fixed. It had to do with picketing on a construction site. In 1951 the Supreme Court, in *Denver Building Trades v. U.S.* ruled that "common situs picketing" was an illegal secondary boycott. Unions could only picket the specific contractor in a dispute, not the entire work site. The ruling, everybody knew, made a picket line on a major construction project nearly worthless, hidden away in some obscure corner. Presidents Truman, Eisenhower, Kennedy, and Johnson all publicly favored amending the Taft-Hartley Law to reverse the Court decision, but no such legislation ever made it through Congress for their signatures. Dunlop told Ford he had a solution that would satisfy all the parties. Dunlop's compromise was a bill that allowed common situs picketing as long as management received a ten-day advance notification, and the picketing was restricted to no more than thirty days. Construction unions would also agree to a legal ban on wildcat strikes. Ford promised to sign such a bill, but didn't reckon with the change in the wind that was sweeping through corporate headquarters.

The contractors' organization, the Associated General Contractors of America, had originally given a green light to changing the law, but, as the bill proceeded successfully through Congress in 1975, reversed itself and began a massive and expensive lobbying campaign against it. Newspapers all over the country, including the *Wall Street Journal*, railed against it on their editorial pages. Dick Cheney, the president's chief of staff, said that no other matter in the Ford administration, including the controversial blanket pardon of Nixon, provoked more mail than this one. Of course, the more than 700,000 letters and telegrams opposing the measure were carefully organized by the talented ultraconservative media manipulator, Richard Viguerie. Cheney also let Ford know that his renomination to the presidency was at stake if he signed the bill. Ford bowed to the political pressure from conservatives and vetoed it. Dunlop resigned a week later. Unionized construction labor fell by half during the rest of the century. In the sunbelt it all but disappeared. This was the last serious attempt at federal labor law reform that had a chance to pass.

ERA

The Equal Rights Amendment (ERA) to ban any kind of discrimination based on gender also had the support of most national leaders. Few spoke openly against it. President Ford's wife, Betty, joined Nixon's wife, Pat, as an advocate of ERA. The CIO favored the idea at its 1946 convention in Atlantic City, and the merged AFL-CIO finally got around to endorsing it in 1973, a year after it had sailed through Congress with overwhelming votes in both Houses. Women were at the time earning approximately $.60 for every $1.00 earned by men in similar work. NOW, the AFL-CIO, and almost every prominent national union leader joined in a vigorous campaign to get the necessary three-quarters of the states to ratify the amendment. The campaign looked hopeful for a few years. Even Governor Ronald Reagan of California said he favored its passage.

The tide, however, was changing. The national discussion about gender rights became diverted in the media and in political debate to the continuing controversy about abortion issues and gay rights. The Equal Rights Amendment fell a few states short, and was not ratified. For the future of gender rights, the resolution of specific issues would have to be found in court, or in highly specific legislative actions. When the Supreme Court made it nearly impossible for pregnant women to protect themselves from employer discrimination in a 1976 ruling, the Pregnancy and Disability Act of 1978 restored that right.

Concession Bargaining

The serious economic problems of no growth, spiking energy prices, and high rates of inflation of the Ford years were summarized by the press in the term *stagflation*. Unemployment rates were rising fast, but so were prices, in defiance of popular economic mythology that blamed high rates of inflation on high employment rates, for example. Foreign-made goods, especially automobiles and electronic products, challenged or replaced domestic manufactures in the marketplace. Both the president and the workforce were set back by these developments. Ford was not reelected in 1976.

Corporations bailed themselves out by restructuring, sometimes called "retrenchment," to weaken or break unions through layoffs, plant closings, or bankruptcy proceedings. They also increased their foreign investments, and undertook a long-range plan to shift the tax burden more heavily to workers. Corporate threats in economic hard times forced concessions or give-backs from labor. Before the end of the decade corporations would also increase the grants, loans, tax exemptions, and cred-its, and win other direct subsidies in research and capital costs from federal and state governments.

The federal minimum wage, the earnings of millions of entry-level workers, would no longer be corrected or adjusted to approximate the consumer-price index. The unwritten corporate program for the rest of the century was the destruction or un-dermining of the remaining parts of the Fair Labor Standards Act of 1938. Minimum wage stagnation, begun in the Nixon–Ford years, was the first consequence.

The advantage of union pay contrasted with nonunion pay for the same or similar work widened from 20 to 30 percent by the end of the decade, which served as another corporate incentive for blocking organizing drives or breaking existing unions. The cost to corporations of violating NLRB codes fell accordingly. Where union organizing drives were once typically successful in two-thirds or more of NLRB certification elec-tions, they fell off to less than half by the middle of the 1970s and have not recovered since.

Union busting, or firms that specialized in providing "counter-organizing" consul-tants to business, became a minor growth industry that would become a multibillion-dollar business over the next fifteen years. One union busting company, Modern Man-agement Methods (3M's), provided consultants in 500 organizing drives in 1978–79 alone. A long dark night for labor and democracy was underway, though not yet fully appreciated by the defenders of either.

Actually, it was Walter Reuther who made the first significant national concession bargaining agreement with General Motors Corporation, when he agreed to accept a cap, or limit, on the cost of living adjustment (COLA), in a contract in 1967. But that was nearly insignificant compared to what followed. Faced with the threat of plant closings and massive layoffs beginning in 1974, unions were forced to accept losses in every aspect of collective bargaining. The number of strikes remained relatively high throughout the decade, but the outcomes were more often stalemates or continued the pattern of trade-offs and concessions. Divisions, or tiers, were negotiated for workers that set lower pay scales for new hires. Promotion practices were slowed or conceded, salary steps to the top took longer to reach, overtime became mandatory, and rates were reduced. Freezes or actual cuts in pay became the trade-off for keeping a job. No major union was spared by the new corporate offensive, and no concession was good enough to stop the pressure for even more give-backs.

Plants closed anyway. Men and women were laid off anyway. Unemployment grew to a new postwar high of 8 percent in 1975, reaching 11 percent by the end of 1981. For black workers the devastation of manufacturing layoffs was far worse because of job discrimination and poor schools that limited job options. Unemployment in the black community was twice that of whites, and four times that of whites for young black workers. No work meant no money. Shops closed, mortgages were foreclosed at rates unseen since the Depression. Entire neighborhoods became half abandoned wrecks. Apartment buildings were burned by landlords for insurance settlements, or because of negligence. The loss of union jobs and benefits was especially hard on workers in the urban Northeast and the big manufacturing centers of the Midwest. A "rust belt" of closed and forgotten factories in once highly unionized states spread in grim contrast to the still growing, mostly nonunion, sunbelt. Crime, drug abuse, homelessness, divorce, and family abandonment rates all soared among unemployed workers. Philadelphia, for example, lost 40 percent of its factory jobs and experienced a 200 percent increase in its crime rate from 1970 to 1980. Voters were frustrated by fuel shortages and high prices nationwide, and angry at unfairly shared losses when they rejected President Ford and cast their ballots for his moderate Democratic Party rival, Jimmy Carter, an ex-naval officer and former governor of Georgia. Despite his personal decency, Carter presided over the continued expansion of the corporate state at the expense of workers everywhere.

The Corporate Vision and Labor Identity

Identity is a complex formulation of objective and subjective influences. Paternalistic employers once tried to win the loyalty of their workers by merging the identity of workers with the company as in a family. Slaveowners did the same with house servants. Stock options as well as wages and pensions linked to company profits seek to accomplish that end in the corporate age: what's good for the company is aligned with the worker, though it doesn't always work out that way. Pension funds that are linked to stock valuations, for example, can wither away in a falling market. Workers sometimes call these plans "golden handcuffs."

Unions once built common loyalties among their members based on the shared realities of power relationships, wealth, and politics. Unions served as a connecting bridge for millions of immigrants between their ethnic and national origins and their integration into full citizenship. In the United States there were always a multiplicity of contending ethnic, religious, regional, and—above all—racial influences that continued to shape people's thoughts of who they were and what it all meant. Class, though quite a real concept to people when polled, seemed to have the least influence on their political behavior. Patriotism increased its prominence as part of identity in times of war or perceived common national danger.

Beginning in the 1920s, and accelerating in the aftermath of the Vietnam War, a host of additional identities and loyalties, all linked to corporate ideals, were put before workers in the press, on radio, and on TV. People were encouraged to develop emotional attachments to products, brand names, celebrities, sports heroes, and teams. Workers were no longer portrayed as producers; they were called "consumers." During economic recessions and times of growing unemployment the public was advised by public figures, including presidents, that it was their civic duty to go shopping. It was the corporation, the ads said, not the intelligence and labor of its employees, that made the things that people wanted. GE, not its workers, brought "good things to life." Dupont advertised that it was its corporate chemistry, not chemists, who improved the lives of its customers in the slogan: "Better living through chemistry." The human environment, on the other hand, that was dangerously polluted by corporate managerial negligence or indifference, was turned over to the public as a problem to be cleaned up at public, not corporate, expense. Multibillion-dollar corporations, with wealth and institutional power greater than most of the nations in the world, enjoyed the same constitutional rights as individuals under the Fourteenth Amendment.

Jobs themselves were portrayed as desirable scarce objects, not as the creative source of all profit and new wealth. Corporations, according to the popular myth, deserved the gratitude of the nation for giving people jobs. Saving jobs, no matter the sacrifice, became the goal of cities, states, and the nation, as well as the workers' union. If workers were fortunate, expressed the proper corporate attitudes, and made concessions when the company needed them, they might be rewarded by being able to keep their jobs and serve their country as good consumers. People purchased clothing that prominently displayed the corporate logo; the discreetly hidden union label was fast giving way to a flood of imports during the 1970s, despite the bright singing commercials of textile worker unionists to "look for the union label."

Harvard sociologist Daniel Bell wrote of a "postindustrial society" in 1973, where fewer and fewer workers could make the things the rest of the society needed. There was real evidence that more domestic labor had less and less to do with making useful things. Technology and a global labor force relieved workers in the United States of many of their traditional jobs, as it had done for centuries. As ever, these changes were largely outside of the control of workers, and contributed to fear and insecurity. Technology and international competition also continued to create new work at the same time, though at different compensation rates and under different circumstances.

There was plenty of dissent expressed by workers because job instability and loss of income meant there was plenty of harm. Those complaints were deflected or redirected away from centers of power, and surfaced in terms of personal or existential dilemmas. The actions of corporations were portrayed as neutral, a part of nature, and free of responsibility. President Carter's response to an outburst of frustration and anger from a poor black woman at a public meeting was to sadly lament that " life is not fair." Government, was, in this view, no longer a place to seek social or economic equity. Carter's own personal solution was prayer, something he confessed to doing repeatedly throughout the day.

Corporate Ideas

A rising, more aggressively antilabor and conservative, corporate community was not so passive. A host of straw men were created in corporate and mass media outlets to explain what was wrong. At business meetings, from foundation-funded "think tanks," and in news bulletins and journals, the seemingly new ideology poured forth. The federal government itself was blamed, but not for what it had done to labor in its executive, judicial, and legislative actions. It was too big. State governments should regain their former role. Welfare destroyed initiative (though most of it went to help support children). Supposedly, liberalism broke down discipline by inflating a sense of entitlement and deflating responsiveness to authority. Workers in the United States were said to be careless and unproductive in comparison to foreign rivals. This cant was called into question when Japanese companies built factories and made their high-quality products with domestic labor in the United States. Corporate explanations for economic hardship, crime, and urban decay drew on racial myths and resonated sympathetically in the suburbs and throughout the sunbelt.

The corporate ideology was augmented as well by a rising religious fundamentalism that blended religion with politics. Not satisfied with their own membership's obligation to follow their doctrines, the religious right sought to bring their practices to the entire community. The sunbelt brought forth most of the new crusaders. The Rev. Jerry Fallwell's "Moral Majority" joined other extremist groups that mastered the use of direct mail, televangelism, and talk radio to advance their broadly conservative and antilabor program. Billions of dollars went into more than 500 radio and television stations around the country that soon reached a regular audience of about a hundred million people. Social ills in the country were blamed on a lapse of faith, not the loss of good jobs or cutbacks in education and public services. The legal termination of pregnancy, gender equality and gay rights, the banning of school prayer, and the teachings of Charles Darwin were among the targets of the wrath of the revivalist ideologues. The religious right had nothing to say about sweatshops, child labor, plant closings, or the subsequent revelations of widespread ethical misconduct and criminal wrongdoing at the highest levels of the Reagan government. The power of the religious right diminished slightly in the 1990s, when many of their own leaders faced criminal and ethical misconduct charges.

Little dissent from corporate orthodoxy came from national labor leaders as the presidency of the AFL-CIO quietly passed from George Meany to Lane Kirkland in 1979. Kirkland completely identified with corporate goals, had trained for a career on their behalf in the foreign service, and, like William Green, offered no leadership whatsoever to labor. The Democratic Party, though the beneficiary of strong AFL-CIO endorsement and financial help from 1976 to 1981, along with President Carter, continued to advance the same agenda originally launched in the Nixon years.

Labor Losses Continue

The Carter administration should be remembered by labor for both its failures and its accomplishments. Democrats in Washington failed to stem the loss of good jobs, union jobs. Carter and the Democratic majorities in Congress had no effect on the decline in manufacturing job losses and plant closings. Capital in the United States had great mobility, which it used to invest in enterprises everywhere, especially in places that provided financial and tax incentives, government subsidized "enterprise zones," docile and inexpensive labor. Latin America and the Caribbean were favored investment areas, especially when nuisance governments could be overthrown by U.S. trained military forces that worked, openly and secretly, with the CIA and the AFL-CIO. At least seven million manufacturing jobs, mostly union, were lost in the United States in the 1977–81 period, and concession bargaining only increased within the nation. (For a nearly firsthand picture of what it was like, see the documentary film, *Controlling Interests*, made in 1978.)

Congress also failed to overturn a filibuster that blocked a proposed reform of national labor law to increase business penalties for unfair labor practices. Legislation to connect minimum wage to the cost of living failed as well, and, despite small adjustments, continued a long decline against inflation. Public services, block grants, and aid to cities suffered further budget cuts. But, if Democrats were hamstrung in dealing with labor, manufacturing losses, and decaying northern and midwestern cities, they had no comparable difficulties with their corporate program.

Corporate tax relief was increased, and the capital gains and maximum income tax rates were reduced, neither of which did very much for people who worked for someone else. By raising interest rates, the cost of checking inflation was passed onto the shoulders of every mortgage holder, debtor, and shopper. Creditors couldn't have been happier. Corporate executives also began to widen the gap between their earnings and everyone else who worked at the company. They deserved it, they told their board members and shareholders. Profits were increasing, labor costs were going down, stock prices were beginning to rise.

In another corporate bonanza, President Carter and his Democratic Party majorities carried out broad-scale deregulation of business practices in 1978, with hardly a murmur of opposition from labor leaders. The changes had special impact on the trucking, airline, and communications industries. Mergers, takeovers, and bankruptcies increased as national codes and standards were eased or eliminated. Union contracts were thrown into confusion or the courts, or tossed out altogether. Thousands of trucking companies turned their drivers into subcontractors working with leased equipment. The Teamsters lost nearly a million members in the decade that followed the deregulation measures of 1978. Services to the public were affected as well. Airport security, for example, fell into the hands of private airline company subcontractors who could employ nonunion labor at, or near, minimum wage. Deregulation of the telecommunications industry had the same profitable, but disastrous consequence for unionized workers and the public.

Lack of enforcement of existing labor laws continued during the Carter years. Sweatshops proliferated, especially on both coasts of the country in the garment industry. Shops in lofts or cellars were quickly set up and taken down. The federal government agreed with the ILGWU that at least 500 sweatshops were functioning in New York in 1979. At the same time in California, the state Division of Labor Enforcement reported that the entire garment industry, of about 100,000 workers, was involved in one or another form of labor law violation. These shops, which employed large numbers of undocumented women immigrants, did not pay minimum wage or overtime rates, employed child labor, disregarded sanitary and safety regulations, and typically imposed 60- to 70-hour work weeks, or paid workers by the piece, all in violation of provisions of the Fair Labor Standards Act of 1938.

One result of the expansion of sweatshop practices was to force all of the textile worker unions to put aside their "no aliens" organizing policy. The United Farm-workers (UFW), the Service Employees International Union (SEIU), and other unions soon followed. Government action to counter the rise in unionizing efforts among immigrant workers followed a few years later. In 2002, the Supreme Court ruled in *NLRB v. Hoffman Plastics Compound, Inc.* that companies that illegally fired improperly documented immigrants for union activities would not be required to restore their lost pay.

Just one step away from recent immigrant workers in terms of the lack of job rights were workers without full-time jobs. Part-time workers, adjuncts, contract employees, and consultants became a fast-growing segment of labor, and one that was most union resistant, over the next decade and more. Part-timers have no protection under the NLRB, sign or work under short-term contracts or verbal agreements, and cannot easily assemble or associate with one another. When they do attempt to unionize, they are easily dismissed and replaced. Altogether, this group began to increase rapidly during the economic slowdowns of the 1970s and expanded to more than 25 percent of the workforce by 1988.

The corporate state showed its cultural power in the public bailout of the Chrysler Corporation in 1979. While money for public facilities and services was drying up, a billion dollars in public revenue was turned over to the automaker as a loan for plant modernization and improvement. Leaders of both political parties backed the deal. So did big labor. Foreign competition threatened one of the nation's big three car manufacturers. Jobs were at stake. The UAW president, Doug Fraser, was given a seat on the company's board of directors in exchange for his support of the deal, a deal that also included wage cuts and no pay increases at Chrysler for two years. The company downsized anyway. Nearly 50,000 jobs were cut. Smaller companies that supplied parts to Chrysler followed the pattern and broke union contracts, or ended collective bargaining altogether. The loan was repaid, eventually. Patriotic symbols filled the ads for Chrysler products. The stockholders were protected. The company was sold to the German automaker, Daimler-Benz, a generation later. Toyota replaced it as third largest auto company in sales in the United States in 2003.

Despite continuing high rates of unemployment, plenty of new jobs were being created. The number of service, professional, and technical jobs was growing rapidly. The most highly educated workforce in history was being assembled. White-collar and professional work was increasing almost as fast as manufacturing jobs were be-ing lost. Office and clerical workers represented almost one-sixth of the labor force by the end of the Carter years. College and university employment, computer-related work, government employment at every level, and the communications and enter-tainment industries all mushroomed during these years, but only a small part of it, mostly among public employees, joined unions. The new jobs had new names. People called what they did a "career." They were employees or professionals, not workers. Skilled employees were called technicians or technologists, no longer craft workers.

No matter what it was called, the new work had much in common with the work of the past. There was a great deal of autonomy on the job, but autonomy had been part of the old work too: coal miners and many craft and semiskilled workers had a great deal of autonomy on the job. Many of the new workers wanted to join unions too, in spite of a very weak, or nonexistent organizing effort by the AFL-CIO. Retail clerks, public employees, and engineers were among those who had established unions in the past and continued to build them.

Professional workers of all kinds ran into trouble, however, at the Supreme Court in December 1980. In the *Yeshiva* decision, the Court majority found that college professors in private colleges and universities who participated in making judgments on such matters as the promotion and tenure of other professors were really managers themselves, and were not protected by the National Labor Relations Law. Professors could be, and were, fired for union activity, and a nationwide campus unionizing drive came to an abrupt halt. Some colleges or universities that had collective bargaining for faculty, like Boston University, lost it. Strikes were broken and union officers were fired. The court decision had a chilling effect among all of those professional and technical workers whose skills and services were evaluated by co-workers or by external licensing or accrediting bodies, not the employer.

Small Victories

Labor leaders were pleased by Carter's appointment of Ray Marshall as secretary of labor. Marshall, like Dunlop, was a college professor who openly favored unions, but turned out to be more of a sympathetic spokesman on behalf of labor than anything else. He was articulate, even eloquent at times. He highlighted the advantages to business in efficiency, morale, and accountability that were a characteristic of effective collective bargaining. Marshall defended the Davis-Bacon Act of 1932 that required contractors working on federal projects to pay "prevailing rates" for labor. Those rates were almost always union rates, and the Business Roundtable lobby was seeking to break those down. Concession bargaining, affirmative action, and the creation of nonunion construction company subsidiaries did finally crush the power of the old trade unions in all but a few cities, but Davis-Bacon was maintained. Marshall was an outstanding speaker at union meetings and conventions, but brought little of substance to labor.

A second Carter appointment of considerable value for her ideas was Eleanor Holmes Norton. Norton was appointed to head the Equal Employment Opportunity Commission (EEOC). To deal with the chronic gap in pay between men and women,

Norton called for a major evaluation of job skills. Feminists were pointing out that women's work was obviously undervalued, in defiance of economic logic, Marxist analysis, or any economic theories. Truck drivers, almost exclusively male, and with far less training, earned far more pay than registered nurses or skilled office technologists, both mainly female. Under Norton's leadership a new strategy of "comparable worth" was taken up to close the gender gap. Public employee unions took the lead in winning wage gains and back pay settlements in campaigns for "comparable worth." Her successor, Clarence Thomas, who was named to head the EEOC by President Reagan, dropped the concept. It awaits revival. Real victories, however small in this mean era, continued to be won as well by workers themselves.

National publicity that highlighted the mistreatment and low wages of textile workers in North and South Carolina helped them to win collective bargaining victories at the mills of J. P. Stevens. The victories stand out, not because of their great size or implications for the rest of labor, but because they were so rare at the time, almost unique.

College service workers fought for and won collective bargaining rights at Yale University and elsewhere. So did graduate students after several legal battles to establish that they were really workers, not trainees or interns. Service people of all kinds, from blackjack dealers and healthcare professionals, to janitors, hotel, and restaurant workers, became the fastest-growing segment of organized labor while manufacturing fell off sharply. In contrast to the stodgy indifference of so many leaders at the top of the AFL-CIO, women and immigrant workers were at the forefront of the successful union organizing drives of the Service Employees International Union (SEIU) and Hotel Employees and Restaurant Employees (HERE).

Adjunct faculty, the rapidly expanding segment of college instructional workers, also began to organize. Adjunct faculty quickly became approximately half the classroom faculty in the nation's colleges and universities, and were especially numerous in revenue-starved public institutions. Adjuncts were paid by the course they taught, or by the hour, at rates that were a small fraction of regular faculty salaries.

The job of professor, as had happened before to other crafts, was broken down into its parts. Adjunct faculty became the mainstay of classroom instruction in most colleges. Research professors did almost no teaching of undergraduates; they concentrated on research and trained graduate students and professionals. At small colleges and universities high tuition costs, adjunct faculty, and teaching assistants subsidized reduced teaching assignments to full-time faculty. The adjunct faculty at the bottom, without tenure protection, could be casually hired and fired. Adjuncts had no pension rights or other benefits. Like migratory or sweatshop workers, they had no permanent place, office, or meeting facilities at the workplace. In California they were known as "freeway flyers," because of their need to juggle several classes at more than one college to make ends meet. Their organizing difficulties were compounded by opposition that came from both administrators and regular full-time faculty. It was a scandalous situation without much voice and with few advocates.

Labor Did It Again: The Election of 1980

The corporate culture was so commanding that workers put their own interests aside when they helped to sweep Republican Ronald Reagan into the White House by more than eight million votes over Carter in 1980. Patriotism, racism, and disappointment with the way things were drove most voters to Reagan. Democrats continued to be blamed for every part of the legacy of the civil rights era, including affirmative action. Carter was accused of foreign policy setbacks in Iran and Nicaragua, but given no credit for successful peace initiatives in the Middle East.

The voter turnout wasn't very high. Carter inspired no particular loyalty from workers. Only about 60 percent of those eligible actually voted, down from 70 percent a generation earlier, on its way further down to only about 50 percent in the election of 2000. Samuel Huntington's recommendation to the Tri-Lateral Commission that "some measure of apathy and noninvolvement on the part of some individuals and groups," would help moderate the excesses in democracy, appears to have taken hold (1975, p. 114). Well over half the voters in the working class (union and nonunion) cast their ballots for the well-known conservative. Reagan, as governor of California, was solidly established as no friend of labor, yet he won over 40 percent of the vote in union households, apparently indifferent to the AFL-CIO endorsement of Carter. Union voter support increased to 46 percent in Reagan's reelection four years later. Only two national unions actually endorsed Reagan in 1980, the Professional Air Traffic Controllers Organization (PATCO) and the Teamsters (IBT). PATCO would be the first among labor to experience his gratitude.

The PATCO Strike and Reagan Evolution

The so-called Reagan Revolution, or Reaganomics, or the New Federalism of the new administration were all continuations of the corporate program launched somewhat ambiguously by President Nixon, and followed by every succeeding administration, regardless of party. The dramatic difference, and the possible reason for renaming the Washington, D.C. airport for him, was the way the new president dealt with the federal air traffic controllers when they went on strike. Fifteen thousand controllers struck in August 1981 because of the sped-up pace of work, the high level of dangerous stress in the work, and the deterioration of workplace facilities. President Reagan acted almost immediately. Those who did not report back to work within forty-eight hours would be fired, he proclaimed. More than two-thirds stayed out and most of those never returned to their jobs.

The government had made plans in advance. Military personnel and hastily trained scabs, now politely called "replacement workers," took over the work and kept planes moving on a reduced schedule. As in the Pullman strike nearly a century before, the government was determined to protect the dominant transportation industry from labor action that might infringe on its profits. If controllers could win their strike, others were sure to follow.

The new controllers were moved into the terminals as quickly as possible to keep traffic moving and break the strike. The AFL-CIO mobilized a huge protest march of nearly 500,000 in Washington, D.C., a few weeks into the conflict, and lobbied hard for a negotiated settlement, but took no stronger action such as a boycott or short-term general strike, as suggested by several member unions. Within a few more weeks PATCO was destroyed. When the strike was over, the "replacements" remained as permanent workers.

Crushing the controllers' strike was a signal to the industry and the nation. The assault on labor that followed is one of the reasons many of his fans would like to add Reagan's image to those already carved into Mt. Rushmore. That he did this, and actually increased his popularity and vote among unionists, and labor generally, is one of the reasons observers began to talk about the end of labor as a conscious force in the nation's life.

Concession bargaining continued with a vengeance, and, for the first time, without regard to business cycles or company profits. Companies that enjoyed long traditions of reasonable labor relations turned hostile to their unions. After winning a 10 percent pay cut from the United Steelworkers, US Steel closed twenty mills anyway. Companies accepted long strikes to win or preserve cuts, suspend work rules, and gain other give-backs from their unions. Well-known national corporations with long-established labor relations like Greyhound Bus, Continental Airlines, Trans World Airlines, Eastern Airlines, Phelps Dodge, American Telephone and Telegraph, and Caterpillar were among the most prominent. In most of these strikes corporate profits were strong and the business cycle was on the upswing.

One of the bitterest of these conflicts took place in Austin, Minnesota, in 1985–86, when members of United Food and Commercial Workers (UFCW), Local P-9, struck Hormel over wage cuts. The meatpakers in P-9 refused to accept the same wage concessions as other union locals, and ultimately lost the support of their national union as they watched strikebreakers cross their picket lines and take over their jobs. Some of those who crossed the lines were lifelong friends, fellow unionists, and family members. The documentary filmmaker, Barbara Kopple, captured the poignancy of this struggle and the atmosphere of the era in her film *American Dream*.

The decline in union density, a marked fall-off in the number of strikes to historic lows, and a decade-long decline in real wages are other reasons for Reagan's glowing popularity among business groups. That corporate taxes on profits were cut in half, and the Soviet Union began to disintegrate, only added to the president's luster.

Though the permanent hiring of "replacement workers" in the course of a strike was upheld as legal by the Supreme Court (*NLRB v. Mackay Radio and Telegraph Company*, 1938) previously, it had seldom been done. Few unions ever settled strikes without making sure that all workers could return to their jobs. Workplace disciplinary problems discouraged employers from keeping scabs and firing regular workers. This "Mackay Doctrine" was specifically cited when striking workers were replaced after a strike at International Paper in 1988–89. That this practice now became common meant a major power shift in collective bargaining. Unions have not recovered since then.

The International Labor Organization (ILO), which seeks to establish some basic worldwide labor standards, maintains the right of striking workers to return to their jobs when a strike is over. Unfortunately for workers, though a participating member of the ILO, the United States has never ratified that convention. The very concept of a strike as a legal right is uncertain if the employer is under no obligation to return those on strike to work. Reagan's dramatic firing and replacing of the controllers encouraged frequent repetition of the practice. If unions are ever to recover their former strength, the right to strike without the fear of job loss must be regained. The AFL-CIO gave priority status to its lobbying efforts to amend the labor law to protect the job rights of legally striking workers. That effort has yet to bear fruit.

Government Strikes Labor

In the dynamic tension that always existed between labor and capital, government found additional ways to strike hard against labor. Reagan's appointee as secretary of labor, Raymond J. Donovan, was unlike his predecessors. He was not from the AFL-CIO, nor was he a university professor. Donovan was a Teamster with close ties to the still unreconstructed organization and its shadowy friends. In office until 1985, Donovan began to overturn or reverse a host of labor policies by simple administrative decisions. The Department of Labor, under Donovan and his successors, removed or ignored minimum wage requirements from federal contractors, and reduced Occupational Health and Safety Standards wherever it could do so.

After a thirteen-year battle to improve sanitation conditions for farmworkers who suffered from parasitic illnesses, hepatitis, dysentery, and intestinal diseases "rarely found in developed countries," the assistant secretary of labor for the Occupational Safety and Health Administration, Robert A. Rowland, opposed the requirement to "provide toilets, fresh drinking water and cleanup facilities wherever more than ten workers are employed in the field." The rule would have covered only about a third, or 500,000, of all farmworkers (*New York Times*, April 11, 1985).

Donovan's office also relaxed child labor and home-work restrictions that restored sweatshop practices. One of his successors, Ann McLaughlin, proudly defended the 1988 lifting of a ban of home-work restrictions on making jewelry, buttons and buckles, embroideries, handkerchiefs, and gloves, that was set in the Fair Labor Standards Act of 1938. Piecework and sweatshops were legally brought back to life. Davis-Bacon (prevailing wage protection), though maintained, was subverted by simple internal code changes in the department. But Donovan and McLaughlin were not acting alone. They were part of a team.

In its New Deal infancy the National Labor Relations Board (NLRB) was criticized for its positive rulings on behalf of labor. Beginning with changes made by FDR, the leaders of both parties sought to maintain at least the impression of a balanced board. The NLRB was supposed to be neutral. For almost two years President Reagan let the cases before the board pile up by not filling vacancies on the NLRB. When he finally got around to it, Reagan's appointees represented the most extreme antilabor ideologues and organizations in the country. His first choice to head the NLRB was John Van de Water, a professional consultant to business on the art of union busting. The Senate refused to confirm Van de Water. The Business Roundtable, the National Right-to-Work Committee, and the conservative think tank, the Heritage Foundation, set the board agenda when they controlled the majority of the seats on the NLRB. The board cut sharply into the rights of unions, and made it harder to pass out leaflets and easier to fire workers. Delays by the board in reaching decisions favorable to labor could take five years. Illegal business actions to break union organizing drives resulted in small fines or reinstatement rulings long after the union defeat. Labor law was used so consistently in favor of business by the NLRB that UAW President Doug Fraser said labor would be better off it could return to the "laws of the jungle." Facing hard times together mended some fences as the UAW rejoined the AFL-CIO in 1981 after a thirteen-year separation.

Reaganomics was really little more than a continuation of deep cuts to business and capital gains taxes begun in the previous administration. The shift in the cost of public services to working and middle-income people through higher local taxes, user fees, and reductions of services had all been underway for a decade. Some of the authors of the new economic schemes admitted in interviews later that there really was nothing new in their "trickle down" economic ideas, that the theoretical spin was just a "Trojan Horse" or "Voodoo Economics" designed to disguise what they were doing (Stockman, 1986, pp. 5, 302, 377). But, neither the White House nor Congress was engaging in voodoo when it came to minimum wage law. The federal minimum wage was frozen at $3.35 an hour from 1981 to 1990, an inflationary time period when the consumer price index nearly doubled. In 1990 the rate was increased to just $3.80. Falling wages and salaries to all of labor were a direct consequence of the losses to those at the bottom imposed by those at the top of government.

Reagan-era deregulation policies and "new federalism" (reheated states' rights) were continuations as well, with their modern origins in the "Conservative Manifesto" of 1937 and the Nixon administration. So were cuts or neglect of public-sector needs to the advantage of private alternatives. More than $25 billion in social services to working-class people, the unemployed, and those with disabilities were cut by the Reagan administration budget in 1981. The only public-sector category to enjoy big increases was the military. Fiery cold war rhetoric about an "evil empire" that required a "star wars" missile defense system brought added billions, huge profits, and secure employment to those in the military-industrial complex. Revenue sharing came to an end as the massive tax cuts and big military expenditures resulted in huge federal budget deficits, and states were left with the burden of maintaining existing health and public services.

Public relief for the private sector, on the other hand, was never more abundant than in this administration, no matter the costs. When the savings and loan banks collapsed in 1987 as a result of deregulation and tax policies that led to wild and previously restricted speculative ventures, it was working taxpayers, not the corporate perpetrators, who took on the cost of half a trillion dollars in public debt to bail out the damaged industry.

The Supremes

The Supreme Court was part of the team effort as well. In 1981, Nixon's one successful extremist appointee, William Rhenquist, was named chief justice by President Reagan on the retirement of Warren Burger. Rhenquist helped lead the Court in major decisions against labor that coincided neatly with the concurrent decline in industry-wide and pattern bargaining, two practices that tended to spread union gains. The first, *NLRB v. First National Maintenance*, in 1981, weakened union job security by expanding the area of nonmandatory bargaining rights of corporations, particularly when it came to partial or full plant closings. The second case, *NLRB v. Bildisco & Bildisco*, in 1984, made it easier for an employer to void an existing union contract through a bankruptcy filing, even if it could be shown that the business wasn't actually failing. The ruling allowed a profitable company to file for bankruptcy, blow the contract and the union away, and then resume operations.

The Supreme Court also reaffirmed restrictive limits on labor action in a decision against longshoremen in 1982. The International Longshoremen's Association (ILA) carried out a 1980 boycott against Russian ships in protest against the intrusion of Russian troops in Afghanistan at the end of 1979. The court ruled the patriotic boycott illegal because it was a political action, not an action "based on legitimate labor issues such as wages or working conditions" (*New York Times*, September 25, 1986, A-19). The Supreme Court ruling upheld a lower court decision against the union that awarded Allied Plywood Corporation $8,055,490 for losses caused by the ILA boycott. The union appealed the amount. While unions in the United States are frequently criticized for their narrow attention to bread and butter issues when it comes to action, it is worth noting that it is the law that confines them, not any inherent timidity on their part.

Convict Labor Revived

Law enforcement agencies struck hard at labor as well. Crime and incarceration increased sharply as another response to high unemployment and a declining standard of living. In 1979 there were about 460,000 inmates in federal, state, and local jails in the United States, the highest incarceration rate by far of any industrial nation. In 1992 that number increased almost threefold to nearly 1,300,000 prisoners, and was still rising. The incarceration rate in the United States rose from 110 prisoners per 100,000 in the population in 1970 to 645 per 100,000 by 1997. The national budget for prisons rose to over $75 billion per year by 1992, an increase in real dollars from 1979 of 166 percent (Gordon, 1996, p. 139). Black and Hispanic workers, especially those without high school diplomas, suffered the highest rates of unemployment and incarceration. Their crimes were more likely to land them in prison and result in longer sentences than the crimes of businessmen or other employed workers or professionals. For black people, the incarceration rate in 1997 was 3,098 per 100,000. Corporate crime by those at the top rarely resulted in jail time.

A revived "prison-industrial complex" resulted as private employers were granted access to the labor of the swelling prison population at rates far below state or federal minimum wage requirements. In many situations prison workers received no compensation at all, or token payments of a few cents per hour. Companies in Oregon can lease convict labor for $3 a day; the Konica copier company pays prisoners to service its machines for less than $.50 an hour. In some cases convicts are leased to work outside the prison, where their supervision includes an armed guard paid for by taxpayers. There are no unions or rights to form them in jail, and no health insurance premiums, social security taxes, workers' compensation deductions, sick leaves, vacations, or overtime. The profit potential of convict labor stimulated a campaign by business interests at the state and local levels for the privatization of prisons that has continued ever since. New profits from the sale or leasing of prison labor, and from charging the state for incarceration of prisoners are appealing to some investors. By successfully connecting crime to race in his presidential campaign advertisements in 1988, George Bush continued the racial appeal to white voters that also began with Nixon twenty years earlier.

Labor's Response to the Corporate State

President Reagan won majorities in every state but one in his landslide reelection in 1984. His Democratic Party rival, Walter Mondale, only carried his home state of Minnesota. Workers in the United States put their needs and identification as workers aside when they increased their vote for an antilabor agenda. A significant number, indeed most, white-collar and professional workers actually thought of themselves as managers, or part of the middle class even when they had no corporate decision-making power, and very little, or no, supervisory authority over other workers. The suburban and sunbelt regions of the country where most of them lived were spared the economic devastation of the urban and rust belt northeastern and midwestern areas. Whiteness and patriotism were claimed by the Republicans with more veracity than Democrats, and millions of workers placed that emotional identity ahead of their own objective material and political well-being.

Many cities and a few states maintained a strong labor presence anyway. Labor participated in coalitions that elected mayors and governors in several states. Women and black candidates won more offices than ever, though their impact on labor issues was never great. In office, well-meaning political leaders invariably faced terrible choices in negotiating with public employee unions. Tax revenues declined or failed to keep up with expenses in most cities. Almost every older industrial city went through a version of the New York City fiscal crisis of the mid-1970s in the decade that followed. Continued cuts in state and federal support for legally mandated services placed a growing budget burden on the more regressive tax shoulders of smaller units of government. Sales taxes, real estate taxes, excise taxes, bridge and highway tolls, and user fees for parks and public services all increased as federal and some state revenue cuts were made. Sharp declines in health, education, housing, transportation, and job training services and programs went on without regard to the race or gender of the mayor. Public employees faced bipartisan layoffs or made concessions in collective bargaining agreements. Losses were all that trickled down to workers from the federal policies of the Reagan–Bush era. Hourly wages for more than three-quarters of the labor force continued falling from the late 1970s to the early 1990s.

Hard at Work

To maintain their standard of living as best they could, workers found alternatives to collective bargaining and political organizing. They worked harder, and they worked longer. They worked more jobs, and more of them went to work than ever before. The long historic trend toward shorter hours and a reduced workweek was reversed in the United States, most dramatically in contrast to workers in western Europe. By the end of the Reagan era, manufacturing workers in the United States were putting in over 300 more hours per year than their counterparts in Germany and France, up from about equal hours per year in 1950. Most of that extra work was in overtime, which reached an average of five extra weeks per year among manufacturing workers by 1988. Employers preferred the flexibility of overtime, and because they saved money on the taxes, training costs, and fringe benefits that hiring more full-timers required. During the same forty years, 1950–90, worker productivity increased in the United States by more than 100 percent. If that productivity increase went to workers, in order to maintain the same standard of living as 1950, workers in 1990 should have had to work only half as much, but instead they worked more, or had a second or third job.

More members of the same household worked in 1990 than in 1950. The extra burden of work for women was worse, since their household labor declined very little, if at all, when they took on a part-time or full-time job to supplement otherwise falling household income. Millions did that. Married women with children increased their participation in the paid labor force from about 25 percent in the 1960s to 66 percent by 1990 (Schor, 1991, p. 25). Teenagers as well as college students who worked part-time jobs also worked more hours at those jobs in 1990 than they did in 1970. Millions of young workers also entered the labor force during these years as unpaid interns who received either college credits for their services or an enhanced opportunity to gain pay at a future time. They could leave their job as an intern and go to another for pay after work.

Though more difficult to confirm statistically, more workers found extra jobs, as "off-the-books" workers than ever before. Salary losses from concession bargaining, the end of good paying manufacturing work, and the decline of minimum wages against inflation drove at least 6 percent of the workforce to hold two or more jobs by 1989. Since this work is usually unreported, no taxes paid, no social security deductions taken, and includes illegal activities, the actual number of workers involved are actually estimated to be at least twice the official estimates (Schor, 1991, p. 31). Women and black workers who lost manufacturing jobs and had to turn to domestic or service work were the fastest-growing segment, along with recent immigrants, in this category. Every worker's family has experienced the two-job, or off-the-books work situation, or knows someone who has done it. It is worth noting that in this era of deregulation and tax cutting for business, waiters and waitresses and similar service workers who depended on tips, had their tips more carefully scrutinized and calculated by their employers and the Internal Revenue Service.

Other Options

Workers also did what they have always done. They started small businesses, went to school to build new skills, and sent more of their children to college than ever to seek to improve or maintain their place in the social and economic order. Polls showed that in the 1980s, for the first time in the nation's history, instead of expecting a better future for their children, most workers hoped that their children would not fall below the level of achievement they had made. Workers, though they called themselves middle class, converted millions of suburban houses to accommodate illegal rentals in one-family zoned communities. To maintain their living standard, workers also increased their indebtedness as never before. Though interest rates were high, loans were readily available for mortgages, cars, college tuition and fees, vacations, and home improvements. The widespread introduction of credit cards made everyday purchases possible with payments spread out over time. The interest rates on ordinary credit cards were especially high for the millions of workers who came to rely on them. Wealthy people were not forced into debt to maintain their standard of living. Debt increased dependency and subordinated independent action by workers. Income lost by strikes or job losses could place entire households in jeopardy.

Hope for a better future for millions of workers came from the legalization of what was once called a racket: gambling on numbers, horses, and sporting events, and in casinos. Games of chance, dice and cards, or betting among workers themselves on sporting events were once crimes in every state, except Nevada. Those activities became legal only when they were turned into profitable businesses, or converted into new forms of regressive taxation by the states. An irony of the ultraconservative era is the expansion of the business of chance when other forms of hope for a better future began to fade away. New York State advertised its lottery game with the inducement, "A dollar and a dream." Conservative religious orthodoxy in almost every faith experienced a revival at the same time as legal gambling, lotteries, and casinos became available.

Gambling wasn't the only profitable industry of distraction and amusement available to workers to help them cope with, or put aside, the dreariness of everyday life. Television and film production, popular music, and sports came increasingly under direct corporate ownership and control. Only a few independent film studios and recording companies survived by serving small selective audiences. Ownership of professional athletic teams began to pass from the hands of wealthy individuals to corporate organizations. Boxing stayed raunchy for a few more decades.

Though cable television and other entertainment choices were abundant, the content of popular culture was more completely driven by the corporate influences of profit and advertising revenue than ever. Public television and radio budgets were slashed and their stations were forced to rely more on corporate and foundation subsidies, or direct appeals to their audiences for funding. The renegade cultural expressions and social idealism of the previous generation faded into self-mockery. Madonna sang out that she was "Living in a material world" in 1985.

Democratic Impulses

Aside from remnants in some union halls, and in the residue of the old and new left, an independent cultural expression that once helped labor to identify its own goals nearly disappeared. Unions continued to fall away from the front-line struggles for gender, ethnic, racial, and related human rights battles. Organized labor was more frequently identified as part of the resistance to the enlargement of minority rights, than as advocates.

The single bright note for the possibility of a labor revival came from the stirrings of a broad-based democratic movement inside the big industrial unions themselves. A "Steelworkers Fight Back" reform campaign challenged the old leadership of the United Steelworkers (USW) when it sought to elect Ed Sadlowski its president in 1977. Rich Trumpka overturned the AFL-CIO backed United Mineworkers of America incumbent, Sam Church, when he won election to the presidency in 1982. A "New Directions" caucus was active throughout the United Autoworkers, and the insurgent, Ron Carey won the presidency of the International Brotherhood of Teamsters (IBT) in 1991 with the help of the even more militant Teamsters for a Democratic Union. An increasing number of unions began to independently oppose the foreign policy of the Reagan–Bush years, especially in Central America and South Africa, even though the AFL-CIO continued its unwavering support. The combined force of these democratic insurgencies ultimately led to the overthrow of the Kirkland leadership of the AFL-CIO itself a few years later (see chapter 10).

New Paternalism

Employers knew that the defeat of democratic worker organizations did not end the tension or costly conflict they continued to experience with their employees. As we have seen, in many work areas unions are, and remain for employers, an accepted, even preferred system of creating order. When there is no independent or democratic union, employers seek to set up a workplace structure of loyalties and discipline to increase efficiency and reduce theft, vandalism, or slacking off. Contracts formally justify stratification, pay scales, and promotion policies that reward some workers more than others. When those practices are arbitrary, morale falls off, and turnover and related inefficiencies increase. George Pullman was hardly unique in creating a company town for his workers, with incentives under his control, in the nineteenth century. Company unions and professional (nonunion) "associations" proliferated in the twentieth. As trade unionism was driven from larger parts of the workplace in the aftermath of the war in Vietnam, a host of new corporate schemes were launched to achieve similar results.

Profit sharing, stock options, and bonuses built company loyalty, but were not enough to ensure discipline. Taylorism imposed by managers in search of economic efficiency always met with worker resistance. Corporate managers and their newly named "human resources" specialists learned to use surveys from the field of sociology. Internal surveys appeared to include workers in the study of plans to improve the workplace. Workplace committees, teams, employee involvement (EI) programs, quality of working life (QWL), or quality circles (Qcs) that seek to improve the product or the process of production were introduced with mixed results.

General Foods Corporation gave work teams the right to hire and fire, reassign work, and play a role in the pace of production. The UAW was enthusiastic about cooperation, and saw it as a way to democratize the workplace. The entire Saturn division of General Motors was planned from the start with the UAW along these lines, with pay itself tied to the success of the new car. The Communication Workers of America (CWA) together with AT&T established QWL programs in 1983 that have continued with partial or mixed results since then. U.S. Steel and the United Steelworkers experimented with plant-by-plant labor-management participation schemes during the 1980s, but could do nothing about job losses caused by shutdowns.

The AFL-CIO was ambivalent about these new approaches, especially when they appeared to create new company unions outside of collective bargaining. The NLRB, hardly a friend of labor, agreed with the AFL-CIO on this matter in hearings during 1992–93 in cases involving two companies with employee committees, Electromation and Dupont Chemical. The board concluded in 1994 that workplace committees that dealt with terms and conditions of employment were legal only if they were negotiated with a properly certified union. Otherwise, they amounted to management-dominated company unions, and were in violation of labor law. From then on, the AFL-CIO endorsed the concept of workplace committees. Business leaders weren't happy though; they objected to the restrictive ruling since more and more technical and professional labor required the participation of employees in decision making. Those workers, their employers claimed, should be exempted from the labor law since, like college professors, they engaged in managerial activity. As the nature of work was changing for all parties, the labor law, founded on the Wagner Act of 1935, did not.

Workers themselves initially welcomed the opportunity to participate in decision making, and when they did, the costs of supervision dropped significantly. Speed-ups and technological innovations that brought job losses or dislocations among workers, became more acceptable when they were incentive driven and democratically decided. By the early 1990s nearly half the large corporate workplaces in the United States applied some of these practices. These initiatives, like most contracts, were set up in a single workplace or with a single corporate entity. They could be withdrawn or restructured according to the dictates of the authority on which they rested. Unlike the Japanese model, on which some of them were loosely based, no corporation guaranteed lifetime job security. The European version carried an elaborate public social safety net of health, unemployment, and other benefits that was missing in the United States. A serious attempt to refashion the domestic workplace to take these approaches into account was undertaken by the administration of President Bill Clinton in 1993 (see chapter 10).

Conclusion

The story of labor in the United States is too often seen only in terms of union, its primary institutional form. Because of the weakness of unions some observers have begun to think of labor history as they did at the end of the 1920s, as finished as an independent force in national life. Thomas Geoghean, an astute labor lawyer, expressed his frustration over setbacks to unions at end of the Reagan–Bush era in the title of his book *Which Side Are You On?: Trying to Be for Labor When It's Flat on Its Back.* But, labor itself wasn't down as far, or as flat on its back, as Geoghean and others realized. He was reflecting on the terrible losses he and the unions he represented had suffered, the decline of traditional strong union density in areas like manufacturing, and the almost impossible task of organizing workers into new or existing unions. Some unions were still comfortably affluent, their leaders and members perhaps too well adjusted to the foreign and domestic corporate program. Big corporations seemed to have those unions just where they wanted them. Lane Kirkland rang no alarm bells from his post at the head of the AFL-CIO, though many commentators were beginning to write about the end of traditional unionism.

There was still plenty of energy on the front lines. Militancy could still be found among the rank and file despite the risks and the sharply reduced number of strikes. Big strikes could still be won, too, and concessions blocked. One example was at the Pittston Coal Company, where workers, whose strike, demonstrations, and use of civil disobedience spread over eleven states in 1989, were able to beat back most company demands for cuts. Professional baseball and football players struck, as did teachers, civil service employees, and airline employees in these hard years for union labor. Though the image of greed was often projected by corporate or media adversaries of labor, workers in the United States continued to be willing to employ radical tactics to win very modest objectives, or prevent losses.

Workers were also organized in thousands of grassroots organizations. Millions of them mobilized, not as workers, but on behalf of dozens of human rights, environmental, and civic issues. They battled for housing for those made homeless, protective shelters for battered women, independent police department review boards, local "living wage" standards, progressive tax reform, improvements to mass transit, and a host of related issues. A day did not pass without demonstrations, protests, or rallies somewhere in the country. Workers went into politics too, and within their communities elected thousands of their candidates to school boards, city, state, and other local offices, and a handful (only two or three) to Congress. A million people gathered in Central Park on June 12, 1982, to protest the cold war and the danger of nuclear weapons.

What workers lacked in all of these struggles was unity and power as workers, the two things they had in unions. A parade of thousands of women, gay rights activists, or peace activists may be an impressive sight, but its focus is broad and the consequences are always uncertain. Big Bill Haywood once observed that workers have more power "with their hands in their pockets," than the militia who would not have uniforms without the labor of those who make them. In India, Gandhi successfully sought to combine economic and political action, as Dr. Martin Luther King Jr. did in connecting his civil rights program to striking workers at the time of his death. Boycotts of products led to changes in hiring practices. None of the various protest or advocacy organizations, no matter how big, had the same economic or political power as workers organized as workers. Only those that could unify around a common political program, like labor, had a chance for real accomplishments. When labor was part of those actions, as it was in the battle for women's suffrage, A. Philip Randolph's role in civil rights, or in the antiwar movement of the Vietnam era, they became powerful forces for democratic change.

Not all labor disputes ended with concessions during this period of increasing corporate hegemony, though real wages and union density fell sharply, and the self-consciousness of labor dissipated almost entirely. The truly great loss to the country arising from the weakness of labor was the damage endured by the democracy itself. That danger was recognized in several places, not least of which included the business community and government.

George P. Shultz worried in public about the harm to the nation posed by the weakness of organized labor. Shultz was no labor advocate. He served Nixon as both secretary of labor and secretary of the treasury, and then was Reagan's secretary of state. Shultz was also head of the Office of Management and Budget, and in the private sector was president of the Bechtel Corporation, one of the largest construction companies in the world. Shultz was on the board of directors of General Motors, Boeing,

Chevron, the Morgan Bank, and Tandem Computers when he spoke at a meeting of the National Planning Association at the end of 1991.

Shultz told his business audience that his career taught him two things about the advantages of a strong labor movement: (1) a healthy workplace required a "system of checks and balances," and (2) "free societies and free trade unions go together." As much as any businessman, he acknowledged, "if I'm running my own shop and I don't have a union, I don't want them." The problem, he continued, was that, "as a society, we have a great stake in freedom, and a lot of that is anchored, somehow, historically," in the labor movement (*New York Times*, December, 13, 1991). His audience knew that corporate tyranny over workers was also a threat to business itself, if weakened purchasing power caused sales to fall and economic confidence to erode. The message was clear: democracy and prosperity were bound together by a strong labor movement. When Shultz first entered the Nixon government in 1969 more than one out of four workers was represented by a labor union. Now, as a consequence of Republican-led government policies in which Shultz played no small part for twenty years, it was down to only one out of eight, and he was worried about the future.

Labor in the United States continued to carry the responsibility of building the wealth of the nation and maintaining its prosperity. With real wages falling and union strength as weak as it had been prior to the New Deal, workers had to be mobilized to rescue what remained of the nation's democratic heritage from the grip of corporate autocracy. Were they up to the job? Were their unions? Could a new organizing momentum be built?

William B. Gould IV. This great-great-grandson of a slave served as
President Bill Clinton's chairman of the National Labor Relations Board.
(Courtesy of William B. Gould IV)

CHAPTER 10

Labor's Recent Past and the Future of Democracy

Corporations have been enthroned and an era of corruption in high places will follow, and the money power of the country will endeavor to prolong its reign by working upon the prejudices of the people until all the wealth is aggregated in a few hands and the republic is destroyed.
—Abraham Lincoln, 1864 (Shaw, 1950, p. 40)

Labor Does It Again

The serious economic problems of rising unemployment, an increasing national debt, continuing inflation, soaring costs for health services, and diminishing public confidence in the credibility of Republican President George H. W. Bush led to hopes for a democratic revival with a Democratic Party victory in 1992. The AFL-CIO was pleased to see that both Houses of Congress and the White House were in the control of the party they endorsed. It was time for labor, after a generation of losses, to make some gains again.

Rising Expectations Unfulfilled

The AFL-CIO turned out over 300,000 people for a demonstration in Washington, D.C., in 1991 to support universal national healthcare and to reform the national labor law. Democratic presidential candidate Bill Clinton, talking the talk of a born-again New Dealer, pledged his support and was elected.

Clinton's appointment policies followed Democratic Party practice. Clinton named Robert Reich, a former head of the Bureau of Labor Statistics, as secretary of labor. Reich quickly assembled a Commission on the Future of Labor-Management

Relations to study the labor law and recommend necessary revisions. The former labor secretary under President Ford, John Dunlop, was selected to head the commission, and UAW president Doug Fraser, still an outspoken proponent of "workplace democracy," was appointed to serve as a member.

The Dunlop Commission Report arrived twenty months later. It was a flop. Corporations lined up against its recommendation of European-style elected workers' councils, and also disliked the idea of government participation in workplace health and safety committees. Corporations said they wanted to keep the government "off their backs." Unions objected to what appeared to allow a new form of company-dominated union in the plan, despite the recommendation of easier "card check" certification procedures to replace costly and hard-fought elections. None of the recommendations had a chance anyway, since both Houses of Congress became dominated by Republicans after the election of 1994. Labor law, to most of the new congressmen and women, needed no improvement. In 1994, Clinton named Stanford University law professor William B. Gould IV to head the NLRB. Gould, one of the nation's foremost authorities on labor law, said he hoped to push the board back to the center of the political spectrum after more than a dozen years on the antilabor right.

Clinton pledged in his campaign to support an end to the use of "permanent replacement" workers, and, insofar as he was able, barred the practice among federal contractors. Legislation to amend the labor law to do so, however, died in a House committee in 1993. No presidential muscle could be found to help it through, even while Clinton's party was still the majority.

The North American Free Trade Agreement (NAFTA), on the other hand, sailed through Congress in 1993 and was signed by President Clinton despite vigorous AFL-CIO opposition and strong dissent from many congressional Democrats. The unions and their friends were caught off balance. After years of backing "free trade" competitive advantages to goods made in the United States and sold in foreign markets, union leaders had to quickly realign themselves to oppose the opening up of new trade and markets with Canada and Mexico. NAFTA encouraged capital flows to build factories and reap extra profits from the cheaper labor sources of Mexico. Hundreds of thousands of good manufacturing jobs were lost, though as many (or more) low or minimum wage service jobs were created in the United States by NAFTA. It was one thing for unions to support corporate trade policy when it meant more good work; when it began to export union jobs, organized labor had to say no. This break with foreign trade policy, along with the conclusion of the cold war, represented the beginning of the end of the old-guard AFL-CIO leadership of Lane Kirkland, and quickly exposed Clinton's commitment to labor to new criticism as well.

Healthcare Killed

National healthcare coverage provided through federally subsidized private insurance companies seemed like a way to please both business and labor. A federal program was also expected to provide some controls on wildly escalating healthcare costs. Universal healthcare was a top priority in the 1992 election campaign. The nation seemed ready for it. The president's wife, Hillary Rodham Clinton, who had a legal background in the insurance business, was put in charge of developing a plan built on the existing private health insurance plans, not a new single-payer (government) program like that used by Canada and other modern industrial nations.

The new healthcare plan was supposed to be realistic and practical for the United States, and the concept initially enjoyed support from business as well as labor. It too flopped. The United States Chamber of Commerce withdrew support before the plan was completed in a little less than a year. When the plan was finished it was 1,350 pages long, and required extensive explanation to baffled audiences around the country. It was far too complex for the evening news. The National Federation of Independent Businesses campaigned hard against it, and the big communications corporations withdrew their original support too, as they shifted position to favor more deregulation of their industry. Some large corporations, already making heavy health insurance payments in union contracts, saw the Clinton plan as a way of bringing down their costs. In any case, it couldn't get the votes to pass.

Afterward, some union cynics argued that the plan was set up to fail, and kill off the chance of national healthcare for at least another generation. Intentional or not, the United States remains the only modern nation that lacks a national healthcare program, and more people in the United State were without any healthcare insurance or public health services at the end of the Clinton administration than before it started.

A Single Point of Light

One accomplishment that was favored by labor can be credited to the Clinton administration: the Family and Medical Leave Act (FMLA) of 1993. With little cost to employers, workers were given the legal right to take an unpaid leave from work of up to twelve weeks in a calendar year for their own medical reasons, or to care for a child or other family member in need. Health benefits, if provided by the employer, continued without interruption; if paid by the employee, the right to continue payment and coverage was also protected. FMLA stands out because there was so little else to show for all of labor's support for Clinton and the Democrats. In 1997, after years of stagnation, the minimum hourly wage was increased, though not pegged to inflation rates.

New Losses

Repeal and deregulation of New Deal–era federal reforms continued, though it was the Republican Congress, not the president, that took the lead. In 1996 Clinton signed a Republican-crafted welfare reform law that, as he repeatedly boasted, would "end welfare as we know it." Aid to Families with Dependent Children was originally part of the concept of social security. More than 85 percent of the Depression-era federal assistance program went to support children in low- or no-income families. Critics said it discouraged work, divided families, and subsidized indolence. Republicans and their corporate allies succeeded in racializing welfare recipients, despite contrary statistical data. Social causation was taken out of the picture, so the public debate was clouded with prejudice.

On the other hand, defenders of the old law said it provided a social "safety net." Experts generally agreed on the need to reform the nearly sixty-year-old system, but favored educational and job training programs, and the provision of high-quality child care services as alternatives to caps, or absolute time limits, on the receipt of public assistance. Minimum wage, it was frequently noted, paid so little that a parent (nearly always a woman) forced into the labor market because of the termination of benefits, would earn barely enough to pay for her own child care. Public "workfare" programs that put welfare recipients to work paid less and led nowhere, prompting union critics to equate the practice with slavery. Food stamps, rent, Medicaid, and other subsidies remained available for what quickly became the fastest-growing segment of the labor force, the "working poor." Now, employers would have their below-poverty-level wages augmented by taxpayers, and the federal government would exercise a disciplinary control over millions of workers. Offend your boss and lose benefits, along with the job. Before the end of the decade, the United States Conference of Mayors complained that two-thirds of those seeking emergency assistance in their city food pantries were people with jobs. What a deal for business. The "reform" of welfare also meant that an additional 200,000 black urban children were living without any parent present, in small groups, in loosely formed gangs, or with other relatives by the end of the decade (*New York Times,* July, 29, 2002, p. A-14). Juvenile crime and incarceration rates also increased.

North Dakota pioneered a "living wage" amendment in 1992 that required businesses that received public support to pay their regular workers enough to keep a family of four above the state poverty line. At the time $6.71 per hour was considered a "living wage," in North Dakota, in contrast to the federal minimum wage of $4.25. Several cities, led by Baltimore, responded to the flood of demand on public services by the working poor by passing or proposing similar local living wage ordinances to relieve taxpayers of the burden of subsidizing the pay of minimum wage workers as welfare wound down.

Deregulation continued to impose secondary losses on labor. The Glass-Steagall Act of 1933 that prohibited banks from owning brokerage firms was ended in the Clinton years. Too much speculation fueled by profitable bank credit to their own brokerage customers, it was said, had led to the stock market crash of 1929. Bank failures destroyed the unprotected life savings of millions of workers and their families. In exchange for insuring much of the banking industry, Glass-Steagall aimed to curb speculation, but, after years of being trimmed back, was finally repealed in 1999. A year later the Commodity Futures Modernization Act likewise removed federal restrictions imposed during the New Deal. Clinton signed the last deregulation measure ten days before he left office, as he was also issuing several sensational pardons to, among others, extremely wealthy and generous criminals. The securities industry had finally gotten government off its back.

Deregulation, new federalism, states' rights, and the absence of labor law reform all continued uninterrupted during the Clinton presidency, or despite Democratic majorities in one, none, or both Houses of Congress. Violations of labor law and long delays in hearing cases continued as Congress repeatedly cut the budgets of the NLRB. Union organizing drives were blocked as much as in the prior administration, with a record 23,580 business violations recorded by the NLRB in 1998 alone. Payment of back-pay settlements and huge consultants' fees were still considered a bargain for business compared to allowing legal elections that might result in union victories. Union representation fell below 10 percent of the nonpublic workforce for the first time in more than seventy years.

Real wages fell during the first two years of the Clinton presidency, then leveled off for a few years, and finally began some recovery in the closing three years. The gap in earnings and wealth between rich and poor, black and white, grew dramatically. The wage advantage of men over women workers stayed about the same, though several formerly restricted occupations began to open for women.

Concession bargaining continued during the Clinton years with threats of plant closings and downsizing that forced new wage cuts, tier-wage systems, and mandatory overtime. Almost eight million people worked two jobs in 1996. In a newspaper poll that year in Stark County, Ohio, an industrial and highly unionized area, it was found that almost 30 percent of respondents lived in households where someone had added an extra job in the previous three years. Almost 20 percent lived in a household where someone had been put out of work by "downsizing" in the previous five years (*New York Times*, June 12, 1996, p. A-16). Incarceration rates continued to soar. Several states, including California, devoted more of their budget to maintaining and building new prisons than was spent for public higher education. Gender and human rights advances were stalled or suffered erosion from court decisions. Public education in large cities was deplorable. It was pretty clear. This government was not going to save labor or democracy. Labor would have to do the job by itself.

New Leadership of the AFL-CIO

Outsiders, including most workers, hardly noticed that the old guard at the top of organized labor was finished. The sharp decline in the membership and representation of the AFL-CIO, and its political insignificance, took its leaders out of public consciousness. After Hoffa's disappearance, no national figure emerged for a generation who could speak for any large body of labor, or provide any significant leadership. Aside from public employees, it was weakness, complacency, and decay that were the most prominent characteristics of the old-guard unions that dominated the AFL-CIO. They were ripe for the overthrow that finally came in 1995.

John Sweeney was no radical. He backed the Clinton healthcare plan, sought a cooperative relationship with employers, and comfortably accepted the near-feudal structure of his own union organization. Under slightly different circumstances he might have been chosen as the successor to Lane Kirkland. As president of the Service Employees International Union (SEIU) for fourteen years, Sweeney was a unique leader whose union had grown from 625,000 to 1.1 million members. Among the old-guard leaders, especially among the construction trades, losses, not gains, were commonplace. Sweeney picked up delegate votes from feminists, gay rights activists, and other union progressives because of his support for some of their issues voiced at prior AFL-CIO conventions. His election victory over Kirkland's hand-picked successor, Thomas Donahue, depended, however, on the votes he received from the democratically revived Steelworkers, Teamsters, United Mineworkers, and the traditionally more independent and progressive United Autoworkers. What made Sweeney's election seem radical was that it happened at all. Not since Samuel Gompers's one-term defeat in 1894 had a challenger defeated the incumbent leadership of the AFL-CIO.

Sweeney's election offered new hope and ignited new prospects for labor. He pledged a new organizing drive to reverse the slide in membership. He provided new openings to social reformers on his staff, and his "New Voices" slate brought a fresh perspective to labor issues. Linda Chavez-Thompson was elected secretary-treasurer with Sweeney. She was the first woman, and the first Mexican American, to hold so high a post in the AFL-CIO. Sweeney, in meetings and speeches, reached out to intellectuals, young people, and activists across a wide spectrum of issues. Campus teach-ins in 1996 sought to reunite labor with the formerly alienated academic left. Money poured into new organizing drives, and into reenergized political campaigns. Sweeney's SEIU built stronger ties to community and independent labor activists like ACORN, the office workers' organization, 9 to 5, and supported social activist inspired labor organizing groups such as Justice for Janitors and Jobs with Justice. Sweeney linked a nationwide antisweatshop campaign with environmental and human rights issues. To expose the mainly corporate gains of NAFTA, Sweeney extended a tentative friendly hand to independent (non-cold-war and State Department affiliated) union organizations in Mexico and Canada.

Cautious efforts on behalf of third-party organizations on the state or local level were encouraged by Sweeney, though never at the political expense of what were deemed pro-labor Democrats. The Working Families Party in New York and the Labor Party, with union support, endorsed major party candidates when they seemed to deserve it, but endorsed their own candidates when they didn't. In several cases unionists ran for and won elected office, either on a third-party ticket or as candidates of a major party.

A mood of near euphoria swept through labor, democratic, and social reform movements with Sweeney's New Voices initiatives. Labor would rise again. The real test of the strength of the new leadership, however, was on the front lines of labor action, in organizing and politics. Could organized labor become a counterweight to the gi-antism of corporate economic, political, social, and cultural power?

Strikes

Like Sweeney, Ron Carey was no radical, though he too benefited from the votes and help that his democratic movement gained from the left when he won reelection to the presidency of the Teamsters in 1996. Carey was a popular leader during the national strike of drivers and warehouse workers against United Parcel Service (UPS) in 1997. The workers at UPS were angry at the increased use of part-timers, an issue that touched a sympathetic nerve among workers everywhere. People also liked the UPS drivers. They delivered presents and desired objects ordered by phone or electronically. Public support helped the unified Teamsters win their strike, significant because it was the first nationwide victory for labor in twenty years.

Carey's leadership of the largest union in the nation came to an abrupt end, however, less than a year later when he was charged with illegally using union funds in his election campaign against James ("Junior") Hoffa Jr. When a new election was ordered by the courts, Hoffa Jr. won the presidency. Most of the old guard, not under indictments or in prison, returned to power along with the son of their former union boss. Carey entered a long legal battle that ultimately cleared him of corruption and perjury charges in 2001, but he remains out of office. The IBT's loyalties are no longer aligned with New Voices. They may be shifting politically as well. President George Bush, in personal attendance at the IBT picnic on Labor Day 2001, singled out Hoffa Jr. for special praise.

Professional athletes know more than most workers that it is their artful and strenuous labor that creates all of the wealth made in the sports industry. Major league baseball players have struck four times since 1970, most recently in 1994, and they have never concluded contract talks without the threat of job action. Professional basketball, hockey, and football players struck or were locked out by owners in contract disputes during the 1980s and 1990s as well. Polls showed that fans generally opposed the labor actions of their heroes, and thought that the huge celebrity salaries were already excessive, and the new demands in every situation unreasonable, selfish, and disloyal. Team owners tried to carry on with third-rate football scabs in 1987 without success. Fans wanted the real thing or nothing.

During the 1990s, strikes continued at the low levels set in the 1980s, and with similarly mixed or frequently negative results. The courts were not inclined to reverse the hostile labor relations environment, and the NLRB lacked the capability to do so, especially after new cuts in its budget were made by Republican congressional majorities in 1995. One of the most bitterly fought labor battles of the 1990s was the strike in 1995 of six unions representing newspaper workers at the *Detroit Free Press* and *Detroit News*. All of the elements of the currently hostile labor-management environment were present in the five-and-a-half year-long struggle. The use of "replacement workers" forced the unions back to work without a contract after nineteen months. Delays at the NLRB allowed damaging violations of labor law to go unchecked for over three years. Separate settlements were made by typographers and photoengravers in 1999. The remaining four unions, including Teamsters, accepted similar terms at the end of 2000. Managers at the two papers estimated their strike losses from declines in circulation and advertising revenue at over $200 million. The unions suffered devastating concessions. There were 30 percent pay cuts to several categories of workers and hundreds of permanent job losses. The new contracts contained "open shop" clauses which said that new workers did not have to join or pay dues or dues equivalents to the unions. Average pay increases were no more than about 2 percent per year, with small bonuses tied to circulation increases. Observers noted that management got what it originally wanted in 1995, but paid a big price. A union spokesperson commented: "The ratifications make sure there is still a union at the paper(s). Are these contracts as good as they were prior to 1995? No. But it's better to have a contract, than no contract at all" (*New York Times*, December 19, 2000, p. A-32).

Aside from the absence of violent attacks, striking workers at the end of the twentieth century were as vulnerable to damaging reprisals as they were at the beginning. Without the legally protected right to withhold their labor, contemporary workers and their unions engaged in collective bargaining with their employers in an atmosphere of coercion and fear. Threats of plant closings and job cuts encouraged concession bargaining, wage cuts and freezes, and tier-wage systems, and more union workers held multiple jobs to maintain household income. Sweeney, and the rest of organized labor, looked for a way to confront the right-to-strike issue or feared for the continuation of collective bargaining itself. To maintain and possibly build the strength of labor, the problems for Sweeney and all of labor were how to organize the unorganized, and to regain some political clout in Washington.

Organizing

Sweeney had to organize more workers every year just to stay even. The size of the labor force grew in almost every year since he assumed leadership, but the percentage of unionized labor remained flat or fell despite his renewed efforts at mobilization. Sweeney sought to replace the old 5 percent allocation of a union's budget for organizing with at least 20 percent. One preferred method of organizing was called the "blitz," an intense, well-financed campaign over a relatively short time span. The speed and intensity of the drive, and the skills of professional organizers, were aimed at preventing or reducing employer reprisals and threats while cards were signed and an election carried out. Sometimes it worked. "Salting" was another tactic. Union organizers, unknown to a nonunion contractor, took jobs with the intention of organizing the rest of the workers. The Union of Needle Industries and Textile Employees (UNITE), which was the newly merged union of the former ILGWU and ACWA, used a long-term foundation building approach to gradually build up support for the union. In a tremendous victory for their persistence after ninety-six years of struggle in North Carolina, the textile workers at Cannon-Fieldcrest finally voted for union representation by UNITE in 2000. California home healthcare workers successfully organized 74,000 workers in 1999, after a long legal struggle to change their status from "independent contractors" to workers. Winning an election is only a first step for a union, as many employers defied the NLRB and resisted or refused negotiations.

Elections to win the right of collective bargaining continued to be lost by unions as well, and in greater numbers than were easily accepted by organizers, given the huge expense. Estimates range between $1,000 and $3,000 as the cost-per-new-member of an organizing campaign. The UAW suffered its second loss attempting to win a representation election at the Nissan Motor company plant in Smyrna, Tennessee, in October 2001. It was a harsh defeat. The vote was 3,103 to 1,486 against the UAW. At the time no foreign-owned auto plant operating in the Untied States had a unionized workforce. The foreign automakers were able to defeat the UAW by offering comparable job security, wage, pension, and health benefits. They carefully selected the region or location in which to build their plants, and used surveys and personality tests in hiring workers for the purpose of preventing unionization. Personality testing in the workplace was a $500 million a year industry by 1999 and growing.

Organizing concepts, strategies, and suggestions percolate throughout labor, academic, and labor journalistic circles. New, or revived, ideas like "wall-to-wall" organizing of large-scale work sites, office buildings, or industrial parks were suggested as alternatives to the single-employer model (Aronowitz, 1998, p. 148). "Open source" unionism (really another old concept revived) would allow workers who have not yet gained a majority to have full union membership, protection, and legal benefits at reduced dues rates while they build for the future. A "card-check" strategy of seeking a majority, or supermajority (70 percent or more), of workers to sign up for union representation is sometimes attempted to avoid the firings, threats, and intimidation that are associated with drawn-out election campaigns. Employers, understandably, don't always go along with a card-check, and insist on an NLRB-sanctioned election procedure.

Deficient strategy and tactics was not the reason for the organizing losses. It was the absence of effective law, poor enforcement of existing law, and deliberately long delays in settling disputes that continued to block labor organization. Employers willingly accepted tens of thousands of minor penalties for violations of current labor law. Those violations, mostly illegal firings for union activity, and the long delays before they were adjudicated allowed companies to break organizing drives at a modest cost. To every worker, such an illegal action could destroy a family or a household's way of life.

Despite massive efforts, the volunteer work of tens of thousands, and the expenditure of hundreds of millions of dollars, the percentage of unionized workers stayed flat or actually fell to about 9 percent of private and 15 percent of public employees during the Sweeney era. To grow, it was estimated that organized labor needed to add about a million new members a year. Sweeney's stepped-up drive added no more than about one-third that, just barely enough to stay even with the rising number of new workers.

Those closest to the problem were not ambiguous. Labor law was used primarily to contain and restrict labor, not to enhance its organizing ability, its bargaining power, or its political strength. The power of government was consistent throughout the history of labor in the United States. Government power was used more often to stifle labor and the democratic forces that it represented, than it sought to enhance them. Until the law provides a level or fair field of encounter, employers will continue to stop labor organizing efforts in the same way they are able to continue to break or contain strikes. Without the democratic political counterweight that only labor can provide, the power in government of a small economic minority will continue to increase its dominance over every aspect of national life. Republican conservative businessmen like George Schultz knew that; so did Democrats like William B. Gould IV, the great-great-grandson of a slave.

It's All Politics

Most of John Sweeney's political energy and AFL-CIO money continued to go to Democratic Party figures, but labor was outspent in the political arena by corporations and wealthy individuals by a ratio of at least 10 to 1, with some estimates claiming that the ratio is higher than 20 to 1. What labor offers instead of big money are votes, but, as we have seen, enough money well spent in crafting images and impressions can turn even the votes of union labor against itself. Checking the power of money in politics will never be easy. The desirability of campaign finance reform to prevent the complete dependence of those in office on their largest contributors ought to be obvious. At least $2 billion was spent during the 1996 elections, but costs had risen to nearly $3 billion to pay for the elections of 2000. The Bush campaign raised about $191 million, while Gore brought in only about $133 million. To become mayor of the city of New York in the 2001 election, Michael Bloomberg spent nearly $70 million of his own money. If the city's public schools for workers are in trouble, it may be fairly argued that it is because men like Bloomberg are taxed so inadequately that they have money to casually toss into such personal vanities as winning elective office. Of course, Bloomberg has no one to answer to but himself, a small advantage to the public over other elected officials who must answer to their corporate sponsors. Will Mayor Bloomberg favor a tax system that will prevent men like himself from the kind of egotistical self-indulgence that has led him to seek office? Not likely.

In public office or out, those who have been elected can expect other advantages from a good business record that labor cannot match. Companies provide good jobs, real careers, to the wives and children of politicians at salaries unions only dream about. Class privileges such as admission to private schools and clubs, and membership on prestigious boards are also carefully distributed by those with the power to do so to those who have served well. Political dynasties have been created with corporate money for the next generation of political leaders. Presidents, governors, and lesser officeholders secure future openings for their sons, daughters, or wives in comparable—or the same—elected positions that they have held with the financial and political help of business interests, not labor.

When they leave office, speaker fees that amount to millions of dollars per year await politicians at the banquet tables of corporations and their foundations. Bill Clinton reported $9.2 million in speaker fees in the first year after he left office. Hilary Clinton was paid an $8 million advance for the publication of her memoirs, prior to taking on her new job as U.S. senator from New York. Corporate law firms scramble to win the employment of former members of government, just as defense industries routinely hire ex-generals and admirals with whom their companies have dealt. Labor can't offer or match what corporations can and do provide for those who serve them.

A highly stratified wage system separates and divides workers. Business leaders know that political figures often represent nothing more than another level of employee expense. A large part of the labor of government is to maintain the wealth that is transferred from labor to property owners by law. Labor can never expect anything of substance from any level of government that is comprised of people who rely so completely on business sponsorship. Nor can any democracy survive plutocratic or inherited influences in positions of legal authority.

Corporate goals are imagined as public and private virtues. The same corporate power that steers government policy seeks to influence workers and unions as well. Corporate terminology, "bottom line" thinking, has crept into everyday speech and calculations. Public matters, the realities that affect everyone's life, such as environmental concerns, health issues, and safety matters, are reduced to calculations and cost considerations. Unions most often accept the corporate view on environmental matters when jobs for members are at stake. Lost jobs hurt workers and lost dues hurt unions.

Corporate ideology in the forms of logos, sponsorships, foundation activities, and scholarships dominate public life. Though their investment share is tiny in comparison to the wealthiest 2 or 3 percent of the population, workers are investors in corporate enterprises. More than half the workforce, with much higher percentages among union members, owns or has pension rights tied to the performance of corporate securities, stocks, and bonds. Private self-interest leads workers to join the chorus of cheers when securities markets advance, share the gloom during downturns, and ignore the degradation of public life and democracy that corporate priorities require. Their identification with business leads workers to vote the corporate ticket. Almost all third-party labor alternatives appear to threaten that corporate interest and hold little appeal for most workers.

Overt corruption of some union leaders, as we have seen, is another consequence of the imbalance of corporate and labor power. Unions in the public sector become similarly bound to government leaders whose budgets determine the contract settlements they must take to union members. Public union leaders are under tremendous pressure to climb on bandwagons of political leaders with whom they negotiate. Future contracts may depend on it.

The Clinton administration followed the Carter administration in its inability to satisfy its obligations to labor in exchange for its votes. On the other hand, President Clinton, again like Carter, had no comparable difficulties with business objectives. He was able to grant telecommunications licenses, pharmacological research subsidies, and marketing certifications, and made trade agreements and granted pardons for business and campaign contributors. Corporate gratitude made the ex-president one of the most highly paid speakers in the nation's history, and contributed to his wife's successful election to the U.S. Senate from her new home state, New York.

For all of the Democratic Party's failure to deliver anything much to labor (except for FMLA of 1993 and a boost in minimum wage in 1997) for its votes in 1992 and 1996, its candidate, Vice President Al Gore, held onto the endorsement of the AFL-CIO in the election of 2000. In the election, Gore won the popular majority vote nationwide, but not a decisive majority of the electoral count because of Florida's disputed outcome. The Supreme Court broke the election deadlock by giving Florida's electors to Republican George W. Bush on a straight party-line 5–4 vote. In the election of 2000, for a change, it could not be said that "labor did it."

2000

Some numbers lend themselves to reflection better than others. Y2K was one of these. It was also a census year that showed some dramatic changes in the social composition of labor. The so-called nuclear family was only 23.5 percent of the households in the nation, the lowest ever. Families headed by single mothers (7.2 percent) and fathers (2.1 percent), and composed of unmarried couples with children (5.1 percent) were all on the rise. Other household arrangements, including gay and unmarried couples without children, group households, and singles with no children, comprised the rest. If the traditional family concept was no longer the dominant social formation among workers, the debate about "family wage" versus "comparable worth" for the achievement of gender equity among workers would have to be revisited. The end of "welfare as we know it" compounded the matter, as nearly all of the new workers forced onto the bottom rung of the labor force were single women raising children.

The Best and Worst of Times

The sustained economic growth of the 1993–2000 period created an atmosphere that further contributed to corporate hegemony. Unemployment rates fell to near record lows. Census data also showed a .5 percent decline in poverty from 1999 to 11.3 percent of the population in 2000. The number of children in impoverished households still remained the highest of any industrial nation at approximately 20 percent of the total. People at the top of the wage and salary scales had the biggest earning gains, while people at the bottom took on hard losses. Median income stayed flat despite the economic boom. The distance between the top and bottom of the income scale was greater than at any time in over fifty years. People in poverty fell even farther below the official line because of cuts in food stamps and various assistance programs, and the greater obstacles they encountered when they sought existing sources of aid. Women earned $.73 for each dollar earned by men in 2000, unchanged from the prior year (*New York Times*, September 26, 2001, p. A-12). Full-time earnings for men dropped a significant one percent from 1999 to 2000, the first decline for men in four years. Plentiful low-wage jobs meant more multiple-job workers, young workers, and people working off-the-books.

The stagnation of labor produced some odd and troubling consequences. Union strength remained in work areas that were either highly profitable (gambling casinos, various service jobs, professional sports), or where the work was not easily supplanted by technology, transferred to foreign shores, or done by new immigrants (public employees, skilled crafts). Sometimes it was a combination of those factors that kept labor in a position of some strength. Union and labor weakness in general persisted in the burgeoning telecommunications, still booming dot-coms, and silicone valley computer related industries. Giant retailers like Wal-Mart, the nation's largest, remained nonunion. Manufacturers kept up the pressure for concessions, give-backs, and union decertification through threats of layoffs or moving abroad. Mining and workplace fatalities in general, after a twenty-year period of decline, began to increase. Another trend that was reversed was farmworkers' pay, estimated to have fallen 20 percent during the last two decades of the century after a period of some successful unionizing efforts and small gains.

As healthcare became more completely privatized, nurses and other healthcare workers lost ground as wages fell, working conditions deteriorated, and the ability to form or maintain unions worsened. Increased workloads and low wages resulted in severe shortages of nurses and teachers in several big urban areas. There were no comparable shortages of casino dealers. Marijuana production, much of it grown in basements and garages, was estimated to be a $4 billion a year crop in Kentucky, the biggest cash crop in the state (and several others) in 2000. A police official observed: "It's kind of like the old moonshine days with neighbors making a living at it" (*New York Times*, February 28, 2001, p. A-10). Was the society well served by overworked and underpaid nurses on the one hand and prosperous casino employees and celebrities on the other? How much child poverty is acceptable? What are the social consequences of a multibillion-dollar illegal substances industry? What about the chronic wage gap between men and women?

Leadership in the continuing social debate did not come from organized labor. John Sweeney may be remembered by some astute members of the public for his plea, "Labor needs a raise." When both political parties responded with an increase in minimum wage in 1997, and again in 2001, Sweeney faded from national attention. He knew how precarious the situation was for labor, but remained cautious in his approaches. His own union, SEIU, continued to spend about $100 million a year on organizing work (half the union budget) and remained the fastest-growing labor organization in the nation. From a strictly business point of view, Sweeney's SEIU was doing well.

Democracy was not doing so well, though, as the election of 2000 indicated. Voter turnout was the lowest in forty years. No election ever cost more, or excluded more black people from voting in the past thirty years. This exclusion was especially true in Florida, the state that determined the outcome. Reg Brown, deputy general counsel to Governor Jeb Bush (candidate George Bush's brother), said that voting in Florida was "a privilege, not a right, for people who have broken the social compact" (*New York Times,* November 3, 2000, p. A-18). Florida denied the vote to 647,000 adults, the highest number in the nation, mainly because they were considered (not all were) ex-felons. In Florida 31 percent of the adult male black population were denied the vote in 2000, the greatest such restriction in the nation.

Labor rights and voting rights were always closely linked. States with restrictive labor laws continue to restrict voting rights as well. In the election of 2000, only nine states had absolute bans on voting by ex-felons, six of which, including Florida, also had right-to-work laws. Two states eliminated or modified restrictions on ex-felon voting soon after the election, but none of the right-to-work-law states did so. The message is clear: if you want to vote or join a union, stay out of those states.

Bushwhacked

From at least the time of the new U.S. Constitution's careful legitimization of slavery in 1789, government has always sought to take the lead in setting labor's relationship to capital. Despite his alleged limitations as an administrator, President George W. Bush wasted no time doing the same. After only three weeks in office Bush alarmed some of his own Republican associates by issuing four executive orders that sought to roll back government labor policies. One of these, the banning of "project labor agreements," provoked thirty-two Republicans, mainly from industrial states in the House of Representatives, to write in protest to Bush. Those agreements essentially protected unionized labor by allowing unions that are involved in federal projects to set wages and benefits for all workers involved, even if some of the workers and contractors were nonunion. If this executive action was sustained, it would further erode the Davis-Bacon law on prevailing-wage rates. While the serious matters went to court, the president gave a clear signal as to the direction of his new administration.

Corporate PAC money and close ties to the energy industry prompted other Bush actions. The new president quickly put aside an international agreement on global warming accords made by his predecessor in Kyoto, Japan, and rejected the similarly new and more restrictive curbs on tolerable arsenic levels in the nation's drinking water. He soon reversed his action on arsenic after a storm of protests came from the public and his own party leaders. With votes from most Democrats in Congress, a tax reduction of many billions for business and the wealthiest citizens passed easily in early 2001. There was almost nothing in it but a few hundred dollars each for most workers. Religious institutions (nonunion for the most part) were, the new president proclaimed, to receive more federal funds to carry out humanitarian aid and social service programs as public agencies (mostly civil service and union) were cut back or eliminated. The president emphatically endorsed the Supreme Court ruling a year later in 2002 that allowed the states to use public funds to pay for education in religious schools through tuition vouchers.

Bush named Eugene Scalia, the son of the ultraconservative Supreme Court Justice Antonin Scalia, to the position of top enforcement official (solicitor) in the Department of Labor. Scalia's appointment was made without the votes of a Senate committee to confirm him, and was regarded as a major setback for labor as Scalia was a well-known critic of the Occupational Health and Safety Administration's ergonomics regulations. Scalia called the new rules "quackery" and "junk science," when they were debated and repealed by Congress a few months prior to his nomination. Though women were 46 percent of the workforce, they experienced 64 percent of all repetitive motion injuries, and 71 percent of all carpal tunnel syndrome cases. Apparently Bush's "compassionate conservatism" didn't extend to the injuries of mainly women office workers.

Labor in a Hostile Environment

Immigrant and low-wage workers, likewise, found little compassion for their circumstances. A few notable examples follow. Farmworkers in the expanding foie gras (duck liver) industry in New York State were mostly from Mexico. The laws that covered 30,000 farmworkers in New York allowed the duck feeders to work seven-day weeks of over sixty hours each for no more than $6.00 an hour. Most of these workers earned less than that. No days off were permitted during the thirty-day duck-feeding schedules. As soon as one crop of ducks was slaughtered, another group's feeding began with no break in between. One worker said of the hard, heavy, labor-intensive, twenty-four-hour daily schedule: "The conditions of the workers are crueler than the conditions for the ducks" (*New York Times*, April 2, 2001, pp. B-1, B-4). As the New York State legislature contemplated legal remedies, it was pointed out that conditions for both ducks and workers were much better in France, the home of the industry.

Immigrant workers had to sue in a U.S. district court to force several discount retailers to pay minimum wage, end twenty-two-hour-long workdays, and cease other violations of federal and state labor laws in New York, New Jersey, and Connecticut in January 2001. The lawsuits were prompted by long delays and failures to reach settlements of charges brought in state labor departments. Once again, the lawsuit, a form of private legal action, was the alternative that labor was forced to use in the absence of good laws and effective law enforcement.

At Wal-Mart, the nation's largest retailer, with over 6 percent of total sales, or $220 billion a year, conditions were even worse. Wal-Mart didn't want to pay anything at all for some of the labor of its nonunion workforce in over 3,200 stores. Managers in Wal-Mart stores in twenty-eight states engaged in "lock-ins," "clock outs," or time-card "manipulation" according to lawsuits and interviews given to reporters. Workers were locked in stores after hours and expected to continue working without pay, or told to clock out and work with no pay or overtime until certain tasks were completed. Workers regularly worked during breaks without pay, or had work hours deliberately deleted by managers from time cards to avoid overtime pay. These charges in 2002 were not isolated or new. Wal-Mart settled a similar class action suit for $50 million on behalf of 69,000 of its employees in Colorado two years earlier. In Texas the class action suit was on behalf of 200,000 active or former Wal-Mart workers who were underpaid an estimated $150 million for their labor. One Wal-Mart store in New Mexico agreed to a $400,000 settlement for 120 workers for unpaid labor. The operating costs for the huge retailer were, unsurprisingly, the lowest by a wide margin in comparison to its largest competitors (*New York Times*, June 25, 2002, pp. A-1, A-18). Settling lawsuits may actually turn out to cost the violator less than proper payment of wages. It certainly appears preferable to employers than enforcement of labor laws on behalf of workers. Lawyers don't mind either.

Wal-Mart, and other private employers, are not alone in facing class action suits brought by workers. The Social Security Administration, one of the last still-standing remnants of the New Deal, settled a bias dispute brought by 2,200 black male workers against it for almost $8 million in 2002. The agency was charged by attorneys who represented the workers with racial and gender discrimination in its promotion, salary evaluation, and discipline practices. The agreement was unusual since it was reached without conclusive litigation, and the agency professed "no admission of guilt, but a promise for change" (*New York Times*, January 16, 2002, p. A-17). After a decade of litigation, thirteen black state troopers won a $5 million lawsuit against New Jersey in July 2002. The troopers were awarded back pay and compensation for emotional distress that ranged from $225,000 to $500,000 each. Labor law prevents unions from offering workers the same kind of monetary victories as lawsuits. The nation's courts, not its laws, promise to everyone the best justice money can buy.

Patriotism, Religion, and Racism

A few months after the September 11, 2001 attacks on the Pentagon and the Twin Towers of the World Trade Center, and in spite of the energy, dedication, and terrible health risks taken by union workers in the aftermath, President Bush announced an executive order that barred union representation for about 500 people in four of the agencies of the Justice Department, and at the offices of the United States attorneys. Union contracts, Bush claimed, might impose restrictions on the abilities of those agencies to protect national security. Employers, including government, continue to prefer to hire, fire, reward, and punish workers without any interference, no matter how democratically workers organize to offset that arbitrary power.

The Patriot Act, passed easily after the attacks, carried the infringement on democratic rights further by enhancing police power at the expense of the Constitution, especially in the loss of privacy rights and the reduction of the rights of people accused of crimes. The president's appeal to patriotism in the aftermath of the attack and to religious faith in the provision of human services and education coincided with his party's continuing reputation for racist indifference to the rights of black citizens (see above, "election" of 2000). His defense against the charge of racism was that he had a black man and a black woman in positions of great importance. That more than thirty million others were continuing to experience losses and hardships in every measurable category (life expectancy, healthcare, unemployment, education, incarceration, etc.) was of apparently negligible importance.

Patriotism, religion, and racism require faith and submission to accepted authority and a suspension of independent reasoning. Democracy, on the other hand, cannot exist without free and open discourse. Though labor is no monolith with only one outlook, in the United States it is overwhelmingly patriotic, religious, and, aside from those who are its victims, largely indifferent to charges of racism and gender discrimination. Labor's unswerving patriotism ties its destiny to the goals and objectives of corporations that are internationally organized. The unwillingness of most of labor to stand against religious intrusion into the public domain aligns it with the most antilabor and undemocratic forces in the nation. Labor cannot afford to let the struggle for human rights be carried only by victims of abuse. Too much is at stake. An injury to one remains an injury to all.

Labor and Democracy, Yesterday

What have we observed in our journey so far? For one thing, the expansion of legal and political rights to workers in the United States never advanced without sharp conflict or war. And, in every surge of democracy, every segment of labor, black and white, men and women, immigrant and native-born, advanced. When democracy receded and political liberties were set back, all of labor lost material gains and workplace achievements as well. As we conclude our reflections on labor's past, a brief review of what we have already observed may help to shed some new light on current and future prospects for both labor and democracy.

Labor and democracy made great strides in the revolutionary era (1774–87), but suffered some reverses in the decades that followed. Momentum was regained in the era of Andrew Jackson (1828–40), when slavery came to an end in the northern states and was under attack in the South. Universal manhood suffrage, public schools, and the opening of a sustained struggle for women's rights accompanied the workingmen's parties of that "age of the common man." When the Civil War split the nation, Lincoln led farmers and workers to defend the democratic idealism of the founders and end slavery as well. Briefly, during Reconstruction (1865–70), democratic opportunity advanced again as voting rights and public schools accompanied opportunities for land ownership for both freed slaves and poor whites. The first national labor organization gained temporary prominence in the immediate post–Civil War era as well. Those advances were soon blocked as the amendments to the Constitution that were added to protect the rights of newly freed slaves, and all citizens, were disregarded. As Jim Crow prospered in the decades that followed, democratic progress on all fronts was also set back, and labor lost one heroic battle after another.

As an emerging world power, the United States entered a Progressive era (1899–1917) that once again extended democratic liberties while the nation made and planned for war. Labor was the leading force for radical democratic change, and pushed all political groups forward until the wartime emergency passed. Then, nearly every democratic accomplishment was blocked or crushed. The same kind of labor-led democratic advances accompanied the New Deal era (1932–46) as the nation confronted Depression and war. A corporate-labor stalemate checked democratic advances in the early cold war, but such advances revived again in the Vietnam War era (1964–71).

In every period of democratic advance there was an expansion of voting and legal rights. Racial repression was forced to give way, though it never went away. Women's rights were brought forward, and women made important legal and economic gains, though they too suffered reverses afterward. The absolute political and social authority wielded by business and institutional powers was trimmed as material gains, public services, and educational opportunities were enhanced. From the time of the New Deal the Democratic Party carried on the rhetoric and bore some of the stigma of that reformist tradition, and, with few exceptions, held onto the endorsement of organized labor.

The post-Vietnam era was marked by declines and reverses for organized labor, a widening gap between rich and poor, a falloff in voter participation, a massive increase in incarceration, and the use of convict labor for profit. The women's rights movement endured a backlash and the wage gap with men widened. By every statistical measure, the harmful consequences of racism increased. Immigrant labor lost some of its legal rights, and corporations appeared indifferent to labor laws. Enforcement of those laws was so lax as to encourage their violation. Democracy in the United States is in a crisis of survival. So is organized labor.

Labor and Democracy, Today and Tomorrow

If labor chooses the road to democracy for the future, that pathway will be as hard to travel as at any time in the past. The setbacks to democracy resulting from the power of concentrated wealth raised alarms from all quarters. The social and cultural force of corporate and business values spread in the nation in spite of enormous ethical and legal scandals. Democracy can't be sustained without a political component that is built by labor to check the power of concentrated wealth.

Rebuilding the house of labor has attracted great attention in recent years. Labor activists inside and outside the unions have been offering up plans for a revival at a heightened pace since John Sweeney's ascendancy. Sweeney, for his part, concentrated AFL-CIO efforts and huge expenditures on organizing and political work, neither of which returned significant results. His friendly critics urged him to place labor at the forefront of the important social issues of the time, and to take a more independent position on all political issues, including foreign policy. Most national unions were discouraged by the mediocre results of the New Voices campaign. Manufacturers continued to threaten to shut down plants, employed union-busting consultants, and violated the NLRB regulations at will. Unionizing grew in Sweeney's service sector, skeptics said, only because the threat of transfer of most of that work to cheaper labor markets elsewhere could not be made.

To his credit, Sweeney continued to rally labor in speeches, at conferences, and in meetings across the country. His success in his own organization, the SEIU, may have narrowed his vision, however. The SEIU grew within the terms set by current labor law. The regional and district leaders of his union operate in the most traditional manner, one that is reinforced by law and past practices. Internal democracy is not one of the strengths of the SEIU.

Undemocratic themselves, most of the big national unions were unwilling to lead a genuine push for other democratic changes in the nation. The law and their own past history inhibited labor leaders from a role as social reformers. Nor were unions able to organize successfully inside the malls, the sunbelt, the suburbs, or the technical and professional areas where most of the growth of the labor force took place in the recent thirty years. There is no national labor news outlet of consequence, no significant newspaper, and no cable channel. Few unions or workers make active use of existing websites or Internet capabilities for organizing drives or international labor actions. There are no union- or labor-sanctioned international strikes, boycotts, or demonstrations, though the largest corporate entities are globally organized. The AFL-CIO historically bonded its destiny to that of the employer, and the employer's vision of the nation. To continue to do so threatens not only labor, but democracy itself.

Patriotism will have to be redefined on labor's terms with the emphasis on democracy and human values, not profit and empire no matter how sweetly the latter are promoted. Corporations organize and act collectively and internationally, while they restrict their employees to national and individual associations and actions. Capital uses global organizations such as the World Bank and the International Monetary Fund to further their ends while labor does not. The largest corporations are not simply national bodies. Their investments, sales, and profits abroad are greater than those from their home base nations. Until labor forms organizations that can match the reach and power of its business counterparts, it will suffer losses and inferiority by comparison. A dictatorship that can break unions inside one country threatens the democratic gains won by labor in another if corporations are free to do business wherever they choose. Indeed, corporations will always choose the lowest cost, least restricted, most heavily subsidized option. Until labor in the United States finds its own independent patriotic voice, not one that is an echo of capital, it cannot hope to rebuild its power or overcome the democratic losses it has endured.

No expansion of the rights of labor has taken place in the United States without a reaffirmation of the radical democratic ideas of Thomas Jefferson and Thomas Paine. Lincoln can be included as well for his linking of that earlier vision to the Civil War and the end of slavery. FDR enlarged the concept of democracy by including the "Freedom from Want" among his "Four Freedoms," for which, he said, World War II was fought. Every expansion of labor and democracy brought forth leaders from among all of the workforce regardless of gender or race, both newcomers and native-born, who enlarged the meaning of liberty and equality. For that, and in their time, they were known as radicals. The secular and universalist ideas they put forth stood in marked contrast to the religious and sectarian ideas of the authorities they opposed. Royal, aristocratic, and religious powers have relied on coercive mythologies that are anathema to democracy, and always have been. For all of their humane and charitable work, religious institutions can only enter into public life at a cost to civil liberties, labor, and democracy. Radical unionists and labor advocates have always had to deal with the ultimately undemocratic and antilabor power of religious institutions, not religious individuals. To create a modern international labor force that is capable of matching corporate power means building a labor program that sidelines the religious, ethnic, national, and racial differences that continue to separate workers. Sweeney warns that labor will either catch up quickly, or fade into insignificance. The greater danger of that insignificance is to the future of democracy itself.

Racism bonds workers to the divisive ideology of their employers at home in the same way as uncritical patriotism bonds them to corporate foreign policy. Racism subverts every democratic value, and can have no place in a modern labor movement. Its use in the past was to break the inherent unity of labor into isolated parts and devalue democracy at the same time. The political construction of "minority districts," join "affirmative action" and the proliferation of lawsuits in maintaining that divisive process. Unless labor takes back the lead in the struggle to destroy all forms of discrimination against workers, it can never regain the power it needs to counter that of business, nor does it deserve to. Sweet-sounding rhetoric and selective advantages for the few will not cut into the deep racism that divides workers. Only vigorous action by workers themselves can do it. The end of racial and gender inequity can never be accomplished by those who profit from its continuance, no matter the guise or moral pretense that cloaks the various schemes.

As long as labor's adversaries continue to win the political allegiance of workers by cultivating their racial, religious, and national fears, labor and democracy will continue to decline. If all of labor can more fully realize that socially useful work possesses inherent dignity and deserves appropriate respect and proper reward, and that no new wealth can ever be made without the mind and hand of labor, it can restore its lost power. If labor can dream its own dreams again, and begin to imagine its own destiny, it also has the possibility of reviving the democratic tradition of the nation.

The struggle for labor's fair share of what it produces has never been an easy one, temptations to withdraw from that battlefield are as plentiful as the casualties, but the historic goals of labor have never failed to honor those who have carried them forward. That story concludes, but doesn't end here.

BIBLIOGRAPHY

Books

Adams, Graham, Jr. *Age of Industrial Violence, 1910–1915: The Activities and Findings of the United States Commission on Industrial Relations*. New York: Columbia University Press, 1966.

American Social History Project. *Who Built America? Working People and the Nation's Economy, Politics, Culture & Society*. 2 vols. New York: Pantheon, 1992.

Aptheker, Herbert. *American Negro Slave Revolts*. New York: International Publishers, 1987.

Angle, Paul M., ed. *Lincoln-Douglas Debates*. Chicago: University of Chicago Press, 1991.

Arnesen, Eric. *Brotherhoods of Color: Black Railroad Workers and the Struggle for Equality*. Cambridge, Mass.: Harvard University Press, 2001.

Aronowitz, Stanley. *False Promises: The Shaping of American Working-Class Consciousness*. New York: McGraw Hill, 1973.

———. *Working Class Hero: A New Strategy for Labor*. New York: Pilgrim, 1983.

———. *From the Ashes of the Old: American Labor and America's Future*. New York: Houghton Mifflin, 1998.

Aronowitz, Stanley, and William DiFazio. *The Jobless Future: Sci-Tech and the Dogma of Work*. Minneapolis: University of Minnesota Press, 1994.

Asher, Robert, and Charles Stephenson, eds. *Labor Divided: Race and Ethnicity in United States Labor Struggles*. Albany: State University of New York Press, 1990.

Atkinson, Linda. *Mother Jones, The Most Dangerous Woman in America*. New York: Crown, 1978.

Aurand, W. *From the Molly Maguires to the United Mine Workers: The Social Ecology of an Industrial Union, 1869–1897*. Philadelphia: Temple University Press, 1971.

Ayers, Edward L. *Vengeance and Justice, Crime and Punishment in the Nineteenth Century American South*. New York: Oxford University Press, 1984.

Babson, Steven. *An Unfinished Struggle: Turning Points in American Labor, 1877-Present*. Lanham, Md.: Rowman & Littlefield, 1999.

Bailey, Thomas R. *Immigrant and Native Workers: Contrasts and Competition*. Boulder: Westview, 1987.

Barrett, James R. *William Z. Foster and the Tragedy of American Radicalism*. Urbana: University of Illinois Press, 1999.

Baxandall, Rosalyn, Linda Gordon, and Susan Reverby, eds. *Words on Fire: A Life of Elizabeth Gurley Flynn*. New Brunswick, N.J.: Rutgers University Press, 1987.

———. *America's Working Women: A Documentary History, 1600 to the Present.* New York: W. W. Norton, 1995.

Bell, Daniel. *The Coming of Post-Industrial Society: A Venture in Social Forecasting.* New York: Basic Books, 1973.

Benson, Susan Porter. *Counter Cultures: Saleswomen, Managers, and Customers in American Department Stores, 1890–1940.* Urbana: University of Illinois Press, 1986.

Berlin, Ira. *Many Thousands Gone: The First Two Centuries of Slavery in North America.* Cambridge, Mass.: Belknap Press of Harvard University Press, 1998.

Berlin, Ira, and Herbert Gutman, eds. *Power and Culture: Essays on the American Working Class.* New York: Pantheon, 1987.

Bernstein, Irving. *The Lean Years: A History of the American Worker, 1920–1933.* Baltimore: Penguin, 1960.

———. *Turbulent Years: A History of the American Worker, 1933–1941.* Boston: Houghton-Mifflin, 1970.

Blackburn, Robin. *The Making of New World Slavery: From the Baroque to the Modern, 1492–1800.* New York: Verso, 1997.

Blau, Joseph L., ed. *Social Theories of Jacksonian Democracy.* Indianapolis: Bobbs-Merrill, 1954.

Blewett, Mary H. *Men, Women, and Work: Class, Gender and Protest in the New England Shoe Industry, 1780–1910.* Urbana: University of Illinois Press, 1988.

———. *Constant Turmoil: The Politics of Industrial Life in Nineteenth Century New England.* Amherst: University of Massachusetts Press, 2000.

Bluestone, Barry, and Irving Bluestone. *Negotiating the Future: A Labor Perspective on American Business.* New York: Basic Books, 1992.

Bodnar, John. *Kinship, Community, and Protest in an Industrial Society, 1900–1940.* Baltimore: Johns Hopkins University Press, 1982.

Bok, Derek C., and John T. Dunlop. *Labor and the American Community.* New York: Simon and Schuster, 1970.

Bonnett, Clarence E. *History of Employers' Associations in the United States.* New York: Vantage, 1956.

Booth, Sally Smith. *Seeds of Anger: Revolts in America, 1607–1771.* New York; Hastings House, 1977.

Bowers, Claude G. *Jefferson in Power: The Death Struggle of the Federalists.* Cambridge, Mass.: Riverside, 1936.

Boyer, Richard, and Herbert M. Morais. *Labor's Untold Story.* New York: Cameron Associates, 1955.

Braudel, Fernand. *The Mediterranean and the Mediterranean World in the Age of Philip II.* 2 vols. New York: Harper, 1973.

Braverman, Harry. *Labor and Monopoly Capital: The Degradation of Work in the Twentieth Century.* New York: Monthly Review, 1974.

Brecher, Jeremy. *STRIKE!* 2d ed. Boston: South End, 1997.

Bridenbaugh, Carl. *The Colonial Craftsman.* New York: New York University Press, 1950.

Brinkley, Alan. *End of Reform: New Deal Liberalism in Recession and War.* New York: Knopf, 1995.

Brody, David. *Workers in Industrial America: Essays on the Twentieth Century Struggle.* New York: Oxford University Press, 1980.

———. *Labor in Crisis: The Steel Strike, 1919.* Urbana: University of Illinois Press, 1987.

———. *In Labor's Cause: Main Themes on the History of the American Worker*. Oxford: Oxford University Press, 1993.

Bruce, Robert V. *1877: Year of Violence*. New York: Bobbs-Merrill, 1959.

Buhle, Paul. *Taking Care of Business: Samuel Gompers, George Meany, Lane Kirkland, and the Tragedy of American Labor*. New York: Monthly Review, 1999.

Buhle, Paul, and Alan Dawley, eds. *Working for Democracy: American Workers from the Revolution to the Present*. Urbana: University of Illinois Press, 1985.

Burbank, David T. *Reign of the Rabble: The St. Louis General Strike of 1877*. New York: A. M. Kelly, 1966.

Burton-Rose, Daniel, ed. *The Celling of America: An Inside Look at the US Prison Industry*. Monroe, Maine: Common Courage, 1998.

Bussel, Robert. *From Harvard to the Ranks of Labor: Powers Hapgood and the American Working Class*. Campus Park: Penn State University Press, 1999.

Caute, David. *The Great Fear: The Anti-Communist Purge Under Truman and Eisenhower*. New York: Simon and Schuster, 1978.

Clarke, Paul F., Peter Gottleib, and Donald Kennedy, eds. *Forging a Union of Steel: Philip Murray, SWOC, and the United Steelworkers*. Ithaca, N.Y.: ILR Press, 1994.

Cohen, Lizabeth. *Making a New Deal: Industrial Workers in Chicago, 1919–1939*. New York: Cambridge University Press, 1990.

Cochran, Bert. *Labor and Communism: The Conflict That Shaped American Unions*. Princeton: Princeton University Press, 1977.

Colchin, Peter. *Unfree Labor: American Slavery and Russian Serfdom*. Cambridge, Mass.: Harvard University Press, 1987.

Commons, John R. et al., eds. *A History of Labor in the United States*. 4 vols. New York: Macmillan, 1921–35.

———. et al., eds. *A Documentary History of American Industrial Society*. 10 vols. New York: Russell & Russell, 1958.

Compa, Lance. *Unfair Advantage: Workers' Freedom of Association in the United States Under International Human Rights Standards*. New York: Human Rights Watch, 2000.

Creese, Gillian. *Contracting Masculinity: Gender, Class, and Race in a White-Collar Union, 1944–1994*. New York: Oxford University Press, 1999.

Cremin, Lawrence A. *American Education: The National Experience, 1783–1876*. New York: Harper, 1980.

Crittenden, Mary Ann. *Why the Most Important Job in the World is Still the Least Valued*. New York: Metropolitan Books, 2001.

Crozier, Michael J., Samuel P. Huntington, and Joji Watanuki. *The Crisis of Democracy: Report on the Governability of Democracies to the Tri-Lateral Commission*. New York: NYU Press for the Trilateral Commission, 1975.

Cunliffe, Marcus. *Chattel Slavery and Wage Slavery: The Anglo-American Context, 1830–1860*. Athens: University of Georgia Press, 1979.

Davis, Michael. *Prisoners of the American Dream: Politics and Economy in the History of the American Working Class*. New York: Verso, 1986.

Davis, Ralph. *The Rise of the English Shipping Industry in the Seventeenth and Eighteenth Centuries*. New York: St. Martin's, 1962.

Dawley, Alan. *Class and Community: The Industrial Revolution in Lynn*. Cambridge, Mass.: Harvard University Press, 1976.

———. *Struggles for Justice: Social Responsibility and the Liberal State.* Cambridge, Mass.: Harvard University Press, 1991.

Debs, Eugene V. *Walls and Bars.* Chicago: The Socialist Party Press, 1927.

Derber, Charles. *Corporation Nation: How Corporations Are Taking Over Our Lives and What We Can Do About It.* New York: St. Martin's, 1998.

De Tocqueville, Alexis. *Democracy in America.* Edited by Richard D. Heffner. New York: New American Library, 1956.

———. *Democracy in America.* Edited by J. P. Mayer, Translated by G. Lawrence. Garden City, N.Y.: Doubleday, 1975.

Diamond, Jared. *Guns, Germs, and Steel: The Fates of Human Societies.* New York: W. W. Norton, 1997.

Dollinger, Sol, and Genora Johnson Dollinger. *Not Automatic: Women and the Left in the Forging of the Auto Workers' Union.* New York: Monthly Review, 2000.

Draper, Alan. *Conflict of Interests: Organized Labor and the Civil Rights Movement in the South, 1954–1968.* Ithaca, N.Y.: ILR Press, 1994.

Dublin, Thomas. *Women at Work: The Transformation of Work and Community in Lowell, Massachusetts, 1826–1860.* New York: Columbia University Press, 1979.

DuBoff, Richard. *Accumulation & Power: An Economic History of the United States.* Armonk, N.Y.: M. E. Sharpe, 1989.

Dubofsky, Melvyn. *We Shall Be All: A History of the I.W.W.* New York: Quadrangle, 1969.

———. *The State and Labor in Modern America.* Chapel Hill: University of North Carolina Press, 1994.

Dubofsky, Melvyn, and Van Tine, Warren. *John L. Lewis: A Biography.* Urbana: University of Illinois Press, 1986.

———. *Labor Leaders in America.* Urbana: University of Illinois Press, 1987.

DuBois, W.E.B. *Black Reconstruction.* New York: Harcourt, Brace, 1935.

Dunlop, John, and Walter Galenson, eds. *Labor in the Twentieth Century.* New York: Academic, 1978.

Eisler, Benita, ed. *The Lowell Offering: Writings by New England Mill Women, 1840–1845.* Philadelphia: J. B. Lippincott, 1977.

Engerman, Stanley L., ed. *Terms of Labor: Slavery, Serfdom, and Free Labor.* Stanford: Stanford University Press, 1999.

Engerman, Stanley L., and Robert W. Fogel. *Time on the Cross: The Economics of American Negro Slavery.* Boston: Little, Brown, 1974.

Erem, Susan. *Labor Pains: Inside America's New Union Movement.* New York: Monthly Review, 2001.

Ewen, Stuart. *Captains of Consciousness: Advertising and the Social Roots of the Consumer Culture.* New York: McGraw Hill, 1976.

Fair Employment Practices Committee. *First Report.* Washington, D.C.: U.S. Government Printing Office, 1945.

Fantasia, Rick. *Cultures of Solidarity: Consciousness, Action, and Contemporary American Workers.* Berkeley: University of California Press, 1988.

Faue, Elizabeth. *Community of Suffering and Struggle: Women, Men and the American Labor Movement in Minneapolis, 1915–1945.* Chapel Hill: University of North Carolina Press, 1991.

Fethering, Dale. *Mother Jones, The Miner's Angel: A Portrait.* Carbondale: Southern Illinois Press, 1974.

Fillipelli, Ronald L., and Mark D. McColloch. *Cold War in the Working Class: The Rise and Decline of the United Electrical Workers*. Albany: State University of New York Press, 1995.

Fine, Sidney. *Sit-Down: The General Motors Strike of 1936–1937*. Ann Arbor: University of Michigan Press, 1969.

Fink, Gary. *Biographical Dictionary of American Labor*. Westport, Conn.: Greenwood, 1984.

Fink, Leon. *Workingmen's Democracy: The Knights of Labor and American Politics*. Urbana: University of Illinois Press, 1983.

Flynn, Elizabeth Gurley. *The Rebel Girl: An Autobiography; My First Life, 1906–1926*. New York: International Publishers, 1955.

Foner, Eric. *Free Soil, Free Labor, Free Men: The Ideology of the Republican Party Before the Civil War*. New York: Oxford University Press, 1970.

———. *Nothing But Freedom: Emancipation and its Legacy*. Baton Rouge: Louisiana State University Press, 1983.

Foner, Philip S. *History of the Labor Movement in the United States*. 8 vols. New York: International Publishers, 1947–88.

———, ed. *We the Other People: Alternative Declarations of Independence by Labor Groups, Farmers, Women's Rights Advocates, Socialists, and Blacks, 1829–1975*. Chicago: University of Illinois Press, 1973.

———. *Organized Labor and the Black Worker, 1619–1973*. New York: Praeger, 1974.

———. *The Great Labor Uprising of 1877*. New York: Monad, 1977.

———. *Women and the American Labor Movement*. 2 vols. New York: The Free Press, 1979–80.

Foner, Philip S., and Ronald L. Lewis. *The Black Worker: A Documentary History*. Philadelphia: Temple University Press, 1978.

Forbath, William. *Law and the Shaping of the American Labor Movement*. Cambridge, Mass.: Harvard University Press, 1991.

Frankfurter, Felix, and Nathan Greene. *The Labor Injunction*. New York: Macmillan, 1930.

Franklin, John Hope, and Loren Schweninger. *Runaway Slaves: Rebels on the Plantation*. New York: Oxford University Press, 1999.

Franklin, Stephen. *Three Strikes: Labor's Heartland Losses and What They Mean for Working Americans*. New York: Guilford, 2001.

Frantzen, Allen J., and Douglas Moffat, eds. *The Work of Work: Servitude, Slavery, and Labor in Medieval England*. Glasgow: Cruithne, 1994.

Fraser, Steven. *Labor Will Rule: Sidney Hillman and the Rise of American Labor*. Ithaca, N.Y.: The Free Press, 1991.

Freeman, Joshua B. *In Transit: The Transport Workers Union in New York City, 1933–1966*. New York: Oxford University Press, 1989.

Friedman, Gerald. *State Making and Labor Movements: France and the United States, 1876–1914*. Ithaca, N.Y.: Cornell University Press, 1998.

Friedman, Leon, and William F. Levantrosser, eds. *Richard M. Nixon: Politician, President, Administrator*. New York: Greenwood, 1991.

Frisch, Michael, and Michael Walkowitz, eds. *Working-Class America*. Urbana: University of Illinois Press, 1983.

Gabin, Nancy. *Feminism in the Labor Movement: Women and the United Auto Workers, 1935–1977*. Ithaca, N.Y.: Cornell University Press, 1990.

Gall, Gilbert J. *The Politics of Right to Work: The Labor Federations as Special Interests, 1943–1979*. New York: Greenwood, 1988.

———. *Pursuing Justice: Lee Pressman, the New Deal, and the C.I.O.*, SUNY Series in American Labor History. Albany: State University of New York Press, 1999.

Genovese, Eugene. *The Political Economy of Slavery: Studies in the Economy and Society of the Slave South*. New York: Vintage, 1967.

———. *Roll Jordan, Roll: The World the Slaves Made*. New York: Vintage, 1976.

Geoghan, Thomas. *Which Side Are You On?: How to be For Labor When It's Flat on Its Back*. New York: Farrar, Straus & Giroux, 1991.

Gerstle, Gary. *Working-Class Americanism: The Politics of Labor in a Textile City, 1914–1960*. New York: Cambridge University Press, 1989.

Gettleman, Marvin E. *The Dorr Rebellion: A Study in American Radicalism, 1833–1849*. New York: Random House, 1975.

Ginger, Ray. *The Bending Cross: A Biography of Eugene Victor Debs*. New Brunswick, N.J.: Rutgers University Press, 1949.

Glickman, Jonathan A. *Concepts of Free Labor in Ante-bellum America*. New Haven: Yale University Press, 1991.

Glickman, Lawrence B. *A Living Wage: American Workers and the Making of a Consumer Society*. Ithaca, N.Y.: Cornell University Press, 1997.

Goldfield, Michael. *The Color of Politics: Race and the Mainsprings of American Politics*. New York: The New Press, 1997.

Golin, Steve. *The Fragile Bridge: The Paterson Silk Strike, 1913*. Philadelphia: Temple University Press, 1988.

Gompers, Samuel. *Seventy Years of Life and Labor: An Autobiography*. New York: E. P. Dutton, 1925.

Goodwyn, Lawrence. *Democratic Promise: The Populist Movement in America*. New York: Oxford University Press, 1976.

Gordon, David. *Fat and Mean: The Corporate Squeeze of Working Americans and the Myth of Managerial 'Downsizing.'* New York: Martin Kessler, 1996.

Gordon, David, Richard Edwards, and Michael Reich. *Segmented Work, Divided Workers: The Historical Transformation of Labor in the United States*. Cambridge: Cambridge University Press, 1982.

Gorn, Elliot J. *Mother Jones: The Most Dangerous Woman in America*. New York: Hill and Wang, 2001.

Gould, William B., IV. *Black Workers and White Unions: Job Discrimination in the United States*. Ithaca, N.Y.: Cornell University Press, 1977.

———. *Agenda for Reform: The Future of Employment Relationships and the Law*. Cambridge, Mass.: MIT Press, 1993.

———. *Labored Relations: Law, Politics and the NLRB—A Memoir*. Cambridge, Mass.: MIT Press, 2000.

Grant, Joanne, ed. *Black Protest: History, Documents, and Analyses, 1619 to the Present*. Greenwich, Conn.: Fawcett, 1968.

Green, James R. *The World of the Worker: Labor in Twentieth Century America*. New York, Hill and Wang, 1980.

Greenbaum, Joan. *Windows on the Workplace: Computers, Jobs, and the Organization of Office Work in the Late Twentieth Century*. New York: Monthly Review, 1995.

Greene, Julie. *Pure and Simple Politics: The American Federation of Labor and Political Activism, 1881–1917*. New York: Cambridge University Press, 1998.

Griffith, Barbara S. *The Crisis of American Labor: Operation Dixie and the Defeat of the CIO*. Philadelphia: Temple University Press, 1988.

Gross, James A. *The Making of the National Labor Relations Board: A Study in Economics, Politics, and the Law*. Albany: State University of New York Press, 1974.

———. *The Reshaping of the National Labor Relations Board: National Labor Policy in Transition, 1937–1947*. Albany: State University of New York Press, 1981.

———. *Broken Promise: The Subversion of U.S. Labor Relations Policy, 1974–1994*. Philadelphia: Temple University Press, 1995.

Gutman, Herbert. *Work, Culture, and Society in Industrializing America*. New York: Vintage, 1977 (1966).

———. *Power and Culture: Essays on the American Working Class*. Edited by Ira Berlin. New York: Pantheon, 1987.

Gyory, Andrew. *Closing the Gate: Race, Politics and the Chinese Exclusion Act*. Chapel Hill: University of North Carolina Press, 1998.

Hacker, Louis. *The Triumph of American Capitalism: The Development of Forces in American History to the End of the Nineteenth Century*. New York: Columbia University Press, 1940.

Halpern, Rick. *Down on the Killing Floor: Black and White Workers in Chicago's Packinghouses, 1904–54*, The Working Class in American History. Champaign: University of Illinois Press, 1997.

Halpern, Rick, and Roger Horowitz. *Meatpackers: An Oral History of Black Packinghouse Workers and Their Struggle for Racial and Economic Equality*. New York: Monthly Review, 1999.

Halpern, Rick, and Jonathan Morris. *American Exceptionalism? U.S. Working Class Formation in an International Context*. London: St. Martin's, 1997.

Haney Lopez, Ian F. *White by Law: The Legal Construction of Race*. New York: New York University Press, 1996.

Harriman, Florence Jaffray. *From Pinafores to Politics*. New York: H. Holt, 1923.

Harris, H. William. *Keeping the Faith: A. Philip Randolph, Milton P. Webster, and the Brotherhood of Sleeping Car Porters, 1925–1937*. Urbana: University of Illinois Press, 1977.

Harvey, Katherine A. *The Best-Dressed Miners: Life and Labor in the Maryland Coal Region, 1835–1910*. Ithaca, N.Y.: Cornell University Press, 1969.

Hattam, Victoria C. *Labor Visions and State Power: The Origins of Business Unionism in the United States*. Princeton: Princeton University Press, 1993.

Haydu, Jeffrey. *Making American Industry Safe for Democracy: Comparative Perspectives on the State and Employee Representation in the Era of World War II*. Champaign: University of Illinois Press, 1997.

Hill, Herbert. *Black Labor and the American Legal System: Race, Work, and the Law*. Madison: University of Wisconsin Press, 1985.

Hobsbaum, Eric. *Workers: Worlds of Labor*. New York: Pantheon, 1984.

Hofstadter, Richard. *The American Political Tradition and the Men Who Made It*. New York: Vintage, 1960.

———. *America in 1750: A Social Portrait*. New York: Random House, 1973.

Holt, Michael F. *The Rise and Fall of the American Whig Party: Jacksonian Politics and the Onset of the Civil War*. New York: Oxford University Press, 1999.

Holter, Darryl. *Workers and Unions in Wisconsin: A Labor History Anthology*. Madison, Wis.: State Historical Society Press, 1999.

Honey, Michael Keith. *Black Workers Remember: An Oral History of Segregation, Unionism, and the Freedom Struggle*. Berkeley: University of California Press, 1999.

Horowitz, Roger. *"Negro and White, Unite and Fight!" A Social History of Industrial Unionism in Meatpacking, 1930–1990*, The Working Class in American History. Champaign: University of Illinois Press, 1997.

Huberman, Leo. *We, the People: The Drama of America.* New York: Monthly Review, 1960.

Hunnicutt, Benjamin K. *Kellogg's Six-Hour Day.* Philadelphia: Temple University Press, 1996.

Huntington, Samuel P., Michael Crozier, and Joji Watanuki. *Crisis of Democracy: Report on the Governability of Democracies to the Trilateral Commission.* New York: New York University Press, 1975.

Ignatiev, Noel. *How the Irish Became White.* New York: Routledge, 1995.

Jackobson, Julius, ed. *The Negro and the American Labor Movement.* Garden City, N.Y.: Anchor Books, 1968.

Jacoby, Sandford M. *Employing Bureaucracy: Managers, Unions, and the Transformation of Work in American Industry, 1900–1945.* New York: Columbia University Press, 1985.

Jenkins, Philip. *The Cold War at Home: The Red Scare in Pennsylvania, 1945–1960.* Chapel Hill: University of North Carolina Press, 1999.

Jones, Jacqueline. *American Work: Four Centuries of Black and White Labor.* New York: W. W. Norton, 1998.

Joyner, Charles. *Down By the Riverside: A South Carolina Slave Community.* Urbana: University of Illinois Press, 1984.

Kazin, Michael. *Barons of Labor: The San Francisco Building Trades and Union Power in the Progressive Era.* Urbana: University of Illinois Press, 1987.

Kelly, Robin. *Hammer and Hoe: Alabama Communists During the Great Depression.* Chapel Hill: University of North Carolina Press, 1990.

Kennedy, David. *Freedom from Fear: The American People in Depression and War, 1929–1945.* New York: Oxford University Press, 1999.

Kenny, Kevin. *Making Sense of the Molly Maguires.* New York: Oxford University Press, 1998.

Kessler-Harris, Alice. *Out to Work: A History of Wage Earning Women in the United States.* Oxford: Oxford University Press, 1982.

Kimeldorf, Howard. *Battling for American Labor: Wobblies, Craft Workers, and the Making of the Union Movement.* Berkeley: University of California Press, 1999.

Kingsolver, Barbara. *Holding the Line: Women in the Great Arizona Mine Strike of 1983.* Ithaca, N.Y.: Cornell University Press, 1989.

Klein, Herbert. *The Atlantic Slave Trade.* Cambridge, Mass.: Harvard University Press, 1999.

Kolchan, Thomas, Harry Katz, and Robert McKersie. *The Transformation of American Industrial Relations.* Ithaca, N.Y.: ILR Press, 1994.

Kornblum, William. *Blue Collar Community.* Chicago: University of Chicago Press, 1974.

Larrowe, Charles. *Harry Bridges: The Rise and Fall of Radical Labor in the U.S.* New York: Lawrence Hill, 1972.

Larson, Simeon. *Labor and Foreign Policy: Gompers, the AFL, and the First World War, 1914–1918.* Rutherford, N.J.: Fairleigh Dickinson University Press, 1975.

Laslett, John. *Labor and the Left; A Study of Socialist and Radical Influences in the American Labor Movement, 1881–1924.* New York: Basic Books, 1970.

LaFeber, Walter. *Michael Jordan and the New Global Capitalism.* New York: Norton, 1999.

Laughlin, Kathleen A. *Women's Work and Public Policy: A History of the Women's Bureau, U.S. Department of Labor, 1945–1970.* Boston: Northeastern University Press, 2000.

Laurie, Bruce. *Working People of Philadelphia, 1800–1850*. Philadelphia: Temple University Press, 1980.

———. *Artisans into Workers: Labor in Nineteenth Century America*. New York: Hill and Wang, 1989.

Leab, Daniel J., ed. *The Labor History Reader*. Urbana: University of Illinois Press, 1985.

LeBlanc, Paul. *A Short History of the Working Class: From Colonial Times to the Twenty-First Century*. Amherst, N.Y.: Humanity Books, 1999.

Le Bon, Gustave. *The Psychology of Socialism*. New York: Macmillan, 1899.

———. *The Crowd*. Charlottsville: University of Virginia Press, 1995.

Lemon, James T. *The Best Poor Man's Country: A Geographical Study of Early Southeastern Pennsylvania*. Baltimore: Johns Hopkins University Press, 1972.

Letwin, Daniel. *The Challenge of Interracial Unionism: Alabama Coal Miners, 1878–1921*. Chapel Hill: University of North Carolina Press, 1998.

Levine, Stephen Brier, David Brundage, Edward Countryman, Dorothy Fennell, and Marcus Rediker. *Who Built America: Working People and the Nation's Economy, Politics, Culture, and Society*. New York: Pantheon, 1989.

Levitt, Martin J., with Terry Conrow. *Confessions of a Union Buster*. New York: Crown, 1993.

Lewis, Ronald L. *Black Coal Miners in America: Race, Class, and Community Conflict, 1780–1980*. Lexington: University Press of Kentucky, 1987.

Licht, William. *Working for the Railroad*. Princeton: Princeton University Press. 1983.

Lichtenstein, Alex. *Twice the Work of Free Labor: The Political Economy of Convict Labor in the New South*. New York: Verso, 1996.

Lichtenstein, Nelson. *Labor's War at Home: The CIO in World War Two*. Cambridge: Cambridge University Press, 1982.

———. *State of the Union: A Century of Organized Labor*. Princeton: Princeton University Press, 2002.

Lichtenstein, Nelson, and Robert Zeiger. *The Most Dangerous Man in Detroit: Walter Reuther and the Fate of American Labor*. New York: Basic Books, 1995.

Lingenfelter, Richard E. *The Hardrock Miners: A History of the Mining Labor Movement in the American West, 1863–1893*. Berkeley: University of California Press, 1974.

Lippman, Walter. *Public Opinion*. New York: Harcourt, Brace, 1922.

———. *The Phantom Public*. New York: Harcourt, Brace, 1925.

Lopez, Ian F. Hanley. *White by Law: The Legal Construction of Race*. New York: New York University Press, 1996.

Lorence, James J. *The Suppression of Salt of the Earth: How Hollywood, Big Labor, and Politicians Blacklisted a Movie in Cold War America*. Albuquerque: University of New Mexico Press, 1999.

Lorwin, Lewis L. *Labor and Internationalism*. New York: Macmillan, 1929.

Lovejoy, Paul E., and Nicholas Rogers, eds. *Unfree Labor in the Development of the Atlantic World*. Ilford, Essex, England: Frank Kass, 1994.

Luger, Stan. *Corporate Power: American Democracy and the Automobile Industry*. New York: Cambridge University Press, 2000.

Lynch, Timothy P. *Strike Songs of the Depression*. Jackson: University Press of Mississippi, 2001.

Lynd, Alice, and Staughton Lynd, eds. *Rank and File: Personal Histories by Working Class Organizers*. Boston: Beacon, 1973.

Lynd, Staughton, ed. *"We Are All Leaders": The Alternative Unionism of the Early 1930's.* Urbana: University of Illinois Press, 1996.

Mancini, Matthew J. *One Dies, Get Another: Convict Leasing in the American South, 1866–1928.* Columbia: University of South Carolina Press, 1996.

Mannix, Daniel, and Malcolm Cowley. *Black Cargoes: A History of the Atlantic Slave Trade.* New York: Viking, 1971.

Mantsios, Gregory, ed. *A New Labor Movement for a New Century.* New York: Monthly Review, 1998.

Marable, Manning, and Leith Mullings, eds. *Let Nobody Turn Us Around; Voices of Resistance, Reform, and Renewal: An Afro-American Anthology.* Lanham, Md.: Rowman & Littlefield, 1999.

McCallum, John. *Dave Beck.* Mercer Island, Wash.: Writing Works, 1978.

McCartin, Joseph A. *Labor's Great War: The Struggle for Industrial Democracy and the Origins of Modern American Labor Relations, 1912–1921.* Chapel Hill: University of North Carolina Press, 1997.

McClure, Arthur F. *The Truman Administration and the Problems of Post-War Labor, 1945–1948.* Rutherford, N.J.: Fairleigh Dickinson University Press, 1969.

McKelvey, Jean Trepp. *AFL Attitudes Toward Production, 1900–1932.* Ithaca: New York State School of Industrial and Labor Relations, Cornell University, 1952.

McWilliams, Cary. *Factories in the Field.* Hamden, Conn.: Archon Books, 1969.

Marx, Karl, and Frederick Engels. *Selected Correspondence, 1846–1895.* New York: International Publishers, 1942.

———. *Basic Writings on Politics and Philosophy.* Edited by Lewis S. Feuer. Garden City, N.Y.: Doubleday, 1959.

Messer-Kruse, Timothy. *The Yankee International: Marxism and the American Reform Tradition, 1848–1876.* Chapel Hill: University of North Carolina Press, 1998.

Milkman, Ruth. *Gender at Work: The Dynamics of Job Segregation by Sex During World War II.* Urbana: University of Illinois Press, 1987.

Mills, C. Wright. *The New Men of Power.* New York: Harcourt, 1948.

———. *White Collar: The American Middle Classes.* New York: Oxford University Press, 1951.

———. *Power, Politics, and People.* New York: Oxford University Press, 1963.

Montgomery, David. *Beyond Equality: Labor and the Radical Republicans, 1862–1872.* New York: Knopf, 1967.

———. *Workers' Control in America: Studies in the History of Work, Technology, and Labor Struggles.* New York: Cambridge University Press, 1979.

———. *The Fall of the House of Labor: The Workplace, the State, and American Labor Activism, 1865–1925.* New York: Cambridge University Press, 1987.

———. *Citizen Worker: The Experience of Workers in the United States with Democracy and the Free Market During the Nineteenth Century.* New York: Cambridge University Press, 1993.

Moody, J. Carroll, and Alice Kessler-Harris, eds. *Perspectives on American History: The Problems of Synthesis.* DeCalb: Northern Illinois University Press, 1989.

Moody, Kim. *An Injury to All: The Decline of American Unionism.* New York: Verso, 1988.

———. *Workers in a Lean World: Unions in the International Economy.* New York: Verso, 1997.

Morgan, Edmund S. *American Slavery, American Freedom: The Ordeal of Colonial Virginia.* New York: Norton, 1975.

Morris, Richard B. *The Basic Ideas of Alexander Hamilton.* New York: Pocket Books, 1957.

———, ed. *Government and Labor in Early America.* New York: Octagon Books, 1965.

————, ed. *A History of the American Worker.* Princeton: Princeton University Press, 1983.

Mort, Jo-Ann, ed. *Not Your Father's Union Movement: Inside the AFL-CIO.* New York: Verso, 1998.

Murolo, Pricilla, and A. B. Chitty. *From the Folks Who Brought You the Weekend: A Short History of Labor in the United States.* New York: The New Press, 2001.

Nadworny, Milton J. *Scientific Management and the Unions, 1900–1932; A Historical Analysis.* Cambridge, Mass.: Harvard University Press, 1955.

National Civic Federation Records, 1894–1949. Manuscripts and Archives Division, The New York Public Library. New York, N.Y.

Nelson, Bruce. *Workers on the Waterfront: Seamen, Longshoremen, and Unionism in the 1930s.* Urbana: University of Illinois Press, 1988.

————. *Divided We Stand: American Workers and the Struggle for Black Equality.* Princeton: Princeton University Press, 2001.

Nelson, Daniel. *Shifting Fortunes: The Rise and Decline of American Labor, from the 1820's to the Present.* Chicago: Ivan R. Dee, 1997.

————. *Frederick W. Taylor and the Rise of Scientific Management.* Madison: University of Wisconsin Press, 1980.

Nettels, Curtis P. *The Roots of American Civilization: A History of American Colonial Life.* New York: Appleton-Century-Crofts, 1938.

Neufield, Maurice, Daniel J. Leob, and Dorothy Swanson. *American Working Class History: A Representative Bibliography.* New York: Bowker, 1983.

Newton, James E., and Ronald L. Lewis, eds. *The Other Slaves: Mechanics, Artisans, and Craftsmen.* Boston, Mass.: G. K. Hall, 1978.

Nicholson, Philip Y. *Who Do We Think We Are?: Race and Nation in the Modern World.* Armonk, N.Y.: M. E. Sharpe, 1999.

Noble, David. *America by Design: Science, Technology, and the Rise of Corporate Capitalism.* New York: Knopf, 1977.

Northrop, Herbert. *Boulwarism: The Labor Relations Policies of the General Electric Company.* Ann Arbor: University of Michigan Press, 1964.

Orleck, Annelise. *Common Sense and a Little Fire: Women and Working Class Politics in the United States, 1900–1965.* Chapel Hill: University of North Carolina Press, 1995.

Orren, Karen. *Belated Feudalism: Labor, the Law, and Liberal Development in the United States.* New York: Cambridge University Press, 1991.

Owens, Sarah M. *Born for Liberty: A History of Women in America.* New York: The Free Press, 1989.

Papke, David Ray. *The Pullman Case: The Clash of Labor and Capital in Industrial America.* Lawrence: University Press of Kansas, 1999.

Parker, Michael, and Jane Slaughter. *Choosing Sides: Unions and the Team Concept.* Boston: South End, 1988.

Perlman, Selig, and Philip Taft. *History of Labor in the United States, 1896–1932,* vol. IV, *Labor Movements.* New York: Kelley, 1966.

Peterson, Merrill D., ed. *Thomas Jefferson, a Profile.* New York: Hill and Wang, 1967.

Phelan, Craig. *William Green: Biography of a Labor Leader.* Albany: State University of New York Press, 1989.

————. *Grand Master Workman: Terrence Powderly and the Knights of Labor,* Contributions in Labor Studies, no. 55. Westport, Conn.: Greenwood, 2000.

Phillips, Kevin. *The Emerging Republican Majority.* New York: Arlington House, 1969.

————. *Boiling Point*. New York: Random House, 1993.

————. *Wealth and Democracy: A Political History of the American Rich*. New York: Broadway Books, 2002.

Preston, William. *Aliens and Dissenters*. Cambridge, Mass.: Harvard University Press, 1963.

Prude, Jonathan. *The Coming of Industrial Order: Town and Factory Life in Rural Massachusetts, 1810–1860*. Cambridge, Mass.: Cambridge University Press, 1983.

Quaglieri, Philip L. *America's Labor Leaders*. Lexington, Mass.: Lexington Books, 1989.

Radosh, Ronald. *American Labor and United States Foreign Policy: The Cold War in the Unions from Gompers to Lovestone*. New York: Random House, 1969.

Rauch, Basil. *The History of the New Deal*. New York: Creative Age Press, 1944.

Richardson, Reed C. *The Locomotive Engineer, 1863–1963: A Century of American Railway Labor Relations and Work Rules*. Ann Arbor: University of Michigan Press, 1963.

Rigal, Laura. *The American Manufactory: Art, Labor, and the World of Things in the Early Republic*. Princeton: Princeton University Press, 1998.

Robertson, David. *Denmark Vesey: The Buried History of America's Largest Slave Rebellion*. New York: Random House, 1999.

Roediger, David R., ed. *The Wages of Whiteness: Race and the Making of the American Working Class*. New York: Verso, 1991.

————. *Covington Hall's Labor Struggles in the Deep South and Other Writings*. Chicago: C. H. Kerr, 1999.

Roediger, David R., and Philip S. Foner. *Our Own Time: A History of American Labor and the Working Day*. New York: Verso, 1989.

Rose, Elizabeth. *A Mother's Job: A History of Day Care, 1890–1960*. New York: Oxford University Press, 1999.

Rosenberg, Daniel. *New Orleans Dockworkers: Race, Labor, and Unionism, 1892–1923*. Albany: State University of New York Press, 1988.

Safley, Thomas Max, and Leonard N. Rosenband, eds. *The Workplace Before the Factory*. Ithaca, N.Y.: Cornell University Press, 1993.

Sale, Kirpatrick. *The Conquest of Paradise*. New York: Knopf, 1990.

Salinger, Sharon V. *Labor and Indentured Servants in Pennsylvania, 1682–1800*. New York: Cambridge University Press, 1987.

Salvatore, Nick. *Eugene V. Debs: Citizen and Socialist*. Urbana: University of Illinois Press, 1982.

Santino, Jack. *Miles of Smiles, Years of Struggle: Stories of Black Pullman Porters*. Urbana: University of Illinois Press, 1989.

Seavoy, Ronald E. *The American Peasantry: Southern Agricultural Labor and Its Legacy, 1850–1995; A Study in Political Economy*, Contributions in Economics and Economic History, no. 200. Westport, Conn.: Greenwood, 1998.

Selden, Bernice. *The Mill Girls*. New York: Atheneum, 1983.

Selections from the Correspondence of Theodore Roosevelt and Henry Cabot Lodge, 1884–1918. 2 vols. New York: Charles Scribner's Sons, 1925.

Sexton, Patricia Cayo. *The War on Labor and the Left: Understanding America's Unique Conservatism*. Boulder: Westview, 1991.

Schiller, Herbert. *Mass Communications and American Empire*. New York: A. M. Kelley, 1969.

Schluter, Herman. *Lincoln, Labor and Slavery*. New York: Russell & Russell, 1965.

Schneirov, Richard, Shelton Stromquist, and Nicholas Salvatore, eds. *The Pullman Strike and the Crisis of the 1890's: Essays on Labor and Politics*, The Working Class in American History. Urbana: University of Illinois Press, 1999.

Schor, Juliet B. *The Overworked American: The Unexpected Decline of Leisure*. New York: Basic Books, 1991.

Serrin, William. *The Company and the Union*. New York: Knopf, 1973.

Shaw, Archer H. *The Lincoln Encyclopedia*. New York: Macmillan, 1950.

Shelton, Cynthia. *The Mills of Manayunk: Industrialization and Social Conflict in the Philadelphia Region, 1787–1837*. Baltimore: Johns Hopkins University Press, 1986.

Sheriff, Carol. *The Artificial River: The Erie Canal and the Paradox of Progress, 1817–1862*. New York: Hill and Wang, 1996.

Sklar, Kathryn Kish. *Women's Rights Emerges within the Anti-Slavery Movement, 1830–1870*. Boston: Bedford/St. Martin's, 2000.

Silverman, Victor. *Imagining Internationalism in American and British Labor, 1939–1949*. Urbana: University of Illinois Press, 1999.

Simpson, Stephen. *The Working Man's: A New Theory of Political Economy, on the Principle of Production the Source of Wealth*. Philadelphia: Thomas L. Bonsal, 1831.

Sitkoff, Harvard. *A New Deal for Blacks: The Emergence of Civil Rights as a National Issue—The Depression Decade*. New York: Oxford University Press, 1978.

Skeen, C. Edward. *Citizen Soldiers in the War of 1812*. Lexington: University Press of Kentucky, 1999.

Sloane, Arthur. *Hoffa*. Cambridge, Mass.: MIT Press, 1991.

Smith, Abbot Emerson. *Colonists in Bondage: White Servitude and Convict Labor in America, 1607–1776*. Chapel Hill: University of North Carolina Press, 1947.

Smith, Adam. "Causes of the Prosperity of the New Colonies." In *An Inquiry Into the Nature and Causes of the Wealth of Nations*. New York: Random House, 1937, pp. 531–33.

Smith, Warren B. *White Servitude in Colonial South Carolina*. Columbia: University of South Carolina Press, 1961.

Solomon, Mark. *The Cry Was Unity: Communists and African Americans, 1917–1936*. Jackson: University Press of Mississippi, 1998.

Steffen, George G. *The Mechanics of Baltimore: Workers and Politics in the Age of Revolution, 1763–1812*. Urbana: University of Illinois Press, 1984.

Stockman, David. *The Triumph of Politics: How the Reagan Revolution Failed*. New York: Harper, 1986.

Stowell, David O. *Streets, Railroads, and the Great Strike of 1877*. Chicago: University of Chicago Press, 1999.

Sylvis, James C. *The Life, Speeches, Labors and Essays of William H. Sylvis*. New York: A.M. Kelley, 1968.

Tawney, R. H. *The Acquisitive Society*. New York: Harcourt, 1920.

———. *Religion and the Rise of Capitalism*. New York: Harcourt, 1926.

Tentler, Leslie. *Wage Earning Women: Industrial Work and Family Life in the United States, 1900–1930*. New York: Oxford University Press, 1978.

Third Grand Rally of the Workingmen of Charleston, Massachusetts. October 23, 1840.

Todes, Charlotte. *William Sylvis and the American Labor Movement*. New York: International Press, 1943.

Tomlins, Christopher L. *The State and the Unions: Labor Relations, Law, and the Organized Labor Movement in America, 1880–1960*. New York: Cambridge University Press, 1985.

———. *Law, Labor, and Ideology in the Early American Republic*. New York: Cambridge University Press, 1993.

Twaddle, Michael, ed. *The Wages of Slavery: From Chattel Slavery to Wage Labor in Africa, The Caribbean and England*. London: Frank Kass, 1993.

Tucker, Barbara. *Samuel Slater and the Origins of the American Textile Industry, 1790–1860*. Ithaca, N.Y.: Cornell University Press, 1984.

Ulrich, Laurel Thatcher. *A Midwife's Tale: The Life of Martha Ballard, Based on Her Diary, 1785–1812*. New York: Vintage, 1990.

U.S. Bureau of the Census. *Historical Statistics from Colonial Times to 1970*. Washington, D.C.: U.S. Government Printing Office, 1975.

Van Woodward, C. *Reunion and Reaction; The Compromise of 1877 and the End of Reconstruction*. Boston: Little, Brown, 1951.

Vittoz, Stanley. *New Deal Labor Policy and the American Industrial Economy*. Chapel Hill: University of North Carolina Press, 1987.

Voss, Kim. *The Making of American Exceptionalism: The Knights of Labor and Class Formation in the Nineteenth Century*. Ithaca: Cornell University Press, 1993.

Walkowitz, David J. *Worker City, Company Town: Iron and Cotton Worker Protest in Troy and Cohoes, N.Y., 1855–1884*. Urbana: University of Illinois Press, 1978.

Wallace, Mike, and Edwin G. Burrows. *Gotham: A History of New York City to 1898*. New York: Oxford University Press, 1999.

Way, Peter. *Common Labor: Workers and the Digging of North American Canals, 1780–1860*. Baltimore: Johns Hopkins University Press, 1993.

Weinstein, James. *The Decline of Socialism in America, 1912–1925*. New York: Vintage, 1967.

———. *The Corporate Ideal in the Liberal State, 1900–1918*. Boston: Beacon, 1968.

Wilentz, Sean. *Chants Democratic: New York City and the Rise of the American Working Class*. New York: Oxford University Press, 1984.

Williams, David. *Rich Man's War: Class, Caste, and Confederate Defeat in the Lower Chatahoochee Valley*. Athens: University of Georgia Press, 1998.

Williams, Eric. *Capitalism and Slavery*. New York: Russell & Russell, 1961.

Wolff, Leon. *Lockout, The Story of the Homestead Strike of 1892: A Study of Violence, Unionism, and the Carnegie Steel Empire*. New York: Harper, 1965.

Yates, Michael. *Longer Hours, Fewer Jobs: Employment and Unemployment in the United States*. New York: Monthly Review, 1994.

———. *Why Unions Matter*. New York: Monthly Review, 1998.

Yates, Michael, Ellen M. Wood, Peter Meiskins. *Rising from the Ashes? Labor in the Age of "Global" Capitalism*. New York: Monthly Review, 1999.

Yellowitz, Irwin. *Industrialization and the American Labor Movement, 1850–1900*. Port Washington, N.Y.: Kennikat Press, 1977.

Young, Jeffrey Robert. *Domesticating Slavery: The Master Class in Georgia and South Carolina, 1670–1837*. Chapel Hill: University of North Carolina Press, 1999.

Zieger, Robert. *American Workers; American Unions, 1920–1985*. Baltimore: Johns Hopkins University Press, 1986.

———. *John L. Lewis: Labor Leader*. Boston: Twayne, 1988.

———. *The CIO, 1935–1955*. Chapel Hill: University of North Carolina Press, 1995.

Zeiger, Susan. *In Uncle Sam's Service: Women Workers and the American Expeditionary Force, 1917–1919*. Ithaca, N.Y.: Cornell University Press, 1999.

Zilg, Gerard Colby. *Behind the Nylon Curtain: A History of the DuPont Family in America.* Englewood Cliffs, N.J.: Prentice-Hall, 1974.

Selected Articles

Baird, Charles. "Labor Law Reform: Lessons from History." *Cato Journal* 10 (spring/summer, 1990): 175–209.

Brody, David. "The Old Labor History and the New: In Search of the American Working Class." *Labor History* 20 (winter 1979): 111–26.

Drucker, Peter. "Age of Social Transformation." *Atlantic Monthly* (November 1994): 53–80.

Eisenberg, Carolyn. "Working-Class Politics and the Cold War: American Intervention in the German Labor Movement, 1945–49." *Diplomatic History* 7, no. 4 (fall 1983): 283–306.

Hoagland, Henry E. "Rise of the Iron Molders' International Union." *Iron Molders' Journal* 49 (June 1913): 295–313.

Kimmeldorf, Howard. "Bringing Unions Back in (Or, Why We Need a New Old Labor History)." *Labor History* 32 (winter 1991): 91–129.

Klare, Karl. "Judicial Deradicalization of the Wagner Act and the Origins of Modern Legal Consciousness, 1937–1941." *Minnesota Law Review* 62, no. 3 (March 1978): 265–339.

Muldoon, James. "The Indian as Irishman." *Essex Historical Collections* 111 (1975): 267–89.

Nicholson, Philip Y. "George Dewey and the Expansionists of 1898." *Vermont History* 42, no. 3 (summer 1974): 214–27.

Pierce, Michael. "The Populist President of the American Federation of Labor: The Transformation of John McBride, 1880–1894." *Labor History* 41, no. 1 (February 2000): 5–24.

Stone, Katherine. "The Origin of Job Structures in the Steel Industry." *Radical America* 7, no. 6 (November–December 1973): 19–61.

Swados, Harvey. "The Myth of the Happy Worker." *The Nation* 185 (August 17, 1957): 65–68.

———. "The UAW—Over the Top or Over the Hill?" *Dissent* (fall 1963): 321–43.

Weiler, Paul. "Promises to Keep: Securing Worker's Rights to Self-Organization Under the NLRA." *Harvard Law Review* 96, no. 8 (June 1983): 1780–81.

Wright, Helena. "Sarah Bagley: A Biographical Note." *Labor History* 20, no. 3 (summer 1979): 398–413.

Young, Alfred F. "George Robert Twelves Hewes (1742–1840): A Boston Shoemaker and the Memory of the American Revolution." *William and Mary Quarterly* 38 (October 1981): 561–623.

INDEX

of 1919–20, 187–89; textile, 213. *See also* New Orleans

labor unions, 220–21, 240–41, 251–52; and concession bargaining, 291–93; and contract unionism, 258–60, 268–69, 271; decline of, 198–99; democratic impulses within, 308–10; goals of after World War II, 242–43; image of, 266–67; organizing tactics, 322–24; socialist, 155–57; and worker activism, 85–88. *See also specific individually listed labor unions*

labor, women's role in, 183–84, 195, 235–36, 241–42

Landrum-Griffin Act (1959), 267–68

Leviathan (Hobbes), 3

Lewis, John L., xii, 183, 188, 198–99, 205, 208–9, 215, 216–17, 229–30, 232, 246

Lincoln, Abraham, 78, 83, 90–91, 95, 194, 331–32

Locke, John, 23, 29, 32

Lodge, Henry Cabot, 147–48

Lovestone, Jay, 256

Lowell, Massachusetts, 70–72, 79–81

Luther, Seth, 61, 76–77

Lynn, Massachusetts, 88

Madison, James, 43, 50

Malcolm X, 271

Manayunk, Pennsylvania, 67–69

Marshall, Ray, 298

Martyr, Peter, 4

Marx, Karl, 82, 86, 91, 100, 130, 148

Mazzochi, Anthony, 274, 286

McBride, John, 130, 138

McCarthy, Joseph, 249, 253, 255

McClellan, John, 267

McGovern, George, 284

McKinley, William, 139–40

McParlan, James, 107–8

Meany, George, 256, 263–64, 273, 282–83, 284, 295

Mechanical Society of Baltimore, 43, 51, 54

Medical Care Act (1965), 273

Mediterranean and the Mediterranean World in the Age of Philip II, The (Braudel), 5

Mexican War, 83–84

Miners Benevolent Association (MBA), 106–7; and the Long Strike, 107–8

Mitchell, John, 143–45, 149

modernism, 164–65

Molly Maguires, 108–9, 114

Mondale, Walter, 305

Morgan, Edmund S., 15

Murray, John, 143–45, 149

Murray, Philip, 242, 244, 246–47, 249, 254

Muste, A. J., 270

National Association for the Advancement of Colored People (NAACP), 130, 160, 178, 221, 266

National Association of Manufacturers (NAM), 145–46, 147, 175, 189, 214, 224, 225, 226

National Civic Federation (NCF), 142–45, 149, 177–78

National Industrial Recovery Act (NIRA), 208, 214

National Labor Relations Board (NLRB), 214, 221, 222, 224–25, 227, 230, 232, 248, 287, 297, 319, 321; Supreme Court decision concerning, 304

National Labor Union (NLU), 98–100; demise of, 100–101

National Negro Congress (NNC), 221

National Organization for Women (NOW), 272

National Recovery Administration (NRA), 208–11; end of, 214–15; as the "Negro Removal Act," 210

National Typographers Union (NTU), 86–87

Native Americans, 8, 9, 21, 44, 46, 91, 96, 116, 126, 270–72

nativism, 76–78

Netherlands, the, 6, 7

New Deal, the, and labor, 206, 221–24, 226, 229

New Orleans, 199; civil rights movement in, 123; dock and cotton strike (1907), 161–63, 187, 207; General Strike of 1892, 122–23

Nixon, Richard, 253, 255, 263, 273, 276, 279; agenda of, 284–85; labor legislation of, 286–87; law and order initiatives, 287–88; and the Supreme Court, 285–86. *See also* affirmative action

Norris-LaGuardia Act (1932), 200

North American Free Trade Agreement (NAFTA), 316

Norton, Eleanor Holmes, 298–99

Occupational Safety and Health Administration (OSHA), 286–87, 329

Olney, Richard, 136–37

Operation Dixie. *See* Southern Organizing Campaign

Paine, Thomas, 39, 64

Palmer, A. Mitchell, 186; and the Palmer raids, 189–90

Panic of 1837, 73–75

Patriot Act (2001), 331

Penn, William, 18